Innovations in Artificial Intelligence and Human-Computer Interaction in the Digital Era

Intelligent Data-Centric Systems

Innovations in Artificial Intelligence and Human-Computer Interaction in the Digital Era

Edited by

Surbhi Bhatia Khan
Department of Data Science, School of Science, Engineering and Environment, University of Salford, Manchester, United Kingdom

Suyel Namasudra
Department of Computer Science and Engineering, National Institute of Technology Agartala, Tripura, India

Swati Chandna
Professor of Information, Media and Design, SRH University Heidelberg, Heidelberg, Germany

Arwa Mashat
Faculty of Computing and Information Technology, King Abdulaziz University, Rabigh, Saudi Arabia

Series Editor Fatos Xhafa
Universitat Politècnica de Catalunya, Barcelona, Spain

ELSEVIER

ACADEMIC PRESS
An imprint of Elsevier

ISBN: 978-0-323-99891-8

For information on all Academic Press publications visit our website at
https://www.elsevier.com/books-and-journals

Publisher: Mara E. Conner
Editorial Project Manager: John Leonard
Production Project Manager: Prasanna Kalyanaraman
Cover Designer: Miles Hitchen

Typeset by TNQ Technologies

Working together
to grow libraries in
developing countries

www.elsevier.com • www.bookaid.org

Contents

List of contributors xiii
Biographies xv
Preface xvii

CHAPTER 1 Introduction to human-computer interaction using artificial intelligence 1
Surbhi Bhatia Khan and Swati Chandna

1.1 Introduction 1
1.2 Human-Computer interaction and its importance 1
    1.2.1 Characteristics of HCI and AI waves 2
    1.2.2 An evolving HCI interaction in the era of AI 3
    1.2.3 Possible research areas 5
    1.2.4 Conclusion 5
    References 5

CHAPTER 2 Augmented and immersive virtual reality to train spatial skills in STEAM university students 7
Hugo C. Gomez-Tone, Jorge Martin-Gutierrez and Betty K. Valencia-Anci

2.1 Introduction 7
    2.1.1 Definition of spatial skills and their components 7
    2.1.2 Importance of spatial skills in STEAM 9
    2.1.3 Spatial skills training 10
2.2 Employing virtual and augmented reality 11
2.3 Motivation and contribution 12
2.4 Methodology 12
    2.4.1 Pilot study with augmented reality 12
    2.4.2 Pilot study with immersive virtual reality 16
2.5 Results 19
    2.5.1 Comparison spatial skill gains between university groups training by augmented reality and between training types (AR and VR) 23
2.6 Discussion 24
2.7 Conclusions and future works 26
    References 27

CHAPTER 3 Introduction to artificial intelligence and current trends 31
Law Kumar Singh and Munish Khanna

3.1 Introduction 31
3.2 History of AI 31
    3.2.1 The growth of AI (1943−56) 31

3.3 Industry 4.0 and AI revolution 35
    3.3.1 Learning about the different kinds of AI.....................................36
3.4 Explainable AI...37
3.5 Applicability of AI in recommendation systems 39
    3.5.1 How do system recommendations function?................................39
    3.5.2 Common obstacles encountered by a recommender system?.....40
    3.5.3 Recommender systems with AI 40
    3.5.4 Machine learning in recommendation systems 40
3.6 Advantages and disadvantages of AI 41
    3.6.1 Decrement in human error 41
    3.6.2 Availability 41
    3.6.3 No risk 41
    3.6.4 Impartial decisions 41
    3.6.5 Faster decision 41
    3.6.6 Unemployment 41
    3.6.7 Lethargic humans 42
    3.6.8 Expensive..42
    3.6.9 Losing creativity 42
    3.6.10 Data maintenance 42
3.7 Symbolic AI and computational AI 42
3.8 Evolutionary computing 43
    3.8.1 Evolutionary algorithm..44
    3.8.2 Benefits and limitations of genetic algorithm............................46
    3.8.3 Application in the real world 47
3.9 Logic-based reasoning 48
    3.9.1 Theorem proof by reasoning..48
    3.9.2 Reasoning as computation of symbols 49
3.10 Models of knowledge representation based on structural analysis 50
    3.10.1 Semantic networks 50
    3.10.2 Frames 50
    3.10.3 Scripts 52
3.11 Rule-binding systems 52
    3.11.1 Model of rule-based systems..52
3.12 Pattern recognition and cluster analysis..54
3.13 Neural networks...55
3.14 AI applications...57
    3.14.1 Gaming 57
    3.14.2 Natural language processing 57
    3.14.3 Expert systems..57
    3.14.4 Speech recognition 59
3.15 Intelligent robots...61
3.16 AI research prospects and future directions...61

3.17 Conclusions 63

References 64

CHAPTER 4 Computational intelligence in human-computer interaction—Case study on employability in higher education 67

Pooja Thakar, Manisha, Anil Mehta, Neetu Goel and Seema Verma

4.1 Introduction 67

4.2 Case study in higher education system 68

4.2.1 Issues of the higher education system in India.............................68

4.2.2 Potential aspects to resolve issues with computational intelligence............68

4.2.3 Contributions of chapter 69

4.3 Background 69

4.3.1 Review of literature 70

4.3.2 Problems faced by the higher education system for employability 70

4.4 Proposed framework: solution with artificial intelligence and human-computer interaction...79

4.4.1 Data sets 79

4.4.2 Approach 80

4.4.3 Experimental setup and measures 81

4.4.4 Machine learning algorithms implemented in the model.............83

4.4.5 Application of model on all datasets 84

4.5 Results and conclusion 84

4.5.1 Results 84

4.5.2 Conclusion and future possibilities 88

References 88

CHAPTER 5 Human-centered artificial intelligence 95

Zainab Aizaz and Kavita Khare

5.1 Introduction to human-centered AI 95

5.2 Human-in-the-loop machine learning, reasoning, and planning............98

5.2.1 For increasing the accuracy of an AI model 99

5.2.2 For achieving the required accuracy of an AI model faster.........99

5.2.3 Model 1 100

5.2.4 Model 2 100

5.2.5 Model 3 101

5.2.6 Model 4 102

5.2.7 Model 5 102

5.3 Data analysis 102

5.3.1 Data labeling..103

5.3.2 Quality control in data labeling 104

5.3.3 Predicting the amount of annotation required 107

5.3.4 Obtaining annotated data from an existing AI design model 108

5.4 Designing and prototyping 109
 5.4.1 Different design approaches of HAI...109
 5.4.2 Some examples of hybrid designs involving humans and AI...................111
5.5 Evaluation and strategies 116
5.6 Case studies..120
 5.6.1 Proposed case study of HAI in loan approval and debt recovery.............120
 5.6.2 Transformation from simple AI to human-centered AI at LinkedIn.........123
 5.6.3 Human-centered AI at Netflix...125
 5.6.4 The HAX toolkit 125
5.7 Limitations of HAI 127
5.8 Conclusion 128
References..128
Further reading 130

CHAPTER 6 **Strategies for efficient and intelligent user interfaces**...................**131**
     S. Suriya, M. Balaji and S. Nivetha
6.1 Introduction..131
 6.1.1 User interface 131
 6.1.2 User interface design...131
 6.1.3 Theo Mandel's golden rules...131
 6.1.4 User interface design process...132
6.2 Strategies required for efficient intelligent user interfaces.....................133
 6.2.1 Intelligent user interfaces 133
 6.2.2 Importance of artificial intelligence and machine learning.................134
6.3 Recent innovations in intelligent user interfaces 139
 6.3.1 Intelligent interface for Tamil letter recognition using machine learning
    techniques..139
 6.3.2 Intelligent interface for online examination system using natural
    language processing techniques 141
 6.3.3 Intelligent interface for online music genre classification system using
    machine learning techniques...152
6.4 Conclusions and future work..168
References..169
Further reading 171

CHAPTER 7 **Uses of artificial intelligence with human-computer interaction in**
     psychology **173**
     Achyut Tiwari, Aryan Chugh and Aman Sharma
7.1 Introduction..173
 7.1.1 Motivation...173
 7.1.2 Contribution...173

7.2 Preliminaries 174
7.3 Role of HCI and AI in psychology 174
    7.3.1 Chatbots 175
    7.3.2 Cyberpsychology 178
    7.3.3 Intelligence amplification..181
    7.3.4 Physiological impacts of COVID-19 182
    7.3.5 AI and human rights..183
7.4 User-centered system development 186
    7.4.1 Key elements of UCDD 186
    7.4.2 Context analysis 187
    7.4.3 Iterative design 187
    7.4.4 Process approach within UCDD 187
7.5 Usability engineering and verification 188
    7.5.1 Usability 188
    7.5.2 The usability engineering lifecycle..188
    7.5.3 Usability heuristics 190
    7.5.4 Usability testing...191
    7.5.5 A/B testing 191
    7.5.6 Test budget...191
    7.5.7 Importance of user-centered design 192
    7.5.8 Google homepage over 20 years..193
7.6 Democratization of information technology 195
    7.6.1 Distribution of information 195
7.7 Challenges..199
7.8 Conclusion and future scope 200
7.9 Discussion 200
References...201

CHAPTER 8 **Managing postpandemic effects using artificial intelligence with human-computer interaction** **207**
    V. Kakulapati, Sheri Mahender Reddy and A. Paramasivam
8.1 Introduction...207
8.2 Background studies..208
    8.2.1 Effect of COVID-19 outbreak..209
8.3 Managing effects of work from home..217
    8.3.1 WFH benefits...218
    8.3.2 Drawbacks of WFH..220
8.4 Managing effects of blended learning 222
    8.4.1 Advantages of blended learning...223
8.5 Managing effects of eLearning..224
    8.5.1 eLearning benefits 226

8.5.2 eLearning drawbacks..226
8.5.3 Inequalities in ethnicity...226

8.6 Discussion 227

8.7 Conclusions and future works 228

References..229

CHAPTER 9 Practical case studies on human-computer interaction **233**
Sheela S.V., Abhinand P. and Radhika K.R.

9.1 Introduction 233
9.1.1 Principles of HCI...234

9.2 Healthcare systems 236

9.3 Digital hearing 238

9.4 Digital humanities...240

9.5 Business intelligence...241

9.6 Case studies...242
9.6.1 Air traffic systems 242
9.6.2 Automotive systems 245
9.6.3 Virtual reality systems..246
9.6.4 Crisis management 248

9.7 Conclusion 249

References..250

CHAPTER 10 Design and development of applications using human-computer interaction **255**
Anunaya Pandey, Sanjeeb Prasad Panday and Basanta Joshi

10.1 HCI design principles 255
10.1.1 Feedback cycles..255
10.1.2 Direct manipulation and invisible interfaces 256
10.1.3 Mental models and representations.....................................257
10.1.4 Distributed cognition 258

10.2 Designing VR applications..259
10.2.1 Current VR landscape 259
10.2.2 VR application design considerations..................................259
10.2.3 VR application evaluation 261
10.2.4 Case study on VR Game difficulty adjustment 262

10.3 Designing automotive applications 263
10.3.1 Automotive interfaces and road safety 264
10.3.2 Users of automotive applications..264
10.3.3 Automotive application tasks and problems.......................265
10.3.4 Empirical measurement of safety and usability 267
10.3.5 Evaluating automotive applications and interfaces 267

    10.3.6 Procedures for iterating on automotive application design 268
    10.3.7 Case study on GPS and distributed cognition 268
  10.4 Designing healthcare applications 269
    10.4.1 Healthcare applications and public health 270
    10.4.2 Users of healthcare applications 272
    10.4.3 Medical applications and interfaces in home healthcare 273
    10.4.4 Evaluating healthcare applications 274
    10.4.5 Case study on the role of HCI in experiential learning through augmented reality 276
  10.5 Designing airline applications 278
    10.5.1 Airline interfaces and flight safety 278
    10.5.2 Mental models and situational awareness 279
    10.5.3 Airline automation and usability heuristics 279
    10.5.4 GOMS model for evaluating airline applications 280
    10.5.5 Case study on how a cockpit remembers its speeds 282
  10.6 HCI for emergencies 284
    10.6.1 Users of emergency applications 284
    10.6.2 Challenges for emergency HCI 286
    10.6.3 Case study: cognitive task analysis for an emergency management game 287
  10.7 Conclusion 289
  References 291
  Further reading 293

CHAPTER 11   Challenges and future work directions in artificial intelligence with human-computer interaction **295**
    Mahesh H. Panchal and Shaileshkumar D. Panchal
  11.1 Introduction 295
  11.2 Research challenges in AI with HCI 298
    11.2.1 Lack of unified concept for XAI systems 300
    11.2.2 Biased decisions and explanation from AI systems 302
    11.2.3 Lack of stakeholder-specific explanations 303
    11.2.4 Exploring research areas in XAI 305
  11.3 HCI for speech-impaired people: a case study 305
    11.3.1 Issues and challenges 307
  11.4 Beyond HCI 307
  11.5 Future work directions in AI with HCI 308
  11.6 Conclusions 309
  References 310

Index 311

List of contributors

Zainab Aizaz
Department of ECE, Maulana Azad National Institute of Technology (MANIT), Bhopal, Madhya Pradesh, India

M. Balaji
Department of Computer Science and Engineering, PSG College of Technology, Coimbatore, Tamil Nadu, India

Surbhi Bhatia Khan
Department of Data Science, School of Science, Engineering and Environment, University of Salford, Manchester, United Kingdom

Swati Chandna
Applied Data Science and Analytics, SRH University Heidelberg, Heidelberg, Germany

Aryan Chugh
Department of Computer Science & Engineering and Information Technology, Jaypee University of Information Technology, Solan, Himachal Pradesh, India

Neetu Goel
Vivekananda School of Information Technology, VIPS-TC, Delhi, India

Hugo C. Gomez-Tone
Universidad Nacional de San Agustín de Arequipa, Arequipa, Peru

Basanta Joshi
Pulchowk Campus, Institute of Engineering, Tribhuvan University, Kathmandu, Nepal

Radhika K.R.
Department of Information Science and Engineering, BMS College of Engineering, Bangalore, Karnataka, India

V. Kakulapati
Department of IT, Sreenidhi Institute of Science and Technology, Hyderabad, Telangana, India

Munish Khanna
Department of CSE, Hindustan College of Science and Technology, Mathura, Uttar Pradesh, India

Kavita Khare
Department of ECE, Maulana Azad National Institute of Technology (MANIT), Bhopal, Madhya Pradesh, India

Manisha
Department of Computer Science, Banasthali Vidyapith, Rajasthan, India

Jorge Martin-Gutierrez
Universidad de La Laguna, Tenerife, Spain

Anil Mehta
School of Legal Studies, Banasthali Vidyapith, Rajasthan, India

S. Nivetha
Department of Computer Science and Engineering, PSG College of Technology, Coimbatore, Tamil Nadu, India

Abhinand P.
Bosch Group, Bangalore, Karnataka, India

Mahesh H. Panchal
Graduate School of Engineering and Technology, Gujarat Technological University, Ahmedabad, Gujarat, India

Shaileshkumar D. Panchal
Graduate School of Engineering and Technology, Gujarat Technological University, Ahmedabad, Gujarat, India

Sanjeeb Prasad Panday
Pulchowk Campus, Institute of Engineering, Tribhuvan University, Kathmandu, Nepal

Anunaya Pandey
Engineering Manager, Microsoft, Noida, India

A. Paramasivam
Department of Mechanical Engineer, Rajalakshmi Engineering College, Chennai, Tamil Nadu, India

Sheri Mahender Reddy
Otto-Friedrich University of Bamberg, Bamberg, Germany

Sheela S.V.
Department of Information Science and Engineering, BMS College of Engineering, Bangalore, Karnataka, India

Aman Sharma
Department of Computer Science & Engineering and Information Technology, Jaypee University of Information Technology, Solan, Himachal Pradesh, India

Law Kumar Singh
Department of Computer Engineering and Applications, GLA University, Mathura, Uttar Pradesh, India

S. Suriya
Department of Computer Science and Engineering, PSG College of Technology, Coimbatore, Tamil Nadu, India

Pooja Thakar
Vivekananda School of Information Technology, VIPS-TC, Delhi, India

Achyut Tiwari
Department of Computer Science & Engineering and Information Technology, Jaypee University of Information Technology, Solan, Himachal Pradesh, India

Betty K. Valencia-Anci
Universidad Nacional de San Agustín de Arequipa, Arequipa, Peru

Seema Verma
Department of Electronics, Banasthali Vidyapith, Rajasthan, India

Biographies

Surbhi Bhatia Khan is Doctorate in Computer Science and Engineering in the area of Machine Learning and Social Media Analytics. She earned Project Management Professional Certification from reputed Project Management Institute, USA. She is currently working in the Department of Data Science, School of Science, Engineering and Environment, University of Salford, Manchester, United Kingdom. She has more than 11 years of academic and teaching experience in different universities. She is the awardee of the Research Excellence award given by King Faisal University, Saudi Arabia, in 2021. She has published 100+ papers in many reputed journals in high indexed outlets. She has around 12 international patents from India, Australia, and the United States. She has successfully authored 3 books and has also edited 12 books. She has completed many projects approved from Ministry of Education, Saudi Arabia, and Deanship of Scientific Research in different universities in Saudi Arabia and from India. Her area of interest is Knowledge Management, Information Systems, Machine Learning, and Data Science.

Suyel Namasudra has received PhD from the National Institute of Technology Silchar, Assam, India. He was a Postdoctorate Fellow at the International University of La Rioja (UNIR), Spain. Currently, Dr. Namasudra is working as an Assistant Professor in the Department of Computer Science and Engineering at the National Institute of Technology Agartala, Tripura, India. Before joining the National Institute of Technology Agartala, Dr. Namasudra was an Assistant Professor in the Department of Computer Science and Engineering at the National Institute of Technology Patna, Bihar, India. His research interests include blockchain technology, cloud computing, IoT, AI, and DNA computing. Dr. Namasudra has edited 4 books, 5 patents, and 75 publications in conference proceedings, book chapters, and refereed journals like *IEEE TII*, *IEEE T-ITS*, *IEEE TSC*, *IEEE TCSS*, *IEEE TCBB*, *ACM TOMM*, *ACM TOSN*, *ACM TALLIP*, *FGCS*, *CAEE*, and many more. He has served as a Lead Guest Editor/Guest Editor in many reputed journals like *ACM TOMM* (ACM, IF: 3.144), *MONE* (Springer, IF: 3.426), *CAEE* (Elsevier, IF: 3.818), *CAIS* (Springer, IF: 4.927), *CMC* (Tech Science Press, IF: 3.772), *Sensors* (MDPI, IF: 3.576), and many more. Dr. Namasudra is the Editor-in-Chief of the *Cloud Computing and Data Science* (ISSN: 2737-4092 (online)) journal, and he has participated in many international conferences as an organizer and session Chair. He is a member of IEEE, ACM, and IEI. Dr. Namasudra has been featured in the list of the top 2% scientists in the world in 2021 and 2022, and his h-index is 29.

Swati Chandna is working as a full-time Professor for Data Science at SRH University Heidelberg, Germany. Additionally, she is the Program Director of the master's in applied data science and analytics program. Earlier from January 2018 till March 2020 she was working as a guest professor at SRH University Heidelberg. In parallel, she was also working as a full-time senior data scientist and has worked for various renowned customers in automobile, heat, and airline industry. From 2013 until 2018, she has worked as a computer scientist at Karlsruhe Institute of Technology, Karlsruhe, Germany, in the area of digital humanities. Her scientific profile includes artificial intelligence, big data analytics, data visualization, natural language processing, machine learning, and data storytelling. She has authored and co-authored many research papers published in various national and international journals and conferences.

Arwa Mashat is an Associate Professor in the Information System department in the Faculty of Computing and Information Technology, King Abdulaziz University, Rabigh, Saudi Arabia. She received her Bachelor degree in Computer Science from King Abdulaziz University, Jeddah, her Master's degree in Educational Technology from Youngstown State University, Ohio, USA, and her PhD in Instructional Design and Technology from Old Dominion University in USA. Currently, she is the Vice Dean for the Applied College and the Vice Dean for the Faculty of Computing and Information Technology in King Abdulaziz University, Rabigh, Saudi Arabia. Her research interests include eye tracking, education technology, online learning, artificial intelligence, and Internet of Things.

Preface

Human-computer interaction (HCI) is a multidisciplinary field that focuses on the design of computer technology and, in particular, the interaction between users and computers in different domains. On the other hand, artificial intelligence (AI) is an area of computer science that emphasizes the creation of intelligent machines that work and react like humans. It deals with the simulation of intelligent behavior in computers. There are many applications of AI in today's world, such as chatbots, healthcare, gaming, business, social media, data security, and many more. HCI looks to see how well the AI can interact with users based on linguistics and user-centered design processes, especially with the advances of AI and the hype around many applications. HCI and AI can mutually benefit from a closer association. An interdisciplinary team of HCI and AI researchers can develop extraordinary applications, such as improved education systems, smart homes, and many more.

This edited book discusses the peculiarities of HCI and AI, which are not usually addressed in traditional approaches. It provides a platform for researchers, academicians, and other professionals from different background areas to show their state-of-the-art knowledge about HCI and AI. Hands-on chapters are contributed by academicians and other professionals from reputed organizations, which improves the quality of this edited book. The summary of the following chapters is explained below:

Chapter 1 explains the introduction of HCI and AI, mentioning broadly the areas of AI and HCI. Then, it highlights the relevance of AI and HCI and also explains how the interaction of HCI is evolving in the era of AI. The possible research areas are described in the context of the latest trends in different applications.

Chapter 2 describes the importance of augmented reality and immersive virtual reality, and it presents a case study demonstrating these new technologies, showing the effectiveness of HCI. This research addressed the issues and recognized the positive impact of spatial skills training needed to strengthen the effective involvement in higher education.

Chapter 3 gives a complete introduction to AI starting with the history of AI followed by advances in AI applications. It also describes some of the techniques of AI followed by a discussion of how AI is being used in a variety of cutting-edge multidisciplinary applications. The pros and cons of AI have been listed with the discussion of some diverse applications.

Chapter 4 discusses the infusion of computational intelligence in the field of HCI by providing an in-depth analysis of previous research work done in the field. This chapter also showcases a case study for prediction of employability in higher education by using data generated and stored after HCI in various tests. This chapter further discusses the prediction model by integrating supervised and unsupervised techniques of AI by providing a generic solution.

Chapter 5 highlights the important human-centered AI (HCAI) aspects, theory, models, and design approaches. It also explains a wide variety of HCAI examples, such as HCAI in industry, healthcare, public security, and autonomous vehicles. The evaluation strategy for successful HCAI designs is compared with the design thinking approach, which is used for solving complex problems using a quantitative approach.

Chapter 6 explains the strategies for efficient intelligent user interfaces and shows how intelligent interfaces play a vital role in recent innovations. The three different intelligent interfaces are discussed in this chapter, namely, Tamil character recognition, an online examination system, and online music genre classification. It presents and gives a very clear insight of how machine learning techniques are integrated with the user interface to efficiently handle tasks.

Chapter 7 describes how the advances in technology will empower tackling problems and difficulties in a more efficient, viable, and productive manner from a psychological point of view. It also focuses on usability engineering and verification discipline dealing with Human-computer interfaces and AI including psychology, human factors, and cognitive science. The design and user design development evolution with time has been demonstrated using a case study.

Chapter 8 discusses the computational issues that are difficult or impossible for current AI algorithms to tackle, which have prompted the investigation of human computation. This study aims to comprehend the effects of the pandemic in different areas with significant benefits and drawbacks that can be learned for the postpandemic outbreak and effective management of the results using AI and HCI technologies.

Chapter 9 mainly deals with the role of HCI systems in the design of various applications. The design aspects are analyzed followed by examining the design of HCI for healthcare systems, digital hearing, digital humanities, and business intelligence. Applied scenarios with reference to case studies are given, such as air traffic control, automotive systems, and many more.

Chapter 10 explains the foundational principles that are used in the design and development of applications while giving examples of relevant application interfaces. The HCI principles, tools, and methods in the context of designing applications in five different verticals have been explored with themes in AI: virtual reality, the automotive industry, healthcare, airlines, and emergency preparedness/response.

Chapter 11 explains the need for explainable artificially intelligent systems and presents paradigms that exist to achieve it, various forms of explanations expected by different stakeholders, and challenges in the field of making transparent systems in the direction of trustworthy HCI. The possible research areas under explainable artificial intelligence are also shown with the future possibilities of integrating AI and HCI, which can be considered open research challenges.

Editors

Surbhi Bhatia Khan
Suyel Namasudra
Swati Chandna
Arwa Mashat

Introduction to human-computer interaction using artificial intelligence

1

Surbhi Bhatia Khan[1] and Swati Chandna[2]

[1]*Department of Data Science, School of Science, Engineering and Environment, University of Salford, Manchester, United Kingdom;* [2]*Applied Data Science and Analytics, SRH University Heidelberg, Heidelberg, Germany*

1.1 Introduction

Artificial intelligence (AI) is a new technology that has become widely accepted in a variety of fields [1]. In recent decades, applications have expanded to encompass virtual support, healthcare, and security in addition to language translation, picture recognition, credit scoring, e-commerce, entertainment, and business. Human—computer interaction (HCI) is the reflection of the confluence of two key technologies, AI and HCI [2], and it aids in the creation of intelligent interactive systems for user interaction. AI is applied in many different sectors in conjunction with HCI by utilizing a variety of algorithms. Users can trust the system because of the transparency this combination offers them.

Today, a variety of interaction techniques are used for face-to-face communication with the modern world. Mobile computing is one of the more advanced technologies available today and has recently emerged as a crucial element in modern life. Technology of many kinds has also been developed. AI is crucial in enhancing the flexibility of interactions with all of these computing systems. By incorporating several interactions, the field of HCI makes usage of this technology simple to understand. In other words, interactions made by AI are extremely clever. By introducing user experience design and explainable artificial intelligence (XAI), HCI and AI are linked together [3]. The primary goal of user experience design is to create products that provide positive user experiences. XAIs describe many types of interactions that are developed to give the end user a setting where they can trust the outcomes. Explainability in AI is a field that is also active in many different areas, such as corporate processes, security, financial and legal judgments, autonomous vehicles, smartphones, and AI for designers.

1.2 Human-Computer interaction and its importance

One of the most crucial fields that combines computer science and psychology is HCI. HCI gives people a means of communication so they can interact with all of the cutting-edge technologies that are currently available, such as our smartphones and multimedia touch screens, for a better user experience. User experience is described as "a person's perceptions and responses that emerge from the usage or expected use of a product, system, or service" [4] by ISO 9241-210, an international standard on ergonomics of human system interaction. User experience describes the steps customers take to use a product (user experience, UX). Both their direct interactions with the product and how it fits into their larger job completion process are covered by this. Even whether different aspects of the experience are directly controlled by the product or only have a little link to it, the entire experience is what is regarded as a component of the UX by taking the user's perspective into account. In essence, it covers how customers and businesses interact.

UX has received a lot of attention recently, but it is not as simple and straightforward to rely on general agreement about its nature and application as it might seem. Their experience on the viewpoints of UX from academia and industry have surely been addressed by the latest research and studies done in this regard. The dynamic, context-dependent, and subjective nature of UX has been emphasized [5]. In addition, it has been stated that UX, which results from interacting with a system, product, service, or item, can be discussed as personal rather than social. The suggested ISO definition of UX looks to be in line with the survey finding, even though the challenges of anticipating use and the aim of UX will need more explanation. Meeting client expectations without passing judgment, causing trouble, or causing worry will be the key focus for articulating and defining an excellent UX. The combination of elegance and simplicity is yet another crucial component that will contribute to and produce items that are a pleasure to own and use. True and false UXs can be distinguished from one another. Client requests being fulfilled or checklist features being offered are not actual UXs. To provide a high-quality UX in a company's offerings, it requires the seamless integration of the services of many disciplines, including engineering, marketing, visual and industrial design, and interface design.

1.2.1 Characteristics of HCI and AI waves

When the personal computer (PC) was originally introduced in the 1980s, its programs were developed using a "technology-centric strategy," oblivious to the demands of common users. The issue of UX progressively emerged as PCs became popular. Human factors, psychology, and computer science were the main forces behind the initiatives that gave rise to the area of HCI. It appears that history is repetitive. The difficulties we were dealing with as we entered the era of artificial intelligence in the 1980s are still there today. Although AI technology has numerous advantages for individuals, it also significantly affects how people work and live. Unfortunately, a "technology-centric design" approach dominates the creation of AI systems. Many AI experts place a heavy emphasis on algorithmic research rather than on practical AI systems that serve users' demands, which causes many AI systems to fail. AI systems that have been trained on skewed data produce biased "thinking," which is easily reinforced and can even be harmful to humans. As a result, some significant AI initiatives were unable to be carried out. The AI incident database, specifically, has gathered over 1000 incidents related to AI, such as self-driving cars that kill pedestrians, trading algorithms that cause "flash crashes" in markets and transfer billions of dollars between parties, and facial recognition systems that detain innocent people. Both the advantages and possible threats presented by AI coexist, much like the "dual-use" characteristics of nuclear energy and biochemical technology. As the creation and application of AI are decentralized global phenomena, entry barriers are low and challenging to regulate. To address the issue, Stanford University set up a research center named "Human-Centric AI" to concentrate on morally sound design. Shneiderman and Xu took the idea a step further by suggesting a human-centered AI (HCAI) strategy. This HCI profession has reached a tipping point, much as the HCI area that PC technology created 40 years ago. This time, it is obvious that there will be more severe repercussions if human-centered design principles are disregarded. The machines that humans use are no longer the "conventional" computers we are familiar with as AI technology permeates all aspects of human life and work. In terms of the primary job we do as HCI specialists, we are witnessing a shift from "conventional" HCI to new human–AI engagement increase. The HCI community has helped build AI systems, but more work has to be done to make HCAI methods implementable and to offer HCI solutions that deal with the particular problems that AI technologies present.

The emergence of HCI [6] started long back when the term was coined in the early 1980s, wherein the focus was on scientific testing explaining the new designs. The patterns evolve from each era, thus providing us with the rich body of knowledge. The design is continuously evolving and striving to address complex and systematic problems using technology and design. Table 1.1 details the emergence of HCI.

The three main waves of growth in AI technology are universally accepted. AI's initial two waves were largely concerned with academic achievement and scientific research. A third wave of AI began to develop in 2006 as a result of cutting-edge innovations like deep machine learning. In the third wave, AI technology changed from being "useless" to "helpful," enabling individuals to use practical AI applications to address everyday issues. Its main objective is to enhance and find landing scenarios for AI applications, front-end programs, interaction technologies, ethical design, etc.

1.2.2 An evolving HCI interaction in the era of AI

The focus of study on human–machine interactions (such as human factors) throughout a specific technologic era is determined by the peculiarities of human–machine relationships in that era. AI technology is enabling machines to play new roles in human–machine systems as we move closer to an "autonomous world" based on AI. Human–AI system interactions mostly take place between humans and autonomous/AI agents within AI systems.

Table 1.1 Emergence of HCI.

Features	Wave 1	Wave 2	Wave 3
Period	1980–90	1990–2000	2000–10
Models	Desktop and mental models	Collaboration and communication	Self-expression and social change
Main characteristic	Mainly emphasized easy to learn and easy to use	Cognitive modeling to interaction design	Value-driven design for making sustainable change
Driving factors	Mental modeling and human factors engineering in software development	Interface, tools, and technologies	Personal devices in social settings
Techniques	Cognitive walkthroughs, heuristic evaluation and usability testing	Facilities encouraging knowledge sharing	Holistic approach focusing on complex interactions with habit-forming technologies

Intelligent agents may be created to display distinctive behaviors, have autonomous traits, and differing degrees of human-like intellect as AI technology develops. In numerous fields of work, exploratory study on human—machine collaboration has begun. Intelligent air traffic management systems, robotic team building for operators, intelligent flight decks, pilot system team building, and highly autonomous vehicle driver system team building are a few examples. Still, there are a lot of unanswered issues. This HCI research and application in the AI era, as well as new designs in the construction of AI systems, will unavoidably result from such novel forms of human—machine collaboration leveraging AI technology, as demonstrated by the history of the computing period. Progressive methods and a paradigm shift in thinking will result from it. This implies that utilizing human—machine collaboration is yet another strategy to harness the advantages of AI technology while lowering any potential security threats. For HCI specialists, creating useable and accessible user interfaces for computer systems is a top priority. When creating user interfaces for AI systems, we confront new difficulties in addition to usability issues. Because machine learning (ML) and the learning process lie at the heart of AI, they are opaque, and the outcomes of AI-based decision-making are often counterintuitive. Intelligent systems based on ML, particularly deep learning neural networks for pattern recognition, are often perceived as "black boxes" by nontechnical users. The user starts to doubt the choices made by his AI system as a result of this "black box" issue. Why are you doing this, why is this the outcome, when did it succeed or fail, and when can I trust you? As a remedy, explainable AI aims to show the user what the machine is thinking and can inform the user as to why explainable AI is gaining increasing attention. The program focuses on three work-related areas: (1) developing new or enhanced ML technologies to produce explainable ML algorithms; (2) creating an explainable user interface model using cutting-edge HCI technology and design principles; and (3) assessing existing psychological explanation theories to support explainable AI. The task of explainable AI may be aided by existing psychology theories on explanation. Measurement, modeling, and mechanism-related aspects of psychology have all been studied. Examples of reasoning techniques include induction, causality, self-explanation, comparison, and counterfactual reasoning. While there is still much to learn about explainable AI, several researchers have come to the conclusion that its main goal should be to guarantee that the intended audience can comprehend what the AI systems produce.

Future HCI projects ought to look toward HCAI-based user-participating solutions, e.g., this is done to engage customers in ways that go beyond the explainability that AI experts have previously overlooked and to explain AI to consumers. Many of the studies that are being conducted now also lack rigorous behavioral science procedures, such as user and experimental validation. HCI should assist verification methods with its expertise. To introduce user-participating experimental assessment, we need to move beyond some unilateral evaluation methodologies from prior research, which only evaluate the performance of AI systems. HCI should make it simpler to evaluate AI technologies as complete human—machine systems.

It is expressive and quite productive to describe computer use as semiotic processes between humans and computers. This could result in several projects at the interface of AI and HCI, with both more accessible methodologies and richer theoretical underpinnings, from a semiotic standpoint. By "increasing the effective use of the intellectual potential of society's problem solvers," they may carry out Douglas Engelbart's goal. User-centered, evaluation-focused system trials using technologies from AI, pattern recognition, and data science can be one way to accomplish this. According to Lieberman [7], speech and handwriting recognition will be significant application fields for HCI and AI technology. Statistical language models received criticism for their subpar first-generation implementations, but Moore's Law will eventually make them powerful enough to successfully tackle speech and handwriting recognition. Research on deep learning has already demonstrated that face detectors can be trained without labeling images with or without faces, and that unsupervised learning can automatically pick up complex concepts like cat faces and human bodies. Numerous publications on interactive ML are available. As "a natural technique to integrate background knowledge into the modeling step," interactive ML is suggested. Allowing users to "operate in tandem with ML systems" was one of the objectives [8]. A technique frequently employed in HCI, the thought-aloud study [8], was utilized to investigate this.

1.2.3 Possible research areas

Applications in business and medicine could greatly benefit from the convergence of AI and human—computer interaction, especially interactive ML. The best interactions, just like human contact and communication, are founded on a thorough comprehension of one another and the effective exploitation of one another's inner states and intentions, similar to a teacher who is aware of what her students comprehend, what they do not, and how they can advance (the Socratic conception of the teacher as midwife). Statistical ML techniques enable developers to produce better UXs by offering users the appropriate level of support and help. Technology that is proactive and supportive could enable transdisciplinary science, smart home management, personal financial management, and monitoring of one's own health. But it could also make programming easier and greatly improve education.

1.2.4 Conclusion

This study reviews the combination of HCI with AI. The papers chosen for the evaluation were divided into HCI, AI, and various application domains. The chapter highlighted the relevance of the fields of HCI and AI. The research directions future research could be conducted on the algorithms to explain and assess their effectiveness and make them more beneficial for application in many areas. The challenges listed in this chapter include emphasizing and inserting novel and unique explainability techniques that are connected to several fields. Moreover, improving model interpretability and accuracy should be also a matter of concern and must be given priority in the future.

References

[1] S. Dick, Artificial Intelligence, 2019.
[2] J.M. Carroll, HCI Models, Theories, and Frameworks: Toward a Multidisciplinary Science, Elsevier, 2003.
[3] F. Xu, H. Uszkoreit, Y. Du, W. Fan, D. Zhao, J. Zhu, Explainable AI: a brief survey on history, research areas, approaches and challenges, in: CCF International Conference on Natural Language Processing and Chinese Computing, Springer, Cham, October 2019, pp. 563—574.
[4] A.G. Mirnig, A. Meschtscherjakov, D. Wurhofer, T. Meneweger, M. Tscheligi, A formal analysis of the ISO 9241-210 definition of user experience, in: Proceedings of the 33rd Annual ACM Conference Extended Abstracts on Human Factors in Computing Systems, April 2015, pp. 437—450.
[5] K. Hornbæk, M. Hertzum, Technology acceptance and user experience: a review of the experiential component in HCI, ACM Trans. Comput. Hum. Interact. 24 (5) (2017) 1—30.

[6] J.H. Carlisle, Evaluating the impact of office automation on top management communication, in: Proceedings of the June 7-10, 1976, National Computer Conference and Exposition, June 1976, pp. 611−616.

[7] B. Myers, Challenges of HCI design and implementation, Interactions 1 (1) (1994) 73−83.

[8] B. Shneiderman, Designing the user interface: strategies for effective human- computer, Interaction 3 (1998).

Augmented and immersive virtual reality to train spatial skills in STEAM university students

2

Hugo C. Gomez-Tone[1], Jorge Martin-Gutierrez[2] and Betty K. Valencia-Anci[1]

[1]*Universidad Nacional de San Agustín de Arequipa, Arequipa, Peru;* [2]*Universidad de La Laguna, Tenerife, Spain*

2.1 Introduction

2.1.1 Definition of spatial skills and their components

Intelligence was defined by Spearman [1] as "the ability to obtain and create new, useful and suitable information from existing sensory information, which is evident in the behavior or mental activity of the subject". Therefore, depending on the information and the tasks that are required, intelligence is not unique, and this posture has been maintained by researchers in the field of human intelligence such as Gardner [2], who established that the human being possesses at least eight intelligences, including spatial intelligence, which serves to capture information, formulate problems, and solve them, becoming a necessary skill to incur in the fields of science and technology.

This spatial intelligence that allows us to mentally represent two-dimensional and three-dimensional spaces, in addition to facilitating the resolution of real or imaginary spatial problems, is known as spatial skills and is directly related to our visual capabilities. Spatial skills has been studied for over a hundred years as an important line of investigation in cognitive and educational psychology. From the researchers who have delved most deeply into this topic such as Carroll [3] and Lohman [4], there is almost a single definition that establishes that it is the ability to generate, retain, recover, and mentally manipulate well-structured visual images and their parts in a bi- and three-dimensional space. Furthermore, this cognitive ability, like any other, comprises and integrates three important aspects [5] shown in Fig. 2.1. First, it is the aptitude, that is, the innate talent of the individual that has been inherited and that is shown without prior training. Then, it is the ability, which is the ease and possibility of learning through some type of training. Finally, it is the dexterity that allows integration and motor execution of the previous ones [6]. Specifically, it is the spatial ability that we are interested in studying since it can be trained and can be measured with standardized psychometric tests.

But the several decades that spatial skills have been studied have not ended in a clear agreement on the components or subcomponents that shape them [7]. Some proposals consider only two components [3]: spatial visualization and mental rotation; some more recent proposals, such as the Cattell-Horn-Carroll Model of Intelligence [8], support 11 spatial skills, and even more recent findings, based on contemporary theories and previous models, determine that visual processing consists of 25 factors [9], many of which are interrelated and are all psychometrically measurable.

Innovations in Artificial Intelligence and Human-Computer Interaction in the Digital Era. https://doi.org/10.1016/B978-0-323-99891-8.00002-4

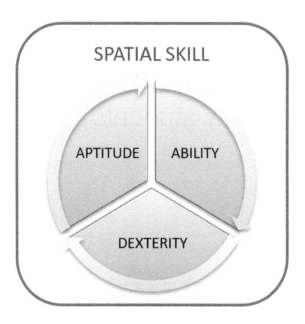

FIGURE 2.1

Conception of spatial skills.

Prepared by authors adapted from H. Sánchez, C. Reyes, Psicología del aprendizaje en educación superior, Lima Visión Univ.
(2003).

The simplification of spatial skills components generally responds to the intentions of researchers to train these skills in the fields of engineering and architecture to create a positive impact. Table 2.1 shows a synthesis of the authors who are most used in research [10].

It is common to recognize between two and five components of the spatial skills that turned out to be almost the same. These have been well defined by McGee [11], Maier [12] as follows:

- Spatial relations (SR) is the skill to perceive the position of an object in relation to a previous position, considering size, distance, volume, or any other distinctive sign.
- Spatial perceptions (SP) is the skill to determine the spatial relationships between objects despite irrelevant information.
- Spatial visualization (SV) is the skill to mentally manipulate visual images. This may involve imagining the rotations of objects in space.
- Mental rotation (MR) is the skill to mentally rotate visual images. These images can be two-dimensional or three-dimensional.
- Spatial orientation (SO) is the skill to orient oneself physically or mentally in space. A person's spatial position is essential to this task.

For the experimental part that will be shown in this chapter, we will use the components proposed by Carroll [3], that is, spatial visualization and mental rotation, when experimenting with engineering students, and to this, we will add the component of spatial orientation when experimenting with architecture students (Fig. 2.2).

Table 2.1 Most followed components in research, adapted from Martin-Gutierrez [10].

Author	Components
McGee [11], Maier [12]	Spatial relations (SR) Spatial perception (SP) Spatial visualization (SV) Mental rotation (MR) Spatial orientation (SO)
Linn and Petersen [13]	Spatial perception (SP) Spatial visualization (SV) Spatial orientation (SO)
Pellegrino et al. [14], Olkun [15]	Spatial relations (SR) - Mental rotation (MR) - Spatial perception (SP) Spatial visualization (SV)
Carroll [3]	Spatial visualization (SV) Mental rotation (MR)

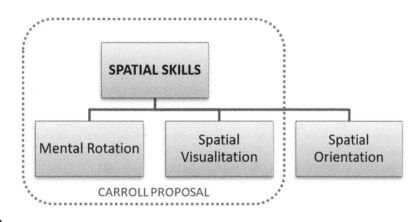

FIGURE 2.2

Component spatial orientation added to Carroll's proposal [3]. Components of spatial skills considered for this research.

Source: Author original.

2.1.2 Importance of spatial skills in STEAM

Since the study of spatial skills began a century ago, it has been maintained continuously and longitudinally that they are an attribute and a very important characteristic that every person must have that is successfully involved in the STEM field (science, technology, engineering, and mathematics) [16]. In the specific case of engineering, it has been shown that the spatial skills have a direct relationship between the retention rates of freshmen in these careers and the best performance in courses of a graphic nature [17−19], but also with the success in other courses of the first year of studies in engineering careers [20] as in mathematics [11]. In general, there is a proven influence of spatial skills in the field of engineering [21−23] that also reaches motivational beliefs and self-directed learning [24,25].

In the specific case of architecture and arts, because they are inside the expanded set of disciplines of science, technology, engineering, arts, and mathematics (STEAM), and since they require in their training several subjects related to drawing and descriptive geometry, it has been demonstrated more recently that there is the same relationship in which the spatial skills are fundamental for success in the design and drawing subjects of the first year of studies [26]. Some other authors have linked spatial skills with spatial creativity, necessary for architectural design [27], by correlating this creativity with spatial visualization and mental rotation, by demonstrating that individuals with spatial abilities excel in shape design, while those with medium and low spatial abilities excel in additive approaches of a simpler nature. The development of spatial skills at the beginning of university studies in architecture provides a foundation on which more complex skills can be built to solve complex problems of architectural design, but the architectural design process can involve so many aspects and skills that neither mental rotation nor originality can cover [28].

2.1.3 Spatial skills training

The highly malleable quality of spatial thinking [29] in general terms and specifically of the spatial skills make this capacity able to be developed with training [18], which according to Baenninger and Newcombe [30] turns out to be more effective when it is specific, that is, short (2 or 3 weeks) and oriented to a specific test of spatial visualization, as it has also been demonstrated in practice through countless investigations, highlighting those carried out at the Michigan Technological University since 1993 [31]. There is also general or indirect training, which coincides in most cases with the instruction of mandatory graphic expression courses. These have also shown effectiveness in the development of this ability, but to a lesser degree despite its longer duration [30,32]. Furthermore, the training methodologies are varied and are based on the resources used, which range from sketches with pencil on paper, physical materials such as blocks, through the use of multimedia platforms and specific software to video games, virtual reality, and augmented reality [33−35].

Among the many investigations in this regard, at least three trends have been found. First are those who consider that the inclusion of informatic technologies such as the computer, three-dimensional modeling software, and animation [36,37] allow greater learning of the spatial skills [38] than traditional methods that are considered insufficient [39]; an example of this is three-dimensional object modeling in Sketch-Up [35]. Second are those who argue that traditional techniques such as hand drawing [15,40,41] or physical manipulation of objects [42] improve spatial skills, and only then do computer-aided design and drawing programs help [40], which are not considered useful in initial training [23]. The latest trend refers to those who claim that the combination of traditional graphic engineering with computer technologies (three-dimensional modeling and visualization) favors the development of space capacity to a greater extent [43,44]. However, "the most important aspect of activities designed to improve space capability is that they are context-specific" [19].

The most recent emerging technologies such as virtual reality, mixed reality, and augmented reality have had a greater evolution in the last decade than along with a significant expansion of applications for these technologies, and they have introduced interactivity and participation in the field of teaching-learning [45]. And within this field, they are demonstrating to be highly effective tools for the formation of space skills and are therefore treated in a special section.

2.2 Employing virtual and augmented reality

The term augmented reality coined in 1990 by Caudell and Mizel [46] is understood as "*the technology that is used to 'augment' the visual field of the user with information necessary in the performance of a current task*," a definition that has not changed much and that can be summarized as follows: "a process of combining or 'augmenting' video or photographic displays by overlaying the images with useful computer-generated data" [47]. According to Azuma [48], the most important features of this technology are the combination of the real with the virtual, real-time interactivity, and registration in three dimensions. The aim of this technology should not replace real experiences, but rather complement them. According to Barfield [49], "*the extension of the real world by means of synthetic images, due to which it is not required that the scene is completely generated by a computer; however, the synthetic image is used as a complement to the real-world scenes*".

Augmented reality has been shown to have a high impact on students' motivation, in their learning [50−52], with a focus on student-centered learning [53] and on improving the quality of education by promoting autonomy and interest in educational material [54]. These qualities are ideal to consider in any type of learning or training in higher education such as spatial skills training. There are experiences that show that augmented reality increased the interest and motivation of students in engineering graphic courses [55−57]. Given the important development of these technologies today, there are various training courses aimed at enhancing spatial skills, specifically visualization and rotation [22,58].

On the other hand, after the term virtual reality was coined in 1992 by Jaron Lanier [59], and different authors have been redefining this concept that today can be synthesized in the definition given by the Encyclopedia Britannica: "the use of computer modeling and simulation that enables a person to interact with an artificial three-dimensional (3-D) visual or other sensory environment. VR applications immerse the user in a computer-generated environment that simulates reality through the use of interactive devices, which send and receive information and are worn as goggles, headsets, gloves, or body suits" [60]. According to Schroeder's definition [61], the two most important characteristics of this technology are immersion and interaction; immersion is understood as the perception of being physically present in a non-physical environment that is created with images, sounds, or other stimuli that provide a totally absorbing environment and interaction, which is understood as the natural action that occurs between the user and the virtual environment. For this research, we will specify virtual reality as immersive virtual reality.

The use of the immersive virtual reality for the training of spatial skills has been given since the appearance of this technology as the experience that sought in university students the learning of tasks of space pursuit and space navigation [62−64]. However, with the further development of technology, lots of research has begun, some oriented to a specific component of the spatial skills such as mental rotation [65] or spatial orientation [66], but mostly the training applied to engineering students consists of the movement, rotation, and scaling of objects or geometric shapes [67], even for students of architecture or industrial design [68].

2.3 Motivation and contribution

In academia, graphic expression teachers find students who have difficulties in solving tasks that require visualization and spatial reasoning skills. Teachers of this subject often argue that spatial skills are necessary to understand graphic expression subjects, but the curricula do not include specific actions for the acquisition of these skills that are fundamental to understanding these subjects. It is true that representation systems improve spatial ability [43], but it is also true that not all students have the same ability to visualize the contents of descriptive geometry and objects in space, so it is necessary to provide them with a good level of spatial ability so that they can follow the contents of the graphic expression with less difficulty.

Virtual and augmented reality technologies are interesting and attractive to students, so specific training that provokes the performance of mental tasks of visualization, rotation, relations, and orientation leads to exercise the mind by training it in these tasks. The training based on augmented reality is a training widely validated by the authors, and in this work, they provide a comparison of training in engineering students from two different countries (Spain and Peru). On the other hand, for the first time, training based on full-scale sketching with virtual reality in an immersive environment through Head Mounted Display (HMD) has been carried out. These trainings can be carried out autonomously by the students, so it is a good strategy for teachers to recommend their implementation.

2.4 Methodology

As explained in the introduction, firstly, it is required to determine the levels of the spatial skills that the students of the engineering and architecture professional careers begin with at the university because they can determine their success, rather than desertion, in the first years of study and secondly to determine the level of effectiveness of training designed with augmented reality and immersive virtual reality. The research presented in this chapter was based on two pilot studies carried out with engineering and architecture students from one Spanish and one Peruvian university.

2.4.1 Pilot study with augmented reality

In this pilot study that used augmented reality to design a short and specific training, the target population was engineering freshmen students enrolled in the graphic engineering subject at two universities: *Universidad Católica San Pablo* (UCSP) located in Peru (Arequipa city) and *Universidad de La Laguna* (ULL) located in Spain (Canary Islands).

The experimental design consisted of inviting students to participate in training sessions to improve their spatial skills; for this, they were informed of the benefits they could obtain not only for the better development of the courses of graphic expression but also in different courses in their first years at the university. Participants were provided with full information about the purpose of the study, and their informed consent was obtained prior to participation in the study. The enrolled participants were subdivided into two groups: an experimental group that received augmented reality training and a control group that would not be trained at all. The measurement data of the spatial skills, as well as the same training, were both carried out in the previous weeks (UCSP) and during the first week (ULL) of the academic year so that the students had not started classes and had not had any contact with any other university subjects. The training was carried out face-to-face on the campus of each university so that the research team had full control over the experimental conditions.

Prior to training, validated spatial skills measurement tests were administered to the experimental and control groups from each university to establish pre-training values. The experimental groups then underwent training, while the control groups received no training. At the end of the augmented reality training, the same measurement tests were given to the experimental and control groups to measure the gains and establish the spatial skills levels at the end of the training.

The 9-h training of self-learning content was carried out on 5 days from Monday to Friday. Each day the training lasted 2 hours, except for the last day, which lasted only 1 hour for evaluation purposes. For the training, an "augmented " was used that contains different sets of tasks designed to train and develop the spatial skills [69]. The purpose of the book is to combine the characteristics of augmented reality with those of a physical textbook; for this, the printed text on paper is associated with the digital content that is displayed with augmented reality, which was achieved with the development of software to access and display the content of the augmented book. The design and evaluation of the interactive system are explained in the article "Design and validation of an augmented book for spatial abilities development in engineering students" [22]. The software, based on tracking markers to visualize three-dimensional objects in augmented reality, was installed on PCs in the computing laboratories of each university.

The measuring instruments used to measure and evaluate the different components of spatial skills were the Mental Rotation Test (MRT) to measure mental rotation, and the Differential Aptitude Test (DAT5-SR) to measure spatial visualization. These standardized measuring instruments are the most widely used in research worldwide.

The MRT was created by Stephen Vandenberg [70] and consists of 20 items in which the participant has figures of a block in three-dimensional perspective and is then shown four figures of blocks with a different orientation, from which he/she must choose the two that correspond to the sample block (see Fig. 2.3). Selecting a correct alternative gives one point and selecting both gives two points; however, selecting a correct one and a wrong one removes the score from that item. The 20 items achieve a maximum score of 40 points.

The DAT5-SR was created by Bennet et al. [71] and consists of several tests, within which the Spatial Relation (SR) subset contains 50 items. This instrument measures the mental dexterity of the participants by assigning them the task of creating a three-dimensional mental image from a two-dimensional figure displayed (Fig. 2.4) The test consists of 50 figures to be recognized where one point is assigned to each correct answer and no points are deducted.

To determine the participants in this pilot study, the technique of non-probabilistic sampling was used for convenience. In both universities, the participants of the study were first-year students of the professional career of Civil Engineering at the UCSP and Electronic Engineering and Mechanical Engineering at the ULL. In both universities, the students were registered in the graphic subject in engineering, which had contents in both universities related to the learning of different systems of representation of objects, which itself constitutes a training of the spatial skills. So, the training was given before or during the first week of the start of the courses so as not to interfere with the results of the proposed training. Table 2.2 shows the distribution of participants per university.

MENTAL ROTATION TEST

MRT

This test is intended to measure the ability to recognize a given object in a sample of different objects. The only difference between the original object (left) and the object to be located consists in a modification of the angle of vision. In the image below we have an example of what to do:

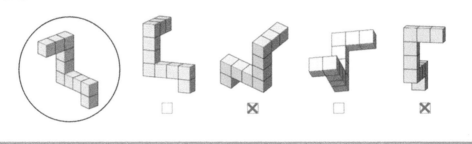

FIGURE 2.3

Explanatory example of MRT.

Prepared by authors, adapted from S.G. Vandenberg, A.R. Kuse, Mental rotations, a group test of three-dimensional spatial visualization, Percept. Mot. Skills. 47 (1978) 599–604. https://doi.org/10.2466/pms.1978.47.2.599.

The "augmented" designed using Bloom's taxonomy has different exercises grouped into four difficulty levels so that each session addresses one level of the book in about 2 hours. The fifth level is an assessment that is designed to be completed in 1 hour.

- Level 1 (knowledge) contains three types of tasks: to identify vertices and faces in orthographic views and axonometric projections.
- Level 2 (comprehension) contains one type of task: to identify orthographic views.
- Level 3 (application/analysis) contains two types of tasks: to identify the spatial relationship between objects to identify how many objects are in contact with a selected object, and to identify the minimum number of views to define an object.
- Level 4 (synthesis) contains two types of tasks: to draw the missing orthographic view.
- Level 5 (evaluation) contains one type of task: to draw the axonometric perspective.

To solve each exercise in the book, the reference markers for each page must be displayed to the computer's webcam, and then the installed software identifies these fiducial markers and determines the corresponding exercise to be displayed (Fig. 2.5). The user then interacts with the augmented content and handles the figures with his or her hands using the general markers in the printed book (Fig. 2.6).

DIFFERENTIAL APTITUDE TEST: SPATIAL RELATIONS

DAT5 -SR

This test consists of 50 exercises. In each one a model or pattern is presented in which some areas are shaded and in others small drawings appear. To the right of each model are four three-dimensional figures. Your task is to find out which of these figures is the only one that could be formed from the model. The model always shows the outer part of the figure.

EXAMPLE

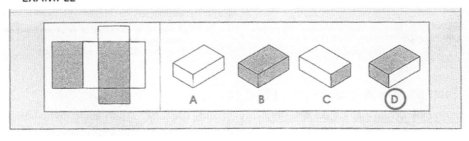

FIGURE 2.4

Explanatory example of DAT5-SR.

Prepared by authors adapted from G.K. Bennett, H.G. Seashore, A.G. Wesman, The Differential Aptitude Tests, Spanish of TEA Ediciones, New York, NY, USA, 1947. https://doi.org/10.1002/j.2164-4918.1956.tb01710.x.

Table 2.2 Participating population and sample size by university.

	UCSP	ULL
Total population	134	378
Experimental group	31	84
Control group	31	25

FIGURE 2.5

Augmented book and fiducial marks.

Source: Author original.

FIGURE 2.6

Students training with the augmented book.

Source: Author original.

2.4.2 Pilot study with immersive virtual reality

In this second pilot study that used immersive virtual reality to design a short and specific training, the target population was architecture students of the first year of studies at the ULL, located in the Canary Islands, in Spain.

The experimental design consisted of recruiting newly admitted students to participate in short training sessions to improve their spatial skills; for this, as in the previous pilot study, they were informed of the benefits, and previous consent was obtained before participation in the investigation. The recruited participants were subdivided into two groups: an experimental group to receive immersive virtual reality training and a control group that would not receive any training.

The spatial skills measurement data, as well as the same training, were both carried out during the first week of the academic year so that the students had not yet started any university subjects. The training was conducted in person within the university campus to have full control over the experimental conditions.

As in the first pilot study, spatial skills measurement tests were administered to both the experimental and control groups as well as before and after the training to measure gains and establish final levels upon completion of it.

The training for this pilot study lasted a total of 3 hours spread over 3 days (Monday, Wednesday, and Friday), for 1 hour a day. For the training, a two-dimensional drawing of six ephemeral architectures (small architectural spaces) was used. Each group was organized into three levels of difficulty according to their degree of complexity. Participants were shown two-dimensional paper drawings of each module: a top, front, and side view, as well as three perspectives with vanishing points. The drawings showed a person inside for better analysis. After observing the drawings for a period of 3 minutes, they were set up with the Head Mounted Displays HTC Vive Cosmos to immerse them in a virtual environment into which the same images had previously been embedded. Then, with these images as aids and using the drawing tools of Google's Tilt Brush application (https://www.tiltbrush.com), they had to draw the proposed module in life-size proportions with the haptic controls.

The Perspective Taking/Spatial Orientation Test (SOT) was added to the two measuring instruments (MRT and DAT5-SR) already used in the first pilot study to measure the spatial orientation, because with these two test, small shapes or manipulable objects could be inspected, imagined, or mentally transformed while learning the distribution of a building or a city that is carried out in larger spaces surrounding the body and involves the integration of the sequence of views that change with one's movement in the environment [72], which requires the ability to orient oneself in an environment and imagine how it looks from different points of view. This skill does not necessarily depend on the mental rotation [73] in which the observer rotates the object in his mind.

The SOT was created by Hegarty and Waller [74] and consists of 12 drawn items so that the participant imagines himself/herself in the position of one of the items, which will become the center of the circle, looking at another item, which will become the top of the circle. The participant's task is to draw an arrow from the center object that indicates the direction to a third object from the new orientation (see Fig. 2.7). In this test, each item has a score that is the absolute deviation in sexagesimal degrees between the chosen answer and the correct answer, so a lower score means being closer to the correct answer.

The participants of this pilot study were students enrolled in the first year of Architecture at the ULL in Spain and were recruited using the technique of non-probabilistic sampling for convenience. To participate in the study, they had to adjust to the "student archetype" for the purposes of this study, which aimed at participants with an interest in video games, a high level of familiarity with computer technologies, and not suffering from color blindness, vertigo, dizziness, or migraine. In addition, participants should not have had experience with the use of HMD. The participants were subdivided into an experimental training group that consisted of 14 students and a control group made up of 16 students that did not complete the training experiment. Both groups were between the ages of 18 and 20.

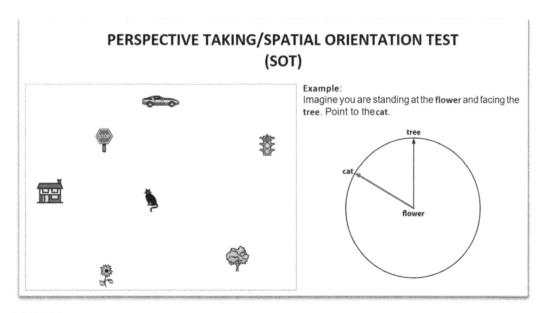

FIGURE 2.7

Explanatory example of SOT.

Prepared by authors adapted from M. Hegarty, D. Waller, A dissociation between mental rotation and perspective-taking spatial abilities, Intelligence 32 (2004) 175–191.

In the first session, all the participants of both the experimental group and the control group took the spatial skills measurement tests. The MRT and DAT5-SR tests were administered 1 day before the SOT measurement test. In the second session, the experimental group was taught how to use the HMD with haptic controls so that they became familiarized with the use of these devices and were taught for 20 min the use of the drawing tools of the Tilt Brush application to draw in three-dimensional free-hand. Then the schedule for training sessions was informed to them.

The material used for this training was six small architecture modules designed by the architects of the research team. Each participant's session was individual and lasted a maximum of 60 min. The participant used the HMD and haptic controls in each session to freely draw two architectural spaces in three-dimensions. The first session drew two basic modules, the second two intermediate level modules, and the last session the two most complex level modules (see Figs. 2.8–2.10). The three sessions took place on Monday, Wednesday, and Friday of the same week. After the end of the training, both groups (experimental and control) were called again to perform the three tests to compare and confirm if there were significant differences.

www.DeepL.com/Translator

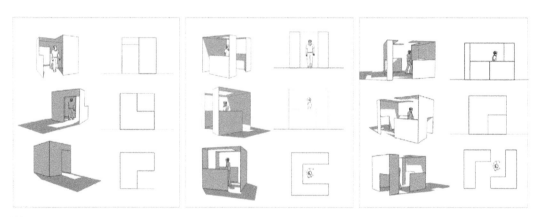

FIGURE 2.8

Examples of basic, intermediate, and advanced drawings given to the students.

Source: Author original.

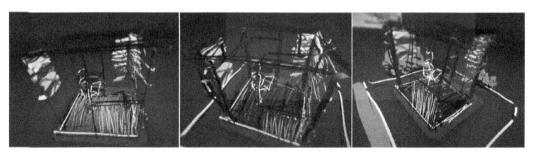

FIGURE 2.9

Example of the drawings made using immersive virtual reality.

Source: Author original.

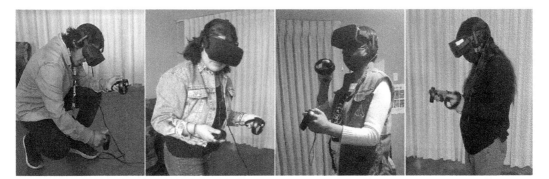

FIGURE 2.10

Students training with immersive virtual reality.

Source: Author original.

2.5 Results

The objective of the experiment was to evaluate whether the students improved the level of the components of the spatial skills after performing the proposed training. The general hypotheses to confirm this study were as follows.

- Hypothesis H1: the two groups conducting augmented reality training significantly improve the spatial skills components measured with MRT and DAT5-SR.
- Hypothesis H2: there is no significant difference in the improvement of spatial skills acquired by the two augmented reality training groups.
- Hypothesis H3: the group conducting immersive virtual reality training significantly improves the spatial skills components measured with MRT and DAT5-SR, in addition to improving the spatial orientation component measured with SOT.
- Hypothesis H4: the two types of training (immersive virtual reality and augmented reality) equally improve the components of the spatial skills measured with MRT and DAT5-SR.

As mentioned above, the augmented reality and immersive virtual reality training sessions were conducted at the two universities by first-year engineering and architecture students. In each university, experimental groups (AR and IVR) and control groups (CT) were organized. Table 2.3 presents the descriptive data of the study groups before starting the training.

A first statistical analysis verifies that the data collected before training follow a normal distribution. The statistical analysis aimed to confirm whether the experimental groups and the control groups were homogeneous in terms of their spatial skills before initiating any experimentation. The Kolmogorov—Smirnov test was applied for the sample of more than 50 people, and Shapiro—Wilk test was applied for the samples of fewer than 50 people, to test the normality of each sample. Table 2.4 shows the results of the analysis of the normality distribution of each study group: experimental groups and control groups.

The results show that spatial visualization (DAT5-SR) and spatial orientation (SOT) data follow a normal distribution in all groups (P-value $> .05$), but mental rotation (MRT) data for some groups did

Table 2.3 Mean values and standard deviation for populations and study samples prior to training.

Group	Pre-MRT Mean value (SD)	Pre-DAT5-SR Mean value (SD)	Pre-SOT Mean value (SD)
Group AR ULL (n = 84)	15.85 (6.55)	25.99 (9.46)	-
Group CT_ar_ULL (n = 25)	17.44 (9.82)	28.40 (10.17)	-
Group AR UCSP (n = 31)	18.52 (7.80)	26.42 (7.47)	-
Group CT_ar_UCSP (n = 31)	16.00 (7.46)	22.94 (8.14)	-
Group IVR ULL (n = 14)	17.21 (8,30)	29.29 (10.67)	46.52 (26.97)
Group CT_ivr_ULL (n = 16)	20.06 (10.81)	28.25 (9.64)	43.49 (27.08)

Table 2.4 Normality test for samples from both universities (experimental and control groups).

	Group	Kolmogorov−Smirnov (a)			Shapiro−Wilk		
		F	gL	Sig.	F	gL	Sig.
MRT_ULL	AR_ULL	0.111	84	**0.012**			
	CTar_ULL				0.917	25	**0.044**
	IVR_ULL				0.901	14	0.115
	CTivr_ULL				0.968	16	0.825
DAT5-SR_ULL	AR_ULL	0.082	84	0.200 ([a])			
	CTar_ULL				0.965	25	0.526
	IVR_ULL				0.949	14	0.548
	CTivr_ULL				0.932	16	0.263
SOT_ULL	IVR_ULL				0.945	14	0.479
	CTivr_ULL				0.885	16	0.052
MRT_UCSP	AR_UCSP				0.908	31	**0.012**
	CTar_UCSP				0.937	31	0.069
DAT5-SR_UCSP	AR_UCSP				0.972	31	0.573
	CTar_UCSP				0.981	31	0.828

AR, *Experimental Group Augmented Reality;* CTar, *Control Group Augmented Reality;* CTivr, *Control Group Interactive Virtual Reality;* IVR, *Experimental Group Interactive Virtual Reality.*
[a]*Greater than this value.*

not have a normal distribution (P-value $<$ .05). Data that followed a normal distribution were analyzed using parametric statistical tests (Student's t test or ANOVA), while data that did not follow a normal distribution were analyzed using nonparametric statistical tests (Kruskal–Wallis).

The ANOVA analysis of DAT5-SR and SOT data and the Kruskal–Wallis analysis of MRT data confirmed that the experimental and control groups were similar in spatial skills levels before training; that is, before training the experimental and control group of UCSP did not have significant differences (P-value $=$ .241 on DAT5-SR and P-value $=$ .411 on MRT). The same result was obtained for the ULL groups; there are no significant differences prior to training with augmented reality (P-value $=$ .244 on DAT5-SR and P-value $=$ .096 on MRT) and the IVR training group (P-value $=$ 0.43 on MRT, P-value $=$ .78 on DAT5-SR and P-value $=$ .89 on SOT).

Based on the results, it is concluded that both experimental groups when compared with their respective control groups are equivalent in terms of visualization and spatial rotation before training. Hence, any differences between the experimental and control groups observed after the intervention will reflect the training sessions and not any other variables or factors.

Next, we proceed to test the research hypotheses. We analyzed if the students obtained gains in the components of the spatial skills after undergoing the trainings. Table 2.5 shows the results of the pretests, posttests, and gain scores. The mean gain values for the pre- and posttests of ULL students who underwent training are 8.06 (SD $=$ 6.27) for the MRT and 8.95 (SD $=$ 5.27) for the DAT5-SR, while the same values for UCSP students are 7.00 (SD $=$ 7.62) for the MRT and 13.06 (SD $=$ 5.79) for the DAT5-SR. In the virtual reality training, the gain scores obtained by ULL students are 6.07 (SD $=$ 4.14), for the MRT, 7.00 ($-$4,62), and for the SOT, 29.72 (SD $=$ $-$41.40).

For the augmented reality training, specific research hypotheses were defined:

- H1AR_ULL: the experimental group shows an enhancement in spatial visualization measured with the DAT5-SR after the proposed training.
- H2AR_ULL: the experimental group shows an enhancement in spatial rotation measured with the MRT after the proposed training.
- H3AR_UCSP: the experimental group shows an enhancement in spatial visualization measured with the DAT5-SR after the proposed training.
- H4AR_UCSP: the experimental group shows an enhancement in spatial rotation measured with the MRT after the proposed training.

To analyze augmented reality training at the ULL, a one-factor ANOVA was performed on the gain values of the component DAT5-SR, $F_{1,107} = 8.586$, P-value $=$ .004, and a Kruskal–Wallis test on the component MRT $\chi^2 = 6.968$, P-value $=$ .008. A significant difference was found in both cases, so research hypotheses H_{1AR_ULL} and H_{2AR_ULL} are accepted.

An analogous procedure was performed to analyze augmented reality training at the UCSP. The results on the gain values of the component DAT5-SR were $F_{1,60} = 108.235$, P-value $=$ .000, and on the component MRT were $\chi^2 = 9.494$, P-value $=$ .002. Also, a significant difference was found in both cases. Therefore, the research hypotheses H_{3AR_UCSP} and H_{4AR_UCSP} are accepted. Thus, it is possible to state that the augmented reality–based training did improve both spatial skills components in both training groups (ULL and UCSP). General hypothesis H1 is confirmed: "the two groups that perform training with augmented reality significantly improve the components of spatial skills measured with MRT and DAT5-SR".

Table 2.5 Mean pretest, posttest, and gain scores (SD) for MRT, DAT5-SR, and SOT.

	Pre-MRT	Post-MRT	Gain MRT	Pre-DAT5SR	Post-DAT5SR	Gain DAT5SR	Pre-SOT	Post-SOT	Gain SOT
Group AR ULL n = 84	15.85 (6.55)	23.90 (8.04)	8.06 (6.27)	25.99 (9.46)	34.94 (9.44)	8.95 (5.27)	–	–	–
Group CTar ULL n = 25	17.44 (9.82)	22.08 (9.94)	4.64 (4.36)	28.40 (10.17)	33.52 (11.77)	5.12 (7.13)	–	–	–
Group AR UCSP n = 31	18.52 (7.80)	25.52 (9.04)	7.00 (7.62)	26.42 (7.47)	39.48 (6.40)	13.06 (5.79)	–	–	–
Group CTar UCSP n = 31	16.00 (7.46)	18.35 (6.72)	2.35 (1.85)	22.94 (8.14)	24.71 (7.23)	1.77 (1.72)	–	–	–
Group IVR ULL n = 14	17.21 (8.30)	23.29 (11.02)	6.07 (4.14)	29.29 (10.67)	36.39 (9.10)	7.00 (−4.62)	46.52 (26.97)	28.03 (19.40)	18.48 (17.57)
Group CTivr ULL n = 16	20.06 (10.81)	22.25 (9.57)	2.19 (−3.94)	28.25 (9.64)	32.06 (8.50)	3.81 (−3.71)	43.49 (27.08)	26.42 (28.37)	17.07 (11.79)

On the other hand, the training carried out with immersive virtual reality was analyzed. We assessed whether trained students made gains in components of spatial ability (including spatial orientation) after undergoing drawing-based training using full-scale three-dimensional sketching techniques in immersive virtual reality environments.

We explored whether there are significant differences between the two groups (experimental and control) after training. Specific research hypotheses were defined to verify the improvement of spatial skills in students through this virtual reality—based training.

- HVR1_ULL: the experimental group shows an improvement in spatial visualization measured with the DAT5-SR after the training.
- HVR2_ULL: the experimental group shows an improvement in spatial rotation measured with the MRT after the training.
- HVR3_ULL: the experimental group demonstrates an improvement in spatial orientation measured with the SOT test after the training.

To compare the mean gain values obtained by both groups, experimental and control, in the three components, the Student's t statistic was used. It obtained P-value $= .01$ for MRT gain, P-value $= .04$ for DAT5-SR gain, and P-value $= .039$ for SOT. In all cases the P-value was less than 0.05, which means that there is a significant difference in the improvement of mental rotation, visualization, and spatial orientation. Thus, it can be stated that the experimental group has obtained greater gains after training compared with the gains obtained by the control group, and the research hypotheses H_{VR1_ULL}, H_{VR2_ULL}, and H_{VR3_ULL} were all accepted. General hypothesis H3 is confirmed: the group that performs the immersive virtual reality training significantly improves the spatial skills components measured with MRT and DAT5-SR, in addition to improving the spatial orientation component measured with SOT.

2.5.1 Comparison spatial skill gains between university groups training by augmented reality and between training types (AR and VR)

Whether there was a significant difference in the gain of mental rotation levels and spatial visualization between the groups that trained with augmented reality and immersive virtual reality or not was checked. The Student's t test was performed for independent samples comparing pairs of training. Table 2.6 shows the P-values for the gain of the MRT and DAT 5-SR levels for every two workouts.

The comparison per pair shown in Table 2.6 indicates that the augmented reality training group at UCSP improved the spatial visualization component more than the AR and IVR groups at ULL (P-

Table 2.6 Comparison of gain levels in spatial skills between training groups.

	Training's comparison		
	$ULL_{AR} - UCSP_{AR}$	$ULL_{AR} - ULL_{IVR}$	$UCSP_{AR} - ULLI_{IVR}$
Gain MRT_AR	t $= -0.757$	t $= 1143$	t $= 0.427$
	P-value $= .450$	P-value $= .256$	P-value $= .672$
Gain DAT5-SR_AR	**t $= 3.615$**	t $= 1.304$	**t $= 3.447$**
	P-value $= .001$	P-value $= .195$	**P-value $= .001$**

value = .001). The mean gain was 13.06 scores versus 8.95 and 7.00 scores respectively. In all training groups, the spatial rotation component improved equally.

In particular, the augmented reality and immersive virtual reality training performed by the experimental groups of the ULL show no significant difference in gain.

Considering the above and that there are no significant differences in spatial rotations between the three pieces of training, the authors consider that general hypotheses H2 and H4 are confirmed: "*there is no significant difference in the improvement of spatial skills acquired by the two augmented reality training groups*" and "*the two types of training (IVR and AR) improve the components of the spatial skills equally.*"

2.6 Discussion

Based on the results obtained, it can be recognized that the spatial skills level of engineering and architecture students, in general terms, at the beginning of their university careers, is not the best and would require mostly some type of training to have levels that allow them to successfully face university studies. The diversity of levels found is due to the fact that the spatial development of people has an early start in life [75], which can be affected by various factors such as differences in the frequency of construction of things in childhood [76] or the use of video games [77]. However, more studies are needed to determine more precisely such factors. In any case, the implementation of training that might even be a mandatory requirement for those students who have weak spatial skills could develop a high capacity in a way that leads to better success for students in terms of grades obtained, as well as in retention and graduation rates as demonstrated in longitudinal studies such as that of Michigan Tech [78].

In addition, it has been found, in this research, that the spatial skills levels of Spanish students are slightly higher than those of Peruvian ones. It is possible that cultural differences in school education are also a factor that affect the development of spatial skills. However, we consider that the recognized importance given to education by European countries such as Spain or countries such as the USA when considering that the impact of this capacity exceeds the professional success of future engineers and architects, reaching an impact on the technologic development of countries, has led to the evaluation and development of these skills even at the school level [79]. In Latin America, particularly in Peru, the knowledge about the benefits that the spatial skills development provides is very incipient, and very few interventions have been made in this regard [32], and government policies are almost nil.

In the experimentation, the gains in the levels of each component of the spatial skills of the control groups were compared with the experimental groups, and it was found that the control groups showed higher scores the second time, despite not having undergone any training. This non-significant difference is a documented phenomenon that responds to the familiarization that the participants obtain and the memory of the test [80] that allows them to respond more quickly. However, this gain is significant in groups that have been trained with augmented reality and immersive virtual reality.

The significant differences that have been found in the levels of spatial skills means that 3 days for immersive virtual reality and 5 days for augmented reality are effective for the development of spatial skills, in agreement with the research supporting that short-term training is effective [30]. This quality of effectiveness in a short time can be extremely useful to balance the levels of spatial skills in freshmen university students the previous week or the first week of starting university studies without affecting the academic load of the students and without requiring important logistic resources from the universities.

Regarding the specific training with augmented reality, the results obtained determined that the proposed training had a positive influence on the improvement of spatial skills levels both in the mental rotation component (measured with the MRT) and in the spatial visualization component (measured with the DAT5-SR), providing results consistent with the results of similar training [80–82]. Moreover, the results show that in terms of mental rotation, both groups, Peruvian and Spanish students, improved this component in a very similar magnitude. However, in terms of the spatial visualization component, the students of the Peruvian experimental group obtained higher gains compared with their counterpart group from the Spanish university. The experimental conditions have been almost identical, except for the fact that in Peru, the training took place 2 weeks before the beginning of the academic semester, when the students did not have any academic activity, whereas in Spain the students were in the first week of the beginning of the semester, which could have caused some distraction. However, we consider that this is not a clear explanation for this difference, and we will continue looking for the causes to use these factors for the benefit of the students who in the future follow this training or others.

Furthermore, regarding specific training with immersive virtual reality, an important difference with respect to augmented reality training should be mentioned. Since architecture students work from the first year with buildings and urban spaces that are larger than them, in which objects must be designed externally and internally, for where they must imagine walking through them, we consider that in addition to spatial visualization and mental rotation, the students need the subskill of spatial orientation, which allows them to orient themselves in space and in which the spatial position of the person in relation to a fixed object is essential. Although many authors have found a direct correlation between the psychometric measures of mental rotation and spatial orientation, which has led them to use only one of them, other researchers, despite recognizing such a correlation [74], have found a dissociation between tasks that depend on mental rotation and spatial orientation processes, concluding that the ability to orient oneself in an environment and imagine how it is seen from different points of view does not necessarily depend on mental rotation [73]. Thus, the training aimed that the participants, based on the interpretation of two-dimensional drawings, build small architectural spaces on a real scale in a virtual environment so that they could enter and exit them and go through them. This way, they could train the spatial orientation apart from spatial visualization and mental rotation.

The results show that the mean gain obtained for the component of spatial orientation is 18.49 degrees (17.57 SD), which when compared with another study that also used immersive virtual reality [83] that obtained 12.81 degrees (13.97 SD), turns out to be considerably higher. The greatest gain may be due to the fact that in our investigation the students could build a virtual space on a real scale to which they could enter, exit, and go through it, while the comparative study used urban routes using the Google Street View application. The significant gain obtained in our experimentation is comparable, as indicated by the same study, with other kinds of training that used GISc, geoportals, and augmented reality. It is necessary to continue investigating the importance of measuring spatial orientation in architecture students and confirm with larger experiments the benefits of the training with immersive virtual reality and the construction of architectural spaces.

Finally, regarding the comparison of the gains in the spatial skills levels between all the training groups, it has been found that the mental rotation improved in the same magnitude with both trainings and in both universities. However, the spatial visualization had different behavior. It has been the training with augmented reality in the Peruvian university that has caused a higher and important increase in the spatial visualization component with respect to training with immersive virtual reality and with respect to the Spanish university. The evidence that shows that people with lower levels of spatial skills obtain higher gains [84] does not fully explain the effect found in this research, and investigations should continue to find the causes.

The motivation generated using these emerging technologies in the students has been recognized by them verbally, as well as their satisfaction at the end of the training. But beyond that, the need to use technologic tools to train the spatial skills of STEAM students in a short time is demonstrated and, in this way, guarantees their good academic performance in the first years, which will guarantee a greater number and quality of professionals, allowing the development of societies.

2.7 Conclusions and future works

There is an important body of knowledge and research developed that shows the benefits of spatial skills training. However, the effects of cultural differences and age groups on the better development of these skills have yet to be deepened. It is also pending to expand the relationship of the spatial skills in the academic development of architecture students and the development of the creativity they require. In the field of engineering, this study contributes to the countless investigations that recognize the positive impact of spatial skills training and therefore its consequent strengthening and success at the beginning of the university studies.

As for experimentation, we conclude that the short training, developed in 1 week, using exercises of drawing orthographic views and axonometric projections with the help of augmented reality has fulfilled its purpose of raising the level of the spatial skills of engineering students from Peru (UCSP) and Spain (ULL). This conclusion is based on the significant difference found in the experimental groups compared with the control groups when the mental rotation component (measured with the MRT) and the spatial visualization component (measured with the DAT5-SR) were measured in those students. The training helped both groups achieve the same development, even though students from Spain and Peru had different levels in the initial measurements. This training using augmented reality could be expanded to become a longitudinal study that allows finding other important relationships such as the academic performance throughout the professional career, the benefits of its application at the pre-university level, or the greater participation of women in the STEAM field. An update of this augmented reality training has recently been released with a new app for mobile devices [85], which may bring new developments in this line of research.

We also conclude that the short training, developed in a week, using full-scale three-dimensional construction exercises of small architectural spaces with the help of immersive virtual reality has fulfilled the objective of raising the level of the spatial skills of architecture students of Spain (ULL). We based our conclusion on the significant difference found in the experimental group compared with the control group when three components of spatial skills were measured: mental rotation (measured with MRT), spatial visualization (measured with DAT5-SR), and spatial orientation (measured with SOT) in architecture students. No references have been found for a similar training, and it remains as a proposal, for future and more far-reaching work in terms of sample size and time, the study of the relationship of spatial orientation with the skills required by architecture students in terms of navigation, and the route of spaces in the initial phases of ideation of such architectural spaces.

Finally, we hope that this research will strengthen European institutional policies for the development of spatial skills in students who are involved with STEAM careers. Also, we hope that in Latin America, the benefits of the development of the spatial skills can be recognized to give way to the first initiatives in this regard in the governmental sphere, in the field of higher education, and the teaching field. Addressing this issue will strengthen the body of professionals responsible for leading the technologic development of the countries.

References

[1] C.E. Spearman, The Abilities of Man, (n.d.).

[2] H. Gardner, Inteligencias Múltiples, Paidós Barcelona, 2005.

[3] J.B. Carroll, Human Cognitive Abilities: A Survey of Factor-Analytic Studies, Cambridge University Press, 1993.

[4] D.F. Lohman, S. ability, g.I.D.ve P. Tapsfield (Eds.), Human Abilities: Their Nature and Measurement Içinde (S. 97-116), Lawrence Erlbaum Associates, Hillsdale, NJ, 1996.

[5] H. Sánchez, C. Reyes, Psicología del aprendizaje en educación superior, Lima Visión Univ., 2003.

[6] J.L. Saorín-Pérez, R.E. Navarro-Trujillo, N. Martín-Dorta, J. Martín-Gutiérrez, M. Contero, La capacidad espacial y su relación con la ingeniería, DYNA-Ing. E Ind. 84 (2009).

[7] H. Stumpf, J. Eliot, A structural analysis of visual spatial ability in academically talented students, Learn, Individ. Differ. 11 (1999) 137−151.

[8] W.J. Schneider, K.S. McGrew, The Cattell-Horn-Carroll Model of Intelligence, 2012.

[9] J. Buckley, N. Seery, D. Canty, Spatial cognition in engineering education: developing a spatial ability framework to support the translation of theory into practice, Eur. J. Eng. Educ. 44 (2019) 164−178.

[10] J. Martín Gutiérrez, Estudio y evaluación de contenidos didácticos en el desarrollo de las habilidades espaciales en el ámbito de la ingeniería, Universitat Politècnica de València, 2010.

[11] M.G. McGee, Human Spatial Abilities: Psychometric Studies and Environmental, Genetic, Hormonal, and Neurological Influences, American Psychological Association, US, 1979, https://doi.org/10.1037/0033-2909.86.5.889.

[12] P.H. Maier, Spatial geometry and spatial ability-how to make solid geometry solid? in: E. Cohors-Fresenborg, et al. (Eds.), Selected Papers From the Annual Conference of Didactics of Mathemathics 1996, 1998.

[13] M.C. Linn, A.C. Petersen, Emergence and characterization of sex differences in spatial ability: a meta-analysis, Child Dev. (1985) 1479−1498.

[14] J.W. Pellegrino, D.L. Alderton, V.J. Shute, Understanding spatial ability, Educ. Psychol. 19 (1984) 239−253.

[15] S. Olkun, Making connections: improving spatial abilities with engineering drawing activities, Int. J. Math. Teach. Learn. 3 (2003) 1−10.

[16] J. Wai, D. Lubinski, C.P. Benbow, Spatial ability for STEM domains: aligning over 50 years of cumulative psychological knowledge solidifies its importance, J. Educ. Psychol. 101 (2009) 817.

[17] S.A. Sorby, B.J. Baartmans, The development and assessment of a course for enhancing the 3-D spatial visualization skills of first year engineering students, J. Eng. Educ. 89 (2000) 301−307.

[18] S. Sorby, Developing 3D spatial visualization skills, Eng. Des. Graph. J. 63 (2) (1999) 21−32.

[19] J.L. Mohler, Compter graphics education: where and how do we develop spatial ability? in: Eurographics Educ. Pap, 2006, pp. 79−86.

[20] S. Sorby, E. Nevin, A. Behan, E. Mageean, S. Sheridan, Spatial skills as predictors of success in first-year engineering, in: 2014 IEEE Front. Educ. Conf. FIE Proc, IEEE, 2014, pp. 1−7.

[21] P. Connolly, M. Sadowski, Measuring and enhancing spatial visualization in engineering technology students, Age 14 (2009) 1.

[22] J. Martín-Gutiérrez, J. Luís Saorín, M. Contero, M. Alcañiz, D.C. Pérez-López, M. Ortega, Design and validation of an augmented book for spatial abilities development in engineering students, Comput. Graph. 34 (2010) 77−91, https://doi.org/10.1016/j.cag.2009.11.003.

[23] S.A. Sorby, Educational research in developing 3-D spatial skills for engineering students, Int. J. Sci. Educ. 31 (2009) 459−480, https://doi.org/10.1080/09500690802595839.

[24] A. Wigfield, J.S. Eccles, U. Schiefele, R.W. Roeser, P. Davis-Kean, Development of achievement motivation, in: Handb. Child Psychol, John Wiley & Sons, Inc., Hoboken, NJ, USA, 2007, https://doi.org/10.1002/9780470147658.chpsy0315.

[25] B.J. Zimmerman, M. Martinez-Pons, Student differences in self-regulated learning: relating grade, sex, and giftedness to self-efficacy and strategy use, J. Educ. Psychol. 82 (1990) 51–59, https://doi.org/10.1037/0022-0663.82.1.51.

[26] K. Sutton, A. Williams, D. Tremain, P.W. Kilgour, University entry score: is it a consideration for spatial performance in architecture design students? This Artic. Was Orig. Publ. Sutton K Williams Tremain Kilgour P2016 Univ. Entry Score It Consid. Spat. Perform. Archit. Des. Stud. J. Eng. Des. Technol. 14 (2) (2016) 328–342, https://doi.org/10.1108/JEDT-10-2013-0073.

[27] J. Suh, J.Y. Cho, Linking spatial ability, spatial strategies, and spatial creativity: a step to clarify the fuzzy relationship between spatial ability and creativity, Think. Skills Creativ. 35 (2020) 100628.

[28] J.Y. Cho, Spatial ability, creativity, and studio performance in architectural design, in: Proc. 17th Int. Conf. Comput. Aided Archit. Des. Res. Asia Chennai 25-28 April 2012, CUMINCAD, 2012, pp. 131–140. http://papers.cumincad.org/cgi-bin/works/BrowseTree=series:acadia/Show?caadria2012_087. (Accessed 13 August 2021).

[29] F. Munoz-Rubke, R. Will, Z. Hawes, K.H. James, Enhancing spatial skills through mechanical problem solving, Learn. Instr. 75 (2021) 101496.

[30] M. Baenninger, N. Newcombe, The role of experience in spatial test performance: a meta-analysis, Sex. Roles 20 (1989) 327–344.

[31] S.A. Sorby, Developing 3D spatial skills for engineering students, Australas. J. Eng. Educ. 13 (2007) 1–11.

[32] H.C. Gómez-Tone, Impacto de la Enseñanza de la Geometría Descriptiva usando Archivos 3D-PDF como Entrenamiento de la Habilidad Espacial de Estudiantes de Ingeniería Civil en el Perú, Form. Univ 12 (2019) 73–82.

[33] K. Samsudin, A. Rafi, A.S. Hanif, Training in mental rotation and spatial visualization and its impact on orthographic drawing performance, J. Educ. Technol. Soc. 14 (2011) 179–186.

[34] J. Martín-Gutiérrez, M.M.A. González, Ranking and predicting results for different training activities to develop spatial abilities, in: Vis.-Spat. Abil. STEM Educ, Springer, 2017, pp. 225–239.

[35] A. Šafhalter, S. Glodež, A. Šorgo, M. Ploj Virtič, Development of spatial thinking abilities in engineering 3D modeling course aimed at lower secondary students, Int. J. Technol. Des. Educ. (2020) 1–18.

[36] M. Ardebili, Using solid modeling and multimedia software to improve spatial visualization skills, in: 2006 Annu. Conf. Expo, 2006, pp. 11.1411. 1–11.1411. 11.

[37] R. Devon, R.S. Engel, R.J. Foster, D. Sathianathan, G.F. Turner, The effect of solid modeling software on 3-D visualization skills, Eng. Des. Graph. J. 58 (1994) 4–11.

[38] L.E.C. Bravo, J.A.T. Ortiz, L.F.V. Tamayo, Evaluación de factores de entorno que afectan el desarrollo de habilidades espaciales en estudiantes de primer semestre en Ingeniería Industrial, Acad. Virtualidad. 6 (2013) 17–32.

[39] A.S. Alqahtani, L.F. Daghestani, L.F. Ibrahim, Techniques used to improve spatial visualization skills of students in engineering graphics course: a survey, Int. J. Adv. Comput. Sci. Appl. IJACSA. 8 (2017) 91–100.

[40] F.F. Pieterse, A.L. Nel, Teaching Graphical Communication to first year engineering students, in: 2013 IEEE Glob. Eng. Educ. Conf. EDUCON, IEEE, 2013, pp. 405–409.

[41] M. Alias, T.R. Black, D.E. Gray, Effect of instructions on spatial visualisation ability in civil engineering students, Int. Educ. J. 3 (2002) 1–12.

[42] J.A.T. Ortiz, L.F.V. Tamayo, L.E.C. Bravo, Evaluación de técnicas tradicionales y TIC para el desarrollo de habilidades espaciales en estudiantes de primer semestre de ingeniería industrial, Rev. Virtual Univ. Católica Norte (2014) 34–50.

[43] C. Leopold, R.A. Gorska, S.A. Sorby, International experiences in developing the spatial visualization abilities of engineering students, J. Geom. Graph. 5 (2001) 81–91.

[44] G. Marunić, V. Glažar, Improvement and assessment of spatial ability in engineering education, Eng. Rev. Međunar. Časopis Namijenjen Publ. Orig. Istraživanja Aspekta Anal. Konstr. Mater. Novih Tehnol. U Područ. Stroj. Brodogr. Temelj. Teh. Znan. Elektrotehnike Račun. Građev. 34 (2014) 139–150.

[45] N. Sala, virtual reality, augmented reality, and mixed reality in education, in: Curr. Prospect. Appl. Virtual Real. High. Educ, IGI Global, 2020, p. 48.

[46] T.P. Caudell, D.W. Mizell, Augmented reality: an application of heads-up display technology to manual manufacturing processes, in: Proc. Twenty-Fifth Hawaii Int. Conf. Syst. Sci, IEEE, 1992, pp. 659−669.

[47] W.L. Hosch, Augmented reality, Encycl. Br. (2023). https://www.britannica.com/technology/augmented-reality. (Accessed 12 March 2023).

[48] R.T. Azuma, A survey of augmented reality, Presence Teleoperators Virtual, Environ. Times 6 (1997) 355−385.

[49] W. Barfield, Fundamentals of Wearable Computers and Augmented Reality, CRC press, 2015.

[50] E.A.-L. Lee, K.W. Wong, C.C. Fung, How does desktop virtual reality enhance learning outcomes? A structural equation modeling approach, Comput. Educ. 55 (2010) 1424−1442.

[51] Á. Di Serio, M.B. Ibáñez, C.D. Kloos, Impact of an augmented reality system on students' motivation for a visual art course, Comput. Educ. 68 (2013) 586−596.

[52] J. Martín-Gutiérrez, M.D. Meneses Fernández, Applying augmented reality in engineering education to improve academic performance & student motivation, Int. J. Eng. Educ. 30 (2014) 625−635.

[53] Y.C. Larsen, H. Buchholz, C. Brosda, F.X. Bogner, Evaluation of a portable and interactive augmented reality learning system by teachers and students, Augment. Real. Educ. 2011 (2011) 47−56.

[54] R. Gurevych, A. Silveistr, M. Mokliuk, I. Shaposhnikova, G. Gordiichuk, S. Saiapina, Using augmented reality technology in higher education institutions, Postmod. Open. 12 (2021) 109−132, https://doi.org/10.18662/po/12.2/299.

[55] T. Serdar, E.-S.S. Aziz, S.K. Esche, C. Chassapis, Integration of augmented reality into the CAD process, in: 2013 ASEE Annu. Conf. Expo, 2013, pp. 23.784. 1−23.784. 10.

[56] T.R. Thornton, Understanding How Learner Outcomes Could Be Affected through the Implementation of Augmented Reality in an Introductory Engineering Graphics Course, North Carolina State University, 2014.

[57] H.C. Gómez-Tone, J. Martin-Gutierrez, L. Valencia Anci, C.E. Mora Luis, International comparative pilot study of spatial skill development in engineering students through autonomous augmented reality-based training, Symmetry 12 (2020) 1401.

[58] A. Dünser, K. Steinbügl, H. Kaufmann, J. Glück, Virtual and augmented reality as spatial ability training tools, in: Proc. 7th ACM SIGCHI N. Z. Chapters Int. Conf. Comput.-Hum. Interact. Des. Centered HCI, 2006, pp. 125−132.

[59] J. Lanier, Virtual reality: the promise of the future, Interact. Learn. Int. 8 (1992) 275−279.

[60] H.E. Lowood, Virtual reality, Encycl. Br. (2023). https://www.britannica.com/technology/virtual-reality. (Accessed 12 March 2023).

[61] R. Schroeder, Possible Worlds: The Social Dynamic of Virtual Reality Technology, Westview Press, Inc., 1996.

[62] J.W. Regian, W.L. Shebilske, J.M. Monk, Virtual reality: an instructional medium for visual-spatial tasks, J. Commun. 42 (4) (1992) 136−149, https://doi.org/10.1111/j.1460-2466.1992.tb00815.x.

[63] H.C. Gomez-Tone, J. Martin-Gutierrez, B.K. Valencia-Anci, Spatial skills training through drawing architectural spaces inside immersive virtual reality, in: Perspect. Trends Educ. Technol, Springer, 2022, pp. 383−393.

[64] H.C. Gómez-Tone, J. Martin-Gutierrez, J. Bustamante-Escapa, P. Bustamante-Escapa, Spatial skills and perceptions of space: representing 2D drawings as 3D drawings inside immersive virtual reality, Appl. Sci. 11 (2021) 1475.

[65] T. Guzsvinecz, É. Orbán-Mihálykó, E. Perge, C. Sik-Lányi, Analyzing the spatial skills of university students with a Virtual Reality application using a desktop display and the Gear VR, Acta Polytech. Hung. 17 (2020) 35−56.

[66] J.S.-K. Chang, G. Yeboah, A. Doucette, P. Clifton, M. Nitsche, T. Welsh, A. Mazalek, Evaluating the effect of tangible virtual reality on spatial perspective taking ability, in: Proc. 5th Symp. Spat. User Interact, Association for Computing Machinery, New York, NY, USA, 2017, pp. 68−77, https://doi.org/10.1145/3131277.3132171.

[67] R. Molina-Carmona, M.L. Pertegal-Felices, A. Jimeno-Morenilla, H. Mora-Mora, Virtual reality learning activities for multimedia students to enhance spatial ability, Sustainability 10 (2018) 1074, https://doi.org/10.3390/su10041074.

[68] N.A.A. González, Development of spatial skills with virtual reality and augmented reality, Int. J. Interact. Des. Manuf. IJIDeM. 12 (2018) 133−144, https://doi.org/10.1007/s12008-017-0388-x.

[69] J. Martín Gutiérrez, M. Contero González, M. Alcaniz Raya, Curso para la mejora de la capacidad espacial. Perspectivas y vistas normalizadas mediante realidad aumentada, Ar-books.com, Madrid, 2011.

[70] S.G. Vandenberg, A.R. Kuse, Mental rotations, a group test of three-dimensional spatial visualization, Percept, Mot. Skills 47 (1978) 599−604, https://doi.org/10.2466/pms.1978.47.2.599.

[71] G.K. Bennett, H.G. Seashore, A.G. Wesman, The Differential Aptitude Tests, Spanish of TEA Ediciones, New York, NY, USA, 1947, https://doi.org/10.1002/j.2164-4918.1956.tb01710.x.

[72] M. Hegarty, D.R. Montello, A.E. Richardson, T. Ishikawa, K. Lovelace, Spatial abilities at different scales: individual differences in aptitude-test performance and spatial-layout learning, Intelligence 34 (2006) 151−176, https://doi.org/10.1016/j.intell.2005.09.005.

[73] M. Kozhevnikov, M. Hegarty, A dissociation between object manipulation spatial ability and spatial orientation ability, Mem. Cognit. 29 (2001) 745−756, https://doi.org/10.3758/BF03200477.

[74] M. Hegarty, D. Waller, A dissociation between mental rotation and perspective-taking spatial abilities, Intelligence 32 (2004) 175−191.

[75] N.S. Newcombe, M. Stieff, Six myths about spatial thinking, Int. J. Sci. Educ. 34 (2012) 955−971, https://doi.org/10.1080/09500693.2011.588728.

[76] S.A. Sorby, N.L. Veurink, Spatial Skills Among Minority and International Engineering Students, 2012, pp. 25.1172.1−25.1172.11. https://peer.asee.org/spatial-skills-among-minority-and-international-engineering-students. (Accessed 6 August 2021).

[77] H. Choi, J. Feng, Using video games to improve spatial skills, in: Serious Games Educ. Appl., 1er Edición, IGI Global, 2016, https://doi.org/10.4018/978-1-5225-0513-6.ch005.

[78] N.L. Veurink, S.A. Sorby, Longitudinal study of the impact of requiring training for students with initially weak spatial skills, Eur. J. Eng. Educ. 44 (2019) 153−163, https://doi.org/10.1080/03043797.2017.1390547.

[79] S. Sorby, T. Drummer, K. Hungwe, L. Parolini, R. Molzan, Preparing for engineering studies: improving the 3- D spatial skills of K-12 students, Int. J. Learn. Annu. Rev. 12 (2007), https://doi.org/10.18848/1447-9494/CGP/v14i02/45218.

[80] N. Veurink, A.J. Hamlin, S. Sorby, Impact of spatial training on " non-rotators ," in: 68th -Year Conf, 2013, pp. 15−22.

[81] C. Roca-González, J. Martin-Gutierrez, M. García-Dominguez, M. del C.M. Carrodeguas, Virtual technologies to develop visual-spatial ability in engineering students, Eurasia J. Math. Sci. Technol. Educ. 13 (2017) 441−468, https://doi.org/10.12973/eurasia.2017.00625a.

[82] M. Contero, J.M. Gomis, F. Naya, F. Albert, J. Martin-Gutierrez, Development of an augmented reality based remedial course to improve the spatial ability of engineering students, in: 2012 Frontiers in Education Conference Proceedings (Ed.), IEEE Computer Society, 2012, pp. 1−5.

[83] C. Carbonell-Carrera, J.L. Saorin, Virtual learning environments to enhance spatial orientation, Eurasia J. Math. Sci. Technol. Educ. 14 (2017) 709−719, https://doi.org/10.12973/ejmste/79171.

[84] L.T. David, Training effects on mental rotation, spatial orientation and spatial visualisation depending on the initial level of spatial abilities, Procedia - Soc. Behav. Sci. 33 (2012) 328−332, https://doi.org/10.1016/j.sbspro.2012.01.137.

[85] R. Llorens Rodríguez, J. Martín Gutiérrez, M.R. Contero González, M.L. Alcañiz Raya, Ejercicios para el entrenamiento de las habilidades espaciales, Colecc. Académica. (2020).

Introduction to artificial intelligence and current trends

3

Law Kumar Singh[1] and Munish Khanna[2]

[1]*Department of Computer Engineering and Applications, GLA University, Mathura, Uttar Pradesh, India;* [2]*Department of CSE, Hindustan College of Science and Technology, Mathura, Uttar Pradesh, India*

3.1 Introduction

People have given a logical name to humankind: *Homo sapiens* (man the wise). AI endeavors to associate human knowledge with machines or PCs. It started in 1956. It took logicians about 2000 years to figure out how the machine could pick things up, see things, remember things, and think.

Artificial intelligence (AI) means the ability to mimic or simulate the human mind's capabilities. AI is a continuously emerging and growing field of computer science. It has a great impact on the quality of life. This chapter will discuss the history of AI, its advantages and disadvantages, the distinction between symbolic and computational AI, evolutionary computing, logic-based reasoning, structural models of knowledge representation, rule-based systems, pattern recognition, cluster recognition, neural networks (NNs), and AI applications, and so on. It will also look at how AI research will progress in the future and where it might go in the coming years, among other things.

3.2 History of AI
3.2.1 The growth of AI (1943—56)

A paper published in the journal *Science* in 1950 by Warren McCulloch and Walter Pitts [1] is often considered to be the earliest piece of work that is today commonly referred to as "artificial intelligence." A direct result of Russell and Whitehead's work on the formal analysis of propositional calculus was the discovery of Turing's theory of computation, which was also a direct result of their work on propositional calculus. According to the researchers, in their model, each neuron is represented as either "on" or "off," with the transition from off to on occurring in response to incitation by a considerable number of nearby neurons, as indicated by the researchers. The researchers hope to demonstrate, among other things, that every measurable limit may be specified by a network of neurons that are interconnected and that all of the canny connectives can be realized by unambiguous network plans. They hypothesized that networks that were accurately described would learn from their mistakes in a manner comparable to that of other networks, which they found to be true. Among the most important and energizing guidelines for modifying the affiliation qualities between neurons to the extent that learning might take place was offered by Donald Hebb [1a]. The chess program written by

Claude Shannon [2] and Alan Turing [2a] was influenced by the work of John von Neumann and was designed for use on conventional computers. Shannon and Turing were both members of the Shannon—Turing team. The development of the world's first NN computer took place during Marvin Minsky and Dean Edmonds' undergraduate years at Princeton, and it was completed at the same time as the actual computer. Aside from that, Princeton served as the residence of John McCarthy, who was at the time a significant player in the field of AI. McCarthy accepted a position at Dartmouth College shortly after graduating, which would subsequently develop into a position at the forefront of his field of expertise. McCarthy invited Noam Minsky, Claude Shannon, and Nathaniel Rochester to collaborate with him to assist him in bringing together examiners from all over the United States who were interested in automata, NNs, and the evaluation of comprehension. Toward the end of the spring semester of 1956, they organized a 2-month workshop at Dartmouth, and they all worked together to make it a reality. However, while the Dartmouth workshop did not result in any big achievements, it did serve to familiarize all of the important players with one another, which was a positive step forward. It would be this group of professionals, as well as their understudies and associates at universities such as MIT, CMU, Stanford, and IBM, among other places, who would come to dominate the area over the next 2 decades. As a result of the workshop, the participants agreed to use McCarthy's alias in the field, which was the following: "Artificial Intelligence (AI) is a term that refers to the study of artificial intelligence." This was possibly the most significant outcome of the workshop.

3.2.1.1 Early excitement, incredible assumptions (1952–69)

Several triumphs were achieved during the early and extended years of AI development, but each was insignificant when compared with the whole scope of the field during that time period. Given the basic nature of personal computers at the time, as well as the restricted programming tools available, it is astonishing how many jobs they were capable of performing. Because computers were thought to be capable of nothing more than number shuffling only 2 or 3 years earlier, it came as something of a surprise when a PC accomplished even the most basic of jobs. The fact that this was not the case provided us with great reassurance and comfort. There are almost a million Xs in Turing's huge list of Xs, which is an exhaustive list of every X that can be executed by a machine. It was once thought that "a machine can never do X," and the intellectual elite were comfortable with that belief for a long time. Despite the fact that it was first accepted, this hypothesis has since been brought into doubt as being incorrect. Virtual intelligence professionals will respond to inquiries by flashing an X one after another after another until the question has been handled, at which point they will stop responding. When it comes to the vast majority of situations, it is likely that this will be how they reply to you. According to some of the most knowledgeable professionals, this stage of AI is referred to as "Look, Ma, no hands!" AI is referred to as "Look, Ma, there are no hands!" by some of the world's most cutting-edge AI experts. "Look, Ma, there are no hands!" say some of the world's most cutting-edge AI experts. Nathaniel Rochester and his IBM colleagues were collectively referred to as the Rochester Group during the period in which they were in command of a substantial chunk of IBM's key AI programs, which included the Watson computer.

The 1950s saw the birth of Herbert Gelernter's Geometry Theorem Prover [3]. The logic theorist's aphorisms can be used to demonstrate hypotheses in a succinct and accessible manner. There were many possibilities open to Gelernter, but he quickly realized that most of them led nowhere. By showing the general hypothesis to be demonstrated through the graph's mathematical description, the search became more focused. Prior to using an outline, a computer can confirm its legitimacy based on its context. When John McCarthy enrolled at MIT in 1958, he departed Dartmouth with three promises:

MIT AI Lab Memo No. 1 was McCarthy's introduction to Drawl, the AI programming language. No one can deny Drawl's unquestionable appeal, and no one can argue against it. The key to McCarthy's success was the use of Lisp and the resources available to him. Securing scarce and costly resources was also a challenge. Thus, he and other MIT students began debating the pros and cons of time-sharing arrangements. Long story short, McCarthy became interested in this project because of his legitimate fears about Digital Equipment Corporation's future as a global leader in personal computer production. As Rosenblatt showed, the connection qualities of a perceptron can be modified to match any input that suggests a possible match.

3.2.1.2 A portion of the real world (1966–74)

This is what will happen 10 years from now: a machine that can play chess is going to be better than the best player in the world. This is what is going to happen. It will still have to be done by hand in 5 years. A computer will be able to show that a new numeric theory is true, but it will still have to be done by hand. People have made many false claims. When simple models were used to solve more complicated problems, they did not work out well at all. Some of the people who worked on AI projects at the time had trouble with this. Things worked this way in the 1950 and 1960s: during history class, a lot of what people learned about computer science looked a lot like the same story line that they had already seen before. The 1950 and 1960s were a time when a lot of people worked on making machines that could both read and write. This did what it was supposed to do to help speed up the translation of Russian logical articles into English quickly and it worked. For many years now, adding punctuation and changing words based on electronic word references have been thought to keep each sentence's meaning the same. This is not true. However, this turned out to be false. If you know a lot about the subject, it will help you figure out how to understand what someone says. Many people have a hard time translating this phrase into other languages, as you can see in the text that comes after this. A way to show this is to say, "the soul wants, but the tissue is hard to work with." If you say, "The vodka tastes good, but the meat is disgusting," that is how you should say it. This shows how hard it is.

"No computer interpretation of broad logical content has occurred, and none is expected in the near future," writes the author. According to Minsky and Papert's Perceptrons (1969) [4], despite the fact that perceptrons appeared to be capable of learning everything they were prepared for, they were actually capable of learning basically nothing of any significance. When both of its input streams were extremely rich in information, a two-input perceptron could not detect it. Despite the fact that their conclusions were not applicable to larger, multifaceted organizations, funding for NN research had practically dried up by the time they were finished. In the late 1980s, the discovery of back-engineering learning calculations for multifacet networks triggered a rush in neural net research. This paved the way for a rise in NN research in the late 1980s [5].

3.2.1.3 Information-based frameworks: the way to control (1969–79)

Throughout the first decade of AI development, critical thinking was portrayed as a general-purpose inquiry component aimed at integrating basic thinking skills to identify intricate arrangements. Such methods have been nicknamed "feeble procedures" since they rely on unstable data about the environment. Furthermore, the presentation of many challenging problems is rendered ineffective. The only way to avoid this is to make better use of data to think in larger steps and address common issues in highly specialized industries. Dealing with a challenging situation, it could be said, needs planning ahead of time on how to tackle it. Feigenbaum and colleagues at Stanford began the Heuristic

Programming Project to see how far the new master frameworks method might be applied to a variety of human abilities. Following that, the clinical conclusion domain drew a lot of interest. Feigenbaum, Buchanan, and Dr. Edward Short created MYCIN to detect blood pollution. With around 450 principles, MYCIN has the ability to advance like a few specialists and significantly better than junior specialists. It also has two significant differences from DENDRAL. The MYCIN rules, unlike the DENDRAL rules, could not be produced using a broad hypothetical model. They need to come from a wide range of specialists who have firsthand knowledge of the events. Second, the standards must be followed to account for clinical data sensitivity. With the continuing development of applications for real-world scenarios, the demand for acceptable data visualization methodologies has increased. There was a wide spectrum of portrayal accents.

Certain logic-based programming languages have been developed, such as Prolog in Europe and the PLANNER family in the United States. Others used a more methodical approach, collecting data on individual products and occurrences and organizing them into a massive, ordered sequence that resembled natural scientific classification. Others took a more deliberate approach, gathering information on specific items and events and organizing it into a vast orderly sequence that resembled natural scientific classification. Others took a more methodical approach, gathering data on specific item and event types and organizing it into a massive ordered sequence that was indistinguishable from natural scientific classification. Minsky [5a] designed a massive ordered sequence that was indistinguishable from natural scientific classification, while others took a more methodical approach, gathering data on specific item and event types and organizing it into a massive ordered sequence that was indistinguishable from natural scientific classification.

3.2.1.4 AI becomes a thriving industry (1980–88)

The first successful implementation of a master framework occurred at Digital Equipment Corporation (DEC) [5]. This program facilitated the development of new personal computer frameworks. Furthermore, the organization was supposed to save $40 million each year by 1986. By 1988, DEC's AI division had produced 40 master frameworks, with more on the way. Du Pont had 100 in use and 500 under development, equating to an annual savings of roughly $10 million. Almost every big company in the United States had its own AI team and was either trying out master framework innovation or was already using it.

The Fifth-Generation project sparked interest in AI, and academics and corporations were able to secure support for similar investment in the United States by exploiting worries about Japanese dominance. To compete with Japan's efforts, the Microelectronics and Computer Technology Corporation was formed. In the United Kingdom, the Alvey report restored funds that had been reduced by the Lighthill report. Furthermore, the burgeoning AI industry included software companies like Carnegie Group, Inference, Intellicorp, and Knowledge that provided tools for developing expert systems, as well as hardware companies like Lisp Machines, Texas Instruments, Symbolics, and Xerox that built workstations optimized for Lisp programming. A number of companies have invested in the development of vision systems for industrial robots. The industry's overall value climbed from a few million dollars in 1980 to more than two billion dollars in 1988.

3.2.1.5 The return of neural networks (1986–present)

Despite the fact that, following Minsky and Papert's *Perceptron* book, the focus of software engineering changed away from neural organizations, research in other areas, most notably physical research, continued. Enormous clusters of basic neurons are similar to massive chemical assemblages in materials. Hopfield [5b] analyzed organizational capacity and streamlining using factual mechanical methodologies, resulting in critical thought cross-preparation. The concepts of NNs have been examined by memory researchers David Rumelhart and Geoff Hinton. We investigate the true stimulus that occurred despite the fact that, following Minsky and Papert's *Perceptrons* book, software engineering mostly ignored the topic of brain organization in favor of study in other fields, most notably physical science. In the 1980s, at least four different organizations looked into the back-spread learning computation invented by Bryson and Ho in Ref. [5c]. People in computer science and neurology have used computing to solve a wide range of issues when they learn. The collection of Parallel Circulated Processing used a lot of energy because there was no way to predict how the results would be distributed [6].

Some experts predict a harsh "artificial intelligence winter," in which AI investment will plummet. NNs may have been seen as rivals to traditional AI at one point because of this, as well as because of real parts on the NN side.

3.2.1.6 Recent events (1987–present)

As an example, speech recognition is a field of study. Several different structures and strategies were tried throughout the 1970s. Several of these were appointed with care. They were also displayed on a few oddly selected autos. Recently, hidden Markov models (HMMs)-based approaches have recently swept the region. The current topic is concerned with two aspects of HMMs. To begin with, they are based on a precise numeric foundation. As a result, discourse analyzers have been able to add to an already long list of numeric outputs generated across a variety of areas. Second, they are created by building a large corpus of actual conversation data in a cycle. This ensures a powerful display, and the HMMs have consistently improved their performance in tough visually handicapped tests. Discourse innovation, as well as the field of manually written character recognition, is being used in a lot of current and consumer devices.

According to Peter Cheeseman's work "In Defense of Probability," the publication of Judea Pearl's *Probabilistic Reasoning in Intelligent Systems* [7] coincided with a renaissance of interest in likelihood and choice hypotheses in AI (1985). The consequence network formalism has been widely employed in judicial processes for decades to aid in effective reasoning when dealing with a variety of problematic material. In its current version, this paradigm is thought to have overcome the majority of the issues associated with probabilistic thinking frameworks developed in the 1960 and 1970s. As a result, AI research on questionable reasoning and master frameworks has been the field's core focus.

Alien Newell, John Laird, and Paul Rosenbloom created SOAR [8,9], the most well-known example of a fully specialized AI architecture. The ostensibly "planned" development seeks to understand the operations of specialists working in real-world situations by using consistent tactile data sources. The findings of this study include the discovery that when the judgments of hitherto limited AI subfields are integrated into a single expert plan, they may all be revised equally.

3.3 Industry 4.0 and AI revolution

The term "fourth industrial revolution," also referred to as "industry 4.0," describes the current era of rapid technologic advancement, particularly in areas driven by AI [10,11]. The development of data-driven AI technologies is providing the impetus for the fourth industrial revolution, known as industry

4.0. The term "industry 4.0" refers to the present trend of exchanging data and automating operations through the use of various technologic tools. The term "industry 4.0" refers to the present trend in industrial technology toward the automation and exchange of data. This trend encompasses the development of intelligent factories, cyber-physical systems, the internet of things, cloud computing, and cognitive computing. The first step in the digital revolution that will eventually lead to industry 4.0 is the acquisition of data, which is then followed by the analysis of that data using AI. Since AI is changing the world by putting human behavior and intelligence into machines and systems, the term "intellect" can be used to describe computing and services.

People are talking about AI right now because they think it will have an effect on businesses of all sizes and in all fields. Industrial AI has the potential to improve the reliability, safety, and dependability of products and services that are already out there. For example, the automotive industry uses computer vision to reduce the number of accidents and help vehicles stay in their lanes, both of which make driving safer. AI is causing a revolution, so the most powerful governments in the world are putting more money into AI research and development. In a similar way, the most powerful and well-known companies in the world are putting a lot of work into researching and developing AI technologies that will give them an edge over their competitors. The article "Real-World Applications of AI" says that AI has a big effect on almost every area, including homes, businesses, hospitals, and even online communities.

3.3.1 Learning about the different kinds of AI

AI is viewed as a field of study and engineering that seeks to recreate certain challenges and behaviors related to the study of human cognition. However, the ever-changing nature of real-world data and events could make it difficult to develop a reliable AI model. Fig. 3.1 depicts the potential of AI, and our goal is to learn about this power so that we can use it to solve the many problems that have arisen as a result of the fourth industrial revolution. To do this, we look into different kinds of AI, like analytical, functional, interactive, textual, and visual AI [12].

Analytical AI: When "analytics" is used as a noun, it refers the process of recognizing, comprehending, and successfully communicating the significance of repeating patterns in data". Consequently, the goal of analytical AI is to identify fresh insights, patterns, and relationships in the data, in addition to supporting humans in making data-driven decisions. Consequently, in the area of modern business intelligence, it has evolved into an essential component of AI that can provide an organization

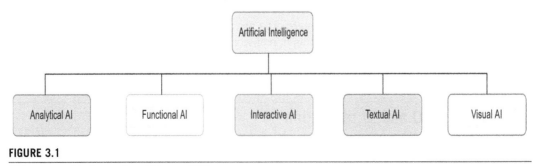

FIGURE 3.1

AI types considering real-world issues [12].

with insights and make suggestions based on its ability to handle and analyze data. In other words, it can reveal details about your organization. In other words, it has become an essential component of AI and may be valuable for businesses. Several machine learning and deep learning techniques can be utilized to develop an AI model that solves a practical problem. Estimating the operational risks of a business could be done with the help of an analytical model that is driven by data.

Functional AI: AI that is functional, much like AI that is analytical, searches through enormous amounts of data to identify recurrent patterns and interdependencies. On the other hand, functional AI is more concerned with carrying out actions than it is with offering advice. For instance, a functional AI model could be used in robots and apps for the internet of things to promote rapid action.

Interactive AI: Interactive AI is often used to make communication automation more efficient and interactive. This is common in many parts of our daily lives, especially in the business world. This is especially true when it comes to virtual assistants, which are a type of AI that can be used in a conversational way. One example of this would be the use of an interactive AI model when making chatbots and other smart personal assistants. A lot of different methods can be used to make an interactive model of AI. Some of these methods are machine learning, frequent pattern mining, reasoning, and AI heuristic search.

Textual AI: Textual AI largely consists of text analytics or natural language processing (NLP), which gives businesses the ability to recognize text, convert speech to text, translate it into other languages, and create their own content. Text analytics are also extensively used in textual AI. Textual AI, for instance, might be used by a company to keep an internal corporate knowledge library and provide customers with appropriate services, like query answers.

Visual AI: Visual AI is frequently capable of categorizing, organizing, and identifying objects, in addition to drawing conclusions from still photos and movies. Therefore, it is possible to think of visual AI as a branch of computer science that aims to teach robots how to learn about images and visual data in a manner that is comparable to how humans do it. This means that the goal of this branch of AI is to teach robots how to learn about images and visual data. This particular variety of AI is utilized rather frequently in a variety of industries including computer vision and augmented reality.

3.4 Explainable AI

In this tech-driven era, AI is creating cutting-edge technologies for more efficient workflow in multiple industries across the globe. There are machine learning and deep learning algorithms that are too complex for anyone but AI engineers and related employees to comprehend. AI has produced self-explanatory algorithms that enable stakeholders and partners to comprehend the entire process of transforming massive, complex, real-time data sets into meaningful, in-depth insights. This is known as explainable artificial intelligence (XAI), in which the outcomes of these solutions can be easily comprehended by humans. It aids AI designers in explaining how AI machines have generated a particular type of insight or outcome for the market success of businesses [13].

For a deeper comprehension of explainable AI through the creation of interpretable and inclusive AI, numerous online courses and platforms are available. There are four primary principles of XAI for interpreting machine learning model predictions. User-benefit, societal acceptance, regulatory and compliance, system development, and owner-benefit models are available for XAI. XAI is required for the implementation of responsible AI to ensure AI model explainability and accountability.

Most people think of black box algorithms when they think of AI. Millions of data points are fed into these algorithms, which then do their "magic" and give out results that users are expected to accept even though they cannot be explained. Even the engineers who made this kind of model cannot explain what it means because it is built directly from the data. Black box models, like NNs, do a great job with hard prediction problems. Even though the results of the algorithms are very accurate, no one can figure out how the algorithms got to those results in the first place. Explainable white box AI, on the other hand, lets people understand the reasoning behind the system's decisions. This has helped the technology become more popular in corporate settings. Black box algorithms are more advanced in terms of technology than these models. However, they are more reliable, which is a good thing for companies with high standards. This is a trade-off for the fact that they are more open.

The principles of explainable AI are a set of four guidelines that enable XAI to efficiently and effectively adopt some fundamental properties. To better comprehend how AI models function, four guiding principles have been developed. These principles apply individually and independently of one another and must be evaluated separately.

Explanation: This is the first major principle that requires an AI model to generate a comprehensive explanation with evidence and reasoning so that humans can comprehend the process of generating high-stakes business decisions. The other three principles of explainable AI regulate the standards for these clear explanations.

Meaningful: This is the second principle of explainable AI, which provides explanations that are meaningful and understandable to human stakeholders and business partners. The more insightful the explanation is, the clearer is the comprehension of AI models. The explanations should not be complicated and should be tailored to both groups and individuals of stakeholders.

Explanation accuracy: This is the third principle for producing meaningful outputs from a complex AI process. It aids in imposing precision on stakeholders' explanations of a system. There can be varying explanations and metrics of accuracy for various groups and individuals. Therefore, it is essential to provide multiple types of explanations that are 100% accurate.

Knowledge limits: This is the fourth and final principle of XAI, which explains that the AI model operates only under specific conditions according to its design with training data sets: the black box's knowledge is limited. It should operate within the bounds of its knowledge to avoid discrepancies or unjustified business outcomes. To maintain trust between an organization and its stakeholders, the AI system is required to identify and declare its knowledge limitations.

XAI aids in enhancing AI interpretability, assessing and mitigating AI risks, and deploying AI with the utmost confidence and trust. With the development of self-explaining algorithms, AI is advancing daily. Employees and stakeholders must have a thorough understanding of the intelligent decision-making process with AI model accountability in machine learning algorithms, deep learning algorithms, and NNs for self-explanatory algorithms.

In some fields, AI algorithms need to be explained before they can be used. This could be because of rules or because of how people act. Think about how brain tumors are grouped. No doctor will feel comfortable going into surgery just because "the algorithm said so." What about making loans? People whose requests were turned down would want to know why. There are some situations where you do not have to give an explanation. Even if predictive maintenance applications were not a matter of life and death, employees would feel safer if they knew why certain equipment might need preventive maintenance. Senior management often understands the value of AI applications, but they also have some worries. Experts say that executives always have a "but" in their minds: "but if you cannot explain how you came up with the solution, I cannot use it." This is because there is a risk of bias in black box AI systems, which could lead to lawsuits, big costs, and damage to the organization's brand and finances. The best XAI solution is one that is fairly accurate and can be explained to practitioners, executives, and end users.

Intelligent software that incorporates XAI principles is characterized by the following:

- **Brings relief to system users**: It provides system users with comfort. They get the logic behind the choices and can support them. For instance, a loan officer would feel more at ease advising a client that their loan application was denied if he is aware of the reasoning behind the decision.
- **Ensures compliance**: By confirming the offered explanation, users may determine if the algorithm's rules are valid and in conformity with the law and ethics.
- **Permits optimization of the system**: When designers and developers read the explanation, they may determine what is wrong and change it.
- **Eliminates prejudice**: When users read the explanation, they may identify any biassed judgment, overturn the system's conclusion, and modify the algorithm to prevent similar situations in the future.
- **Enables employees to act on the output of the system**: For instance, an XAI could predict that a specific corporate client will not renew their software license. The initial response of the manager may be to offer a discount. However, what if poor customer service was the reason for the departure? In its explanation, the system will state this.
- **Gives individuals the ability to act**: XAI permits parties impacted by particular decisions to contest and potentially alter the outcome (such as mortgage granting situations).

3.5 Applicability of AI in recommendation systems

A recommendation engine is a data-driven system that proposes goods, services, and information to consumers. Nevertheless, the suggestion might be influenced by a range of things, such as the user's past and the actions of similar users. Recommendation systems are rapidly becoming the dominant method for exposing users to the whole of the digital universe via the lens of their experiences, actions, preferences, and interests. And in a world of information density and product saturation, a recommendation engine enables businesses to present customers with individualized information and solutions in an effective manner [14].

A recommendation engine may greatly increase revenue, click-through rates, conversion rates, and other key metrics. It may have a favorable impact on the user experience, leading to increased customer retention and satisfaction. Consider Netflix as an example. Instead of requiring you to go through hundreds of box sets and film titles, Netflix provides you with a far tighter selection of potential favorites. This feature saves you time and enhances the user experience. With this feature, Netflix was able to reduce cancellation rates, saving the corporation around one billion dollars annually. Companies such as Amazon have employed recommender systems for over 2 decades, but in the past few years, it has spread to other areas such as banking and tourism.

3.5.1 How do system recommendations function?

Shopping has always been and will continue to be an important human activity. Not so long ago, we asked our friends for advice before purchasing a certain product. Therefore, it is human nature to purchase products advised by our more trusted friends. The digital age has taken into account this antiquated practice. Consequently, every online store you visit today may use a recommendation engine. Using algorithms and data, recommendation engines select and propose the most relevant goods for a particular consumer. As the saying goes, it resembles an automated store clerk. When requesting one item, he offers another that you may be interested in.

Developing product recommendation algorithm models is a rapidly expanding field of study.

3.5.2 Common obstacles encountered by a recommender system?

1. **A lack of data**: Data sets containing rows upon rows of values that are empty or include zeros. Therefore, it is crucial to identify strategies to use dense and information-rich portions of the data collection.
2. **Latent relationship labeling is flawed**: The same items with different labeling might be overlooked or ingested inappropriately, indicating that the information is not correctly assimilated.
3. **Scalability**: The multitude of goods and clientele has rendered the conventional strategy ineffective. This becomes difficult when data sets grow in size and might result in a decrease in performance.

3.5.3 Recommender systems with AI

To fulfill the increased demand for recommendations, numerous AI-based algorithms have been developed and deployed into recommender systems as a result of the rise of big data. The following section discusses seven various AI-based strategies that have enhanced recommender systems.

1. recommender systems using deep NNs
2. perceptron-based multilayer recommender systems
3. auto-encoding recommendation systems
4. recommender systems based on convolutional NNs
5. recommender systems based on recurrent NNs
6. recommender systems based on generative adversarial networks
7. recommender systems based on graph NNs

3.5.4 Machine learning in recommendation systems

Algorithms are used by recommendation engines to suggest services or products to clients. Recently, these engines have begun applying machine learning methods to improve the accuracy of item predictions. The algorithms adapt based on the data collected from recommendation systems. The two kinds of machine learning methods for recommendation systems are collaborative and content-based filtering. Modern recommendation systems, however, integrate both.

Content-based filtering takes into account the similarity of product qualities, while collaborative approaches measure similarity based on consumer interactions. Generally speaking, the essence of machine learning is to build a function that predicts the relative usefulness of objects. With so much information on the internet and so many people utilizing it, it has become crucial for businesses to search for and present clients with information that matches their requirements and preferences.

3.6 Advantages and disadvantages of AI

There are numerous advantages to using AI, which is a rapidly developing field, some of these advantages are stated below [9].

3.6.1 Decrement in human error

The term "human blunder" is used to describe this phenomenon because humans make mistakes from time to time, whereas computers, if properly programmed, do not make any mistakes"". A list of options is prepared for consideration based on the most recent data that has been obtained and after the data has been subjected to a set of exact criteria. In the presence of these factors, the risk of errors occurring is reduced, and the likelihood of demonstrating a better level of precision at precision is increased.

3.6.2 Availability

A typical day for the ordinary person will consist of 5−6 h of labor, excluding breaks, if no breaks are taken during the day. People who are naturally prone to working long hours need a reward that will help them prepare for the next day's work-life cycle. They must make every effort to maintain a flawless reputation in both their professional and personal lives on a weekly basis, regardless of the circumstances. On the other hand, machines and AI can work together without becoming bored or exhausted after completing the same activity over and over again.

3.6.3 No risk

One of the primary advantages of AI is that it exposes us to a variety of risks by allowing AI robots to do our work. Metal-bodied equipment is intrinsically protective and can survive harsh circumstances, whether incapacitating a terrorist, traveling to space, or scanning the most vital parts of the ocean. AI allows robots to do jobs more precisely while being free from fatigue.

3.6.4 Impartial decisions

Emotions absolutely impact people. However, AI is completely rational and practical. AI has a big advantage over humans because it does not have one-sided views. This allows it to make more accurate decisions.

3.6.5 Faster decision

Because they are realistic and employ acceptable strategies, machines are faster and more precise than humans. Humans, on the other hand, are emotional, which might have an impact on their productivity at work. AI has a big impact on people's lives, and while it has a lot of advantages, it also has a lot of disadvantages.

3.6.6 Unemployment

Humans are being displaced from jobs that are no longer needed by AI. As a result, the number of open positions has significantly fallen. Many jobs are being lost as a result of AI. The chabot is an excellent example of this. Personnel, on the other hand, are in excruciating pain.

3.6.7 Lethargic humans

AI does the majority of the tedious and meaningless tasks. Because we will not have to memorize data or answer puzzles to conduct business, we'll think less critically in general. People may face difficulties in the future as a result of their reliance on AI.

3.6.8 Expensive

Because AI-based frameworks are so sophisticated, they need a large amount of research and resources to design, maintain, and upgrade. The underlying investigation, as well as the framework development, have a significant impact on the cost of a solution. NN applications require amazing hardware with faultless processing capability to handle complex data. Keeping such equipment and essentials in good working order requires a lot of money, which raises the price.

3.6.9 Losing creativity

Despite their variety, AI systems can only accomplish preprogrammed tasks. They need effort and imagination since they are devoid of assumptions. They just preserve rule-based estimation and, regardless of how they can participate in the dynamic, do not reflect the character of the human psyche. Due to a lack of imagination, AI systems cannot come up with new ways to deal with new situations.

3.6.10 Data maintenance

It will be more difficult to keep up with information protection and security as humans become more reliant on technology. It will be hard to get back data that was lost, which could put both the business and its customers at risk. As humans become increasingly dependent on technology, it will be more challenging to stay up to date with information protection and security. Data recovery is likely to be difficult, putting business and customer safety at risk.

3.7 Symbolic AI and computational AI

AI in today's world is all about NNs. It is, however, no longer the same as it once was. In actuality, during the prior 6 decades, the situation was completely different. The field is mostly made up of symbolic AI, which is also called "rule-based AI," "classical AI," and "good old-fashioned AI."

The term "symbolic AI" [6] refers to a number of approaches to AI research that emphasize human-readable representations of logic, issues, and search. It necessitates the deliberate incorporation of human data and operational concepts into computer programs. The instruction had a confident tone in the early years of AI development. This is because neural groups, which are also called "connectionist AI," are taking off.

Let's look at the benefits and drawbacks of symbolic AI.

At the dawn of AI and registration, symbolic artificial consciousness showed early development. We can easily imagine, express, and investigate the logic that underpins rule-based programs.

Symbolic AI awareness is useful when the rules are obvious and we can easily acquire, include, and convert them into visuals. Indeed, the great majority of computer programs today are constructed on rule-based frameworks, including those used to build deep learning applications.

Consider the field of computer vision, which aims to teach computers to recognize the content of images and movies. Assume we have a photo of our cat and need to create a program that can tell the difference between different photos of your pet. It is simple to make a standard-based application that takes new images as data sources, scans the pixels in the original feline image, and tells us whether or not our kitty appears in the shots we send it.

Computational intelligence (CI) refers to robots' ability to learn a task through information, trial perception, or experimental observation. Despite being widely regarded as the soft computing equivalent, CI is primarily a collection of nature-inspired computational techniques and approaches to dealing with difficult real-world issues where numeric or traditional modeling can be futile for a variety of reasons: the cycles may be too perplexing for numeric thinking, the interactions may contain a few vulnerabilities, or the interaction may contain a few vulnerabilities. In fact, some real-world problems cannot be converted into parallel programming languages for computer processing (unique values of 0 and 1). It falls under the category of AI [15]. Computer intelligence is made up of fuzzy logic, NNs, learning theory, probabilistic approaches, evolutionary computation, and other things. These things make computers smart.

3.8 Evolutionary computing

Evolutionary computing is a branch of software development that is actively being researched. As a one-of-a-kind work of art, artwork inspired by the natural process of evolution has been created (Table 3.1). The numerous species in our world each have unique traits that enable them to thrive in their particular environments, illustrating the force of evolution. Natural evolution has naturally inspired academics, which is unsurprising given how much time and effort they invest in their job. Most people use evolutionary computing with a type of critical thinking called evolutionary computation, which is about trying out new ideas and learning from them, and this is how most people use it.

In a given environment, a population of humans makes progress toward survival and reproduction. People's performance in reaching fitness-related goals is influenced by their surroundings. It discusses their odds of surviving as well as duplication. A stochastic trial and error (called "build and test") type critical thinking measure is also available in a range of application settings. As a result of their ability to solve problems, they will be used to come up with more realistic solutions [16].

All of these solutions are based on the same premise: a society with limited resources must work together to make decisions (endurance of the fittest). As a result, the community's overall health improves. We can establish as many applicant configurations as we want that are components of the capacity domain because there will only be one quality function that needs to be raised. Then, as a theoretical fitness measure, we apply quality capacity to these, higher and better. To seed the future, the

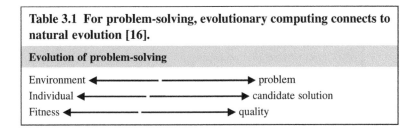

Table 3.1 For problem-solving, evolutionary computing connects to natural evolution [16].

Evolution of problem-solving	
Environment ⟷	problem
Individual ⟷	candidate solution
Fitness ⟷	quality

best up-and-coming arrangements are picked based on fitness criteria. This is accomplished by recombination and mutation. A recombination administrator is someone who brings together at least two candidates. This process is repeated until an appropriate application (response) or computational line is discovered.

The premise of developmental frameworks is structured by two major powers.

- Mutation and recombination boost population diversity and collaborate nicely with inquiry.
- Selection acts as a motivator in the population, broadening the normal arrangement. In the majority of cases, the combination of diversity and incentive leads to increased wellness perceptions in long-term populations.

3.8.1 Evolutionary algorithm

This method definitely fits within the category of creating and testing computations. The fitness work heuristically evaluates arrangement quality, whereas the variety and selection operators drive the inquiry interaction. Evolutionary algorithms (EAs) (Algorithm 3.1) have a few things that make them stand out from all the other techniques that make and test things.

- Because they are population-based, EAs analyze a large range of potential solutions on a regular basis.
- The majority of EAs employ recombination to combine information from newcomers to create a new one.
- These are unpredictably distributed.

The following terms are important in evolutionary computing (Fig. 3.2).

- *Individual*: It implies a solitary solution.
- *Population*: It is a gathering, everything being equal.
- *Chromosomes:* These are when genes are joined to shape a string of qualities.
- *Gene*: These are boundaries that are characterized in a solution to the issue addressed.
- A *fitness score*: It is the value of an objective function. Each chromosome has a fitness score, which is taken from the chromosomes by utilizing a fitness function. It decides the fitness of the solution set.

Algorithm 3.1 Pseudopodia of evolutionary algorithms [8].

Begin
INITIALIZATION population with random candidate solutions
EVALUATE each candidate
REPEAT UNTIL (termination condition is satisfied) *DO*
    1. SELECT parents
    2. RECOMBINE pairs of parents
    3. MUTATE the resulting offspring
    4. EVALUATE new candidate
    5. SELECT individual for the next generation
OD

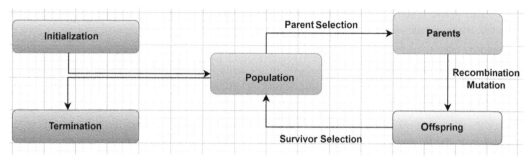

FIGURE 3.2

Flowchart of evolutionaryalgorithm [16].

- *Trait:* It is the element of a solitary solution or individual.
- *Genome:* It is the arrangement of all chromosomes (traits) for an individual.
- *Genotype:* It is the crude genetic data in the chromosomes.
- *Phenotype:* It is expressive of the chromosomes as far as the model.

3.8.1.2 Fundamental genetic algorithm flow

1. Represent the problem with a chromosomal area that is appropriate for it, and address each solution with a human string of a consistent length. Select crossover and mutation probabilities according to how well each individual is performing. Any of them can be reproduced using this procedure.
2. Using the fitness function, determine the prevalence of each chromosome in the population. During reproduction, the fitness function determines which chromosomes are chosen for pairing.
3. To finish the new population, go back to the previous steps and do the same things again:

A. Selection: This is a method of selecting chromosomes from a population at random depending on their evaluation function. The higher a person's fitness function is, the better are his or her chances of being chosen. Selection intensity, also known as selection pressure, is defined as giving better people a preference. Convergence rates will be higher if the selection intensity is higher. The genetic algorithm will work harder to find the best choice if there is not enough selection pressure. Any time there is too much pressure to choose, an incorrect and imperfect solution will come together quickly.

B. Crossover (recombination): It is the process of creating a child by combining the solutions of two parents. As a result, the population benefits from better individuals. Although reproduction does not produce new strings, it does produce clones of previously successful strings. Crossover administrators are introduced into the breeding pool to produce children that outperform their parents.

There are three steps to it.

(I) Individual threads are selected for mating by the reproduction administrator.
(II) Cross-site is determined at random, along with string length.
(III) The quality status of the two strings is shifted as a result of the cross-site.

A crossover probability is a criterion for determining the likelihood of a crossing. In the event of a crossover, both parents' chromosomes are used to make children. There will be no crossover as long as the offspring are direct descendants of their parents.

CMutation: This eliminates the probability of the method being detected at least once in a particular area. Both retrieving genetic data and changing genetic data that make you feel awful require mutation.

Crossover uses the present answer to identify better ones, while the mutation process aids in the exploration of the full search space. It necessitates the swapping and flipping of components such as 0 to 1 and vice versa. A metric for determining how chromosomes are mutated is mutation probability. There is no mutation if no offspring are produced as a result of the crossing. When a mutation occurs, the entire chromosome is changed. It prevents the algorithm from colliding with the neighborhood's boundaries.

4. For new chromosomes, the fitness function is re-evaluated.
5. Replacement: In the last advance, new people are added by removing individuals from the previous population. It refers to the process of determining who will be replaced and who will remain in the population.
6. This is an iterative process in which the problem is rehashed until the optimum answer is found.
7. For search termination, some of the parameters employed include maximum generations, elapsed time, no change in fitness, stall generation, and stall length restriction.

3.8.2 Benefits and limitations of genetic algorithm

It is straightforward to parallelize, and it reliably solves problems. It increases the number of options available and facilitates the search for the finest global solutions. Because it can be applied to a wide range of optimization problems, this technique performs well and is commonly employed. On the other hand, discontinuities exist on the reaction surface and have no bearing on the optimization process as a whole. It generates a list of potential multimodal problem solutions. This is a bold statement given the challenges and problems in evaluating the objective function. It is extremely likely that it can be altered to efficiently address a range of difficulties. It can also manage noisy functions and search areas that are huge and tough to comprehend.

There are several disadvantages, such as the difficulty in locating local optima due to a lack of fitness function recognition. A significant number of reactions are required to test fitness function. It is a tad vague in terms of setting. This should be carried out in tandem with a local search engine optimization effort. It is impossible to successfully leverage inclination and include explicit data at the same time. Population size, mutation rate, crossover rate, selection strategy, and strength all influence the difficulty of establishing discrete borders. Things are not as seamless with unimodal functions. Premature convergence can be a major limitation in genetics. When the population for an optimization issue converges too rapidly or too early, the results are bad. Even with the help of genetic operators, parental solutions are unable to produce offspring who are superior to their parents. Premature convergence can occur when genetic variation is lost.

3.8.3 Application in the real world

Genetic algorithms are employed in a range of applications in the real world. Engineering design, traffic and freight routing, robots, and multicriteria shortest path problems (MSPPs) are among the subjects covered.

- Engineering design

To make the design cycle process faster and more cost-effective, engineers have relied largely on computer modeling and simulation [17]. A genetic algorithm was utilized to optimize and develop a suitable solution. The genetic algorithm is a currently being investigated adaptive search approach for civil, structural, and mechanical engineering applications. Civil, electrical, and mechanical engineering difficulties being investigated include arch dams, large-scale hydropower projects, buildings and building components, digital filters, gas turbines, and nuclear power plant thermal cycles, to name a few. The majority of this work is carried out in close partnership with industry, ensuring that the most up-to-date engineering design techniques, constructability, and cost are all taken into account. Indeed, it has been suggested that the development of a really successful generic technique involves constant interaction between theory and practice.

- Traffic and shipment routing (traveling salesman problem)

Many sales-oriented businesses have successfully dealt with this issue as a result of the time and money savings. The employment of a genetic algorithm is also used to accomplish this. This study takes into account fuel costs, freight rates, currency rates, transportation demand, global transportation capacity, and ship pricing [18]. In the transportation business, one method for determining decision-making parameters on foot composition that is helpful from a profitability standpoint is described. The foot composition's income is computed using a simulator that is dependent on market conditions. This technique can be used to establish decision-making criteria based on foot composition to optimize ship trade behavior. The rules, which are written as a vector, are optimized using a genetic algorithm. The technique was tested on conveyor ships traveling between Asia and Europe. The simulation determined the most effective decision-making methods.

- Robotics

One of the most important branches of AI is robotics. As a result of the large number of patients who require physiotherapy, the demand for rehabilitation services has risen considerably in recent years. Patients require applied exercises in rehabilitation modalities such as passive, assistive, and resistance exercises to regain their ability to move, walk, and perform basic functions. Rehabilitation for those with mobility issues is a time-consuming and difficult process that requires patience. It has an effect on the therapist's mental health as well. Rehabilitation equipment is updated on a regular basis based on patient desires and well-being to address these difficulties. Meanwhile, there has been a significant surge in study into the use of robots in the field of rehabilitation. The author presents a novel chaotic map based on the degree of freedom of each joint [19], which is utilized to select the desired joint route coordination. In addition, for hip and knee joint rehabilitation, an effective technique for a 3DOF robot using an optimal intelligent control system is described. The genetic algorithm optimizes the angles and speeds of the knee and hip joints, which are then calculated using artificial NNs to arrive at the desired path.

- Multicriteria shortest path problems

For many years, academics and decision-makers working on MSPPs relied on weighted linear combinations of the criteria to reduce MSPPs to the classic shortest path problem. MSPPs can be solved with algorithms and approximation methods, but their complexities prevent them from being used in real-world situations. The multicriteria EA technique is used to solve MSPPs on networks with multiple independent criteria [20]. The EA technique has been shown to analyze the underlying network space thoroughly, develop massive candidate path sets, and generate high-quality approximations to the optimum MSPP solution(s).

3.9 Logic-based reasoning

To solve a particular problem, a logical approach can give us two options in AI:

1. Reasoning as a means of proving a theorem
2. Reasoning as a computation of symbols

A "precise model" is a simple and unambiguous method of expressing the structure of a program. It is critical to use the first-order logic (FOL) language and, more specifically, the inference rules defined in the FOL specification to properly describe reasoning in the context of proving a theorem. Lambda calculus is a precise paradigm when it comes to thinking in terms of symbol processing, just as arithmetic has long been thought to be.

3.9.1 Theorem proof by reasoning

Let's discuss the logic that goes into proving the theorem.

3.9.1.1 First-order logic description of the world

To describe an object or scene in the world in the language of FOL, let us grab some important things, i.e., terms.

- People, monuments, and other items are shown using individual constant symbols.Other symbols are frequently represented by the letters x, y, and z, as well as other related characters.Symbols that bind one object to another object, e.g., root ( ), mother ( ), are known as function symbols. Furthermore, predicate symbols are combined with first-order language. We can think of them as functions that are formed over terms and have one of two outputs: is it true or false.

After writing the syntax of the first-order language, we can learn about its semantics. Semantics allows us to refer to real-world formulations made up of genuine elements represented by distinct constant symbols. A "universe" is a grouping of various objects. Predicate symbols are used to describe the relationships that exist between objects in the universe. Function symbols represent the functions defined in the universe. An interpretation is the assignment of specific objects, relations, constant symbols, and predicate symbols to individual constant symbols and predicate symbols. To put it another way, interpretation is the process of imbuing first-order linguistic objects with meaning.

We can now look into the potential of connecting FOL formula computations to the lifestyle that they represent. First, we want to test if a specific formula describes a "piece" of the globe correctly.

And if this is the case, we can be confident that the calculation formula was accepted as part of the assignment syntax [21].

3.9.1.2 Reasoning by the method of resolution

The final section illustrates a logical reasoning-based AI system's local processing component. In practice, however, this kind of thinking is insufficient for building AI systems. It was invented by J. Alan Robinson and allows us to build faster and more powerful logic-based reasoning systems.

The approach to resolution is based on a contradiction-based theorem. To prove a hypothesis, we must first disprove it, then demonstrate how the findings violate commonly held assumptions. Follow these steps to learn how to implement this strategy.

- If we have to show a formula, ψ, which is our hypothesis, concluded from a group of formulas $\phi 1$, $\phi 2$, ..., ϕn, which are our truism, then we do the following.
- We make the negation of the formula $\neg\psi$, and join the negation with the group of formulas $\phi 1$, $\phi 2$, ..., ϕn, and then we try to show the blank clause, shown, which represents the false logical value [21].

3.9.1.3 Techniques for converting formulas to normal forms

While describing the resolution procedure, all alternatives have left out a crucial stumbling block to its actual usage. We use the resolution approach to calculate formulas in artificial systems, which can be displayed in specialized forms called normal forms. We will update the FOL calculative formulas in this part to make them work in normal form. Let's have a look at the transformation process.

1. First of all, a calculative formula gets changed into negation normal form.
2. It is then converted to prenex normal form by stacking quantifiers in front of it.

3.9.1.4 In reasoning systems, specific forms of FOL calculative formulas

Conjunctive normal form (CNF) calculative formulas are frequently used in reasoning systems to develop more efficient formula-compliment algorithms. As we all know, a CNF calculative formula is a joining of clauses. By deleting conjunction symbols, formulas can be reduced down into more fundamental concepts.

It is a method of making judgments based on data. Formulas are commonly saved in the definite form, also known as the clause form, in this system.

3.9.2 Reasoning as computation of symbols

Newell and Simon's system hypothesis characterizes thinking as the process of calculating symbols in relation to physical symbols. This hypothesis decreases the amount of thought required to automatically update symbol-based expressions.

We can easily figure out what the goal of this writing method is by looking at how many times the second protocol is used, then how many times the first rule is used to close the operation A. Our calculations of symbols will not take into account what that word means. We must, however, make sure that our reasoning is correct for the sake of our work.

Lambda calculus (λ-calculus) was coined by Alonzo Church and Stephen C. Kleene, and it is the most often used term in this concept of thinking as a symbol computation. It was written in answer to

David Hilbert's Decisions problem from 1928 (difficulty in making decisions). Professionals utilize lambda calculus as a method of performing mathematics. It uses reasoning to figure out the symbols.

Let's discuss some notions in lambda calculus that can be seen as somewhat peculiar to one novice reader:

The variables that can be shown in each step of lambda calculus are taken as functions.

Lambda abstraction (|->) is the second well-known peculiar notation in lambda calculus.

For example, in (λy. y+5)6, (λy. y+5) is treated as a function, and 6 will be considered an argument.

Here we can see λ joins variables in the same way as quantifiers can do.

3.10 Models of knowledge representation based on structural analysis

The formation of ontologies is one of the most important goals in developing an underlying model of knowledge portrayal, which is one of the most challenging but crucial actions in the field of knowledge representation. One of the functions of ontologies is to represent knowledge. According to the discipline of software engineering, ontology is defined as "the traditional determination of a specific space that is characterized in such a way that it may be used to cope with a variety of issues with the assistance and support of general reasoning techniques." Ontology is described as the determination of a specific space that can be used to solve a variety of problems using general reasoning techniques, as opposed to the determination of a specific space that cannot be used to solve a variety of problems using general reasoning procedures. This decision is made with the goal of instilling uncertainty in the minds of the public. It might be considered a reference book on the subject because it describes, among other things, ideas, objects, and their interactions. If we eliminate the domain of knowledge from the traditional reasoning technique, we will be able to perform automated reasoning, which is exactly what we propose to do to achieve our goal. The use of underlying models is common in the context of addressing spatial knowledge. In this context, situational knowledge, semantic networks, frames, and scripts are all common models.

3.10.1 Semantic networks

In 1969, as a result of their studies into NLP, Allan M. Collins and R. Quillian proposed semantic networks. They had a thought that led to information in the form of a group of connected ideas that help us understand this knowledge. Through this approach, knowledge systems were built. Let's look at math to see that the new ideas that are created refer to the ideas that were already defined.

Each of these shapes is made up of a quadrilateral, and each of these shapes is made up of a polygon, and so on (Fig. 3.3). Consider the following example of description logic to show how we talk about including big ideas in our descriptions.

3.10.2 Frames

In 1975, Marvin Minsky presented the frames. A semantic framework is viewed as an enlargement of a frame system. Nodes are replaced by complicated structures called frames in this expansion, which allows us to describe objects and classes in a point-by-point manner. We talk about "object frames" when there is an instance of an object, and "class frames" when there are classes.

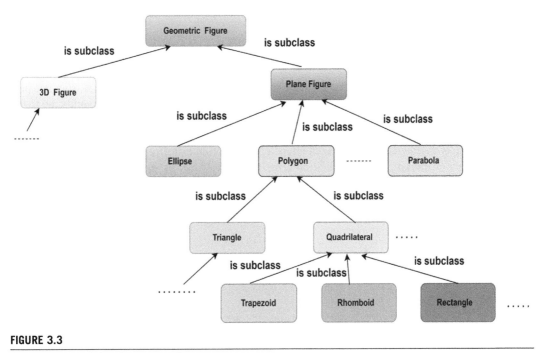

FIGURE 3.3

Semantic network for above example.

The traits and features of the object or idea displayed inside the frame are displayed in each slot of the frame. A frame is made up of slots that are used to display the characteristics and traits of an object or an idea that is displayed within it. Each location has facets that are used to store a variety of different points of view from a variety of different people.

1. **Value**: The information regarding the current value of the slot is contained within the facet.
2. **Range**: It is a list of values that are allowed for slots.
3. **Default**: It has a default value for the slot.
4. **Belongs to a class (for an object frame)**: This object has a pointer to a class in which the object is a member, which is specified by the class name.
5. **Is a subclass of (for a class theme)**: A pointer to one of the classes of which it is a subclass is used to represent each instance of this class; each instance represents a different subclass of the class represented by the pointer.

The inheritance property, which is dependent on the property of ontologies, serves as the frame system's primary reasoning mechanism because it is dependent on this feature. This subclass inherits all of its superclasses' traits, showing the concept of broad concept inclusion. In the event that one subclass is refreshed or altered, the superclass will likewise be changed. If we make a frame of an object that portrays some gadget, it can have characteristics like voltage, temperature, pressure, and so forth. Each characteristic is addressed by a slot [21].

3.10.3 Scripts

Roger Schank and Robert P. Abelson proposed the scripts for NLP in 1977. The promise of brain research underpins this strategy. This model's purpose is to give generalization patterns for various sorts of remembered events.

For example, if a kid goes to the center with his/her mother for the test, she knows from her past encounters what the grouping of steps to be performed are: the first step is to enter the facility, go to the front counter, hang tight for a number in line, meet with the specialist, and the specialist poses an inquiry, "Where does it hurt?" Subsequent to having an exam, a prescription is given by the specialist, and the last step is to leave the facility. Such a type of information is utilized in AI for anticipating the course of events or thinking. How explicit an errand ought to be dealt with to arrive at a particular objective? The message ought to be organized. In the event that the message lacks data, it gets tumultuous and the sequence gets upset.

There are a lot of things that make up a script. These are the parts that make up the structure of a script.

- *Agents*: These are the items that can create an impact on one article and that can be affected by different articles. For instance, a kid, a mother, and a specialist are agents.
- *Props*: These are the articles that happen in scripts. For instance, a clinical thermometer and a prescription are props.
- *Actions*: These comprise rudimentary occasions that are utilized for developing the entire occasion.
- *Preconditions*: These are the propositions that should be valid at the beginning of inference with the assistance of a script.
- *Results*: These are propositions that should be valid toward the finish of inference with the assistance of the script.

3.11 Rule-binding systems

In logic-based and rule-based systems, deductive reasoning is applied (Fig. 3.4). The type of expression utilized for knowledge representation is the primary difference between these models. In FOL, the expressions used in logic-based reasoning are formalized as lambda expressions. In rule-based systems, the terms as alleged rules are treated in the same way:

In the event that a specific condition is satisfied, carry out a specific action.

This is of extraordinary use for planning knowledge bases that are created by specialists and experts in the field.

3.11.1 Model of rule-based systems

The functioning memory principally contains portrayals of facts that are utilized in the reasoning process in certain parts of the world. Other data required in the reasoning process is saved in the functioning memory, which is working theories. It addresses the design of the variable bindings.

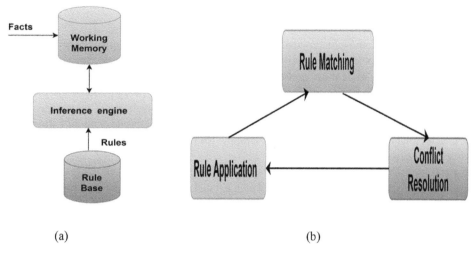

(a)   (b)

FIGURE 3.4

A rule-based system: (A) a module scheme and (B) a reasoning cycle [21].

We have effectively referenced the type of RULE in the accompanying articulation:

R: If condition is met, then action is taken.

The standard's consequence is the action, while the standard's antecedent is the circumstance. An antecedent is defined as a logical proposition. It is the result of a string of fortuitous events.

The fact that facts exist in a functioning memory to the extent that they can substitute variables in the condition while maintaining the condition's relevance is demonstrated by the satisfaction of the standard condition. As a result of the declarative rules' standard conditions, action is usually a logical endpoint. Making a decision changes what is in your working memory, which creates a new reality and changes the values of certain variables [21].

In any case, in the event of reactive rules, an action can be a sure technique to affect the outside climate of the framework, like the exchanging of the fan. The rule base stores every one of the rules. The inference engine is the one that controls the reasoning based on rules and memory. It has three stages, which are given next.

1. The inference engine finds for rules the same facts that are put away in the functioning memory during rule coordination with the stage. The arrangement of rules that are chosen fundamentally is called a "conflict set."
2. There are times when conflict resolution is needed, and the inference engine chooses one standard from its memory to be used.
3. After applying the last principle, the process is done when the system returns and no matching rule is left to apply in the memory.

Rule-based systems are basically used in lexical analysis in interpreting programs or in the NLP of natural language.

3.12 Pattern recognition and cluster analysis

In pattern identification and cluster analysis, patterns can be objects, phenomena, structures, or metrics. The concept is not limited to visible images. In the realm of pattern recognition, there are three fundamental approaches. A feature vector addresses a feature space pattern in an approach-based manner. If the pattern is intrinsic in nature, either synaptic pattern recognition or the primary technique is used. The third strategy makes use of neuronal organizations. The process of pattern recognition entails classifying an obscure pattern into one of a few established classifications known as classes. Cluster analysis is a completely free technique for pattern recognition. Its primary function is to classify a collection of endeavors.

The issue of pattern recognition is addressed in an overall manner. We expect that there are N classifications (classes) ($\omega1$, $\omega2$, ..., ωN) into which a pattern can be classified. Allow us to expect that each pattern is addressed by an n-dimensional feature vector:

$$(x1, x2, ... xn) = X$$

To play out pattern recognition, we ought to have a training set that is portrayed as if it were: Y = ((x1, y1), (x2, y2), ... (xm, ym)) and (yj = k), where j is a learning set vector and k 1, ..., N is the correct classification of the pattern addressed by the vector Xj.

Preprocessing, feature extraction, and feature selection are three of the steps that come before classification in a pattern recognition framework.

During the preprocessing task, noise expulsion, smoothing, and normalization are all performed. The sign separation approach is used to complete the commotion evacuation. Normalization is the process of scaling pattern features to get a position with nearly equivalent reach. To lower the dimensionality of the feature, we want the number of pattern features in the classification phase to be as small as possible. The cost of estimating a feature, the rate of computation failure, and the rate of classification errors all rise as the feature's dimensionality rises. Dimension reduction is the most important task throughout the feature extraction procedure. Several components are connected and repurposed to achieve the decrease. The third stage involves assessing which features have the greatest discriminatory power. Finally, we want to know which features resulted in the fewest errors during the categorization process. A feature space is a collection of vectors that deal with patterns in the aforementioned manner.

Pattern recognition, like cluster analysis, is a tough task. We can see that there are various test patterns, but we have no idea how to organize them. To classify these patterns by clustering them together, cluster analysis is required. Patterns in the same location as a related cluster should be combined. Patterns from different clusters should be distinct from one another at the same time. As a result, the concept of similitude is crucial in cluster analysis. Because pattern recognition emphasizes patterns, we use a specific measurement to characterize the distances between patterns in an example collection. We consider two patterns comparable if the variation between them is minor. K-means clustering is a well-known approach for data partitioning. Cluster analysis strategies are classified into two types.

In the first method, we know how many clusters ought to be categorized; this method is based on partitioning. In the second method, we do not know the number of clusters categorized, called hierarchic methods.

3.13 Neural networks

A NN is made up of a succession of hubs, or units, that are linked together by joins. Each link has a numeric weight given to it. In NN, weights are the fundamental method of long-term accumulation, and weight refreshes are utilized to achieve learning. A portion of the units are externally connected and could be categorized as information or yield units. The weights are changed to fit the information/ yield behavior of the network with the climate that created the data sources. Each unit has an information interface with other units, a set of yields that are linked to other units, a current activation level, and a technique for estimating the activation level at the next scheduling step based on its information sources and weights. Each unit performs a proximal computation based on the contributions of its neighbors, but it has no overall effect on the unit structure. The great majority of NN execution happens during programming, and concurrent control is utilized to update all units in a defined group. To build a NN for a certain task, first decide how many units to use, what sort of units to employ, and how the network's units will be connected. It also demonstrates how to encode the models in terms of how much information and money the network generates. This section goes over network weights and how they were determined using a learning method on a set of project training models.

Neurons (Fig. 3.5) are the essential working units of the brain. The human brain is composed of 100 billion neurons. These neurons send data to and from the brain and to the different brains of the body [22].

A NN (Fig. 3.6) has different layers. The principal layer is the information layer. It gets the data signs and passes them to the accompanying layer. Weights are arbitrarily assigned to the interconnections. The weights are increased with the information signal, and a bias is added to the result of information and weight. The input layer does a wide range of estimations and highlight extractions; it is known as the hidden layer. The weighted amount of the input is taken care of in the activation function to choose which hub to fire for feature extraction. Then, at that point, this stream to the hidden layer is determined and taken care of by the activation work in each layer to choose which hubs to fire. Regularly, there will be more than one hidden layer. Lastly, there's the output layer, which conveys the eventual outcome [23].

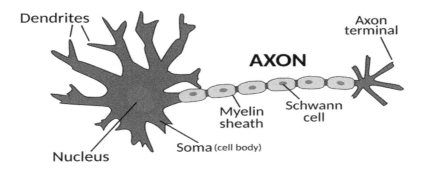

FIGURE 3.5

A biologic neuron of the brain.

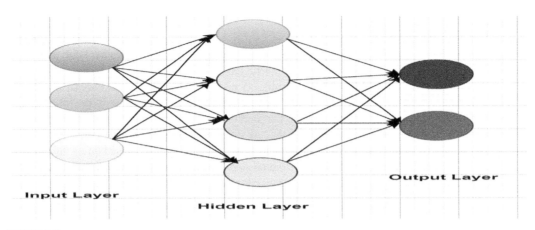

FIGURE 3.6

Neural network structure.

There are various types of NNs:

1. **Convolution neural networks (CNNs)**

It contains five sorts of layers: input layer, convolution layer, pooling measure, completely associated, and output layer. Each layer has a particular purpose, such as summing up, interfacing, or actuating. CNNs have promoted picture grouping and item recognition. However, CNNs have also been used in other areas, such as forecasting, prediction, and NLP [24].

2. **Recurrent neural networks (RNNs)**

This uses successive information, for example, time-stepped information from a sensor or spoken gadget, which comprises a grouping of terms. All the inputs in the repetitive network are autonomous of one another, not at all like in a conventional NN. However, the yield of every component depends upon the calculation of the previous components. RNN is used in time scheduling, determining, and slant analysis [24].

3. **Feed-forward NNs**

Information is taken care of in a forward manner, starting with one layer, then onto the next, the forward way as it were. Each perceptron in one layer is associated with each perceptron in the following layer. There are no input circles or feedback loops [24].

4. **Multilayer perceptron**

The network has a point toward the complex neural nets where input information goes through different layers of fake neurons. In the following layer, each and every hub is associated with every one of the neurons, making it a totally associated NN. There is an input and output layer having different hidden layers in the middle, i.e., at least three layers altogether. This NN has bidirectional engendering that incorporates forward and reverse proliferation. In this, inputs are duplicated with the weights and afterward enacted in the activation work, utilizing the reverse spread, as it would decrease the misfortune that can be brought about simultaneously. Weights are self-adjusted by the distinction between the anticipated output and the weights adjusted by the machine by taking in qualities from NNs. SoftMax employs these nonlinear functions as yield layer activation work. Because of the presence of a thick, completely associated network and a back-spread network, it is utilized in profound learning. The weakness of this network is that it is delayed because of a number of covered-up layers that make the network complex. A portion of the applications are machine translation, speech recognition, and complex classification.

3.14 AI applications

A considerable number of fields are affected by AI, and some of them are mentioned subsequently.

3.14.1 Gaming

An AI intelligence application has been discovered in the gaming sector. It makes the savvy nonplayable characters (NPCs) cooperate with the humans. It likewise notices the human instinct while messing around and improves the highlights of the game. One of the most proficient elements in the games is hunting. Pathfinding is another significant system in gaming. Pathfinding is the technique for deciding how to get an NPC from one point on a guide to another. It ordinarily utilizes choice trees as a typical method for control. The AI's capacity to be productive in battle is significant in situations like this. If nothing else, it will make the AI more human or, if nothing else, to show up [25].

3.14.2 Natural language processing

In NLP, AI is utilized in speaking with an insightful framework utilizing a characteristic language like English that is utilized in NLP. NLP is required when we need a robot or machine to chip away at our directions when we need to hear discourse-based choices. NLP governs how computers perceive and decipher human discourse. NLP enables machines to comprehend written or spoken text and perform tasks such as interpretation, watchword extraction, and subject arrangement. Because NLP is a part of AI, the two words can be used together.

The most famous instances of NLP in real life are remote helpers, similar to Google Assistant, Siri on Apple, and Alexa on Amazon. It comprehends and interprets the human language, as in "Hello, Alexa, what is the temperature in Delhi?" [26]. NLP consists of five steps (Fig. 3.7).

Lexical analysis involves separating the entire piece of text into sections, sentences, and words. It analyses the structure of the words. The syntactic analyzer checks the grammar of the words and their relationships. The semantic analyzer checks the meaningfulness of the sentence from the dictionary. The meaning of the sentence will match the previous sentence, so it checks the previous history and then combines the sentences to create the meaning of the sentence. The pragmatic analyzer tries to draw its meaning from what is said and what it is meant to be [27].

3.14.3 Expert systems

It is a space in which AI invigorates the conduct and judgment of human experts. It deciphers the issues of a human being by procuring information from its own knowledge base. The information is added by

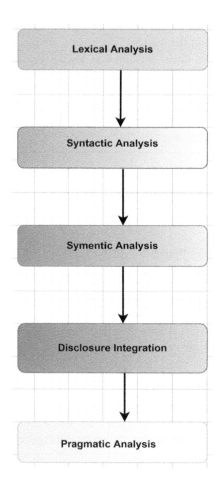

FIGURE 3.7

Basic steps of NLP.

the people who are working in the specific domains. The programming is utilized by nonspecialists to acquire information. Accounting, medicine, gaming, automobiles, coding, and other fields make use of it [15].

AI programming uses data from an information base to take care of issues. This requires the human master to be around there and jellies the human master's information. Thus, expert systems are applications created to tackle complex issues in a specific area, such as mastery, with exceptional human insight. There are various characteristics of expert systems (Fig. 3.8) like elite levels, straightforwardness, total solidity, and exceptional responsiveness. The expert systems are equipped for various activities, including inciting, helping with human dynamics, showings, and bearings, determining plans, finding and deciphering information sources and giving appropriate yields, foreseeing results, defense of finishes, and ideas for elective responses to an issue [15].

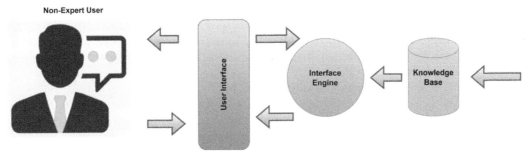

FIGURE 3.8

Components of an expert system [15].

There are five components of an expert system.

1. Documentation repository:

The knowledge base addresses current realities and rules in an expert system. It has information about the area to deal with the problem and to come up with ways that are relevant to the space.

2. Inference engine:

The work of the inference engine is to obtain important information from the given information base in an expert system, decipher it, and discover the arrangement according to the issue. This has explanatory and troubleshooting capacities.

3. Knowledge acquisition and learning module:

There are some restrictions in this section that make it hard for expert systems to get more data from different sources and store it in the knowledge base.

4. User interface

This is the main way for a customer who is not an expert to connect with the expert system and figure out what to do.

5. Explanatory module:

This module helps in giving the client a clear understanding of the accomplished end.

3.14.4 Speech recognition

Change in speech to message or recognizing speech incorporates catching and digitalizing sound waves, changing essential semantic units or phonemes, making phonemic words, and theoretically examining words to ensure the right spelling of words that sound similar. This is called "automatic speech recognition" or "speech to message," which means understanding the voice on a computer and playing out the necessary assignment. It encourages the strategies and advancements that allow for speech recognition and text conversion [22].

The computer makes a contribution to the type of sound vibrations. This is done by a simple computerized converter that converts the sound wave into the advanced structure that can be perceived by the computer. A bunch of complex calculations are run on the information to perceive the discourse and return a book result. Information may likewise be changed into various structures contingent upon the need. For example, the Google Speech to Message Converter, as Siri and Google partner, takes the sound info but can give a voice reaction. If you ask the device, "What is the weather like in Agra?" it will also give you a clear answer [21].

The working of speech recognition is shown in Fig. 3.9.

The principal objective of speech recognition is for a machine to have the option to "tune in," "comprehend," and "follow up on" the data given through voice input. Programmed speaker recognition wants to break down, separate, show, and show off information about the speaker's personality [28].

The speaker recognition framework works in three phases: 1. analysis, 2. extraction of features, and 3. modeling.

These are the types of speech recognition software.

1. Speaker dependent

Those who will utilize the framework train the speaker's subordinate frameworks. These frameworks are capable of achieving a high preference order tally with a precision of over 95% for word recognition. The downside of this process is that the framework only responds precisely to the person who created it. This is the most well-known PC programming methodology.

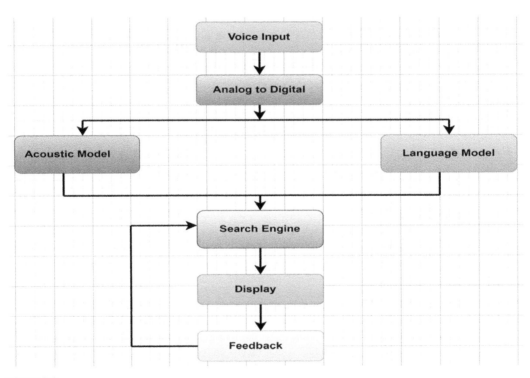

FIGURE 3.9

Mechanism of speech recognition [28].

2. Speaker independent

Speaker independent is a framework that is ready to react to a word regardless of who is speaking. As a result, the framework must respond to a wide range of speech instances and articulations, with the articulation being of the objective word. The order word tally is generally lower than the speaker-subordinate one, but great precision can still be maintained within handling restrictions. Modern prerequisites need speaker-free voice frameworks all the more regularly. For example, the AT&T framework is utilized in the phone framework.

Instances of speech recognition are carried out at the front and back ends of the clinical reports. Front-end speech recognition is where the provider coordinates the speech recognition engine. Verbally communicated words are displayed as seen. The despot is answerable for adjusting and shutting down the document. Back-end recognition, in any case, called surrendered speech recognition, is where the provider coordinates into a mechanized correspondence system. The voice is coordinated through a speech recognition machine, and the draft document is seen. It is directed by the principal voice record to the article chief (where the draft archive is adjusted and the report settled). Back-end or conceded recognition is generally utilized in business as of now.

In cars, for initiating a call, playing music, selecting radio stations, etc., the approach can be used. In fighter planes, speech recognition is used to set radio frequencies, control the autopilot systems, and set weapon release parameters, among other things, like in a car.

3.15 Intelligent robots

People became more familiar with the first mechanized machines, which were robots. Some time ago, robots were made for making exceptional undertakings. These seasons of machines were made with no AI for dull assignments. These days, AI is incorporated with robots to foster the development of robots that can carry out various undertakings and, furthermore, learn new things with a better view of the climate. AI in advanced mechanics assists robots with carrying out essential errands with a human-like vision to identify or perceive the different items. Robots are created through AI preparation. An enormous number of datasets are used to prepare the PC vision model, so advanced mechanics can perceive the various items and complete the activities with the correct outcomes. Using AI in mechanical technology and the types of datasets that are used to make the AI model for robots are being looked at by them. The AI in mechanical technology not just assists with learning the model to play out specific assignments, but it additionally makes machines astute to act in various situations. To prepare for the AI calculation, it takes preparing information and attempting to comprehend the situations or perceive different objects. It generates a massive number of datasets, assisting advanced mechanics with perceiving and handling various types of items or carrying out the ideal activity in the correct way. Image annotation is the process of making AI useful in advanced mechanics [29].

3.16 AI research prospects and future directions

Now, we should put some light on the eventual fate of AI. It is said that there will be an enormous development and display later on for AI, and the increment is found in the period over the next decade. In addition, AI has made an effect by spreading its underlying foundations in the IT area and has had consistent freedom in different ventures as well. In any case, the vast majority of individuals believe that AI will eliminate the positions and pay for them. They accept that machines will assume control over the work environment and that this will make them jobless. In any case, the fact of the matter is a long way from these suppositions. The rise of AI will pave the way for new enterprises that we would never have imagined and assist businesspeople in staying aware of the changing advertising track continuously. Businesses can upgrade their tasks, computerize their work interactions, and improve client encounters. When self-sufficient activities are handled by AI, the eventual fate of AI is beyond any cutoff, any vehicle without a driver, and robots that can deal with any type of assignment. Children will acquire information by receiving smart guides, online mixed-media reference books, practical conflict games, global communication, unified government, and enterprises immediately. The most important future scope of AI in the medical field is the classification of diseases [30−36].

To the degree that AI is prevailing with regard to discovering issues in the general public, we are currently confronting a portion of the main problems. It is amazing that lawful responsibility should be talked about. When a doctor relies upon the judgment of the clinical master framework, who is at fault if the finding is not right? Up until this point, courts have held that clinical master frameworks expect comparable parts as clinical course readings and reference books; specialists are responsible for understanding the thinking behind any decision and for using their own judgment in deciding whether to recognize the framework's ideas. In arranging clinical master frameworks as subject matter experts, it is anything but a figure specialist's choice can straightforwardly influence the existence of a patient. It could be illegal for specialists to not follow expert system advice if they do not use it.

Consequently, the advancement of AI treated as a research region has been firmly influenced by the logical disciplines. It appears that AI will be created along these lines in the near future. How about we attempt to discover the most significant possibilities of AI?

The critical hindrances in the space of critical thinking, normal language handling, mechanized picking up, arranging, and innovativeness result from our absence of mental models for two nonexclusive psychological cycles, which are idea appreciation and articulating a judgment. Any consequence of research identified with these cycles would be extremely valuable to computer reproduction. Communication among humans and AI frameworks requires considerably more successful strategies. In the field of AI, advanced models of syntax analysis are produced for phonetics, demonstrating their proof. In any case, AI needs sufficient models for semantic analysis to be created in the not-so-distant future. To disentangle the secret of the human cerebrum, then, at that point, we need headway in the neuro-imaging and electrophysiology procedures in neuroscience so we can build more compelling connectionist models. Models of life forms and physiologic cycles and their transformative components will be boundless wellsprings of motivation for creating general strategies for critical thinking. Arithmetic should assist us with formalizing models of science, brain research, semantics, and so forth that could be utilized in AI. In computer science, new compelling ways to write programs and build frameworks should be found [21].

A portion of the issues are starting to emerge with regard to the utilization of keen specialists on the "information highway" Consolidating requirements are made into canny specialists so that they cannot harm the records of different clients. The risky truth is about the administrations that include money-related exchanges. On the off chance that those exchanges are finished by the insightful specialists for somebody, is that person responsible for the obligations brought about by those exchanges? Would it be workable for the wise specialists to have the actual resources and perform electronic exchanges for their own benefit? Could they own stocks and bonds in an equivalent manner to how organizations keep their own stocks and bonds? It appears to be preposterous as no program has been allowed lawful status for the financial exchanges. Additionally, programs are not considered drivers to authorize the traffic guidelines on genuine roadways. Associations will depend vigorously on AI systems for their everyday cooperation, computerizing business tasks, and information examination. The coming days will show the effect of the capacity and cognitive ability of AI in advancing change. In California, there do not appear to be any legitimate approvals on the vehicles to restrict the speed of mechanized vehicles, in spite of the fact that the originator of the vehicle would be viewed as at risk in the event of mishaps. The law presently cannot seem to find the new improvement in innovation. These points, among others, are shrouded in diaries like "AI and Society," "Law," "Computers and Artificial Intelligence," and "Artificial Intelligence and Law" [22].

Historically, researchers in automatic facial recognition and biometric technology have focused on developing precise algorithms [37]. When this technology is integrated into operational systems, engineers and scientists are being asked whether these systems conform to societal norms [38]. This line of inquiry is motivated by the notion of 'trust' in AI systems. In this work, researchers adapt XAI to face recognition and biometrics, presenting four XAI principles for face recognition and biometrics [39]. Four case studies demonstrate the principles by illustrating the problems and issues inherent in developing algorithms capable of generating explanations. Let us focus on four recently published studies where AI has been successfully applied for real life problems.

One study [40] came up with a way to combine infrared and visible images by fuzziness and CNNs. The main goal of this work is to find a way to keep thermal radiation characteristics in existing infrared and visible image—based methods. This is because fuzzy systems and CNN have been combined to make a new, strong, and adaptable method. In the beginning, the suggested method kept the features of infrared images while also taking visible images. As a result, the right target location can be seen, which helps with processing and is also important for improving the accuracy and focus of the image that comes out.

Deep learning has become more common in the field of wind energy forecasting in the last few years. Many models for predicting how much wind energy there will be are based on deep learning. An article [41] talks about them (CNN, RNN, and deep belief network). While RNN-based models are good at finding relationships in a time series, CNN-based models are good at finding connections between time series, too. Time series-based RNNs, limited Boltzmann machines, CNNs, and algorithms based on auto-encoders are some of the methods that are shown.

The current article [42] examines common techniques for dealing with imbalanced data in data ecosystems (data that is large, heterogeneous, and complex in nature, and that is generated from multiple autonomous sources with distributed and decentralized control), as well as a Keras-based comparative data modeling framework for balanced and imbalanced datasets.

Individuals with low eyesight find it difficult to interact with dynamic material such as videos and movies. The concept of MagVi, a fully integrated program aiming at expanding access to dynamic content, is introduced in an article [43]. The video magnification program is the first component, which employs video saliency models to identify the most important regions of interest (ROIs) in a range of films. The program's second component allows visually challenged people to examine the selected ROI in a mobile app while panning, zooming, and altering the font size of the text dynamically across the interface.

3.17 Conclusions

This part accentuates the different points that go under AI. We have talked about the historical backdrop of AI, systematic AI, and computational AI, evolutionary AI, logic-based reasoning, structural models of knowledge representation, rule-based systems, rule-based systems, NNs, and different applications of AI. This assumes a significant part in expanding human capacity as it outperforms people on an IQ test and turns out to be superior to people with numerous abilities or knowledge. This technology is intended to learn all by itself and look like a human brain with physical and mental abilities. It is anything but completely creating space for computer science, as there is considerably more to investigate and explore. It is the forgery of brain research that has caused the machines to zero in on philosophical debates. It is demonstrated that AI is a field of computer science with human traits notwithstanding. It assists the climate in developing and reacting reasonably to help individuals. There is one more truth about AI: undertakings that are performed by AI can be both viable and risky. It will influence the work of the wide populace; human work will be supplanted by robots. Thus, it can have both positive and negative effects on AI development. However, the eventual fate of AI is splendid.

References

[1] W.S. McCulloch, W. Pitts, A logical calculus of the ideas immanent in nervous activity, Bull. Math. Biophys. 5 (4) (1943) 115−133.

[1a] D.O. Hebb, The Organization of Behavior: A Neuropsychological Theory, Wiley and Sons, New York, 1949, ISBN 9780471367277.

[2] C.E. Shannon, XXII. Programming a computer for playing chess, Lond. Edinb. Dublin Philos. Mag. J. Sci. 41 (314) (1950) 256−275.

[2a] A.M. Turing, Digital computers applied to games. Faster than thought, 1953.

[3] H.L. Gelernter, Realization of a geometry theorem proving machine, in: IFIP Congress, June 1959, pp. 273−281.

[4] M.L. Minsky, S.A. Papert, Perceptrons, Expanded edition, 1988.

[5] J. McDermott, R1: a rule-based configurer of computer systems, Artif. Intell. 19 (1) (1982) 39−88.

[5a] M. Minsky, A framework for representing knowledge, in: P.H. Winston (Ed.), The Psychology of Computer Vision, Prentice-Hall, New York, 1975.

[5b] J.J. Hopfield, Neural networks and physical systems with emergent collective computational abilities, Proceedings of the national academy of sciences 79 (8) (1982) 2554−2558.

[5c] A.W. Starr, Y.C. Ho, Nonzero-sum differential games, J. Optim. Theory Appl. 3 (1969) 184−206.

[6] What Is Symbolic Artificial Intelligence?—TechTalks, November 18, 2019. By Ben Dickson, www.bdtechtalks.com.

[7] J. Pearl, Probabilistic Reasoning in Intelligent Systems: Networks of Plausible Inference, Elsevier, 2014.

[8] M. Cheney, D. Isaacson, J.C. Newell, S. Simske, J. Goble, NOSER: an algorithm for solving the inverse conductivity problem, Int. J. Imag. Syst. Technol. 2 (2) (1990) 66−75.

[9] S. Kumar, Advantages and disadvantages of artificial intelligence, Medium (2019). Retrieved April, 6, 2020.

[10] A.D. Maynard, Navigating the fourth industrial revolution, Nat. Nanotechnol. 10 (12) (2015) 1005−1006.

[11] Beata Ślusarczyk, Industry 4.0: are we ready? Pol. J. Manage Stud. 17 (2018) 20.

[12] I.H. Sarker, AI-based modeling: techniques, applications and research issues towards automation, intelligent and smart systems, SN Comput. Sci. 3 (2022) 158, https://doi.org/10.1007/s42979-022-01043-x.

[13] D. Gunning, M. Stefik, J. Choi, T. Miller, S. Stumpf, G.Z. Yang, XAI—explainable artificial intelligence, Sci. Robot. 4 (37) (2019) eaay7120.

[14] Q. Zhang, J. Lu, Y. Jin, Artificial intelligence in recommender systems, Complex Intell. Syst. 7 (1) (2021) 439−457.

[15] Expert Systems in Artificial Intelligence (AI): Types, Uses and Advantages" www.mygreatlearning.com.

[16] A.E. Eiben, J.E. Smith, Introduction to Evolutionary Computing, vol 53, Springer, Berlin, 2003, p. 18.

[17] G.N. Bullock, M.J. Denham, I.C. Parmee, J.G. Wade, Developments in the use of the genetic algorithm in engineering design, Des. Stud. 16 (4) (1995) 507–524.

[18] K. Hiekata, S. Wanaka, Y. Okubo, Mining rules of decision-making for fleet composition under market uncertainty using a genetic algorithm, J. Mar. Sci. Technol. (2022) 1–10.

[19] W.A. Azar, P.S. Nazar, An optimized and chaotic intelligent system for a 3DOF rehabilitation robot for lower limbs based on neural network and genetic algorithm, Biomed. Signal Process Control 69 (2021) 102864.

[20] P. Mooney, A. Winstanley, An evolutionary algorithm for multicriteria path optimization problems, Int. J. Geogr. Inf. Sci. 20 (4) (2006) 401–423.

[21] M. Flasiński, Introduction to Artificial Intelligence, Springer, 2016.

[22] S. Russell, P. Norvig, Artificial Intelligence: A Modern Approach, Global Edition 4th. Foundations 19, 2021, p. 23.

[23] An Ultimate Tutorial to Neural Networks in 2021" www.simplilearn.com.

[24] Neural Networks—What are they and why do they matter?" www.sas.com. (By Leigh Ann Herhold).

[25] Z. Abd Algfoor, M.S. Sunar, H. Kolivand, A comprehensive study on pathfinding techniques for robotics and video games, Int. J. Comput. Games Technol. (2015), 2015.

[26] NLP, Machine Learning and AI, Explained, June 9,2020. By Inés Roldós, www.monkeylearn.com.

[27] GyanSetu! What Is Natural Language Processing? Intro to NLP in Machine Learning, 2020-12-06. Retrieved 2021-01-09.

[28] B.H. Juang, L.R. Rabiner, Automatic Speech Recognition—A Brief History of the Technology Development, vol. 1, Georgia Institute of Technology. Atlanta Rutgers University and the University of California, Santa Barbara, 2005, p. 67.

[29] K. Sennaar, AI in Agriculture—Present Applications and Impact, 2019. Available at: emerj.com/ai-sector-overviews/ai-agriculture-present-applications-impact/. (Accessed 1 August 2019).

[30] L.K. Singh, H. Pooja Garg, et al., An enhanced deep image model for glaucoma diagnosis using feature-based detection in retinal fundus, Med. Biol. Eng. Comput. 59 (2021) 333–353.

[31] M. Khanna, A. Agarwal, L.K. Singh, S. Thawkar, A. Khanna, D. Gupta, Radiologist-level two novel and robust automated computer-aided prediction models for early detection of COVID-19 infection from chest X-ray images, Arabian J. Sci. Eng. (2021) 1–33.

[32] L.K. Singh, H. Pooja Garg, M. Khanna, An artificial intelligence-based smart system for early glaucoma recognition using OCT images, Int. J. E Health Med. Commun. 12 (4) (2021) 32–59.

[33] S. Thawkar, S. Sharma, M. Khanna, L. kumar Singh, Breast cancer prediction using a hybrid method based on butterfly optimization algorithm and ant lion optimizer, Comput. Biol. Med. (2021) 104968.

[34] L.K. Singh, H. Garg, Pooja, Automated glaucoma type identification using machine learning or deep learning techniques, in: O. Verma, S. Roy, S. Pandey, M. Mittal (Eds.), Advancement of Machine Intelligence in Interactive Medical Image Analysis. Algorithms for Intelligent Systems, Springer, Singapore, 2020.

[35] L.K. Singh, H. Garg, M. Khanna, R.S. Bhadoria, An analytical study on machine learning techniques, in: Multidisciplinary Functions of Blockchain Technology in AI and IoT Applications, IGI Global, 2021, pp. 137–157.

[36] L.K. Singh, M. Khanna, A novel multimodality based dual fusion integrated approach for efficient and early prediction of glaucoma, Biomed. Signal Process Control 73 (2022) 103468.

[37] W. Yang, S. Wang, J. Hu, G. Zheng, J. Yang, C. Valli, Securing deep learning based edge finger vein biometrics with binary decision diagram, in: IEEE Transactions on Industrial Informatics, vol 15, July 2019, pp. 4244–4253, https://doi.org/10.1109/TII.2019.2900665.

[38] L.K. Singh, M. Khanna, S. Thawkar, J. Gopal, Robustness for authentication of the human using face, ear, and gait multimodal biometric system, Int. J. Inf. Syst. Model Des. (IJISM) 12 (1) (2021) 39–72.

[39] L.K. Singh, M. Khanna, H. Garg, Multimodal biometric based on fusion of ridge features with minutiae features and face features, Int. J. Inf. Syst. Model Des. 11 (1) (2020) 37–57.

[40] K. Bhalla, D. Koundal, S. Bhatia, M. Khalid, I. Rahmani, M. Tahir, Fusion of infrared and visible images using fuzzy based siamese convolutional network, Comput. Mater. Cont. 70 (2022) 5503–5518.

[41] Z. Wu, G. Luo, Z. Yang, Y. Guo, K. Li, Y. Xue, A comprehensive review on deep learning approaches in wind forecasting applications, CAAI Trans. Intell. Technol. (2021).

[42] G. Mohindru, K. Mondal, H. Banka, Different hybrid machine intelligence techniques for handling IoT-based imbalanced data, CAAI Trans. Intell. Technol. 6 (4) (2021) 405–416.

[43] Thakur, P., Dalvi, T., John, V., & Chandna, S. Magvi: Towards Saliency-Driven Video Magnification Application for the People With Low Vision.

Computational intelligence in human-computer interaction—Case study on employability in higher education

Pooja Thakar[1], Manisha[2], Anil Mehta[3], Neetu Goel[1] and Seema Verma[4]

[1]*Vivekananda School of Information Technology, VIPS-TC, Delhi, India;* [2]*Department of Computer Science, Banasthali Vidyapith, Rajasthan, India;* [3]*School of Legal Studies, Banasthali Vidyapith, Rajasthan, India;* [4]*Department of Electronics, Banasthali Vidyapith, Rajasthan, India*

4.1 Introduction

The new area of research has two major areas for improvement: data mining and human—computer interaction (HCI). This conceptual approach is known as the theory of mental modeling and induction based on data on HCI. The characterization of person in HCI studies has also undergone major changes. The definitions of computer and human have changed a lot. Recently, a new definition of a person has emerged as multilayered nodes and weights, combined with new learning algorithms (for example, deep learning), and it has become a topic that unites people and computers [1]. HCI data collection methods have helped identify cognitive processes that can be replicated using fuzzy ensembles. Fuzzy ensemble modeling can serve as a user-oriented method for designing HCI [2—5]. Assistive systems must learn from the given data to adapt appropriately. Theoretical induction based on HCI data is known as data mining. The study of interaction data reveals what the system knows about its human user. Let's say that HCI is an interaction between computing machines, each of which has its own limitations and inclinations. Inductively learning a recursive function means, in a sense, extracting a feature graph that is represented in incremental blocks over time, a process very similar to extracting HCI data [6—9].

HCI techniques can be applied to the design to evaluate intelligent systems. We can obtain data from HCI and use it to learn more effectively to build smarter systems. With the application of machine learning technology in HCI, systems are becoming more intelligent. Artificial intelligence and machine learning clubbed with HCI have made great progress in many fields and have demonstrated strong research and development potential.

HCI is very prominent in the case of higher education when a student applies for any vacancy in their last year of education. Their performance in the tests conducted for employability is a true example of HCI, where they are tested for their psychological/cognitive/aptitude capabilities as well [10]. The chapter further takes a case study in higher education system, where a system collects the data with HCI techniques by conducting employability tests of the students. The results of the student's employability tests conducted with HCI are further used for analysis and prediction with machine learning algorithms. This combination may act as a basis for creating intelligent systems for higher education.

4.2 Case study in higher education system

The main focus of any education system is to impart quality education. Education should help in the holistic development of the student. All the more the higher education system should not only focus on quality education but must make students ready for industry with knowledge and confidence. Thus, to attain the highest level of excellence, the prerequisite is to make our teaching–learning systems excellent and customized for an individual student.

By the end of 2030, it is forecasted that the higher education system of India will adopt innovative and transformative approaches. This has already begun with new education policy in place that was introduced in 2020. It is estimated that India will emerge as the key largest provider of global talent. It is said that every fourth graduate in the world will be produced by the higher education system of India [11]. It can be easily foreseen that potential is very high and the opportunity to grow is massive, whereas a very limited number of institutions impart education at par with global standards and in unison with industry.

4.2.1 Issues of the higher education system in India

In India, the existing education system has lots of potentials, but it faces many issues as well. The first and foremost problem that the higher education system of India faces today is the ever-growing gap between academia and industry. Students'' poor performance in industry and unemployment has become a national issue. There is a severe shortage of skilled and well-trained employees. Students are not able to obtain jobs per their skill sets, and employers are not satisfied with the performance of students and invest huge amounts in their training every year. Institutes not only play a pivotal role to measure the annual performance of students, but government accreditations and aid are also dependent on it.

We are in dire need of a system that could help students improve their essential skills pertaining to the industry by early detection and guidance. Such a system will also help the management of institutes to take informed decisions and design better policies. Teachers will be able to plan their teaching pedagogy in a well-defined manner. Institutes need to gear up and compete to entice the best students to their respective campuses. They also have to cope with the ever-increasing demand of the industry. Such a system can be built with the help of knowledge stored in the database of students collected at institutes. Timely and correct information will help institutes identify the gray areas of students. Once identified, better decisions can be made, and better policies can be introduced to train students and make them industry ready.

4.2.2 Potential aspects to resolve issues with computational intelligence

Although every institute strives to follow the best of the pedagogies, they face many problems such as dropout students every year, unemployed students, and low-grade achievers. It has been revealed by many researchers that numerous factors are contributing to these problems, which are not always associated with academic progress results. It also includes factors like socio-demographic details, personality preferences of an individual, non-cognitive skills, and cognitive skills of a person.

Understanding and inspecting these factors is a complex and continual process. It may require past and present information about a student. Such data can be congregated from scholastic details and students' performance at various levels. To investigate such complex data necessitates scientific research. We need powerful models to interpret, identify, and analyze students' performance. Statistical methods have been deemed to be less appropriate due to the lack of lucidity and a vast amount of data. Models obtained using them are generally black box in nature, where they may be able to obtain good prediction accuracy rates but are very complicated to understand and interpret due to complex correlations among large numbers for attributes.

Institutes collect students' details from their admission till they pass their program. This enormous amount of data collected remains dormant and adds no value to any managements' decision or policymaking. This data can be put to use with the help of artificial intelligence and data mining techniques.

The advantages of artificial intelligence, machine learning, and data mining have begun to expand in many disciplines. Over a decade, we have seen its growing roots in the education sector. A new research discipline has emerged, popularly known as "educational data mining" (EDM). "EDM is concerned with researching, designing, developing, and applying machine learning techniques to discover patterns in educational data, which is otherwise difficult or impossible to analyze due to the massive volume" [12]. With the advancements of artificial intelligence, HCI, and data mining, the higher education sector of India is also set for robust growth, buoyed by strong demand for quality education and ample employment opportunities.

4.2.3 Contributions of chapter

The major contributions of this chapter are as follows:

1) Case study of using HCI tests (employability tests) for further analysis and prediction.
2) Provides a comprehensive review of literature on employability prediction.
3) Presents a generalized prediction model that is scalable in any context of the higher education system, thus providing a generic solution to the prediction of employability.

4.3 Background

The infusion of computational intelligence in the field of education has opened many avenues for research, including its usage in the progressive growth of students and informed decision-making capabilities. All the research done in the past 2 decades falls under a few categories, as follows.

➤ Survey papers in the domain of education where computational intelligence is applied.
➤ Academic performance prediction of students with the help of artificial intelligence techniques.
➤ Comparison of artificial intelligence techniques in predicting academic performance of students.
➤ Correlation among various significant factors and employability of students.
➤ Employability prediction of students with the help of artificial intelligence techniques.

4.3.1 Review of literature

In the last decade, EDM has aroused the interest of the research community. Most of the research is focused on predicting the academic performance of students [13−19] in EDM. Only some researchers have worked toward predicting the employability of students [20,21]. A few recent studies created employability models [22,23]. All of them are either applied to one course, institute, or university. The need is to create a model with universal application capabilities.

Almost all of the research emphasized including all types of parameters such as English aptitude, cognitive skills, logical skills, psychometric parameters, and background with academic attributes for better prediction [24−26]. The majority of universities and institutes conduct training and take various types of aptitude tests and nowadays with HCI. Such test data can be used for predicting the employability of students at the initial stage of their course enrollment.

Let us look in detail at the studies done to predict the employability of students. Jantawan et al. recognized the attributes that may influence the employment of graduates based on original data obtained from the graduates themselves 12 months after graduation [23]. In another study, by Jantawan and Tsai, it was recognized that three factors—work province, type of occupation, and time to find work—directly affect the employability of a graduate [27]. Mishra et al. predicted the employability of students and compared various data mining algorithms [20]. Most of the efforts in this direction have taken academic attributes only into consideration, yet many researchers have discovered a significant correlation between employability factors and nonacademic factors [28]. The details of the research papers [17,23,26,29−100] related to the domain are given in Table 4.1.

It is clear from the above research that elementary work has been done in the direction of employability prediction of students. Moreover, very few attributes (mostly academic attributes) are taken into consideration; they are generally academic results leaving socio-demographic, cognitive, background, co-curricular, and personality factors aside. Nevertheless, many researchers have clearly exposed a positive correlation between aforesaid factors and employability factors. Inclusion of cognitive ability test results with the help of HCI can act as major predictors of employability. Moreover this type of study in the Indian context with unified approach for entire higher education system is not done. This chapter tries to resolve the issues faced by the higher education system in India in terms of employability prediction.

4.3.2 Problems faced by the higher education system for employability

The economic strength of any country is highly dependent on its higher education system, as it is this system that supplies a skilled and proficient workforce in the diverse sectors of the economy. Thus, the development of the country, specifically a developing nation like India, is highly reliant on its quality workforce. India with the youngest population in the world can only thrive with a state-of-the-art higher education system that is not only self-reliant but is the powerhouse of talent. It has become important for the government to invest in training and skill development along with basic education. It will help in the holistic development of the workforce and will also provide excellent manpower to the world. It cannot be done in isolation. At one end government takes the initiative to train, measure, and regulate the quality of the workforce shaped by higher educational institutions. On the other end, institutes must work hard to ensure the quality of education and training provided to this workforce is on par with the industry.

Table 4.1 Review of papers published.

S. no.	Year	Author(s)	Methodology	Data sets used
1.	2021	Shah, Nimse, Choudhary, and Jadhav	Naïve Bayes, Support vector Machine (SVM), and k-Nearest Neighbor (KNN)	Data collected from a university or college [97]
2.	2020	Pulido, Durán-Domínguez, and Pajuelo-Holguera	Deep Learning	Data of 2058 students collected for introductory programming courses in the first 2 weeks during six-semesters course [96]
3.	2019	Czibula, Mihai, and Crivei	Relational association rules	Bolyai university of Romania; three real academic datasets collected from the university [98]
4.	2018	Borges, Esteves, Nardi Araújo, Oliveira, and Holanda	PCA (Principal Component Analysis)	Two public datasets that describes students' achievements and their social and personal characteristics. The first dataset (dataset I) contains 649 students of the Portuguese subject and is described by 33 attributes. The second dataset (dataset II) is characterized by the same attributes and refers to final achievements of students in the math subject [100]
5.	2017	Asif, Merceron, Ali, and Haider	Classification algorithms trees and KNN	Data was gathered from students' grades in a 4 year information technology program at a Pakistani engineering university. 210 undergraduate students from the 2007—08 and 2008—09 academic years [99]
6.	2014	Dacre Pool, Qualter, and Sewell	Exploratory and confirmatory factor analyses, t-test	Primary data of undergraduate students from UK university [29]

Continued

Table 4.1 Review of papers published.—cont'd

S. no.	Year	Author(s)	Methodology	Data sets used
7.	2014	Saranya, Ayyappan, and Kumar	Naïve Bayes algorithm	Primary data [30]
8.	2014	Cairns, David, Gueni, Fhima, Andrew Cairns, and Khelifa	Clustering technique	Profiles of employees during training [31]
9.	2014	Archer, Chetty, and Prinsloo	Shadowmatch commercial software	Primary data from university of South Africa [32]
10.	2014	Arora and Badal	Association analysis algorithm with Weka tool	Primary data from engineering college of Ghaziabad, India [33]
11.	2014	Pena-Ayala	Statistical and clustering processes	Papers published from year 2010–13 [34]
12.	2014	Vanhercke, Cuyper, Peeters, and Witte	Conceptual paper	Conceptual paper [35]
13.	2013	Potgieter and Coetzee	Statistical tools, multiple regression analysis, and Statistics	Primary data from an open distance Learning higher education institution [25]
14.	2013	Jantawan and Tsai	Tree Method and Bayesian Method with Weka tool	Primary data of employees from the Maejo university, Thailand [23]
15.	2013	Bakar, Mustapha, and Nasir	Using K-Means (clustering analysis) and expectation maximization algorithms	Primary data from Malaysia's ministry of higher education [37]
16.	2013	Singh and Kumar	Weka tool, classification Methods, Bayesian network, naïve Bayes, multilayer perceptron, IBL, decision table	Only academic record of 50 Students from an engineering college [38]
17.	2013	Finch, Hamilton, Baldwin, and Zehner	Two-phase, mixed-methods study	30 hiring managers and 115 employers were interviewed one-on-one [26]
18.	2012	Jackson and Chapman	Online survey	211 business graduate supervisors and 156 business academicians; the performance of Australian business graduates was evaluated [39]

Table 4.1 Review of papers published.—cont'd

S. no.	Year	Author(s)	Methodology	Data sets used
19.	2012	Dejaeger, Goethals, Giangreco, Mola, and Baesens	Neural networks (NN), decision trees, logistic regression, and SMSVM	Primary: "IESEG School of Management" (Lille) in France and "University of Verona" in Italy Secondary: (Tae) data Set from "the University of Wisconsin—Madison" in United States [40]
20.	2012	Osmanbegoviand Suljic	One R-test, chi-square test, gain ratio test, and info gain test, Weka software package, naïve Bayes, multilayer perceptron algorithm, J48, decision tree	Primary data from the university of Tuzla [41]
21.	2012	Sen, Uçar, and Delen	K-fold cross-validation Methodology, SMSVM, artificial neural networks (ANN), decision trees, and logistic regression	Primary data from "Ministry of National Education" in Turkey [42]
22.	2012	Agarwal, Pandey, and Tiwari	Decision rule with decision tree approach in Weka tool	Primary data from community college database [43]
23.	2012	Pandey, Bhardwaj, and Pal		21 research papers [44]
24.	2012	Srimani and Patil	Classifiers, random tree, random forest	Primary data [45]
25.	2012	Sukanya, Biruntha, Karthik, and Kalaikumaran	Bayesian classification Method	Primary data [46]
26.	2012	Yadav and Pal	Decision tree, Weka	Primary data from "V. B. S. Purvanchal University," Jaunpur, India [47]
27.	2011	Torenbeek, Jansen, and Hofman	Structural equations modeling, correlation matrix	Primary data from university in Netherlands with seven different courses [48]
28.	2011	Gokuladas	Statistical correlation and multiple regressions	Primary data from databases of engineering college [49]

Continued

Table 4.1 Review of papers published.—cont'd

S. no.	Year	Author(s)	Methodology	Data sets used
29.	2011	Yongqiang and Shunli	Association rules analysis	Henan Institute of Engineering Zhengzhou, China [50]
30.	2011	Sakurai, Tsuruta, and Knauf	Decision tree, evaluated with cross-validation	"Tokyo Denki University" Chiba New Town, Japan [51]
31.	2011	Pandey and Pal	Association rule	"PSRIET Ranjeetpur Chilbila" Pratapgarh, UP, affiliated With "Dr. RMLA University," Faizabad, India [52]
32.	2011	Aher and Lobo	Weka tool, classification and clustering algorithms	Walchand Institute of Technology, Solapur [53]
33.	2011	Suthan and Baboo	A combination of chaid and Latent class modeling (LCM) (hybrid chaid algorithm)	[54]
34.	2011	Sharma and Mavani	Decision tree, Sota, naïve Bayes In KNIME	SIES College of Management Studies, India [13]
35.	2010	Gokuladas	Statistical analysis: correlation and regression analysis	Primary data from databases of engineering colleges [56]
36.	2010	Ayesha, Mustafa, Raza Sattar, and Khan	K-Means clustering, Model developed in DMX Queries. Available in visual Studio 2005	Primary data from University of Agriculture, Faisalabad [57]
37.	2010	Kovacic	Classification tree Models, chaid, exhaustive chaid, and Quest in SPSS 17 and Statistica 8	Primary data from open polytechnic Management System, New Zealand [58]
38.	2010	Shargabi and Nusari	Association rules (Apriori), clustering (K-Means) and decision trees (ID 3 and J48) inWeka tool	Primary data from university of science and technology [59]
39.	2010	Yani, Shen, and Shao	Rough Set theory	"Huzhou Teachers College," Huzhou Zhejiang, China [60]

Table 4.1 Review of papers published.—cont'd

S. no.	Year	Author(s)	Methodology	Data sets used
40.	2010	Ningning	Neural network, rough Set theory	Huzhou Teachers College, China [61]
41.	2010	Knauf, Sakurai, Tsuruta, and Takada	Decision tree	Primary data from "School of Information Environment" and "Tokyo Denki University," Chiba New Town, Japan [62]
42.	2010	Huacheng Zhang and Huimin Zhang	Decision tree algorithms	Primary data from "Guilin University of Electronic Technology," Guilin, China [63]
43.	2010	Xiangjuan and Youping	Decision tree, ID3	Primary data from Zhejiang Education Institute, Hangzhou, China [64]
44.	2010	Liu and Zhang	Decision tree algorithm, C4.5	Primary data from Shenyang Ligong University, Shenyang, China [65]
45.	2010	David and Balakrishnan	Clustering, K-means algorithm, and decision tree, J48	Set of 125 real datasets [66]
46.	2009	Baker and Yacef		Secondary data from PSLC Datashop [67]
47.	2009	Siraj and Abdoulha	Neural network, cluster analysis, logistic regression, and decision tree	Primary data from Sebha University in Libya [14]
48.	2009	Zhu, Yanli Li, and Xiang Li	Association rule, Apriori algorithm	Primary data from China University of Geosciences [69]
49.	2009	Qingxian, Linjie, and Lanfang	Modified Apriori algorithm	Primary data from Yantai University, Yantai, China [70]
50.	2009	Ahmed, Norwawi, Hussain, and Ishak	Association rules, Apriori algorithm, Weka tool	Primary data from University Utara, Malaysia [71]
51.	2009	Nayak, Agarwal, Yadav, and Pasha	Proposed the use of RDF, ontology, and XML	Proposed training institute with teaching—learning setup online [72]

Continued

Table 4.1 Review of papers published.—cont'd

S. no.	Year	Author(s)	Methodology	Data sets used
52.	2009	Wook, Yahaya, Wahab, Rizal, Isa, Awang, and Seong	Clustering and decision trees, as well as an ANN	Primary data from National Defense University of Malaysia [73]
53.	2009	Pei-Ji, Lin, Jin-Niu, and Yu-Lin	Apriori algorithm	Primary data from "Inner Mongolia University of Science and Technology," Baotou, China [74]
54.	2009	Ramasubramanian, Iyakutti, and Hangavelu	Rough Set theory	Primary Data [75]
55.	2008	Selmoune and Alimazighi	OLAP and association rules, Apriori algorithm, Delphi 7.0, Windows Xp, Oracle 9i	Primary data from Houari Boumediene University of Sciences and Technologies [76]
56.	2008	Shangping and ping	Genetic algorithm and a novel Mining algorithm, Armnga (Ga + Apriori)	Primary data from Hua Zhong Normal University [77]
57.	2008	Bresfelean, Bresfelean, and Ghisoiu	J48 and farthest first algorithms	Primary data from "Faculty of economics and business administration," Cluj-Napoca [78]
58.	2008	Dimokas, Mittas, Nanopoulos, and Angelis	Datawarehouse, MS SQL Server 2005, Olap Server, MS visual Studio 2005, MS Sharepoint Server 2007, and statistical analysis	Primary data from Aristotle University of Thessaloniki [79]
59.	2008	Zhang and Liu	Statistical approach, association rules, Apriori algorithm	Primary data from "Wuhan University of Science and Technology," Wuhan, P.R. China [80]
60.	2008	Zhao	OLAP	Primary data from Dezhou University, China [81]
61.	2008	Villalon and Calvo	Grammar trees, regular expressions on the grammar tree	[82]
62.	2008	Pumpuang, Srivihok, and Praneetpolgrang	Bayesian network, decision forest, C4.5, and Nbtree.	Primary data from Kasetsart University, Bangkok, Thailand [101]

Table 4.1 Review of papers published.—cont'd

S. no.	Year	Author(s)	Methodology	Data sets used
63.	2008	Romero, Ventura, Espejo, and Hervas	Decision tree, rule induction, statistical classifier, fuzzy rule Learning, and neural networks	Primary data from seven Moodle courses with "Cordoba University." Learning Management Systems (LCMS) [16]
64.	2007	Ogor	Clementine 10.0 software, statistical evaluation using some measures of F-test and central tendency	Primary data [85]
65.	2007	Haddawy and Hien	Bayesian network, naïve Bayes algorithm	Primary data from Asian Institute of Technology [86]
66.	2007	Brefelean	Decision trees (J48 algorithm)	Primary data collected from online survey conducted in "the faculty of economics and business administration" in Cluj-Napoca [102]
67.	2007	Nghe, Janecek, and Haddawy	Bayesian network and decision Tree	"Can Tho university" (CTU), Vietnam; and "the Asian Institute of Technology" (AIT), Thailand [17]
68.	2006	Radaideh, Shawakfa, and Mustafa	Decision tree, rough Set theory, ID3, C4.5, and naïve Bayes in Weka toolkit	Primary data from Suranaree University of Technology [88]
69.	2006	Aksenova, Zhang, and Lu	MSVM and rule-based Models	Primary data from California State University, Sacramento [89]
70.	2005	Rasmani and Shen	Fuzzy approaches	Primary data [90]
71.	2005	Delavari, Reza Beikzadeh, and Amnuaisuk	Decision tree, BM intelligent miner tool	Primary data from Multimedia Uuniversity (MMU), Malaysia [91]
72.	2004	Talavera and Gaudioso	Naïve Bayes	Primary data from LMS used for collaborative activity [92]
73.	2004	Salazar, Gosalbez, Bosch, and Vergara	Clustering and decision rule, C4.5 algorithm	Primary data from academic database of "the Industrial University of Santander" (IUS) [93]

Continued

Table 4.1 Review of papers published.—cont'd

S. no.	Year	Author(s)	Methodology	Data sets used
74.	2003	Bidgoli and Iii	Genetic algorithm, PCA classifier KNN to calculate the fitness function for genetic algorithm	Primary data from LMS of Michigan State University [94]
75.	2002	Kotsiantis, Pierrakeas, Zaharakis, and Pintelas	C4.5 algorithm, naïve Bayes algorithm, 3-NN algorithm, Ripper, Winnow	Primary data from Hellenic Open University [95]

A graduate must be proficient in academic knowledge along with employability skills before they present themselves in the industry. The term employability signifies "that a person possesses the skills, ability, and potential to justify a job and to be successful in his/her chosen profession." A report published by India Today in July 2016 exposed that barely 7% of graduates in engineering are job worthy for core engineering professions in India. Another report and study of ASSOCHAM, April 2016, also depicted that most of the professional workforce participants passing from higher education institutes are not ready for industry. It is quoted that "out of 15 lakh engineering graduates produced every year, 20%—30% of them do not find jobs and many others get jobs well below their technical qualification" (ASSOCHAM, 2016). It is also explained that one of the most important constraints is a scarcity of employability skills. The Associated Chambers of Commerce and Industry of India's recent paper (ASSOCHAM, 2017) discloses that the placement scenario is grim in campus hiring. Compared with last year the packages offered are also being curtailed by 40%—45%. Our reliance on degrees rather than skills is seen as a stumbling barrier to economic development. It is emphasized that for India, skill development is critical from both socio-economic and demographic points of view (ASSOCHAM, 2018).

There is a huge disconnect between academic knowledge and the employability skills needed in the real world. These discoveries have glinted grave concerns of the misalliance between the needs of the job market and the education system. Nothing could be more damaging to our long-term economic success and social cohesion than a large number of educated, unemployed adolescents who feel disempowered in every meaning of the word. As a result, it is critical to address this issue fully as soon as possible. That is the only way to emerge as a modern, prosperous, and ever-progressive society. The focus should not be only to provide higher education but the skill development of Indian youth that will help in strengthening the economy of the country.

Today's job market needs and in-demand skills are immensely different from the ones of 10 or even 5 years down the line, and the pace of change is only set to accelerate. The new type of job requires newly enhanced skills. These new types of skills either do not exist or the population is new to the domain. To meet the new requirements, we need to build a skill system that is in line with the business needs and is proficient in opening opportunities for all people. The need is to transform the way employers invest in their workforce and utilize the skills of their employees. This right investment at the right place can be a breakthrough and will help in meeting new skill requirements.

The institute's importance in bridging this enormous gap is undeniable. Along with theoretical learning, there is an urgent need for substantive intervention at the college level to improve students' basic employability skills. The need of the hour is to raise and strengthen educational standards. The educational system will have to adapt to support the nation's economic strategy by focusing more on imparting skill-based information to create a job-ready and employable workforce.

From the time students enroll until they graduate, institutions collect a massive quantity of data on them, including a wide range of attributes. However, this information is unused and does not aid in any decisions or policy making aimed at improving student performance. Not only do universities play a vital role to measure the annual performance of every single student, but government aid and accreditations are also dependent on it. With technologic advancement, machine learning, and data mining tools, it is possible that institutes could use their old records to create knowledge, "knowledge" that could predict the employability of students well in advance. By giving sufficient feedback and time to the students, they will be able to focus and work on their weak areas. Furthermore, institutes will be able to provide personalized guidance to the students and strategize their policies per the specific needs of students.

According to studies, most of the earlier effort in the field of education has been focused solely on the prediction of academic success. Only a smidgeon of an effort is made to anticipate students' employability. Furthermore, previous research on student employability prediction is either based on a specific type of course or a single university/institute, making it inapplicable in various contexts. The need for unification is pressing. This establishes the foundation of contemporary research questions.

We need a framework that can work in any setup with any type of higher education system that is generic enough to be used as a solution to predict student employability in the very early stages of student admission to the institute. Such a setup will help students in finding problem areas and focus their efforts for improvement. Teachers can plan their pedagogies in such a way as to impart the best of the education per the need of the students. Their efforts can be given the right direction. Management can frame better policies for the growth and focused development of students, which in return will bring laurels to the institution. Government accreditations and aid can be utilized in the right direction. Ultimately, it will help in the economic growth and pride of the country. The next portion will describe in detail the proposed framework specifically designed for generalized employability prediction at the early stages of student enrollment.

4.4 Proposed framework: solution with artificial intelligence and human-computer interaction

It has been observed that most of the research is done on students' academic performance prediction, being analyzed from one course or one institute. Analogous to this, very few existing pieces of research for students' employability prediction are also based upon only one course or one institute. In such a way the issue of scalability is not addressed. It generates the necessity of a generalized model, and a model of clustering and classification has been proposed.

4.4.1 Data sets

Data on engineering and master students in computer applications courses were gathered from various institutions across India and classified into five zones: North India, South India, East India, West India, and Central India. These institutes' training and placement officers were contacted to acquire data to guarantee the data's authenticity. Data is huge, multivariate, heterogeneously incomplete, and imbalanced. It also contains lots of missing values. The final dataset consists of around 7000 tuples and 151 columns. The dataset was obtained from previous research datasets collected between 2000

Table 4.2 Datasets from five zones of India.

Datasets	States	Instances in the dataset (attributes 150)
North Zone	Haryana; Himachal Pradesh; Punjab; Uttar Pradesh; and Uttarakhand	2554
East Zone	Bihar; Jharkhand; Orissa; and West Bengal	834
West Zone	Gujarat; Goa; Maharashtra; and Rajasthan	1604
South Zone	Andhra Pradesh; Karnataka; Kerala; and Tamil Nadu	1370
Central Zone	Chhattisgarh; and Madhya Pradesh	781

and 2016 [103–105]. The dataset thus obtained is further categorized and separated into five zones of India. The data not only contains the primary details of a student, but various tests conducted by the institutes for checking the aptitude and technical skills of the students have also been included. These tests are generally conducted with the help of HCI by professionals nationwide. Such tests have been conducted in all the institutes and taken into consideration, and their results have also been included.

The proposed generalized model was applied on each dataset separately described in Table 4.2.

4.4.2 Approach

A predictive generalized model is developed by combining classification and clustering approaches to deal with such data. The suggested extended model provides a generic approach for predicting student employability. The results show how the model performs in different parts of India. As a result, this generic model can be used in a variety of settings.

A generalized prediction model has been designed by combining unsupervised and supervised machine learning techniques (clustering and classification). The model has the capability to predict students' employability in the early years of admission of a student. The model first implements the pre-processing, which automatically selects relevant attributes, and raw data is refined. A novel approach is used for pre-processing the raw data to convert it into a refined dataset with reduced dimensionality automatically. It finds a relevant set of attributes and provides a refined dataset, which can further be readily used for better classification and provides better results.

Then it is taken a step further for ensemble classification at the next level. Instead of selecting a single classification method, the voting ensemble method is employed to improve classification accuracy. The foundation learners are simple CART, random tree, K-star, and random forest. Thus, it integrates more than one classifier to predict students' employability. After that rules are generated to facilitate decision-making. These rules can help in identifying problem areas of students. Timely corrective actions can be taken to help in improving student performance in final placement drives to make them industry ready. The generalized model thus works on the complex dataset, selects a relevant set of attributes automatically, and integrates classification algorithms to predict student employability. The model is scalable enough to be applied in any context [106]. The model is applied on datasets of five zones of India. A logical diagram of the model is presented in Fig. 4.1.

4.4.3 Experimental setup and measures

RapidMiner Studio 7 + version is used to implement the proposed model. The version also implements extended algorithms designed for Weka toolkit.

Because there is no separate test data set, k-fold cross-validation (k = 10) is used as an estimation method to get a good notion of classifier performance. This technique divides the "training set" into 10 equal sections, nine of which are used to train machine algorithms and one of which is used to test these learning algorithms. On the same dataset, this method is used 10 times. As a result, each training set will serve as a test set once.

Performance metrics include accuracy percentage, weighted mean recall, weighted mean precision, root-mean-squared error (RMSE), root-relative-squared error (RRSE), and Kappa statistics. The number of right predictions made divided by the total number of predictions made in percentage is called accuracy percentage. A model can forecast the value of the majority class for all predictions and achieve high classification accuracy in a scenario with a large class imbalance. This is a problem with the dataset utilized in the study, so accuracy may not be the only perfect indicator of the model's performance. Other performance measurements include weighted mean precision and weighted mean recall, RMSE, RRSE, and Kappa statistics.

Accuracy is the percentage of correct predictions or a relative number of correctly classified examples. TP represents *true positive* and TN represents true negative, as represented in Eq. (4.1).

$$accuracy = \frac{TP + TN}{TP + TN + FP + FN} \tag{4.1}$$

Weighted mean recall is the (weighted) average of all per-class recall metrics derived from individual class recalls. After multiplying the scores by their respective class proportions, the sum of recall scores is from all classes. It is based on *recall* value, as represented in Eq. (4.2).

$$Recall = \frac{True\ Positive}{True\ Positive + False\ Negative} = \frac{True\ Positive}{Total\ Actual\ Positive} \tag{4.2}$$

Weighted mean precision is the (weighted) average of all per-class precision measurements obtained using individual class precisions. After multiplying the scores by their respective class proportions, the sum of precision scores is from all classes. It is based on precision value, as represented in Eq. (4.3).

$$precision = \frac{True\ Positive}{True\ Positive + False\ Positive} = \frac{True\ Positive}{Total\ Predicted\ Positive} \tag{4.3}$$

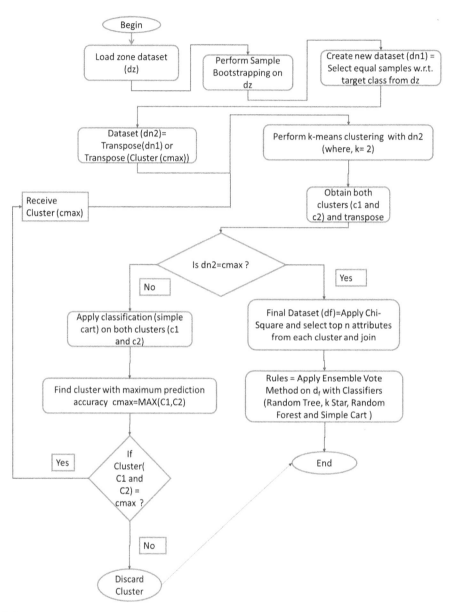

FIGURE 4.1

Logical diagram of proposed generalized model.

The *RMSE* is the standard deviation of the residuals (prediction errors). The residuals represent the distance between the data points and the regression line. The RMSE is a measure of how evenly these residuals are spread out, as represented in Eq. (4.4).

$$RMSE = \sqrt{\frac{1}{N} \sum_{i=1}^{N} (y_i - \widehat{y}_i)^2} \tag{4.4}$$

For RRSE, the total squared error is equal to the relative squared error. It divides it by the total squared error of the simple predictor to normalize it, as represented in Eq. (4.5).

$$E_i = \sqrt{\frac{\sum_{j=1}^{N} \left(P_{(ij)} - T_j\right)^2}{\sum_{j=1}^{N} \left(T_j - \overline{T}\right)^2}} \tag{4.5}$$

The kappa statistics for categorization are widely considered to be a more reliable measure. It is seen to be superior to a basic percentage correct prediction computation because it considers the possibility of a correct forecast occurring by chance, as represented in Eq. (4.6).

$$k = \frac{p_o - p_e}{1 - p_e} = 1 - \frac{1 - p_o}{1 - p_e}, \tag{4.6}$$

4.4.4 Machine learning algorithms implemented in the model

The dataset is largely categorical with some numeric values. Classification techniques in supervised learning are a clear choice. The process of feature selection is also guided by the machine learning algorithm. To the rescue comes the unsupervised learning approach of clustering. It was applied to the set of attributes instead of instances.

For the aim of grouping, the k-means clustering algorithm is used. It uses the kernel approach to approximate the distance between clusters and objects. Because it is essential to total over all elements of a cluster to determine one distance, the procedure is quadratic.

CART, K-star, random tree, and random forest are some of the major classification approaches employed in the model. CART is a binary decision tree that is built by continually splitting a node into two child nodes, starting with the root node, which holds the entire learning sample. K-star is an instance-based classifier of the lazy learner category. It employs a distance function based on entropy. A test instance is based on a similarity function that determines the class of training instances that are similar to it. Overfitting is not a problem for the random tree classifier. It consists of a collection of distinct decision trees, each of which was created using different samples and subsets of the training data. Random forest produces a large number of categorization trees. It is not too tight. On huge databases, it performs well. It can manage a large number of input variables without deleting any of them. The suggested model included the aforementioned classifiers since they outperformed other classifiers.

4.4.5 Application of model on all datasets

The model was applied to each dataset separately. The model works in a layered approach. The first layer implements the pre-processing approach automatically. In this, raw data is converted to refined data. Then it is taken further at the next layer for classification. An ensemble method of voting with four classifiers, namely, random tree, K-star, simple CART, and random forest, is used. The next layer generates rules to facilitate decision-making.

4.5 Results and conclusion

Employability prediction of students can be enhanced by implementing the proposed model. Results prove the fact that the generalized model performs better than individual classifiers. The model is also scalable in many contexts. The generalized model has been applied on five zone datasets and the results have been calculated.

4.5.1 Results

The proposed model has been applied on five zone datasets, and the results have been calculated. Table 4.3 depicts the results obtained after applying the generalized model in terms of classification accuracy, weighted mean precision and weighted mean recall, RMSE, RRSE, and Kappa statistics. Figs. 4.2–4.7 visualize the results obtained in chart form. Fig. 4.2 represents employability prediction accuracy of all the five zones, which reaches above the 80% mark, and the average of all the zones is 89.01%. Figs. 4.3 and 4.4 represent employability prediction in terms of weighted mean precision and weighted mean recall of all five zones, which reaches above the 80% mark, and an average of all zones is 89.01% and 89.27%. Figs. 4.5 and 4.6 represents RMSE and RRSE. Fig. 4.7 visualizes Kappa statistics. All the above results showcase that the proposed model can be applied to any dataset in the education system of India where basic parameters along with specific parameters such as aptitude, academic, demographic, cognitive, and psychometric tests are taken into consideration, even if data is multidimensional and imbalanced in nature.

The results showcase that the proposed model performed well in all cases of zones. The accuracy level reaches 91.54% in the case of South Zone. The least prediction accuracy was recorded in the case of North Zone, with 84.07%, which is still appealing. The decision tree obtained for South Zone with the highest accuracy percentage is shown in Fig. 4.8.

Table 4.3 Results of five zones.

S. no	Zone	Accuracy (%)	Weighted mean recall (WMR)	Weighted mean precision (WMP)	Root-mean squared-error (RMSE)	Root-relative squared-error (RRSE)	Kappa statistics
1.	East	89.75	89.75	89.93	0.305 ± 0.033	0.610 ± 0.065	0.795
2.	West	91.12	91.12	91.34	0.275 ± 0.038	0.549 ± 0.075	0.823
3.	North	84.07	84.07	84.19	0.38 ± 0.016	0.759 ± 0.033	0.681
4.	South	91.54	91.54	91.84	0.283 ± 0.046	0.566 ± 0.093	0.831
5.	Central	88.57	88.57	89.08	0.311 ± 0.049	0.622 ± 0.098	0.771

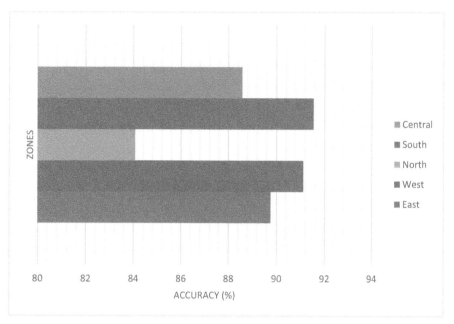

FIGURE 4.2

Employability prediction accuracy of five zones.

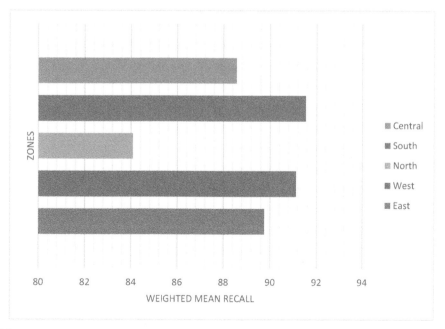

FIGURE 4.3

Weighted mean recall score of five zones.

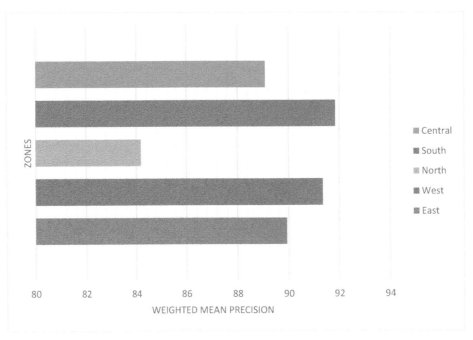

FIGURE 4.4

Weighted mean precision values of five zones.

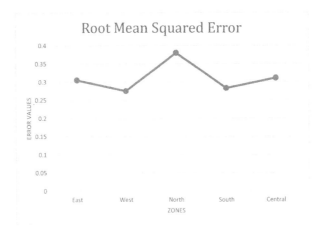

FIGURE 4.5

Root-mean-squared error values of five zones.

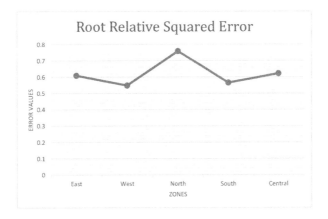

FIGURE 4.6

Root-relative-squared error values of five zones.

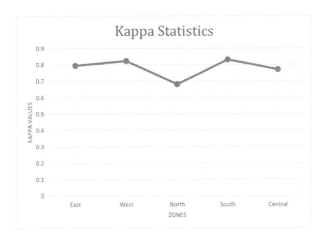

FIGURE 4.7

Kappa values of five zones.

```
CART Decision Tree

quantscore < 540.0
|   quantscore < 97.0
|   |   UgPgsem1=(A)|(C)|(O)|(D): Placed
|   |   UgPgsem1!=(A)|(C)|(O)|(D): Unplaced
|   quantscore >= 97.0
|   |    Computerprogscore < 620.0: Unplaced
|   |    Computerprogscore >= 620.0: Placed
quantscore >= 540.0
|   quantscore < 600.0
|   |   quantscore < 560.0: Placed
|   |   quantscore >= 560.0: Unplaced
|   quantscore >= 600.0: Placed
```

FIGURE 4.8

CART decision tree for south zone.

It was also observed that logical test results, English test results, and quantitative test results played a significant role in the prediction of employability in all five zones of India.

4.5.2 Conclusion and future possibilities

The results prove that prediction performance for students' employability can be enhanced by applying the proposed model. It is also proved that the model is robust in nature and can be applied to any type of imbalanced and multidimensional dataset of the education system in various contexts. Moreover, clustering applied on features set at the stage of preprocessing helps in the prudent selection of features that eventually improves the performance of predictive algorithms. The results clearly depict that the model is superior to commonly used methods of predicting students' employability in terms of universal applicability. The results prove that there is no significant difference existing in the Indian education system with respect to zones as far as the prediction of employability of students is concerned. The model also helps in reducing dimensionality and can further be used for domains other than education. Taking the base of the proposed model, it can be tested on various types of datasets in the future.

References

[1] S. Basheer, S. Bhatia, S.B. Sakri, Computational modeling of dementia prediction using deep neural network: analysis on OASIS dataset, IEEE Access 9 (2021) 42449−42462, https://doi.org/10.1109/ACCESS.2021.3066213.

[2] S. Basheer, K. Nagawanshi, S. Bhatia, S. Dubey, G.R. Sinha, FESD: an approach for biometric human footprint matching using fuzzy ensemble learning, IEEE Access (2021), https://doi.org/10.1109/ACCESS.2021.3057931.

[3] S. Bhatia, M. Alojail, A Novel Technique for Behavioral Analytics Using Ensemble Learning Algorithms in E-COMMERCE, IEEE Access, 2020, pp. 1−9. ISSN: 2169-3536.

[4] G. Mohindru, et al., Different hybrid machine intelligence techniques for handling IoT-based imbalanced data, CAAI Trans. Intell. Technol. 6 (4) (2021) 405−416.

[5] S.S. Kshatri, D. Singh, B. Narain, S. Bhatia, M.T. Quasim, G.R. Sinha, An empirical analysis of machine learning algorithms for crime prediction using stacked generalization: an ensemble approach, IEEE Access 9 (2021) 67488−67500, https://doi.org/10.1109/ACCESS.2021.3075140.

[6] R. Jiang, et al., Flow-assisted visual tracking using event cameras, CAAI Transac. Intell. Technol. 6 (2) (2021) 192−202.

[7] S. Chandna, F. Rindone, C. Dachsbacher, R. Stotzka, Quantitative exploration of large medieval manuscripts data for the codicological research, in: 2016 IEEE 6th Symposium on Large Data Analysis and Visualization (LDAV), IEEE, 2016, pp. 20−28.

[8] T. Wang, A. Hussain, M.N.M. Bhutta, Y. Cao, Enabling bidirectional traffic mobility for ITS simulation in smart city environments, Future Generat. Comput. Syst. 92 (2019) 342−356.

[9] S. Bhatia, A comparative study of opinion summarization techniques, IEEE Transac. Comput. Soc. Syst. 8 (1) (Feb. 2021) 110−117, https://doi.org/10.1109/TCSS.2020.3033810.

[10] R.A. Sheikh, S. Bhatia, S.G. Metre, A.Y.A. Faqihi, Strategic value realization framework from learning analytics: a practical approach, J. Appl. Res. High Educ. 14 (2) (2022) 693−713, https://doi.org/10.1108/JARHE-10-2020-0379.

[11] Indian Education Sector in India Industry Report, May 2021, India Brand Equity Foundation (IBEF). Available: https://www.ibef.org/industry/education-sector-india.aspx.

[12] C. Romero, S. Ventura, Educational data mining: a review of the state of the art, IEEE Transac. Syst., Man, and Cybernet. Part C (Appl. Rev.) (2010) 601–618.

[13] M.A. Sharma, Accuracy Comparison of Predictive Algorithms of Data Mining: Application in Education Sector. Advances in Computing, Communication and Control, Springer Berlin Heidelberg, 2011, pp. 189–194.

[14] F.A. Siraj, Uncovering Hidden Information within University's Student Enrollment Data Using Data Mining, Modelling and Simulation, 2009, 2009. AMS'09. Third Asia International Conference on. IEEE.

[15] P.A. Pumpuang, Comparisons of classifier algorithms: bayesian network, C4. 5, decision forest and NBTree for Course Registration Planning model of undergraduate students. Systems, Man and Cybernetics, 2008. SMC 2008, in: IEEE International Conference on. IEEE, 2008.

[16] C.S. Romero, Data Mining Algorithms to Classify Students, EDM, 2008, pp. 8–17.

[17] N.T. Nghe, A comparative analysis of techniques for predicting academic performance, in: Frontiers In Education Conference-Global Engineering: Knowledge Without Borders, Opportunities Without Passports, 2007. FIE'07. 37th Annual. IEEE, 2007.

[18] A.A. Saa, Educational data mining and students' performance prediction, Int. J. Adv. Comput. Sci. Appl. 7 (5) (2016) 212–220.

[19] C. El Moucary, Data Mining for Engineering Schools Predicting Students' Performance and Enrollment in Masters Programs, 2011.

[20] T.D. Mishra, Students' employability prediction model through data mining, Int. J. Appl. Eng. Res. 11 (4) (2016) 2275–2282.

[21] K.C. Piad, Predicting IT employability using data mining techniques, in: Digital Information Processing, Data Mining, and Wireless Communications (DIPDMWC), 2016 Third International Conference on, IEEE, 2016.

[22] Pl Chen, W. Cheng, T.T. Fan, Study on the BP neural network evaluation model of employability, in: Proceedings of the 22nd International Conference on Industrial Engineering and Engineering Management 2015, Atlantis Press, 2016.

[23] B. Jantawan, C.-F. Tsai, The application of data mining to build classification model for predicting graduate employment, Int. J. Comput. Sci. Inf. Secur. 11 (10) (2013) 1–7.

[24] N.Y. Rahmat, Determination of constructs and dimensions of employability skills based work performance prediction: a triangular approach, Int. J. Econ. Financ. Issues 5 (2015) 1S.

[25] I.A. Potgieter, Employability attributes and personality preferences of postgraduate business management students, SA J. Ind. Psychol. 39 (1) (2013) 1–10.

[26] D.J. Finch, An exploratory study of factors affecting undergraduate employability, Educ. Train. 55 (7) (2013) 681–704.

[27] B. Jantawan, C.F. Tsai, A classification model on graduate employability using bayesian approaches: a comparison, Int. J. Innov. Res. Comput. Commun. Eng. (2014) 4584–4588.

[28] P. Thakar, A. Mehta, Manisha, Role of secondary attributes to boost the prediction accuracy of students' employability via data mining, Int. J. Adv. Comput. Sci. Appl. (2015) 84–90.

[29] L.D. Pool, P. Qualter, P.J. Sewell, Exploring the factor structure of the CareerEDGE employability development profile, Educ. Train. 56 (4) (2014) 303–313.

[30] S. Saranya, R. Ayyappan, N. Kumar, Student progress analysis and educational institutional growth prognosis using data mining, Int. J. Eng. Sci. Res. Technol. 3 (4) (2014).

[31] A. Cairns, H. Awatef, et al., Towards custom-designed professional training contents and curriculums through educational process mining, in: IMMM 2014, the Fourth International Conference on Advances in Information Mining and Management, 2014.

[32] E. Archer, Y. Bianca Chetty, P. Paul, Benchmarking the habits and behaviors of successful students: a case study of academic-business collaboration, Int. Rev. Res. Open Dist. Learn. 15 (2014) 1.

[33] R.K. Arora, D. Badal, Mining Association Rules to Improve Academic Performance, 2014.

[34] A. Peña-Ayala, Educational data mining: a survey and a data mining-based analysis of recent works, Expert Syst. Appl. 41 (4) (2014) 1432−1462.

[35] D. Vanhercke, N. De Cuyper, E. Peeters, H. De Witte, Defining perceived employability: a psychological approach, Person. Rev. 43 (4) (2014) 592−605.

[36] I. Potgieter, M. Coetzee, Employability attributes and personality preferences of postgraduate business management students, SA J. Ind. Psychol. 39 (1) (2013) 01−10.

[37] N.A.A. Bakar, A. Mustapha, K.Md Nasir, Clustering analysis for empowering skills in graduate employability model, Australian J. Basic Appl. Sci. 7 (14) (2013) 21−28.

[38] S. Singh, V. Kumar, Performance analysis of engineering students for recruitment using classification data mining techniques, Int. J. Comput. Sci. Eng. Technol. 3 (2) (2013) 31−37.

[39] D. Jackson, E. Chapman, Non-technical skill gaps in Australian business graduates, Educ. Train. 54 (2/3) (2012) 95−113.

[40] K. Dejaeger, et al., Gaining insight into student satisfaction using comprehensible data mining techniques, Eur. J. Oper. Res. 218 (2) (2012) 548−562.

[41] E. Osmanbegović, M. Suljić, Data mining approach for predicting student performance, Econ. Rev. 10 (2012) 1.

[42] B. Şen, E. Uçar, D. Delen, Predicting and analyzing secondary education placement-test scores: a data mining approach, Expert Syst. Appl. 39 (10) (2012) 9468−9476.

[43] S. Agrawal, G. Pandey, M. Tiwari, Data mining in education: data classification and decision tree approach, Int. J. e-Edu., e-Bus., e-Manage. e-Learn. 2 (2) (2012) 140−144.

[44] U.K. Pandey, B. Kumar Bhardwaj, Data mining as a torch bearer in education sector, Tech. J. LBSIMDS (2012) 11.

[45] P.K. Srimani, M.M. Patil, A classification model for edu-mining, PSRC-ICICS Conf. Proc. (2012).

[46] M. Sukanya, S. Biruntha, D.S. Karthik, T. Kalaikumaran, Data mining: performance improvement in education sector using classification and clustering algorithm, in: International Conference on Computing and Control Engineering,(ICCCE 2012), 12, 2012.

[47] Yadav, S. Kumar, S. Pal, Data mining application in enrollment management: a case study, Int. J. Comput. Appl. 41 (5) (2012) 1−6.

[48] M. Torenbeek, E.P.W.A. Jansen, W.H.A. Hofman, Predicting first-year achievement by pedagogy and skill development in the first weeks at university, Teach. High. Educ. 16 (6) (2011) 655−668.

[49] V.K. Gokuladas, Predictors of employability of engineering graduates in campus recruitment drives of Indian software services companies, Int. J. Sel. Assess. 19 (3) (2011) 313−319.

[50] H. Yongqiang, S. Zhang, Application of data mining on students' quality evaluation, in: Intelligent Systems and Applications (ISA), 2011 3rd International Workshop on, IEEE, 2011.

[51] Y. Sakurai, S. Tsuruta, R. Knauf, Success chances estimation of university curricula based on educational history, self-estimated intellectual traits and vocational ambitions, in: Advanced Learning Technologies (ICALT), 2011 11th IEEE International Conference on, IEEE, 2011.

[52] U.K. Pandey, S. Pal, A Data mining view on class room teaching language, Int. J. Comput. Sci. Issues (2011) 6.

[53] S.B. Aher, L.M.R.J. Lobo, Data mining in educational system using Weka, IJCA Proc. Int. Confer. Emerg. Technol. Trends (ICETT) 3 (2011).

[54] G.P. Suthan, S. Baboo, Hybrid chaid a key for mustas framework in educational data mining, IJCSI Int. J. Comput. Sci. Issues 8 (2011) 356−360.

[55] M. Sharma, M. Mavani, Accuracy comparison of predictive algorithms of data mining: application in education sector, in: Advances in Computing, Communication and Control. Springer Berlin Heidelberg, 2011, pp. 189−194.

[56] V.K. Gokuladas, Technical and non-technical education and the employability of engineering graduates: an Indian case study, Int. J. Train. Dev. 14 (2) (2010) 130−143.

[57] S. Ayesha, T. Mustafa, A. Raza Sattar, M. Inayat Khan, Data mining model for higher education system, Euro. J. Sci. Res. 43 (1) (2010) 24−29.

[58] Z. Kovacic, Early Prediction of Student Success: Mining Students' Enrolment Data, 2010.

[59] Al-shargabi, A. Asma, A.N. Nusari, Discovering vital patterns from UST students data by applying data mining techniques, in: Computer and Automation Engineering (ICCAE), 2010 the 2nd International Conference on, 2, IEEE, 2010.

[60] Z.-min Yan, Q. Shen, B. Shao, The analysis of student's grade based on Rough Sets, in: Ubi-media Computing (U-Media), 2010 3rd IEEE International Conference on, IEEE, 2010.

[61] G. Ningning, Proposing data warehouse and data mining in teaching management research, in: Information Technology and Applications (IFITA), 2010 International Forum on, 1, IEEE, 2010.

[62] R. Knauf, Y. Sakurai, S. Tsuruta, K. Takada, Empirical evaluation of a data mining method for success chance estimation of university curricula, in: Systems Man and Cybernetics (SMC), 2010 IEEE International Conference on, IEEE, 2010, pp. 1127−1133.

[63] X. Wu, H. Zhang, H. Zhang, Study of comprehensive evaluation method of undergraduates based on data mining, in: Intelligent Computing and Integrated Systems (ICISS), 2010 International Conference on, IEEE, 2010, pp. 541−543.

[64] B. Xiangjuan, G. Youping, The Application of Data Mining Technology in Analysis of College Student's Performance, Information Science, 2010.

[65] Z. Liu, X. Zhang, Prediction and analysis for students' marks based on decision tree algorithm, in: Intelligent Networks and Intelligent Systems (ICINIS), 2010 3rd International Conference on, IEEE, 2010.

[66] J.M.D. Balakrishnan, Significance of classification techniques in prediction of learning disabilities, Int. J. Artifi. Intell. Appl. (2010) 10.

[67] R.S.J.D. Baker, K. Yacef, The state of educational data mining in 2009: a review and future visions, JEDM-J. Edu. Data Min. 1 (2009) 3−17.

[68] F. Siraj, M.A. Abdoulha, Uncovering hidden information within university's student enrollment data using data mining, in: Modelling and Simulation, 2009. AMS'09. Third Asia International Conference on, IEEE, 2009.

[69] L. Zhu, Y. Li, L. Xiang, Research on early-warning model of students' academic records based on association rules, in: Computer Science and Information Engineering, 2009 WRI World Congress on, 4, IEEE, 2009.

[70] Q. Linjie, L. Lou, Data mining and application of teaching evaluation based on association rules, in: Computer Science and Education, 2009. ICCSE'09. 4th International Conference on, IEEE, 2009.

[71] A.M. Ahmed, N.Md Norwawi, W. Hussain Wan Ishak, Identifying student and organization matching pattern using Apriori algorithm for practicum placement, in: Electrical Engineering and Informatics, 2009. ICEEI'09. International Conference on, 1, IEEE, 2009.

[72] A. Nayak, J. Agarwal, V.K. Yadav, S. Pasha, Enterprise architecture for semantic web mining in education, in: Computer and Electrical Engineering, 2009. ICCEE'09. Second International Conference on, 2, IEEE, 2009, pp. 23−26.

[73] M. Wook, Y. Hani Yahaya, N. Wahab, M. Rizal Mohd Isa, N. Fatimah Awang, H. Yann Seong, Predicting NDUM student's academic performance using data mining techniques, in: Computer and Electrical Engineering, 2009. ICCEE'09. Second International Conference on, 2, IEEE, 2009, pp. 357−361.

[74] P.-ji Wang, L. Shi, J.-niu Bai, Y.-lin Zhao, Mining association rules based on apriori algorithm and application, in: Computer Science-Technology and Applications, 2009. IFCSTA'09. International Forum on, 1, IEEE, 2009, pp. 141−143.

[75] P. Ramasubramanian, K. Iyakutti, P. Thangavelu, Enhanced data mining analysis in higher educational system using rough set theory, Afr. J. Math. Comput. Sci. Res. 2 (9) (2009) 184−188.

[76] N. Selmoune, Z. Alimazighi, A decisional tool for quality improvement in higher education, in: Information and Communication Technologies: From Theory to Applications, 2008. ICTTA 2008. 3rd International Conference on, IEEE, 2008.

[77] D. Shangping, P. Zhang, A data mining algorithm in distance learning, in: Computer Supported Cooperative Work in Design, 2008. CSCWD 2008. 12th International Conference on, IEEE, 2008.

[78] V.P. Bresfelean, M. Bresfelean, N. Ghisoiu, C.-A. Comes, Determining students' academic failure profile founded on data mining methods, in: Information Technology Interfaces, 2008. ITI 2008. 30th International Conference on, IEEE, 2008, pp. 317−322.

[79] N. Dimokas, N. Mittas, A. Nanopoulos, L. Angelis, A prototype system for educational data warehousing and mining, in: InInformatics, 2008. PCI'08. Panhellenic Conference on, IEEE, 2008, pp. 199−203.

[80] X. Zhang, G. Liu, Score data analysis for pre-warning students in university, in: Wireless Communications, Networking and Mobile Computing, 2008. WiCOM'08. 4th International Conference on, IEEE, 2008.

[81] H.-l Zhao, Application of OLAP to the analysis of the curriculum chosen by students, in: Anti-counterfeiting, Security and Identification, 2008. ASID 2008. 2nd International Conference on, IEEE, 2008.

[82] J.J. Villalon, R.A. Calvo, Concept Map Mining: a definition and a framework for its evaluation, in: Web Intelligence and Intelligent Agent Technology, 2008. WI-IAT'08. IEEE/WIC/ACM International Conference on, 3, IEEE, 2008.

[83] P. Pumpuang, A. Srivihok, P. Praneetpolgrang, Comparisons of classifier algorithms: bayesian network, C4. 5, decision forest and NBTree for Course Registration Planning model of undergraduate students, in: Systems, Man and Cybernetics, 2008. SMC 2008. IEEE International Conference on, IEEE, 2008.

[84] C. Romero, S. Ventura, P.G. Espejo, C. Hervás, Data Mining Algorithms to Classify Students, EDM, 2008, pp. 8−17.

[85] E.N. Ogor, Student academic performance monitoring and evaluation using data mining techniques, in: Electronics, Robotics and Automotive Mechanics Conference, 2007. CERMA 2007, IEEE, 2007.

[86] Hien, N. Thi Ngoc, H. Peter, A decision support system for evaluating international student applications, in: Frontiers In Education Conference-Global Engineering: Knowledge Without Borders, Opportunities Without Passports, 2007. FIE'07. 37th Annual, IEEE, 2007.

[87] V.P. Bresfelean, Analysis and predictions on students' behavior using decision trees in Weka environment, in: Information Technology Interfaces, 2007. ITI 2007. 29th International Conference on, IEEE, 2007.

[88] A.Q. Al-Radaideh, E.M. Al-Shawakfa, M.I. Al-Najjar, Mining student data using decision trees, in: International Arab Conference on Information Technology (ACIT'2006), Yarmouk University, Jordan, 2006.

[89] S.S. Aksenova, Du Zhang, M. Lu, Enrollment prediction through data mining, in: Information Reuse and Integration, 2006 IEEE International Conference on, IEEE, 2006.

[90] K.A. Rasmani, Q. Shen, Subsethood-based fuzzy rule models and their application to student performance classification, in: Fuzzy Systems, 2005. FUZZ'05. The 14th IEEE International Conference on, IEEE, 2005.

[91] N. Delavari, M.R. Beikzadeh, S. Phon-Amnuaisuk, Application of enhanced analysis model for data mining processes in higher educational system, in: Information Technology Based Higher Education and Training, 2005. ITHET 2005. 6th International Conference on, IEEE, 2005.

[92] L. Talavera, E. Gaudioso, Mining student data to characterize similar behavior groups in unstructured collaboration spaces, in: Workshop on Artificial Intelligence in CSCL. 16th European Conference on Artificial Intelligence, 2004.

[93] A. Salazar, J. Gosalbez, I. Bosch, R. Miralles, L. Vergara, A case study of knowledge discovery on academic achievement, student desertion and student retention, in: Information Technology: Research and Education, 2004. ITRE 2004. 2nd International Conference on, IEEE, 2004, pp. 150−154.

[94] B. Minaei-Bidgoli, W.F. Punch, Using genetic algorithms for data mining optimization in an educational web-based system, in: Genetic and Evolutionary Computation—GECCO 2003. Springer Berlin Heidelberg, 2003.

[95] S. Kotsiantis, C. Pierrakeas, P. Pintelas, Efficiency of Machine Learning Techniques in Predicting Students' Performance in Distance Learning Systems, Educational Software Development Laboratory Department of Mathematics, University of Patras, Greece, 2002.

[96] J.A. Gómez-Pulido, A. Durán-Domínguez, F. Pajuelo-Holguera, Optimizing latent factors and collaborative filtering for students' performance prediction, Appl. Sci. 10 (16) (2020) 5601.

[97] B. Shah, T. Nimse, V. Choudhary, V. Jadhav, An experiment to determine student performance prediction using machine learning algorithm, Int. J. Adv. Res. Sci., Commun. Technol. 7 (1) (2021) 2581−9429.

[98] G. Czibula, A. Mihai, L.M. Crivei, S prar: a novel relational association rule mining classification model applied for academic performance prediction, Proc. Comput. Sci. 159 (2019) 20−29.

[99] R. Asif, A. Merceron, S.A. Ali, N.G. Haider, Analyzing undergraduate students' performance using educational data mining, Comput. Educ. 113 (2017) 177−194.

[100] V.R.P. Borges, S. Esteves, P. de Nardi Araújo, L.C. de Oliveira, M. Holanda, Using Principal Component Analysis to support students' performance prediction and data analysis, in: Brazilian Symposium on Computers in Education (Simpósio Brasileiro de Informática na Educação-SBIE), 2018.

[101] P. Pumpuang, A. Srivihok, P. Praneetpolgrang, Comparisons of classifier algorithms: bayesian network, C4. 5, decision forest and NBTree for Course Registration Planning model of undergraduate students, in: 2008 IEEE International Conference on Systems, Man and Cybernetics, IEEE, 2008, pp. 3647−3651.

[102] V.P. Bresfelean, Analysis and predictions on students' behavior using decision trees in Weka environment, in: 2007 29th International Conference on Information Technology Interfaces, IEEE, 2007, pp. 51−56.

[103] P. Thakar, M. Anil Mehta, Unified prediction model for employability in Indian higher education system, J. Adv. Res. Dynam. Control Syst. 10 (02-Special Issue) (2018) 1480−1488.

[104] P. Thakar, A. Mehta, Manisha, A unified model of clustering and classification to improve students' employability prediction, I.J. Intell. Syst. Appl. 9 (2017) 10−18.

[105] P. Thakar, A. Mehta, Manisha, Cluster model for parsimonious selection of variables and enhancing students' employability prediction, Int. J. Comput. Sci. Inf. Secur. 14 (12) (2016) 611.

[106] P. Thakar, A. Mehta, M. Sharma, Robust prediction model for multidimensional and unbalanced datasets, Int. J. Inform. Syst. Manage. Sci. 1 (2) (2018). Available at SSRN, https://ssrn.com/abstract=3364973.

Human-centered artificial intelligence

Zainab Aizaz and Kavita Khare

Department of ECE, Maulana Azad National Institute of Technology (MANIT), Bhopal, Madhya Pradesh, India

5.1 Introduction to human-centered AI

Artificial intelligence (AI) can be referred to as the intelligence created in machines that is similar to human intelligence. It can be speculated that AI is presently a hot-button topic that is being used in online shopping, agriculture, machinery, education, cybersecurity, government policymaking, and in day-to-day life. With the advent of neural networks, researchers have remodeled the human brain. For 5 decades, tumultuous experimentation on convolutional neural networks and deep neural networks (DNNs) has been performed, extracting out their potential to overtake other AI algorithms in the terms of accuracy and performance. DNNs require enormously large amounts of input data to produce high-accuracy output. DNNs excel in other AI algorithms in terms of their high accuracy in pattern identification and versatility. We are dwelling in the era in which the best researchers are plumbing into the depths of deep learning, and we are seamlessly using it in search engines, self-driven cars, satellite imaging, and so on.

In the book, *AI Superpowers—China, Silicon Valley, and the new world order* [1], the extent of the intervention of AI in our lives is shown. AI has taken over the countries' economies and will be a major factor determining the development of a country, in more years to come. The book reveals that the United States has achieved a breakthrough in technology and research by implementing AI in all of its sectors, which underwent acceleration more due to the standard of living of the country that attracts elite researchers from around the world to settle there. The book also provides insights into China where AI has acquired government, technology, and business, and AI has even trickled to the depths of the kindergartens where kids at a very young age are introduced to the potential of AI. A well-known prediction has existed since the beginning of the robotic era and has gained fame from kids' television showing that robots are going to take over all the tasks that humans do, threatening that the day is not far away when the robots will rule the world. This possibility appears to be converting into reality with the help of fast-paced growth in AI technologies. But the decision lies in our hands, and we still can control the flow of automation, whether robots will rule us or we will rule over the robots. One more danger of robotic dominance is the failure of systems, resulting in crashes such as accidents due to self-driven cars, autonomous missiles, and space vehicles. Humans must take actions presently to ensure that the direction in which AI is moving exponentially may not lead us to a condition where human intervention becomes extremely difficult, and the technology is saturated to such an extent that to

Innovations in Artificial Intelligence and Human-Computer Interaction in the Digital Era. https://doi.org/10.1016/B978-0-323-99891-8.00004-8

control the machines, complete redesigning is required. An example of such a system can be of a photograph taken using a smartphone, in which the focus and apertures are calculated using the algorithm, while the level of zoom, image location, and applied filters are decided by the users. Unless the user clicks, the camera cannot capture the image, and therefore, even after the use of advanced AI algorithms, the prominent control lies in the hands of humans.

According to Shneiderman [2], the idea of machines replacing humans should be disapproved by us, and a more human-friendly design of AI-based systems should be invented wherein robots are not given entire control over the tasks they are programmed to perform. The concept of conventional AI is that humans design AI algorithms that are autonomous and human work is done by algorithms; on the contrary, the concept of human-centered artificial intelligence (HAI), as shown in Fig. 5.1, is that AI algorithms are designed in such a way that they do the work of humans, but they are under control of humans, and not completely autonomous. Humans control their actions, decisions, and execution. AI systems are not grown up in a cultural environment as humans, and since they lack basic common sense, they are not expected to fulfill the emotional requirements of an adult who relies completely on a robot. The growth of AI systems seems to be ever increasing, and therefore, some ways are required to gain larger control of the designs of AI-based autonomous systems. HAI is a model of AI in which humans will have their abilities enhanced due to the combination of humans and AI working together to achieve escalated performance. The goal is to design devices that are able to initiate, predict, calculate, and provide results in outstanding ways owing mainly due to the intervention of humans in the AI loop. Therefore, HAI magnifies the outputs achieved by ordinary AI by using the human inputs while working on the same embedded platform. Fig. 5.2 shows the potential areas where HAI can be useful such as military, healthcare, business, education, and agriculture. In these areas, the human—AI combination can prove to be a game changer. Finally, the key vision behind the introduction of HAI is to design the systems in such a way that without human augmentation, the algorithms of the AI do not complete, and sufficient control lies in the hands of humans. This ensures that human interaction,

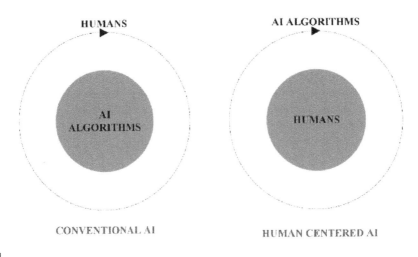

FIGURE 5.1

Goals of human-centered intelligence.

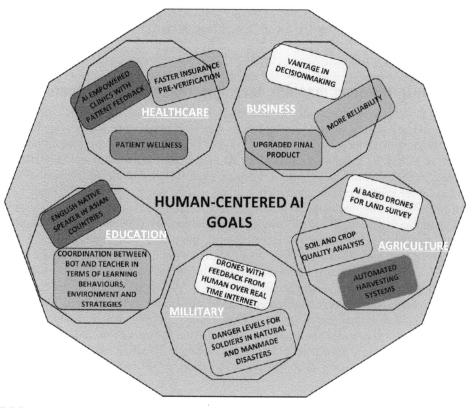

FIGURE 5.2

Areas benefitting from HAI.

human ethics, and human emotions are not threatened by machines in the future, and the threats due to robots do not encompass their benefits.

Highlights of the chapter

1. Complete coverage of the HAI aspects, theory, models, and design approaches
2. Wide variety of HAI examples such as HAI in industry, healthcare, public security, and autonomous vehicles
3. Quantitative analysis showing the relation between accuracy and data annotation
4. Illustrative case studies

The rest of the chapter is organized as follows. Section 5.2 shows human-in-the-loop machine learning and demonstrates four different models showing the inclusion of humans in the AI loop. Section 5.3 describes the essentials of data analysis in HAI with a focus on data annotation, crowdsourcing, and the relation between data annotation on accuracy. Different design approaches of HAI are presented in Section 5.4. The chapter also shows various hybrid designs that can be used in HAI-based systems. Section 5.5 presents the evaluation methods and the design flow of HAI models.

Section 5.6 provides detailed case studies of Netflix and LinkedIn, throwing light on the Microsoft HAX toolkit. Finally, Section 5.7 presents limitations of HAI, and Section 5.8 presents the conclusion.

5.2 Human-in-the-loop machine learning, reasoning, and planning

We still need to walk far to experience the full potential of AI. The idea of HAI is to increase human convenience and beneficence from the AI rather than AI replacing the humans. There are various ways that putting humans in the loop can help improve ways of living. Fig. 5.3 shows some of the ways HAI can benefit us. Firstly, by avoiding the bias of the AI model, since data fed to the AI models is itself biased, these models tend to become biased. Humans when included in the AI loop will create more jobs, and as for the process of data annotation, humans will be always be required. People who label data will be required more in number than people who design algorithms. Humans can augment the rare data by adding to data that is not sufficient to train an algorithm. HAI promotes the requirement of lesser data, and since AI becomes more perfect with more data, with humans in the loop, the requirement of a large amount of data ceases. AI alone cannot perform in applications such as building space vehicles and aircraft. Manufacturing of aircraft parts requires extremely high levels of precision, failing which disastrous consequences occur. Therefore, if AI-powered machines are manufacturing the aircraft, by including humans, the desired level of precision can be achieved. Similarly, more sophisticated applications can be created if subject experts are included in the loops of models. Humans in the loop will promote consistency and increase the accuracy of the models. Humans in the AI loop can help to increase the efficiency of various applications such as biomedical and healthcare, public safety, autonomous driving, and industry. At an airport, if the visa entry of a person is rejected,

FIGURE 5.3

Goals of HAI.

he or she will require a human who will be held accountable for the issues of his rejection; we cannot expect a robot to do this job. Therefore, humans will always be needed for transparency and accountability. Increasing safety and security has so much reliance on the human-in-the-loop paradigm. For example, an AI-driven vehicle requires human inputs for a safer drive, and this is shown in Section 5.4.2.2. Finally, AI is always there to make the human task easier, but when humans are included in the loop, they make the task of AI easier by providing data annotation.

Let us consider the example of the treatment of an aneurysm in the brain. The disease is commonly known to occur from weakened capillaries (blood vessels) in the brain. The treatment of this disease requires magnetic resonance imaging (MRI) for detection and for treatment. MRI scan images show the location and condition of the affected blood vessels, and an AI algorithm can be applied for the recommendation of the most appropriate medication and further treatment. In a real-world situation, the treatment is prescribed by a doctor, who uses his expertise to first monitor the blood pressure, sugar level, and blood composition of the patient, which can be a dependent factor in determining the correct medications to be given. The aneurysms tend to rupture if a slight increase above a tolerable limit occurs in the blood pressure. The medications prescribed depend upon blood pressure levels on daily basis. The decision to perform surgery or not also depends upon the doctor with the experience from the previous patients since aneurysms can be treated with only medication or with surgery. If doctors' opinions can be inserted into the loop of this application, the results of the AI algorithm can be highly accurate, and the risks will be very low. On the other hand, without human intervention, a 100% appropriate treatment is difficult to achieve. Thus, before we enter into the all-robot age, there are still many such applications left where an AI algorithm requires human inputs for providing near-perfect outputs. For robots to become self-sufficient in the medical field, human-in-the-loop is a crucial requirement, and ignoring that, even small errors can produce catastrophic results. What are the basic principles of machine learning with humans in the loop? For humans and AI to combine effectively, there should be clear goals that reflect the output of the applications created. These goals can be any one or more than one of the following.

5.2.1 For increasing the accuracy of an AI model

For the application in which the human experience can provide tremendous gain in computation, such as handwritten digit recognition, computer vision, etc., by taking inputs from users, a lot of tasks of the algorithm can be reduced. Suppose that in the applications where one human input is 100% accurate and compared with that many loops of AI algorithm are required for achieving 90% accuracy for the same, then this application can use inputs from humans once in a while to increase their accuracy.

5.2.2 For achieving the required accuracy of an AI model faster

Now the question arises, where to put humans in the AI loop? There can be five models that define the position of humans in the AI loop where inputs from humans can be effectively used. First is at the beginning before training takes place, i.e., at the point of data annotation. Secondly, after the algorithm finishes with the classification task, humans can be consulted for the verification or confirmation of the outputs.

5.2.3 Model 1

In this model, one can implement humans in the AI loop during data annotation. Data annotation is a technique in which the data is labeled and characterized before entering the AI model or application. An annotated data produces better outputs compared with the raw data for the same number of iterations. Data annotation requires human inputs such as labels and tags that categorize data into different groups, more precisely called active learning. One factor that determines how model 1 performs is the employment of the correct person for the annotation process. The success of active learning depends on the type of application and on the type of labels. There can be three broad categories of labels: labels corresponding to the majority class, labels near the decision boundary, and noisy labels. The labels corresponding to the majority class are obvious and simple to understand, and these can be easily classified even without the need of the human-in-the-loop. For the labels that are near the decision boundary, rethinking the class definition must be performed by the humans to label them effectively. For the noisy labels, even humans cannot label them effectively; for example, in medical images, even doctors cannot identify all classes by looking at the labels. Therefore, the key to handling the noisy labels is to use a semi-supervised strategy. In the book by Monarch [3], it is shown that retraining the model a number of times from newly annotated data increases the accuracy of the model. This includes overfitting as well, which if it occurs in one iteration can be corrected by following subsequent iterations if the data annotation is performed perfectly (Fig. 5.4).

5.2.4 Model 2

In this model, humans can be used after the completion of the AI algorithm. The difference between model 1 and model 2 is that in model 1, humans are involved in the input loop while training the data, but in model 2, humans are involved in the supervision or for taking final decisions in the output loop. There are two kinds of supervision that humans in the output loop can perform. One is the objective supervision, and the other is the subjective supervision. In objective supervision, an individual expert is usually involved in giving inputs or making a decision. An example can be of a judge in a court case where all the classification can be performed by AI algorithm using the evidence, the number of trials, appeals, etc. The final judgment is provided by a human judge as a supervisor who uses his experience and observation to decide. Due to the complexity in decision-making in the court case, an AI algorithm cannot perform as well as a human. In the case of subjective supervision, crowd intelligence can be used to give their feedbacks, which is the AI algorithm. In this model, the feedback by the crowd is not used back in the training; rather the human decisions are used and output is processed (Fig. 5.5).

FIGURE 5.4

Model 1: humans are used for data annotation.

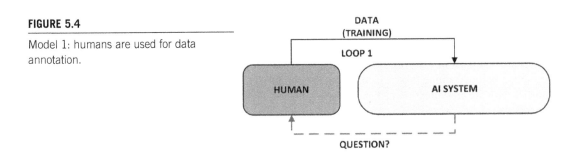

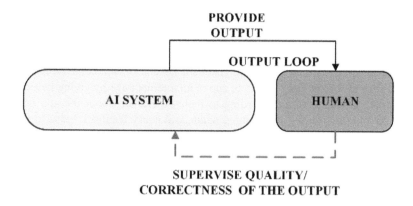

FIGURE 5.5

Model 2: humans are used to assess or decide after the AI system provides output.

5.2.5 Model 3

The quantity of uncertainty in the output is given by confidence level. In this model, the consultation from humans is dependent on the confidence level of the output, calculated by the algorithm. If the confidence level is less than a specified level, the humans are used for the confirmation or decision, and if the confidence level is high enough and the algorithm is sure that it is very close to the correct value, then the human is not consulted. The difference between model 2 and model 3 is that in model 2, the inputs from humans are mandatory every time classification is performed, while in model 3, the inputs from humans depend upon the specified confidence level. For higher accuracy, the value of confidence level must be equal to or more than 90% (Fig. 5.6).

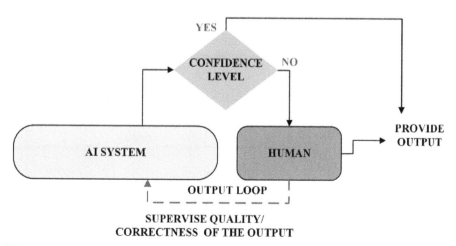

FIGURE 5.6

Model 3: humans are used to assess or decide after the AI system provides output based on a confidence level.

5.2.6 Model 4

This model is a hybrid of the two models, model 1 and model 2; i.e., human inputs can be taken during data annotation and as well as after the completion of the AI algorithm. In the case of subjective supervision, crowd intelligence can be used to give their feedbacks, which the AI algorithm uses later also. An example can be taking feedback of an app or an internet page by giving five stars to the users and requesting them to fill the stars according to their experience about the app or the page. The feedback is stored and used during the training again, and every feedback helps to make the AI algorithm better (Fig. 5.7).

5.2.7 Model 5

This model is a hybrid of model 1 and model 3. It uses humans both for data annotation and for decision-making after the AI system provides output. The consultation from humans is dependent on confidence level as in model 3 (Fig. 5.8).

5.3 Data analysis

The essence of successful AI is the availability of feedback by a human. This is proved by the dominance of supervised learning over unsupervised learning. For an autonomous vehicle, it is easy to drive through the streets because it is told by humans in lengthy (in terms of data inputs) training. The same is the case with home devices that they are trained "heavily," and therefore they understand the human command, "switch off the light." Since the performance of AI majorly depends on the amount and quality of data being fed as input, it is an important task to arrange and label random data. This means that raw data must be handled before feeding to the AI algorithm to convert it to "quality data." By quality data, we refer to data that is right pertaining to the application it is meant for: it helps an AI algorithm to train itself faster, i.e., data that is diverse and rich in the information content. The process of labeling and putting the data into categories is called data annotation. It is a crucial step in preparing the data for training machine learning applications. It is a preliminary task of feeding the right data to an algorithm, which it needs to

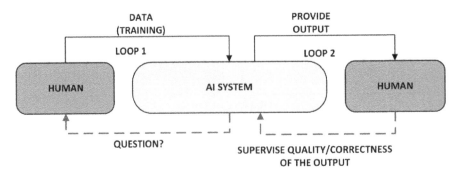

FIGURE 5.7

Model 4: humans are used both during data annotation and after the output is given by the AI system.

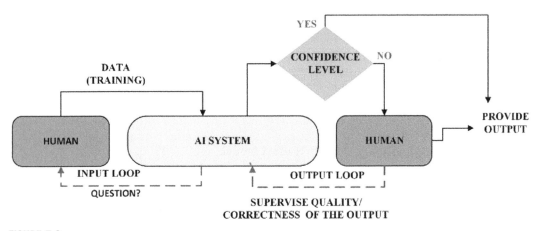

FIGURE 5.8

Model 5: humans are used both during data annotation and after the output is given by the AI system.

learn from and which makes its task easier. An annotated data produced is better compared with raw data since the output and accuracy it produces are better compared with that of raw data when other parameters of the algorithm are kept the same. Machine learning algorithms find it complex and time consuming to compute the attributes in the absence of annotated data. Moreover, the more the data is annotated, the smarter the algorithm performs. For an effective machine learning application that requires data annotation, a prominent requirement is to include humans in the AI loop. The time to collect, reorganize, and prepare the data for the application is sometimes more than that of designing algorithms. Many organizations invest a large percentage of their project estimates in the data annotation process.

5.3.1 Data labeling

By labeling the data, designers prepare them for a better start of the machine learning algorithm. The data labeling can be assumed to be analog to a mechanical machine that has not run for a long time, its parts are not lubricated, and it can be said that it is "cold" due to lack of mechanical activity. Now this machine is started, so initially, it will move with difficulty, and the small gears and other parts do not move swiftly and will create unpleasant noise. After some time, the machine actually gets used to the motion and will continue its work in a satisfactory and progressive way. For humans to label the data, it is essential that the labeling process is planned to make human inputs on data that is statistically harder than the algorithm can identify (Fig. 5.9).

Transfer learning is a technique in which the information of one process is stored and is used in other processes also. In machine learning applications, transfer learning can be applied when the annotated data of one system can be used by the other system provided that the domains of the two systems are the same. An example can be that labeled images of roses can be used both for object detection algorithms and flower classification algorithms. This provides cheap annotated data being available. Labeling or annotation can be performed in two ways.

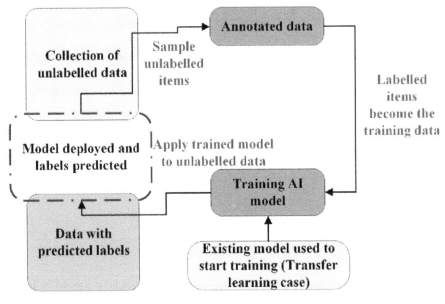

FIGURE 5.9

Model of data annotation in AI system with human-in-the-loop using transfer learning.

5.3.1.1 Simple data labeling

In simple data labeling, the annotation does not require precise efforts by the designer. A good example of this kind of data labeling can be tagging posts on social media. The data annotation of social media can be performed by producing HTML forms and then allowing its filling, and then each form now is rated by the public. The ratings can be considered as new labels, and the process of data labeling completes in this way.

5.3.1.2 Complex data labeling

In complex data labeling, the annotation process is practically complicated even though it is logically feasible. An example suited for this type is recognizing the objects in a video. Suppose that the designer wishes to train the user by drawing the bounding box around each object. Allowing users to draw the bounding boxes to annotate requires a graphical user interface in the application available at the user end. This task is not simple as creating the HTML forms and requires long hours of programming by the designers if they intend to provide an inbuilt bounding box facility with the video.

5.3.2 Quality control in data labeling

Errors are a part of human actions and errors occur in all designs created. In some, more, and in some, less. Therefore, what can be the requirement of quality control? If errors occur in data labeling, overcoming bad training requires unexpectedly more time and effort. The quality control strategy in data labeling ensures minimum error in data annotation. Of course, the errors cannot be avoided completely, but to some extent, they may be mitigated by proper planning and strategic approach.

Error propagation during data labeling also depends on the type of application. For example, in the case of an application in which the feedback of the quality of a certain brand is desired from the public, a small percentage of bad annotation does not spoil the ultimate result. On the other hand, unprecedented and disastrous outcomes are sure to occur in the case of autonomous vehicles if there is a small percentage of bad annotation. For some algorithms, the error is tolerated during the training process, while for some algorithms, a small error reflects in the output. Therefore, quality control is necessary before visualizing the data annotation into a design. There can be two ways to enhance the quality control, where one way could be to employ sensible and appropriate humans for data annotation. The other way can be the application of a check before approving the labels. In the case of appropriate people who can label correctly, the benefit is the ease of labeling and satisfaction, but the drawback is a lack of diversity of the labels. On the contrary, for applying a check before approval of a label to enter into the data annotation process, additional overhead will be required, and an extra expert must be hired for the quality control process.

5.3.2.1 Crowdsourcing

Crowdsourcing is the technique for inviting a large crowd for a purpose [7]. It can be paid or unpaid. It is the most important and reliable way for the annotation purpose of machine learning algorithms. Social media these days provides an easier alternative for crowdsourcing. Similar to it is the technique of outsourcing. Outsourcing is performed by paying people per hour, solely as a temporary job offered. It does not involve social media, and it is more reliable and effective than crowdsourcing. The advantage of using crowdsourcing is that in very little time, a big workforce helps to complete the task. For example, for a feedback form to fill online, in only a few minutes, thousands of unpaid crowd-sourced people can help to finish the task of form filling. This means that for applications that need annotation on quick notices with a short turnaround time, crowdsourcing can help to a greater extent, but at the same time, maintaining the quality of labels is essential.

5.3.2.2 Finding appropriate people for data labeling

Quality control over data labeling requires appropriate people, and to be hired, there may be three things to consider. First is the type of the task to be performed, second, the span of the task, and finally, the time required to annotate the data. In case when the type of task is considered, expert annotators are required in fields of medical urgency, court cases, and business analytics, and for tasks such as types of social media content, the home assistant does not require only experts. When the span of the task is considered, for a medical urgency, the number of experts required may be up to two or three and not more than that, but there can be hundreds of people used for data annotation of social media content. Finally, the time required decides the appropriate people as feedback can be taken from people urgently in cases of general and random annotators, while a time slot or appointment may be required for experienced annotators. Therefore, there can be three types of annotators of the data:

Annotators from crowdsourcing: These annotators are effective and dominate the annotation when quick processing is required in cases of applications like listing the companies that are in the news in the past week, tagging social media content, etc.

Annotators hired on contract: These are the annotators who can be trained to perform annotation based on a set of rules that exist for the selection of particular labels to be applied to the input dataset. Quality can be maintained by proper training of the annotators. This category also includes people who already work in the same organization by whom the algorithm is designed and the application is being built. These workers are less suitable for annotation, they may not work as effectively as required because they have their own roles to play in the organization, and they have to perform annotation based on orders by the organization. Most research papers consider the annotators from crowdsourcing and hired on contract by paying for each task because these people perform annotation by free will or for getting this paid task again. Thus, their performance is not forced, and this kind of annotation promotes honest and correct opinions in data labeling, accelerating the quality control operation.

Expert annotators: These are the annotators who can give labels to the most challenging decisions that cannot be given by ordinary humans. An example is a court case where not a single hearing or evidence can guarantee a correct decision; rather the decisions are based on the entire criminal record, past and present pieces of evidence, and sometimes on burdens of proof, etc. Therefore, in a machine language application of these types, the need for an expert annotator is mandatory.

5.3.2.3 Applying checks to approve labels before entering the system

This is the most effective way of controlling the quality of the data annotation [3]. In this method, the annotated labels are compared against some standard answers already kept for this purpose. These standard answers are called the "ground truth." It is essential to apply checks to both training data and the testing data. But when wrong data is sampled for ground truth, the error again increases to a very large value. Before the selection of ground truth data, several important steps are needed to be taken. An example is checking using random samples for the data, and if the nature of the data being considered is very different from the inputs required in the algorithm, then random data should not be considered. Rather, the data that is much closer to the nature of input data should be considered for random samples. The selection of correct data for ground truth is the key to the success of this method. Let us assume an example of input samples to be images having 55% sunflower, 20% lily, 20% rose, and 5% lotus. We can have three ways for creating our baseline for guessing by random chance:

Random baseline: In this, any one out of four labels may be used based on a random guess of the annotator. Therefore, chances of labeling any one out of four are 25%.

Mode baseline: In this, the annotator labels by seeing the highest percentage of the existing labels. Therefore, the chances of labeling a sunflower are 55%.

Frequency baseline: The labeling by annotator depends on the label frequency of each of the given images. Therefore, chances of labeling a sunflower are 55%, labeling a lily is 20%, and so on. The calculation of baseline is considered by squaring the probability of each of the images. Fig. 5.10 shows the three different accuracy calculations that can be expected by random chance. Most commonly used out of these is the sum of squared frequencies, which is neither too low nor too high and provides a safer side option. In Ref. [3], it is recommended that the baseline can be selected by the annotator after a series of observations of outputs by the system. This method is more practical since the accuracy depends upon the type of application and the type of data.

5.3.2.4 Data annotation using end users

This is an uncommon feature that is not discussed much in literature and is supposed to make the application more accurate and satisfactory. Decision inputs for data annotation from the end users ultimately make the application more satisfying and help to provide the services the users actually want to get from the design.

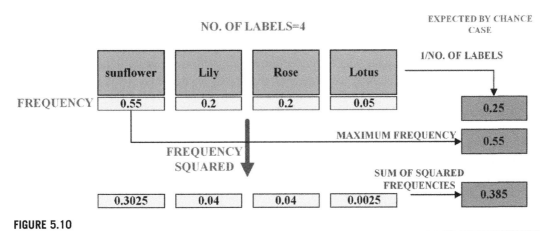

FIGURE 5.10

Three different ways to find accuracies for selection of ground truth through random chance.

Numerous applications rely on customers for both annotation and training of data. An example of this type of annotation is the Google search or any other search engine. The ability of search engines enhances with every single search. The person searching any term is the end user, who is gradually making the search engine smarter and more versatile. The drawback of data annotation from the users is that the model may end up getting the data that is "favorite" of more people as compared with "less favorite" data. This means that for the data that is common or more popular among those end users providing annotation, the algorithm will end up being accurate for that popular data and will not work accurately for less common ones.

Have you ever come across CAPTCHA? A very good example of end user data annotation is the CAPTCHA. The full form of CAPTCHA is a completely automated public Turing test to tell computers and humans apart. This is the test on the internet we sometimes need to give and is a mandatory task that we need to complete to progress further. CAPTCHAs are, although, telling us that they discriminate between humans and the robot only, but it is very possible that we are generating training data for a company. Although the task they give is not very hard for a machine learning algorithm, they take human inputs and get their annotations done in an intelligent and simple way!

5.3.3 Predicting the amount of annotation required

How much annotation is required? There are certain ways to determine this. The following gradient on accuracy can help in the prediction of applied annotation:

When accuracy is more than chance: Even if the accuracy of our model is more than chance, it is the accuracy that signals that more annotations are required at this point. It also signals that the annotation strategy used by us is correct and is resulting in progressive accuracy.

When accuracy is consistent: This is the case of consistent accuracy, and that too when it is lower than expectations or the state of the art. This means that classification is performed correctly, and the annotations are helping in the right direction. At this point, active learning can be used.

When accuracy is high enough: This shows that the design is accurate enough for our use case and that it can be used now for the application for which it is designed.

An estimation of the magnitude of data annotation, provided in the graph in Fig. 5.11, indicates that the number of annotations should increase exponentially to achieve an increase in accuracy. For a simple task of prediction of disaster, the number of annotations required to increase the accuracy to a higher value is shown in Table 5.1.

When accuracy is equal to the industry: When the accuracy is more than the highest accuracy in the industry, we can maintain this accuracy by progressively finding those items that are still able to spoil the output. The items that are uncertain and are new must also be considered as well as their confidence level to be used before their use to achieve the highest stable accuracy. As shown in the table, a meaningful increment in accuracy can be achieved when the number of annotations increases exponentially to the powers of 10. If $m = 3$, the successive number of annotations required are 1000, 10,000, 100,000, and 1,000,000.

5.3.4 Obtaining annotated data from an existing AI design model

If an AI algorithm can provide the annotated data, a lot of money spent on annotations can be saved. Any annotated data does not guarantee good performance. Effective annotations can be obtained by extracting those predictions from an existing AI application that is rated with high confidence. Taking all the data from the available model also does not solve the problem as it promotes the perpetuation of the biases that are already existing in the design. Therefore, available

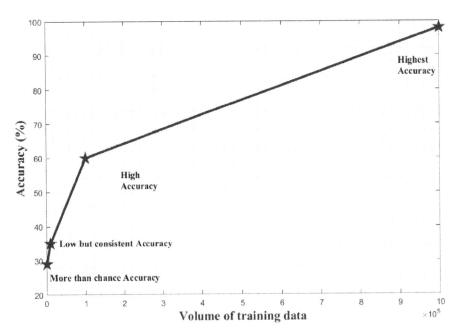

FIGURE 5.11

Increase in the accuracy with the increase in training data.

Table 5.1 Number of annotations required for a given level of accuracy.

Accuracy	Number of annotations
More than chance	10^m
Low but consistent	10^{m+1}
High	10^{m+2}
Highest	10^{m+3}

data can be used along with human annotation. When using labels generated already from computers, we should not rely completely on the confidence level. The confidence level may give illusive decisions in case the domain of existing data and the design to which we are applying it are different. Model-based outliers can be used to remove the predictions that possess the lower value of overall activation. This shows that they are not of the same category or may be dissimilar from the data that was used for training our model. At this point, representative sampling can be used to select some data that could not be labeled automatically, and therefore, it can be reserved for sampling by a human.

5.4 Designing and prototyping

Designing is the planning and preparation before creating a specific object, an application, or a service. Unlike a rational explanation, the designing of AI incorporating humans in the loop through prototype models will be more useful to understand the dilemmas in HAI.

5.4.1 Different design approaches of HAI

In the field of management, people are considered to be resources, and therefore a field emerges called "human resources." But HAI views people as humans who have different perceptions, needs, interests, cultural ethics, etc. These different characteristics of humans play a big role in the design approach [11]. The strategic goal of every HAI is the inclusion of humans in one or more ways in the execution of AI. A number of different design approaches involving ways of the mutual dependence of AI and humans are demonstrated in this section.

5.4.1.1 AI system coupled with society

This design aims at the societal influence of AI, while society demands the AI. The technical aspects of this design are independent of political, socio-economic, and cultural effects that are its direct consequences. A design represents the ideology of the designer when it is linked to society [12]. One example can be human−AI interaction at an airport, where the AI enriches itself from the behaviors, perspectives, and demands of numerous ethnicities and cultures. The social connection of AI strengthens with such a type of design approach. Similarly, Pee et al. [4] elucidated the human−AI relationship in a hospital, in which the AI systems design is based on continuous learning toward diverse requirements of a larger group of people. They found various ways of knowledge manifestation and expressed the more uncommon effects implying a paradox in the human–AI relationship. In this design, a prominent role is played by the designer. It is the designer who plays the role of identifying the gaps in attaining a specified AI design. The designers' capabilities such as perception, decision-making, and responsible behavior in creating such a design have a direct influence on the societal behavior of the application. For instance, the social media sites in the blink of an eye are influencing a bulk of people toward a certain incident or phenomenon and at the same time deviating them from another incident. It all depends on how AI aligns itself with the inputs and directions given particularly. Thus, the role of the designer can have a huge effect on society. This is the reason why university curriculums are equipped with courses such as ethical technologies, environment and ethical designing, etc., to teach the forthcoming engineers the role of a technology that does not ruin the ethical values of the humans that are directly getting influenced by it. An example of how AI influences society in a recent scenario is portrayed by Eisenstat [5], who was supposed to handle the political content on Facebook in 2016. The political content has a direct influence on the perceptions of society as a whole. The filtering of the content had impacted the United States' elections that year on a large scale. With such a design goal, AI seems to have drastic consequences on society. The human–AI interactions in the social media applications have direct ethical repercussions on the societal behavior of AI, and therefore, for the perusal of this type of design, the role of designers is crucial for the realization of such AI designs.

5.4.1.2 Collaborative AI design

This design involves the co-development of AI systems by people and system designers. People here are referred to as the beneficiaries of the application such as end users (end users can be the customers or the employees). This design includes the needs of diverse groups. Thus, the aim is to create a design that is useable, accessible, and useful for one or more of the groups that participate in the system design. This means that during the entire design process inputs from people and system designers of diverse backgrounds will be used. This helps to achieve the overall satisfaction of enterprises that develop these applications, and the risk of underperformance is also eliminated to a certain extent. Users help to co-develop the design. An important requirement here is that the user should have a clear understanding of what AI systems can do and what they cannot do. The duration of collaboration between people and designers is very small and limited to the time of the project, and any manipulation or changes are not allowed after the finalization of the design. The extent of involvement of people can be extended when the design is called inclusive design. In such a design, the system design is modified not only for the users but for a large group of people. Ethical considerations are required to determine who can be included and who cannot. A number of designs differ based on the psychology, culture, ethnicity, and lifestyle of people on which the design depends. Ethically speaking, inclusive designs provide more freedom to the designers than co-developed designs. Designers may be claimed to be partial if some groups are not included in the design process. This problem can be avoided by employing a team that is comparatively diverse in ethical aspects, but in this case, when different perspectives collide, the solutions contradict each other. For a truly collaborative design, a diverse team may be required.

5.4.1.3 Interaction-based AI design

In such a design, the AI system develops, understands, improves, and mutates itself, after interacting with a human. The AI system also amalgamates the effect of the AI system (itself) on humans. An important example of human–AI interaction can be the Netflix streaming television series in which the users' preferences and choices are remembered, and DNNs are used to assess the next most possible choice for the user. The interaction between AI and human enables learning and further self-development of the application. A limitation here is that harmful interactions are also learned by AI systems, and they undergo large loops and exist in the future behaviors of the system. The designers can adopt the use of weights for this application. Potentially important interactions and experiences can have double or triple the weight of the harmful interactions. One way to change human behavior toward technology is the concept of persuasive technology [13]. This demonstrates the modifications in human behavior due to interaction with technology, and later the term was coined as persuasive technology. This is the ability of technology to alter human emotions, perceptions, and actions when they receive the services, and the effects can be attained in a short duration or may take a longer time depending upon the individual human response. AI-based product designing firms use AI systems to persuade users to use their products [6]. The AI systems interact with the users and help them realize how technology can make lives worthwhile. Recently, a lot of research has been carried out to study the AI systems that help in changing people's perception toward buying and using a particular product from the market.

5.4.1.4 Demand-based AI design

Every AI application is designed to satisfy a human requirement or a demand. Therefore, all AI systems are built keeping in view the needs of people in various contexts. A particular AI system is expected to fulfill one or two requirements of people, and not many specific outputs are expected from a system, and there is no necessity for them to be versatile. The demand-based or requirement-based AI has moral considerations also. Let us consider an example of an application that provides banking solutions. It is expected to solve all the requirements of the users. The designer, in the favor of making it user-friendly and attractive, applies a gaming environment in the background. The result will be that most of the users will indulge or at least deviate from their prime focus, which is banking. This behavior implies irresponsible economic behavior, and the AI system has persuaded unprofessional behavior. Since the goal of AI is to make tasks easy and convenient, it is undesirable to satisfy human requirements that do not belong to the particular context for which the AI system is built. A summary of design approaches of HAI is provided in Table 5.2. A prototype is a preliminary example of an AI system that helps users and stakeholders to understand and evaluate the design. A prototype can be drawn on paper, can be built in portable form on hardware, or it can be a software program, etc. With the help of prototypes, designers can also understand the basic behavior of their designs, and at the same time, the scope of evaluation also widens among members of the team. This makes prototyping of designs an essential requirement of designers.

5.4.2 Some examples of hybrid designs involving humans and AI

AI has brought a tremendous driving force for the progress of societal growth and the economy. One way to visualize AI is to compare it with collaborative decision-making [18]. When two or more parties amalgamate to make decisions, the results are increased innovation, more profit, and lucrative strategic solutions. The collaboration of humans and computers can provide coordination of the workflow on a large scale.

Table 5.2 Summary of different design approaches of HAI.

Design approach	Aims of research	Contributions	References
Societal AI design	Analysis of changes in society due to the application of AI. Understanding of cultural, political, and psychological aspects of the AI design	Improvement in dynamic behavior and socio-economic aspects of AI investigation of impact of AI on moral and ethical values of all people influenced by the design	Cooley [12], Margolin and Margolin [14]
Collaborative AI design	A conglomeration of different groups, implying democracy, solely for the development of AI models Designers from different ethnic groups and different countries can promote a wide exploration of the design space Investigation of potential factors for useable AI models that are harmed due to people's behavior, notions, and unethical inputs	By inclusion of users in the design process of AI systems, more user satisfaction is obtained, and more needs of the users are handled Some committees that are excluded till now can be included in the groups that participate in the AI design, which promotes diversity in design	Spencer et al. [15]
Interaction- based and persuasive AI design	Interface designs that produce significant AI designs The persuasive approach invites people to perform a particular behavior	Enable desirable characteristics for the intended users Recognizing the triggers that affect the ethical behavior of AI design	Ford et al. [16]
Demand- based AI design	Development of AI models that satisfy the emotional needs of people and at the same time intellectual needs are taken care of	Recognizing AI designs that promote unethical behavior Examples of unethical behavior are addiction, complete reliance on automated design, and lack of feedback by a human	Gilmore et al. [17]

5.4.2.1 HAI in industry

A daunting task for AI designers is to manage the complex, risky, and uncertain industrial environment [19]. In the present scenario, some factors such as risk control, social networks, and technology configuration in industries are dominated by advancements in socio-technical environments. These environments allow the flow of information and knowledge by using AI. Business intelligence is an advanced version of business management through the help of AI. Therefore, AI affects the competitiveness of organizations by controlling their resources and technical expertise (Fig. 5.12).

5.4.2.2 HAI in medicines and healthcare

The accelerating research on potentially large amounts of medical devices will immanently change the systems of medical care. It is our belief that machine learning and human relationship will become the milestones of future medical management. Instant care and mediation provided to the patients will be assisted by low-power, portable, and high-speed, efficient devices that will be based on a conglomeration of advanced robotic design, machine learning, and advanced computing fields [26–28]. The medical field is said to be very challenging, and the hardest entrance exams are required to be cracked to get into medical studies at a good university. This is because of rules and terminologies that are mammoth-sized and are difficult to memorize. The rules are also unstructured and need to be modified with time. Moreover, the disease space of the human body is not searchable exhaustively. This implies that 100% replacement of doctors by AI should be inaccurate and at the same time not acceptable.

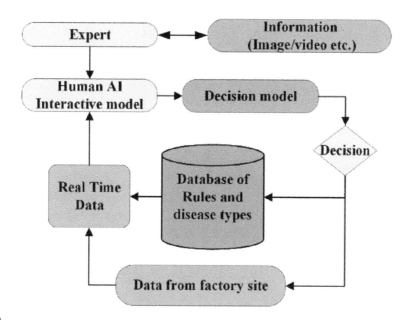

FIGURE 5.12

Coordination between human and AI system in industry.

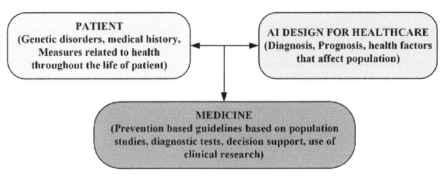

FIGURE 5.13

Workflow of an AI healthcare system.

Watson's system, which was developed by Ando et al. [20], has memorized the rules better than an individual human (Figs. 5.13 and 5.14).

It understands human language, mines patient data, and compares the available conditions with the conditions existing in its memories, and it suggests medication based on the prevailing conditions.

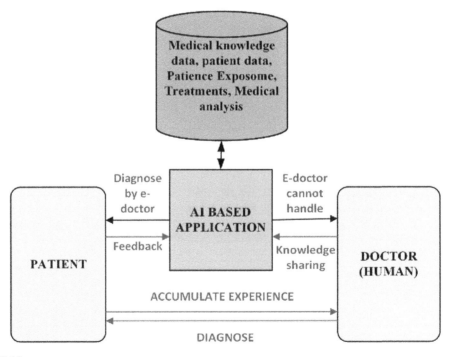

FIGURE 5.14

Coordination between humans and AI system in a healthcare application.

Since human diseases cannot be stored because of huge data due to different symptoms, classifying human diseases alone is not possible, and a doctor is needed to be involved. Fast diagnosis and medication can be achieved if a large storage-based AI system is combined with a doctor's diagnosis. Therefore, hybridizing AI with humans is a necessity for the successful and complete treatment of a disease.

5.4.2.3 HAI in public safety

Safety of people is required in various critical areas such as in the places where a threat to the general public is present, and investigations are required to explore places that are vulnerable to terror attacks. Similar to this are the issues of national security, financial security, web security, public security, and terrorism. AI augmented with humans can provide strong support to the big challenges in the security area. In national security applications, the combination of humans and AI can work well. Human intelligence can be utilized in making judgments, predictions, detection, and the final disposition, and on the other hand, massive data processing can be handled by the AI algorithm. Sentiment analysis [21] is an example of text mining that extracts subjective information in source data. Due to the internet, social media, and networking, sentiment analysis is easily possible. It also helps in the prediction of unusual and anomalous events that can cause harm to life and threaten public safety. Sentiment analysis is not possible to be performed by humans without the assistance of AI. A hybrid system that processes huge data of sentiment analysis using AI, where the final decisions are taken by humans, will benefit immensely in this area. This system can be called a hybrid HAI public security system. A hybrid system can also be built for monitoring public safety. Video streams from the surveillance cameras in streets provide huge data for this purpose. These videos have abnormal individual postures and uncommon crowd behaviors. When AI finds the suspected data, human experts can be introduced into the system, and they can decide the further course of steps to be taken for public security, which can be dependent on their domain knowledge (Fig. 5.15).

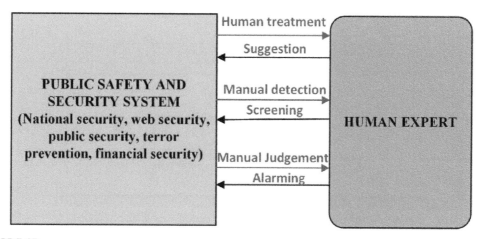

FIGURE 5.15

Coordination between human and AI system in public security and safety.

5.4.2.4 HAI in autonomous vehicles

Rashevsky [22] first gave the concept of autonomous driving. Autonomous vehicles are the latest trend in AI. Completely autonomous driving is facing challenges, and failures occur due to major bottlenecks that are unsolved in the process of amalgamation of 5G communication protocols, transportation systems, vehicle networks, and human−robot driving [29−31]. When a human driver and AI work together, they share vehicle control with each other. This is an example of human−AI collaboration showing complementarity between the driver and the automated driving machine. Humans understand the scenes better and are robust, but they are affected by physical factors such as fatigue. Human−AI driving can improve the conditions by causing fewer accidents. Another affecting factor is improper vision due to bad weather. At this time, the AI-based driving system can show the images using sensors that can be useful to the driver and provide more information that could not be achieved without the help of an AI-based machine-assisted driver. Fully autonomous driving is also facing difficulties in differentiating between natural scenes and traffic scenes. The architecture shown in Fig. 5.16 is divided into three layers for the assistance of the driver. First of all, sensors detect and collect data from the roadside and near the vehicle. The layer that makes the decision first processes the data collected from the sensors, and then it hands it to the geographic information system database that provides real-time decisions. After this, the next action for the human driver is to follow the instructions provided by the AI-based driving system.

5.5 Evaluation and strategies

Evaluation is predominant to create an error-free design. Without evaluation or testing, a design is incomplete and imperfect as its performance behavior is unknown. Evaluations can be performed early

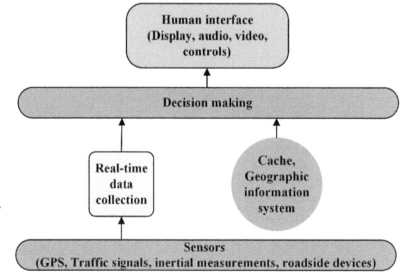

FIGURE 5.16

Coordination between human and AI system in an autonomous vehicle.

or late, but an appreciative launch of a new design requires many evaluation cycles from the beginning till the end of the design. Sometimes problems persist at some stages, but the designers must move ahead and launch the ultimate design. In the present scenario, testing a design may be not as simple as it was earlier. This is because now the users' expectations are elevated due to previous experiences, and a new design must perform better than the previous one to exist and to be used by many customers. Evaluation starts when team members can be consulted for a review of the design, and it ends after a number of tests and finally after the opinion and recommendation of an expert. The final evaluation can be considered as the "expert review." When considering the expert review, it should be comprehensive and broad. It should include all features, whether novice or expert, to provide complete advice on the design as a whole.

For a successful evaluation, where the strategic flow is shown in Fig. 5.17, the flow is similar to the design thinking approach [23] of the general product design flow. In a design thinking approach, complex problems that are improperly defined can be solved, considering the human needs associated with them. A human-centric approach is used to reframe the problem, brainstorming sessions are conducted to create unique ideas, and hands-on sessions are adopted for creating prototypes and for final testing. The design thinking approach can be used by anyone to tackle and solve complex problems of everyday life. The left side of Fig. 5.17 shows the flowchart that demonstrates the five steps used in the design thinking approach. The first step in design thinking is to empathize, which means finding the core of the problem by observing, involving, and empathizing. Analogous to it is the hypothesis step of the HAI system, in which the problem is defined, data is generated, and a plan is

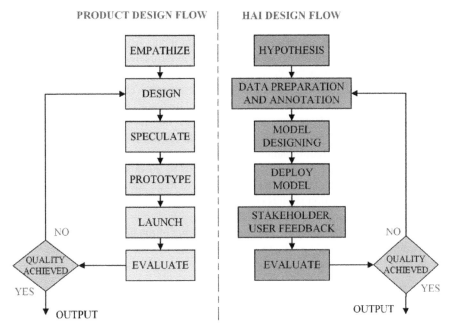

FIGURE 5.17

Flowchart of design thinking approach versus HAI systems.

created for further investigation, shown at the left side of Fig. 5.17. In the design and speculate steps, the information gained in the empathize step is put into the design, and the problem space is expanded by brainstorming. These steps in principle are analogous to data preparation and model designing of the HAI design flow. The HAI design flow includes feedback from stakeholders, users, and experts to create designs that have a higher level of user satisfaction. For the software models, the prototype stage of the design thinking approach may be skipped and replaced by the deployed model step. The prototype step exists when HAI designs are needed to be necessarily prototyped. Examples of such designs are robotic arms, autonomous vehicles, public safety systems, etc. The post-evaluation phase can be determined by a score out of 10 that can be used to rate the answer to these questions. An unsatisfactory score may lead to reanalyzing the entire design flow beginning from the revision in the mode of data collection, revisiting the questionnaires once used before the initiation of the design process, and using more participants for the attainment of more inputs for a better design. Crowdsourcing may be useful in such cases. By using the crowdsourcing technique, hundreds of people can give feedback on the requirements and the expectations from the design. Crowdsourcing especially is important for human-centered design since the number of inputs and feedbacks directly contribute to the collaborated designing approach of the HAI. Although the participants providing feedback are virtual, ultimately the designers are interested in the amount and quality of the inputs and not with the physical presence.

In the book by Heer and Bostock [7], many important applications benefitted by using crowdsourcing, by getting a larger number of diverse ideas to develop the "citizen science app"[8]. Presently, we all have observed the ads before streaming any video on YouTube. Mostly the ads aim to collect funds for people suffering from chronic disease, natural calamities, and other forms of deprival of food and facilities. They are an example of crowdsourcing. During design cycles of human-centered systems, it is beneficial to get quick and relevant feedback and inputs from the people who might be the future users of the same system. Similarly unfulfilled goals in the evaluation stage may lead to rigorous sessions to replan and restructure the design, prototype redesigning, reformulation of algorithms, increment in iterations, and multiple revisions from the experts. The algorithm testing may now include heuristic approaches. Fig. 5.18 shows the important questions that are required to be answered during the evaluation process. Important among these are the questions regarding satisfaction of stakeholder, user, and reviewer satisfaction. As far as the HAI is considered, human intervention during the evaluation stage is predominant to answer these questions. At this point, the inclusion of crowdsourced and outsourced humans will not be beneficial to the desired level. Humans included in this stage should be either users, stakeholders, or experts to make the design readily acceptable after evaluation. A number of evaluation studies conducted [9] do not consider the entire design but rather evaluate only planning, prototyping, or design flow.

An evaluation strategy is demonstrated in which the effect of the healthcare app is seen on a small section of the community [9]. HAI is shown to be proven more useful for the weaker sections of the society due to the following reasons:

1. Lower expectations
2. Potentially fewer requirements
3. Fast changes can be observed due to the flexible behavior of people

The AI-based human-centered app is called "Shifra" [10], and it aimed to provide pre-pregnancy and post-pregnancy care, family health, hygiene, neonatal care, and sex education. This care was

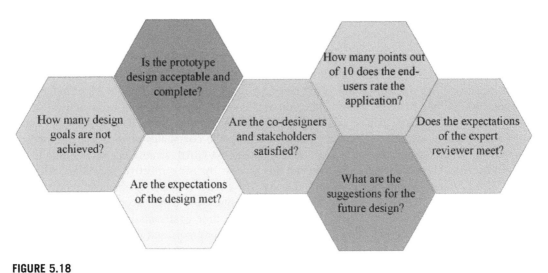

FIGURE 5.18

Important questions to be answered during evaluation.

taught using lectures and instant query—response sessions. The application was non-profit and provided knowledge to a population of refugees. The app was designed collaboratively with some senior members of the refugee group, investors, and engineers to implement the human-in-the-loop principle. Inclusion of these members was done entering their opinions in continuous iterations. It also included experts to talk to in case of each of the topics mentioned above. The storage is provided for keeping the views of the senior members and experts, and these views are included in the annotated dataset. When it comes to taking feedback, Shifra app uses scores to rate. For a score less than 3, it is considered a bad evaluation, a score between 4 and 6 is considered sufficient, between 7 and 9, it is good, and finally, a score of 10 is excellent, and this type of feedback allows an improvement. Many modifications can be performed on an urgent basis by asking the designer to modify the app based on the score given by the team members and experts. The use of the app then is continued, again allowing the cycle of using feedback, improving, and then using again. For research that includes a bulk of human participants and data has to be collected from them, it is required for an organization to demand ethics approval. Acquiring personal data belonging to a larger group of people from a university also involves the same process of the ethics approval form. This process requires the complete information of the design being built, the purpose, the stakeholders, and the expected number of people being served. From ethics approval to data collection, designing, and finally using, Shifra app consumers and stakeholders were asked to give feedback for it, and the app got an average score of 9/12 and was rated very effective in curtailing the problem of poor refugee communities living on minimal facilities in Australia. One phase in the lifetime of the evaluation was the inclusion of a group of students from universities who were continuously involved in the evaluation and development phase of the app. The contribution of students was inclined more toward the social cause related to the consumers of the app, but some of them also agreed that they are involved to observe and experience how the autonomous healthcare facilities under the roof of AI can become technologically successful.

5.6 Case studies

5.6.1 Proposed case study of HAI in loan approval and debt recovery

Due to the strides made by AI algorithms in business and finance, one area where AI can definitely give a hike is finance. According to an estimate of financial experts, for the first time in India, AI will enable more than 300 million first-time loans, and credit appliers will be successful in loan approval. Most finance companies use the CIBIL score [32] for loan lending purposes. The CIBIL score is a measure of the worthiness of a customer to take a loan. Generally, the companies provide a loan based on tedious documentation, processes of legacy, and the customer's CIBIL score. Recently, starting in the previous decade, AI has been all set to overhaul this process by using effective algorithms. Already, around 32% of finance companies have started using AI for a number of their financial services, one among them being ICICI bank [33]. For most young creditors, the CIBIL score is the only way to assess the credibility of lending. The CIBIL score for first-time applicants is not available, which makes it impossible to determine the applicant's worthiness for credit, and this is one of the reasons why more than 48% of first-time loan applicants do not get approval [33]. This is a big loss for the financial firms. Using complex algorithms, predictive analysis, and digital footprints, it is now possible to assess the credibility of loan applicants. AI makes this possible by assessing online shopping patterns, the history of electricity and telephone bill payments, and even social media profiles. Since 80% of the Indian population does not have a credit score, AI can create a temporary CIBIL score for the ones not having it. Even though AI in the recovery field is quite nascent, for some finance companies, AI has helped them to manage their collection debts. Manual debt collection is based on the financial cycle of systematic manual tasks, which takes longer and is prone to error. This process is worsened by variables such as missed payments, unpunctual traceability of the debtors, and vulnerable communication between debtors and finance companies. The proposed case study highlights the loan approval and recovery of finance debts at some of India's large banking financial companies, popular for low-interest rates on business loans, term loans, medical loans, SME loans, working capital loans, etc. In the recovery field, there are two basic ways in which AI can help in boosting the process of debt collection. First is by erasing the requirement of manpower, and secondly, AI enables decision-making that is powered by algorithms. Our case study investigates the contribution of HAI in the recovery area. The case study targets a firm called Zoom Solutions in the city of Bhopal, India, which provides AI services for loan approval and recovery collection to various other finance companies namely, Bajaj Consumer Finance private limited, Ashok Leyland Finance Limited, Hinduja Finance Limited, and HDFC bank, etc. Generally, little is known about how firms like these manage mass collection and the factors that affect collection recoveries. Zoom Solutions services is a specialized collection agency for the assessment and collection of finance depts. The purpose of this study is to analyze how human inputs can trigger loan approvals and recovery rates. We studied their comprehensive datasets. In the process of debt collection, firstly written reminders are sent, and phone calls are made to remind the debtor again, but if no responses are received, finally, legal action is taken. For recovery analysis, an optimization function is derived, which is the collection rate. The company claims that the collection rate has been enhanced by the use of human inputs in the applied AI. The collection of debt if not done online till the due date, is followed by two steps: the awareness calling and the final fieldwork. In awareness calling, an employee politely reminds the customer about the failure of the payment in spite of many online reminders. The caller for this job is smart and is able to convince the customer to

Table 5.3 The collection rate values for various payment modes.

Payment status	Collection rate, C	Company I	Company II	Company III
Full payment	1	0.956	0.921	0.937
Zero payment	0			
Some payment	$0 < C < 1$	0.044	0.079	0.063

complete the payment online. Here the caller connects with the customer empathetically and understands the possible reason. Some 3.5% of customers are fraudulent, and they intentionally want to skip the installments. For such kind of debtors, there will always be a requirement of a final field visit and to contact them physically. Some 3% of customers have genuine problems such as death, loss of service or business, accidents, etc. When even awareness calling does not turn successful, fieldwork becomes mandatory. Zoom Solutions applies AI for enhancing the loan approval and debt recovery process and has successfully elevated its percentage collection in 2 years. The dependent variable is created by observing payments in a standard duration that can be taken as a certain number of months. This ensures consistency in all the claims. For this study, we used 8 months as the standard time to observe. Table 5.3 shows the fraction of customers that yield full, zero, or partial credit payments. The actual figures for full and zero payments are not disclosed. We define collection rate, C, as the sum of payments made by an account over a time period in months, m, divided by the amount that is pending termed as pending due, pd. The collection rate is then defined Eq. (5.1) as follows:

$$C_{j,m} = \frac{\sum_{k=1}^{m} payment_k}{pd} \tag{5.1}$$

One more task Zoom Solutions performs is to classify and analyze the customers for lending by using AI.

Currently, finance companies have started using a new term, called the "social loan quotient," SLQ, to determine the creditworthiness of a loan applicant. It is an effective parameter for a debtor, which calculates his/her "willingness to pay." The range of SLQ score is $0-995$.

For this case study, we investigated the AI analysis of Zoom Solutions for three companies (I, II, and III) with their identities not disclosed. The flowchart of AI applied to financial companies is shown in Fig. 5.19, where HAI is shown at the profile building and maintaining stage. At the profile building stage, more than 80% of the information is taken from payment patterns of electricity and telephone bills and through online shopping as well, where only a few cases reported in-person feedback at the profile building stage. The main human inputs are taken at the profile maintenance, recovery payments, and delinquency check through feedback. This feedback appears as brief questionnaires for the customers every time they are connected to the company, either online or in person. Some of the feedback is made mandatory before proceeding further in online and in-person visits of the customer, but they contain very few questions because the company does not want to irritate the customers. Zoom Solutions calculates SLQ by using social media websites, education and career of the customer, remuneration details and bills from sites such as the income tax department, and finally financial history to determine the credit worthiness of the customer. Human inputs have generally become an important

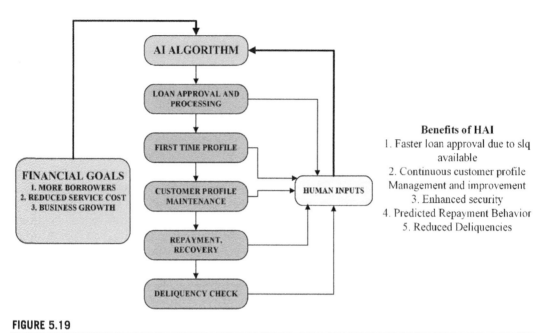

FIGURE 5.19

Achieving better finance using HAI.

stepping stone to increasing the accuracy of the *SLQ*. According to a report by Zoom Solutions, human inputs have helped companies to reframe their loan strategies, revise the interest rates, building *SLQ* thresholds based on the data of just a few months. The dataset we used was provided for three companies: I, II, and III. We used the dataset of 900 debt holders from three companies. The categories in which our comprehensive dataset are divided are some of the contractors and some of the debtor characteristics. The common independent variables are age (in years) of the debtor, the postal codes of the area where the debtors belong, the geographic coordinates, sex, education, family income, number of family members, initial loans taken, initial loans paid, and type of service such as government, business, private. Fig. 5.20 shows the variation in the average percentage collection rate for 300 customers of each company, every 2 months after HAI is applied. Zoom Solutions consistently updated the companies about the changes in the collections and provided them with the weekly collection rate and other statistics. For Company I for the first 2 months, the collection rate, *C*, decreased, which may be due to no relevant steps taken after the first few inputs in the 2 months by Company I. While for Company II, in the first 2 months only, 0.05% change is visible, which shows that the human inputs have been seriously used by the company for revising their finance models, which might have affected the collection rate.

In a similar fashion, for the next 6 months also, there is a significant increment in the values of collection for Company III, and for the next 6 months for all three companies, there is an increment in the collection rates that positively affect the company's growth. Fig. 5.21 shows the percentage variation in average *SLQ* taken over a duration of 8 months. Firstly, the SLQ is taken for 300 customers of each company, and the average is calculated. For every month, this average is observed. For

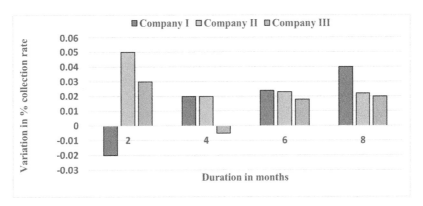

FIGURE 5.20

Percentage collection rate variation over 8 months after HAI is applied.

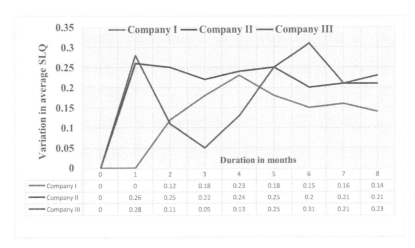

FIGURE 5.21

Variation in *SLQ* after application of HAI.

company I, the average *SLQ* first increases for the first month but then decreases and finally increases. For the other two companies also, variation in *SLQs* demonstrates that consistent human inputs affect the finance and loan approval process to a greater extent and that viable alterations can be made in the finance models using HAI.

5.6.2 Transformation from simple AI to human-centered AI at LinkedIn

LinkedIn, founded in 2002 in the United States, is an online employment-oriented company through which users can receive better career opportunities. By the end of the year 2017, there were straightforward and sarcastic comments on social media about the job search and job recommendation service LinkedIn provided to its users. One example of this is a recommendation of an assistant scientist, wine sales manager, gardener, hairstylist, etc., all to one person. For any individual who is interested in the wine sales manager job, it is almost impossible that he or she is also interested in the assistant scientist job or vice versa. Exasperated by a number of similar social media posts, the AI researchers and product designers were given a task to completely remove this inefficient behavior of the job recommendation application. At LinkedIn, AI is like "oxygen," which means that the entire work such as news feed, advertisements, job recommendations, advanced pages, etc., is built and operated using AI. After preliminary research and talks conducted with design teams, the product designers concluded that the perspectives of engineers designing the job recommendation application and the users who receive the job recommendations are entirely different. It was desired that engineers have empathy toward the users and that engineers should work upon the relevance of the job recommendations. The team adopted a strategic approach for executing this task, which is depicted in Fig. 5.22. The goals were researching the existing AI, transforming the AI culture, and then designing a new HAI. Fig. 5.19 shows the observations when the research on existing AI was conducted, and it was concluded that they lacked the amount, clarity, and accuracy in data provided by the users. To improve this condition, leveraging the data from users became necessary. The user inputs are a crucial part of implementing better AI and shifting the AI culture at the company. The team conducted multiple workshops for improving the relevance by transforming the AI culture, a part of which was relevance humility, which means the company has high-level humility for the users by providing them relevant job offers that benefit them. They included more new job titles that the AI could

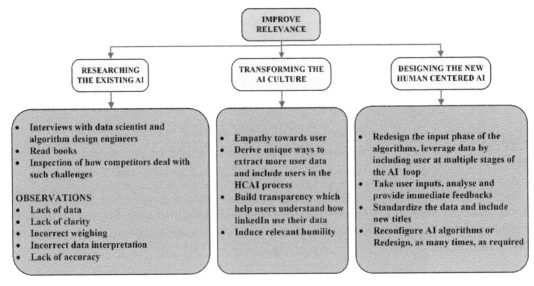

FIGURE 5.22

Strategic approach for transforming the AI culture to human-centered AI at LinkedIn.

understand. When inquired by the principal UX researcher at LinkedIn, Carolyn Chang, about the HAI experiences at LinkedIn, in some internet articles and videos, she reported that by the middle of the year 2021, they were able to redesign the AI by converting the company's AI culture to HAI. One of the ways they could accomplish this was by utilizing user data and providing immediate feedback to improvise the user experience.

5.6.3 Human-centered AI at Netflix

Netflix is an entertainment company, where HAI is extensively used to make informed decisions on every aspect of the business. In a talk with Michelle Ufford, Lead, data engineering, and analytics team, Netflix, she shared how the Data Engineering & AI research team at Netflix does exactly that. She described their analytics environment and how data is used across a variety of roles and then delved into how Netflix is tackling common analytic challenges affecting data quality. Netflix is using AI and big data to drive business performance. Netflix is a very successful business at the moment and has attracted a massive number of 150 million subscribers around the world. Everything they do is by using user data. Evidently, at each and every step for all the applications and products, Netflix uses human inputs. The first place where they use the data is by understanding users as consumers, and they exactly understand what users are watching, browsing, and what they are skipping. They have huge volumes of data, which makes the understanding of consumers become more and more granular. For example, if a user watches a horror movie up to 70% and suddenly stops watching, it indicates that it is probably too scary for the user to finish. So, they release the top-10 scariest movies for the user, making the interface highly granular. Secondly, they use this data for understanding well that there are lots of different genres that people like to watch, and if they produce content of all those genres, they can attract a huge number of consumers. By this their content usage has reached 81%, which is 51% higher than their competitors (TV cable operators, Prime video, etc.). What is worth noticing is that 76% of what users watch is from the Netflix recommendation list only. They frequently fine-tune their algorithm to understand the users and recommend the content that the users really enjoy. By using user input data, they also generate thumbnails. They take care of the short time in which users have to select between titles of say 10 movies. They use these thumbnails, such as a scene that is watched in one film, for a similar scene to be put in the front view of the other recommended videos. Another area Netflix uses HAI and big data is in streaming optimization. When a user sits at home, the streaming speed of broadband varies, so they use the data, and not to compromise the video quality, they increase the streaming speed. Therefore, they monitor the speed of particular users. Finally, Netflix also used HAI in their pre-production and post-production for finding locations for shooting movies, the actors, the scenes, etc., taken from the most successful movies. Fig. 5.23 shows how massively huge quantities of data are generated, processed, and stored at Netflix. Fig. 5.24 shows that every kind of team uses the user data at various stages of their AI designs. Due to this reason, Netflix is also famously known as a data-driven company.

5.6.4 The HAX toolkit

The HAX Toolkit Project (HAX refers to human-centered AI experiences) is a collaboration between Microsoft Research and Aether, for HAI ethics and its associated effects in engineering and research. This Toolkit offers a predefined set of practical tools for generating human-AI experiences. The tools

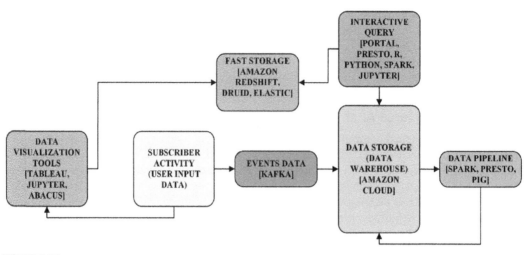

FIGURE 5.23

Storage and pipeline of user data at Netflix. Square brackets show the applications used.

Information source: www.google.com.

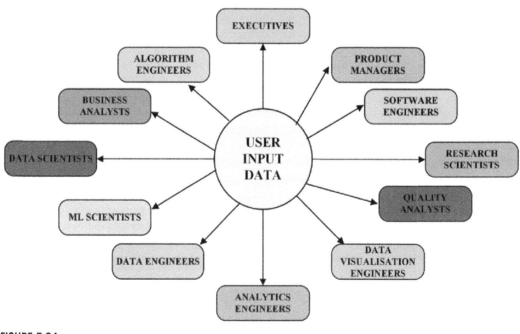

FIGURE 5.24

Human data used at all levels of AI at Netflix.

are constructed on observed needs, validated by applying a lot of research, and tested with expert teams. The proposed Microsoft HAX toolkit includes the following:

1. Guidelines for HAI Development
2. HAX Workbook
3. HAX Design Patterns
4. HAX Playbook
5. HAX Design Library

For HAI development [25], the toolkit provides a comprehensive set of 18 guidelines. These guidelines act as a resource for AI designers for building HAI designs. The HAX Workbook is a tool for structuring early conversations across the multiple roles needed to implement the guidelines for human–AI interaction. The HAX design patterns provide flexible and actionable solutions for dealing with recurring human–AI interaction problems. All of these patterns have a similar structure that guides you to a particular problem, the pattern that can be solved, to the solution of that problem. The patterns also describe when to use, how to use, user benefits, and common mistakes to avoid. The HAX Playbook is a tool for actively and systematically exploring common human–AI interaction failures.

The Playbook enumerates failures important to your AI product scenario, so you can design ways for your end users to recover efficiently. The HAX Design Library provides several designs and tools to apply to user projects for better HAI implementation.

5.7 Limitations of HAI

Before pondering over the great leaps attainable by HAI, one must also consider the opposite direction in which advances in technology can be threatening too. HAI does not guarantee that human dominance over AI would produce better results. Some of the challenges associated with the implementation of HAI are as follows.

1. HAI implementation requires measurable, precise, agreed-upon, and realistic goals. According to Shneiderman [24], excessive automation or excessive human interaction can both be harmful. There are three categories of applications that have their own allowed limits of automation and human control. The first category is the consumer applications such as social media, advertisements, and search engines, where the dominance of automation over human control has produced very good results. The second category is the consequential applications such as financial and legal systems, where dominant human control is proven to be effective in providing effective and more appropriate results. The third category is the life-critical applications such as cars, airplanes, pacemakers, intensive care units, where the HAI implemented requires extremely precise and careful implementation.
2. Humans make errors, and when added to the AI loop, some people may not do their tasks correctly. In hundreds of people, helping in the attainment of the goal through crowdsourced or outsourced inputs, it is not possible to assess the performance of each and every individual. Wrong data inserted by them leads to reduced accuracies and inefficient systems.
3. Due to the dissemination of information, there will always be social and organizational pressures.

5.8 Conclusion

The exceptional results from AI have elevated our expectations, triggering intense research in this field. It is only some years back that the threat of robotic dominance over humans gave rise to the concept of HAI. In this chapter, the concept of HAI is explained in which the focus is applied on various models that show where in the AI loop humans can fit and what will be the requirements for implementing those models. Data collection and annotation are predominant in HAI. Without data annotation, efficient HAI design is not possible. The quality control over data and the amount of data annotation required are discussed. The chapter presents various approaches to HAI design, such as AI systems influenced by society, AI systems created by cooperation between common users and engineers, AI systems that modify themselves after they interact with humans, and AI systems that are built based on user demands. Some prototype models of human—computer interaction and AI in the fields of industry, medicine and healthcare, public safety, and autonomous vehicles are described. The evaluation strategy for successful HAI designs is compared with the design thinking approach, which is used for solving a multitude of day-to-day problems. It is emphasized that the major factors that differentiate and determine the success of HAI are data analysis and stakeholder and user feedback. A case study of a human-centered app called "Shifra" is discussed. The chapter finally presents real-world case studies and limitations of HAI. In the case studies section, it is demonstrated in what ways thriving companies such as LinkedIn and Netflix use HAI in almost all of their operations such as designing, user experience, advertisements, etc.

By expanding the goal of AI by including human-centered designs, a bright future awaits AI researchers, engineers, developers, business founders and leaders, and many others who expand their goals to include HAI ways of thinking. With the advent of HAI, human dignity and security and above all human identity will be preserved, and the shape of the future of technology will be enlarged to serve human needs better. Humans can be considered as super tool builders, who can improve our health, lifestyle, family well-being, education, jobs, and much more. The promise of startling advances through HAI energizes discussions while evoking huge investments in medical, industry, space sciences, and military innovations. This compelling prospect of HAI will in near future enable people to see, think, create, and act with remarkable clarity. Major goals for the future can be peace and prosperity of nations of the world, elimination of malnutrition, safe vehicles, education for all, improvement in global communication, prevention of terrorism, excellent medical facilities even in remote and rural areas, and healthy entertainment services.

References

[1] K.-F. Lee, AI Superpowers: China, Silicon Valley, and the New World Order, Houghton Mifflin Harcourt, Boston, 2018.

[2] B. Shneiderman, Human-centered artificial intelligence: three fresh ideas, AIS Trans. Hum.-Comput. Interact. 12 (3) (2020) 109—124, https://doi.org/10.17705/1thci.00131.

[3] R. Monarch, Human-in-the-Loop Machine Learning, Manning publications, 2021.

[4] L.G. Pee, S.L. Pan, L. Cui, Artificial intelligence in healthcare robots: a social informatic study of knowledge embodiment, J. Assoc. Inf. Sci. Technol. 70 (4) (2019) 351—369, https://doi.org/10.1002/asi.24145.

[5] Y. Eisenstat, Perspective, 2019. https://www.washingtonpost.com/outlook/2019/11/04/i-worked-political-ads-facebook-they-profit-by-manipulating-us/.

[6] N. Eyal, R. Hoover, Hooked: How to Build Habit-Forming Products, 2014, ISBN 1494277530.

[7] J. Heer, M. Bostock, Crowdsourcing graphical perception: using mechanical Turk to assess visualization design, in: Proceedings of CHI 2010, ACM, New York, NY, 2010, pp. 203−212.

[8] M.L. Maher, J. Preece, T. Yeh, C. Boston, K. Grace, A. Pasupuleti, A. Stangl, NatureNet: a model for crowdsourcing the design of citizen science systems, in: Proceedings of the Companion Publication of the 17th ACM Conference on Computer Supported Cooperative Work and Social Computing (CSCW Companion '14), ACM, New York, 2014, pp. 201−204.

[9] V.J. Palmer, D. Piper, L. Richard, et al., Balancing opposing forces—a nested process evaluation study protocol for a stepped wedge designed cluster randomized controlled trial of an experience based codesign intervention, Int. J. Qual. Methods 15 (1) (2016) 1−10.

[10] R. Bartlett, J. Boyle, J.S. Smith, N.N. Khan, T. Robinson, R. Ramaswamy, Evaluating human centred design for public health: a case study on developing a healthcare app with refugee communities, Res. Involv. Engagem. 7 (2021).

[11] J. Auernhammer, Human-centered AI: the role of human-centered design research in the development of AI, in: S. Boess, M. Cheung, R. Cain (Eds.), Synergy - DRS International Conference, 2020. Held online, https://doi.org/10.21606/drs.2020.282.

[12] M. Cooley, Architect or Bee? the Human/Technology Relationship. Slough: Langley Technical Services, 1980.

[13] B.J. Fogg, Persuasive Technology Using Computers to Change what We Think and Do, Elsevier Inc, San Francisco, 2003.

[14] V. Margolin, S. Margolin, A "social model" of design: issues of practice and research, Des. Issues 18 (4) (2002) 24−30, https://doi.org/10.1162/074793602320827406.

[15] J. Spencer, J. Poggi, R. Gheerawo, Designing out stereotypes in artificial intelligence: involving users in the personality design of a digital assistant, in: Paper Presented at the Proceedings of the 4th EAI International Conference on Smart Objects and Technologies for Social Good, Bologna, Italy, 2018, https://doi.org/10.1145/3284869.3284897.

[16] K.M. Ford, P.J. Hayes, C. Glymour, J. Allen, Cognitive orthoses: toward human-centered AI, AI Mag. 36 (4) (2015), https://doi.org/10.1609/aimag.v36i4.2629.

[17] D. Gilmore, et al., User-centered design in practice, in: Paper Presented at the User Centered Design in Practice -Problems and Possibilities, Stockholm, Sweden, 1999.

[18] M.O. Ball, C.Y. Chen, R. Hoffman, et al., Collaborative decision making in air traffic management: current and future research directions, in: L. Bianco, P. Dell'Olmo, A.R. Odoni (Eds.), New Concepts and Methods in Air Traffic Management, Springer Berlin Heidelberg, Berlin,Germany, 2001, pp. 17−30, https://doi.org/10.1007/978-3-662-04632-6.

[19] P. Hu, S. Zhou, W.Z. Ding, et al., The comprehensive measurement model of the member importance in social networks, in: Int. Conf. On Management and Service Science, 2010, pp. 1−4, https://doi.org/10.1109/ICMSS.2010.5577405.

[20] R.K. Ando, M. Dredze, T. Zhang, Trec 2005 genomics track experiments at IBM Watson, in: 14th Text REtrieval Conf, 2005, pp. 1−10.

[21] Y.Y. Zhao, B. Qin, T. Liu, Sentiment analysis, J. Softw. 21 (8) (2010) 1834−1848.

[22] N. Rashevsky, Man-machine interaction in automobile driving, Prog. Biocybern. 42 (1964) 188−200.

[23] R. Razzouk, V. Shute, What is design thinking and why is it important? Rev. Educ. Res. 82 (3) (2012) 330−348, https://doi.org/10.3102/0034654312457429.

[24] B. Shneiderman, Human-centered artificial intelligence: reliable, safe & trustworthy, Int. J. Hum. Comput. Interact. 36 (6) (2020b) 495−504, https://doi.org/10.1080/10447318.2020.1741118.

[25] S. Amershi, D. Weld, A. Vorvoreanu Fourney, B. Nshi, P. Collisson, J. Suh, S. Iqbal, P. Bennett, K. Inkpen, J. Teevan, R. Kikin-Gil, E. Horvitz, Guidelines for human-AI interaction, in: Proceedings of the 2019 CHI

Conference on Human Factors in Computing Systems, Association for Computing Machinery, New York, NY, USA, 2019, pp. 1−13. Paper 3, https://doi.org/10.1145/3290605.3300233.

[26] S. Namasudra, S. Dhamodharavadhani, R. Rathipriya, Nonlinear neural network based forecasting model for predicting COVID-19 cases, Neural Process. Lett. (2021), https://doi.org/10.1007/s11063-021-10495-w.

[27] S.S. Kshatri, D. Singh, B. Narain, S. Bhatia, M.T. Quasim, G.R. Sinha, An empirical analysis of machine learning algorithms for crime prediction using stacked generalization: an ensemble approach, IEEE Access 9 (2021), https://doi.org/10.1109/ACCESS.2021.3075140.

[28] M. Abouyoussef, S. Bhatia, P. Chaudhary, S. Sharma, M. Ismail, Blockchain- enabled online diagnostic platform of suspected patients of COVID-19 like pandemics, IEEE Internet Things Mag. 4 (4) (December 2021) 94−99, https://doi.org/10.1109/IOTM.1001.2100046.

[29] Z. Aizaz, K. Khare, Energy efficient approximate booth multipliers using compact error compensation circuit for mitigation of truncation error, Int. J. Circ. Theor. Appl. (2022) 1−19.

[30] Z. Aizaz, K. Khare, State-of-Art Analysis of Multiplier Designs for Image Processing and Convolutional Neural Network Applications, 2022 International Conference for Advancement in Technology, ICONAT), 2022, pp. 1−11.

[31] Z. Aizaz, K. Khare, Area and power efficient truncated booth multipliers using approximate carry-based error compensation, IEEE Trans. Circuits Syst. II: Express Br. 69 (2) (2022) 579−583.

[32] www.cibil.com.

[33] https://www.icicibank.com/blogs/personal-loan/artificial-intelligence-in-loan-assessment-how-does-it-work.

Further reading

[1] N. Zheng, Z. Liu, P. Ren, et al., Hybrid-augmented intelligence: collaboration and cognition, Front. Inf. Technol. Electron. Eng. 18 (2017) 153−179, https://doi.org/10.1631/FITEE.1700053.

[2] P. Wang, D. Peng, L. Li, L. Chen, C. Wu, X. Wang, P. Childs, Y. Guo, Human- in-the-Loop design with machine learning, in: Proceedings of the 22nd International Conference on Engineering Design (ICED19), Delft, The Netherlands, 5-8 August 2019, 2019, https://doi.org/10.1017/dsi.2019.264.

[3] S. Namasudra, Data access control in the cloud computing environment for bioinformatics, Int. J. Appl. Res. Bioinf. (IJARB) 11 (1) (2021) 40−50.

[4] A. Singhal, S. Chandna, A. Bansal, Optimization of Test Cases Using Genetic Algorithm 1, 2012.

[5] Z. Aizaz, K. Khare, A. Tirmizi, Efficient approximate multipliers for neural network applications, in: J. Nayak, H. Behera, B. Naik, S. Vimal, D. Pelusi (Eds.), Computational Intelligence in Data Mining. Smart Innovation, Systems and Technologies, vol 281, Springer, Singapore, 2022.

Strategies for efficient and intelligent user interfaces

S. Suriya, M. Balaji and S. Nivetha

Department of Computer Science and Engineering, PSG College of Technology, Coimbatore, Tamil Nadu, India

6.1 Introduction

6.1.1 User interface

The user interface (UI) is gateway for human and computers to interact with each other. It is also called a human—computer interface. The overall objective of a UI is to make interactions of a user to be simple and efficient against a computer with minimal efforts being involved. In turn, the UI helps a computer in better understanding and addressing user interactions. The different types of UI are graphical user interfaces, command line interfaces, form-based interfaces, menu-based interfaces, natural language interfaces, and touchscreen graphical user interfaces.

6.1.2 User interface design

User interface design (UID) provides a visual layout that holds different elements, which in turn helps the user to interact with an application or a web site in an efficient and friendly manner. It also focuses on elements on the UI that might lead to easy understanding and accessing the required functionalities of a user who interacts with the system.

6.1.3 Theo Mandel's golden rules

Theo Mandel [2] has stated three golden rules for UID, as shown in Fig. 6.1. These rules have later become the principles that drive UID. The rules are (1) place the user in control, (2) reduce the user's memory load, and (3) make the interface consistent.

Place the user in control refers to a few considerations, as stated by Roger [3],

- Interaction modes should not lead a user to undesired actions.
- Interactions should be flexible.
- Users are permitted to perform interruptible and undoable interactions.
- Interactions should be customizable.
- No technical process needs to be revealed to end users.
- There should be direct interactions through the elements that appear on the UI.

Reduce the user's memory load refers to a few considerations, as stated by Roger [3],

Innovations in Artificial Intelligence and Human-Computer Interaction in the Digital Era. https://doi.org/10.1016/B978-0-323-99891-8.00005-X
131

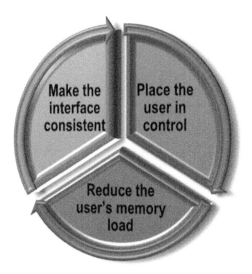

FIGURE 6.1

The three golden rules for user interfaces.

- ✔ Have a visual portrayal to recognize the past interactions.
- ✔ Inherit the meaningful defaults.
- ✔ Have intuitive interface shortcuts.

Make the interface consistent refers to a few considerations, as stated by Roger [3],

- ✔ Maintain consistency.
- ✔ Inherit existing interactive models.
- ✔ Sustain the context of users' tasks.
- ✔ Have a friendly appearance and feeling of integrity.

6.1.4 User interface design process

The analysis and design process of UI, as shown in Fig. 6.2, involves four iterative steps, namely, interface analysis, interface design, interface construction, and interface validation. Interface analysis involves investigation of end users who will interact with the computer. Requirements are collected based on the category of end users. Interface design focuses on elements that might appear on the screen of the UI with which the end user interacts. Interface construction involves development of a prototype. Interface validation is concerned about efficiency of the interface in handling user requests, ease of usage, flexibility, and end user feedback about the interface.

The basic UID principles, shown in Fig. 6.3, are user familiarity, consistency, minimal surprise, recoverability, user guidance, and user diversity. User familiarity refers to inheriting the familiar terminologies, used by end users, toward the new interface being developed. Consistency insists in maintaining the similarity between the functionalities irrespective of their formats being implemented. Minimal surprise targets at being the same with existing common functions that can be easily

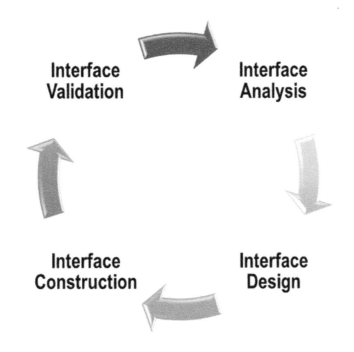

FIGURE 6.2

User interface design process.

predictable by the end users. Recoverability is concerned about recoverability features offered to the end users via the interface, especially about undo facilities of the interface, confirming the destruction of a user activity before being executed and so on. User guidance focuses on the help facilities offered to the end users through the interface. User diversity deals with different types of end users.

6.2 Strategies required for efficient intelligent user interfaces
6.2.1 Intelligent user interfaces

Any UI that can interact with end users in an intelligent way using artificial intelligence (AI) techniques is termed an intelligent user interface. To improve the efficiency of the interaction, AI techniques are incorporated while designing the interface. Hence the integration of AI techniques and human—computer interactions results in intelligent user interfaces, as shown in Fig. 6.4.

Lieberman et al. [4] has addressed the importance of integrating AI concepts with UI from the perspective of reasoning and recognition features offered by artificial intelligence. Bader et al. [5] has highlighted algorithmic decisions getting along with human decisions. A framework of algorithm decisions and human decisions is framed from the two perspectives of detachment from decisions and attachment to decisions. Dudley et al. [6] has introduced interactive machine learning toward UI. The proposed system makes end users to interact with the UI, which works with the support of interactive machine learning. The various interface elements of the interactive machine learning approach are review, feedback, inspection, and overview of a task.

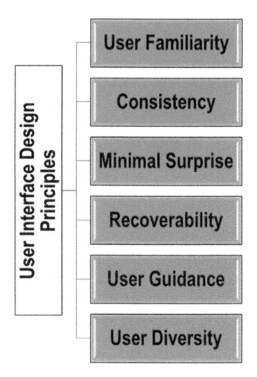

FIGURE 6.3

User interface design principles.

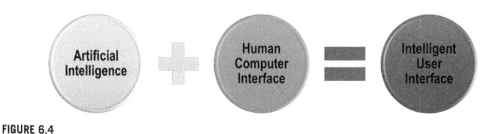

FIGURE 6.4

Intelligent user interface.

6.2.2 Importance of artificial intelligence and machine learning

AI helps computers to mimic the capability of a human mind from the perspectives of learning, problem solving, decision making, and so on. AI is a computing technology that focuses on human intelligence. A subset of AI is called machine learning (ML), which has the capability to learn by itself. A subset of ML is called deep learning, which has the capability to teach itself without the support of humans, as shown in Fig. 6.5.

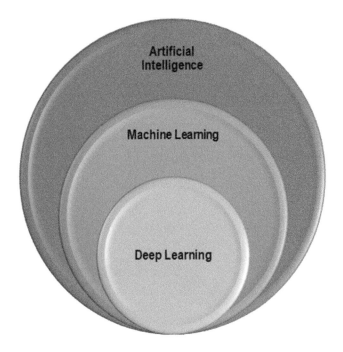

FIGURE 6.5

Artificial intelligence, machine learning, deep learning.

Knowledge can be gained only through learning along with experiences. A human brain is the best example for this fact, as shown in Fig. 6.6. It is applicable to various senses like vision, sound, touch, smell and taste. Traditional programming approaches have focused on generating results over the target data by applying logical solving techniques via any programming languages. Hence a computer is fed with input data along with a suitable program to generate the output, as shown in Fig. 6.7. The ML paradigm, as shown in Fig. 6.8, enables the computer to generate a suitable program for the given dataset using the desired results as input. This output program is also called a model. It is the best approach for decision-making problems. ML paradigm is a new era to build decision-making systems without much burden on manual efforts or relying more on fixed rule-based systems.

Making machines to learn eradicates issues related to the following like lack of human expertise in a particular domain, uncertainty in a scenario that keeps on changing over time, and challenges in translating human expertise into computational methods. ML learns by itself, predicts, and makes improvements without being explicitly programmed. The requirements to develop a ML system are data preparation, basic or advanced algorithms, automation process, scalability, and ensemble modeling. In ML, a target is technically called a "label." A target represents a dependent variable. Tom M. Mitchell [7] defined ML as "A computer program is said to learn from experience E with respect to some class of tasks T and performance measure P, if its performance at tasks in T, as measured by P, improves with experience E." In simple words, ML helps a system to improve its performance by

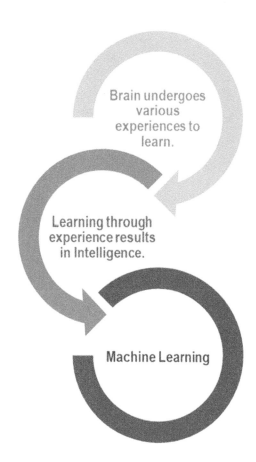

FIGURE 6.6

Evolution of machine learning.

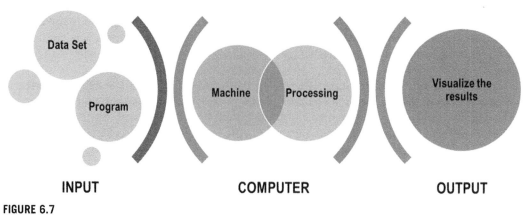

FIGURE 6.7

Traditional programming.

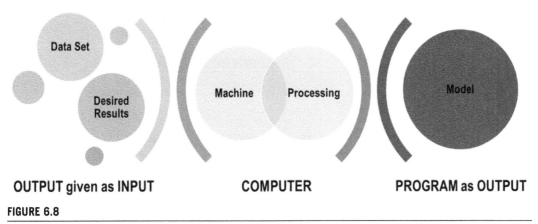

OUTPUT given as INPUT   COMPUTER   PROGRAM as OUTPUT

FIGURE 6.8

Machine learning paradigm.

executing task over time with experience. There are four different types of ML namely: supervised learning, unsupervised learning, semi-supervised learning, and reinforcement learning, as shown in Fig. 6.9. The bird's eye view of different operations offered by different types ML is shown in Fig. 6.10.

1. Supervised learning:

In this type of ML method, algorithms work with labeled training data over defined variables. Explicit identification of input and output of the algorithm will be done. The user has to train the supervised learning algorithm using labeled inputs and desired output. Supervised learning techniques are best suitable for binary classification, multiclass classification, regression modeling, and ensembling.

2. Unsupervised learning:

In this type of ML method, algorithms train on the unlabeled data. Algorithms train on the data by making predictions that are predetermined. Unsupervised learning algorithms work over unlabeled data to track patterns that help to train the system. Suitable applications are clustering, anomaly detection, association mining, and dimensionality reduction.

3. Semi-supervised learning:

This method is a fusion of supervised learning method and unsupervised learning method. Algorithms start their training with labeled data and are free to make predictions based on their understanding of the dataset. Areas where semi-supervised learning technique can be used are machine translation, fraud detection, and labeling data.

4. Reinforcement learning:

In this type of ML, rules are defined clearly to train the machine. Applicable areas are robotics, video gameplay, resource management.

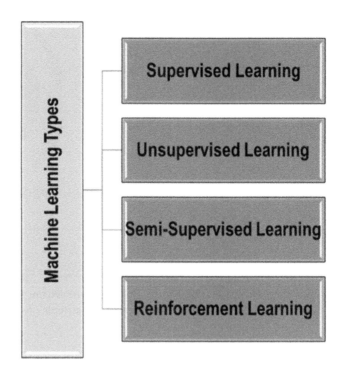

FIGURE 6.9

Types of machine learning.

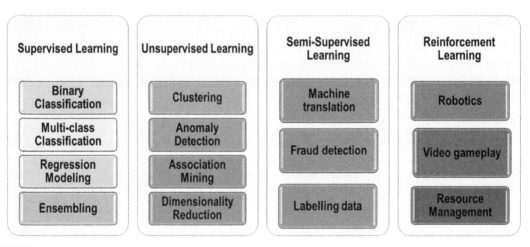

FIGURE 6.10

Bird's eye view of different operations offered by different types of machine learning.

6.3 Recent innovations in intelligent user interfaces
6.3.1 Intelligent interface for Tamil letter recognition using machine learning techniques

Character recognition is done with help of ML techniques as described in a detailed manner in Table 6.1. The UI of the intelligent interface for Tamil letter recognition using ML techniques, as shown in Fig. 6.11, is a webpage that is designed using flask, HTML, and JavaScript. This webpage allows the user to give a handwritten Tamil character as input that can be tested in the background to classify the input into the correct Tamil character. To get handwritten input from the user, a sketchpad is created. A sketchpad is similar to that of a white board, where the user could write any character using the mouse or the touch pad. The webpage contains three buttons, "clear image," to erase the input given in the sketchpad, "save image," to accept the image and resize the image to a required size, and "classify image," which triggers the background execution. Once the handwritten input is given by the user, the input is extracted as an image, and the image is resized to 160×160. The resized image is stored in the directory, so the image can be fetched for classification. The resized image is fetched from the directory and is tested in the background. Once the image is tested, as in the case of background execution, the five characters whose accuracies are highest are stored in a text file "temp.txt," which is then fetched by the front-end code and is displayed in the table in a webpage. Each test scenario of the UI along with the expected result and actual results are tabulated in Table 6.2.

Every image is an arrangement of dots (a pixel) arranged in a special order. If the order or color of a pixel is changed, then the image would change as well. A weight matrix is defined that extracts certain features from the image. Sometimes when the images are too large, the need to reduce the number of trainable parameters becomes the next focus. It is then desired to periodically introduce pooling layers between subsequent convolution layers. Pooling is done for the sole purpose of reducing the spatial size of the image. Pooling is done independently on each depth dimension; therefore the depth of the image remains unchanged. The most common form of pooling layer generally applied is the max pooling. Three hyperparameters would control the size of output volume.

1. The number of filters: The depth of the output volume will be equal to the number of filters applied. The output is stacked from each filter to form an activation map. The depth of the activation map will be equal to the number of filters.
2. Stride: With higher stride values, we move a larger number of pixels at a time and hence produce smaller output volumes.
3. Zero padding: This helps us to preserve the size of the input image. If a single zero padding is added, a single stride filter movement would retain the size of the original image.

A CNN consists of a number of convolutional and subsampling layers optionally followed by fully connected layers. The input to a convolutional layer is an m x m x r image, where m is the height and width of the image, and r is the number of channels, e.g., an RGB image has r = 3. The convolutional layer will have k filters (or kernels) of size n x n x q, where n is smaller than the dimension of the image, and q can either be the same as the number of channels r or smaller and may vary for each kernel. The size of the filters gives rise to the locally connected structure, which is convolved with the image to produce k feature maps of size $m - n + 1$. Each map is then subsampled typically with mean or max pooling over p x p contiguous regions, where p ranges between two for small images (e.g.,

Table 6.1 Machine learning techniques for Tamil letter recognition.

Machine learning techniques	Accuracy	Purpose
Offline handwritten Tamil character recognition using convolutional neural networks (CNNs) [8]	Overall accuracy of 97.7%	To utilize the CNN technique to achieve good recognition results on both training and testing datasets
Tamil handwritten character recognition using feature extraction [9]	Around 85%	Deals with three feature extraction techniques to grasp features from various Tamil characters possessing variations in style and shape
Tamil text recognition by using K-nearest neighbor (KNN) classifier [10]	Overall 91%	To get an efficient output, and this approach has increased the speed and accuracy of character recognition
Effective printed Tamil text segmentation and recognition using Bayesian classifier [11]	Overall accuracy of 96.3%	To recognize Tamil characters irrespective of the characteristics of the text such as font style, color, and size
Novel approach for multiclass classification to recognize Tamil characters using binary support vector machines [12]	About 98.08%	Each node of the hybrid decision tree exploits an optimal feature subset in classifying the Tamil characters effectively
Novel method for pattern recognition problems in terms of linear regression [13]	Around 91%	To effectively recognize the Tamil characters using linear regression that works on nearest subspace approach
Tamil text recognition using fuzzy technique [14]	Accuracy ranged from 90% to 100%	To recognize cursive Tamil handwritten words with fuzzy logic
Kohonen neural network-based self-organizing maps to recognize handwritten Tamil character [15]	Accuracy ranges from 89.5% to 98.5%	To yield promising and feasible output with higher performance than other existing techniques.

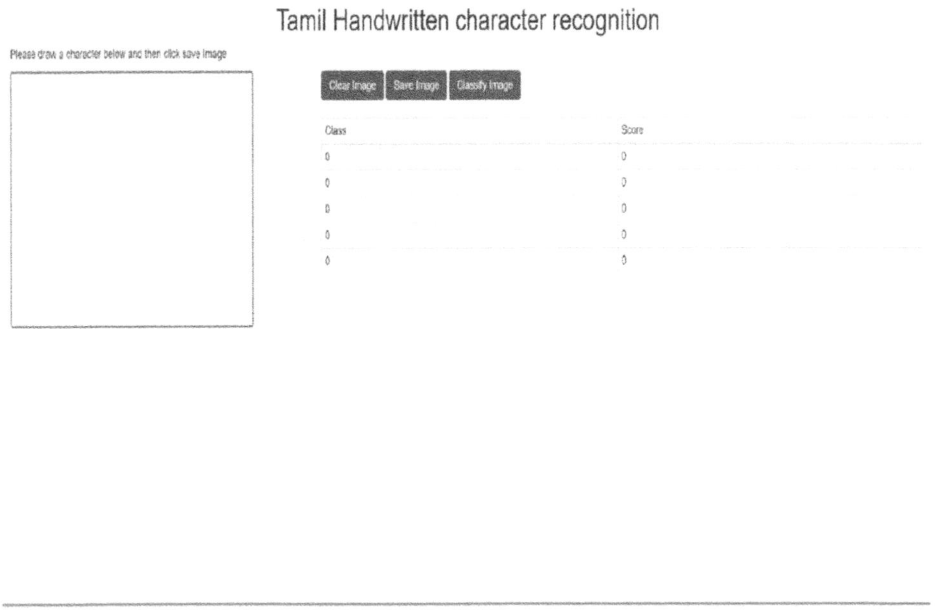

Tamil Handwritten character recognition

Please draw a character below and then click save image

| Clear Image | Save Image | Classify Image |

Class   Score

0   0

0   0

0   0

0   0

0   0

FIGURE 6.11

Intelligent interface for Tamil letter recognition.

MNIST) and is usually not more than five for larger inputs. Either before or after the subsampling layer, an additive bias and sigmoidal nonlinearity are applied to each feature map. The figure below illustrates a full layer in a CNN consisting of convolutional and subsampling sublayers. Units of the same color have tied weights.

6.3.2 Intelligent interface for online examination system using natural language processing techniques

An online examination system survey is done with help of ML techniques as described in a detailed manner in Table 6.3. The user interface of the intelligent interface for the online examination system using natural language processing (NLP) techniques is shown in Fig. 6.12. The online examination system acts as a master for the entire workings of the system. It stores all the details about the students and the faculty members. It authenticates the students and the faculty members each time they log onto the system. It receives the chapter inputs from the faculty member and the test type and subject from the students and generates necessary questions and answers for those generated questions. The test is now open for the students to attempt. Once the student completes the test and submits it, the answers given by the students are extracted by the system, and those answers are evaluated by comparing with those answers that were generated by the system and using similarity measures to compute the score using NLP techniques. These grades are then stored in a sheet from where the faculty could view the results of the students. The UI of this system can be designed as shown in Fig. 6.12.

Table 6.2 Testing the user interface for Tamil letter recognition.

Module name	Test scenario	Expected result	Actual result	Pass/ fail
Testing the user interface	Check the design of the sketchpad	The handwritten input given by the user must be visible on the sketchpad without any time delay	The input given using the mouse or the touch pad is displayed in the sketchpad without any delay.	Pass
	Check the functionality of "clear image" button	The handwritten input present over the sketchpad must be erased on clicking the "clear image" button	On clicking the "clear image" button, the input present over the sketchpad is erased	Pass
	Check the functionality of "save image" button	The functionality of this button is to extract the image as a screenshot	On clicking the "save" button, the handwritten input is extracted as a screenshot	Pass
	Check the functionality of "classify image" button	The data present in the temp.txt file must be displayed as the result	This button, on clicking, triggers the background execution, and finally fetches the results present in the temp.txt file and displays the output in the table	Pass

The UI used for this intelligent interface is the web-based UI or web UI. The web-based UI accepts input and provides output by generating web pages that are viewed by the user when using the web browser. Three webpages have been designed to implement the online examination system. The first webpage is designed to implement the user authentication module to authenticate the students. The second webpage gets the inputs of the test type and the subject from the student and proceeds to the next page. The final webpage will display the questions of the selected type and subject, and it records the answers from the students, validates those answers, and displays the results. Each test scenario of the UI along with the expected result and actual results are tabulated in Table 6.4.

6.3.2.1 Objective answer evaluation

The answer for the objective type of question is generated along with the process of question generation. A variable "SCORE" is used to keep track of user's attempts. For every correct answer given by the user, the score is increased by 100. For every wrong answer given by the user, the score remains the same. The final score is divided by the number of questions to get the final result. If the final result if greater than 33.33, then the user is declared to "PASS," or else the user is declared to "FAIL."

Table 6.3 Machine learning techniques for online examination system.

Paper	Keypoints
Checkpoint: an online descriptive answers grading tool [16]	✔ Natural language processing (NLP)-based descriptive answer checking and grading application. ✔ Four important modules: grammar check, stop word removal, stemming, comparison with keywords and grading. ✔ Process: 　1. Parse the answer 　2. Similarity between the answer keywords and the parsed answer 　3. Grade the answers based on similarity ✔ Provides an accuracy of 98% ✔ Future work: reduce execution time
Online descriptive examination and assessment system [17]	✔ Pattern-matching technique algorithm ✔ Process: 　1. The descriptive answer and the standard answer is converted to graphical form 　2. Similarity measures are applied 　3. Calculation of similarity score is made ✔ Provides an accuracy of 70%
Use of syntactic similarity-based similarity matrix for	✔ Similarity matrix for evaluating descriptive answers

Continued

Table 6.3 Machine learning techniques for online examination system.—cont'd

Paper	Keypoints
evaluating descriptive answer [18]	✔ Based on word-to-word syntactic similarity measure ✔ The solution is in the form of points or sentences ✔ Similarity measure is applied for the answer keywords and the answer given as input ✔ Accuracy equals around 70% ✔ Future work: handle the synonyms in answer content
Algorithm for automatic evaluation of single sentence descriptive answer [19]	✔ Process: 1. Converts both single sentence answer and standard answer into graphical form 2. Match the nodes and labels in an intelligent way (similarity measures) 3. Calculate similarity score using similarity matching between teacher nodes and student nodes ✔ Future works: evaluation of multiple sentence answers
An examination system automation using natural language processing [20]	✔ NLP to assign marks to answers ✔ Answer keywords are stored by the teacher; stop words from students'

Table 6.3 Machine learning techniques for online examination system.—cont'd	
Paper	**Keypoints**
	answers are removed
	✔ Keyword existence in the answer is calculated using sparse matrix
	✔ Sparse matrix equals count of each and every keyword in the answer
	✔ High accuracy of about 95%
	✔ Future work: to track malpractice, where student has copied from the other student
Intelligent online exam management and evaluation system [21]	✔ Uses pair-wise approach
	✔ RA is reference answer
	✔ SA is student's answer
	✔ Both are provided to the AEE algorithm as input after text preprocessing
	✔ Similarity between RA and SA is computer using cosine similarity and scores are calculated
	✔ Provides accuracy of about 80%
Comparative analysis of computer-assisted valuation of descriptive answers using WEKA with different classification algorithms [22]	✔ Process: the answer given by the student passes through the following stages: 1. Tokenizer 2. Vectorization 3. Training 4. Filter 5. Classification
	✔ Provides an accuracy of 70%
	✔ Future works:

Continued

Table 6.3 Machine learning techniques for online examination system.—cont'd

Paper	Keypoints
	1. Improving grammatical errors and recognition 2. Using NLP and AI to make the system better

Evaluation of the descriptive type answers using hyperspace analog to language (HAL) and self-organizing map (SOM) [23]	✓ Uses HAL and Kohonen SOM
	✓ Process:
	  1. Students' answer is given as an input to HAL, which builds high-dimensional semantic space for words
	  2. Each word is represented as a vector
	  3. HAL vectors are given as input to SOM and form the document map, so nearby neurons contain a similar document
	  4. SOM results are compared with clustering methods, and results are produced
	✓ Future works: refine the system to deliver education through online class

Automatic assessment of descriptive answers for online examination using semantic analysis [24]	✓ Uses NLP and ANN
	✓ The modules of the system are
	  1. Question answering
	  2. User authentication

Table 6.3 Machine learning techniques for online examination system.—cont'd

Paper	Keypoints
	3. Subjective examination 4. Feature extraction using NLP 5. Classification using semantic analysis 6. ANN for evaluation of marks
AI-based symmetric answer evaluation system for descriptive answering [25]	✔ Uses HAL and SOM ✔ Process: the evaluation process will have both the teacher's and students' answers; model's answer is stored in a database 1. The system reads and extracts the keywords from both the answers using TF/IDF keyword extraction algorithm 2. Latent semantic analysis and SOM are applied to the text 3. Scores are allotted using cosine similarity
Online examination with short text matching [26]	✔ Predefined answers are stored in a database ✔ Core functionality is selection of random questions from the question database based on a constraint of difficulty level

Continued

Table 6.3 Machine learning techniques for online examination system.—cont'd

Paper	Keypoints
	✔ Uses text mining to extract useful keywords from the students' answers ✔ The text is then passed through classification algorithm ✔ Finally, analysis of the text is done

Neural models for key phrase detection and question generation [27]	✔ A two-stage neural model to generate questions from documents
	✔ First model: question and answer corpus was used to train the neural model
	✔ Two neural models:
	  1. To rank entities
	  2. Points to key phrase start and end boundaries
	✔ Used sequence-to-sequence model to generate questions based on key phrases
	✔ Experiments were conducted on the Stanford Question Answering Dataset (SQuAD) and NewsQA datasets

Neural generation of diverse questions using answer focus, contextual, and linguistic features [28]	✔ Uses encode–decode recurrent neural network model (RNN) for automatic question generation ✔ Model also captures meanings

Table 6.3 Machine learning techniques for online examination system.—cont'd

Paper	Keypoints
	✔ Maps a source sequence to a target sequence ✔ Encoder has multilayer bidirectional long short-term memory (LSTM) ✔ Decoder has unidirectional LSTM ✔ Baseline model has four different token level supervision features, sentence encoder, and copy mechanism ✔ Experiments were conducted on the SQuAD datasets
Learning to generate questions with adaptive copying neural networks [29]	✔ RNN to generate questions ✔ Adds a copying mechanism component onto a bidirectional LSTM ✔ Experiments were conducted on the SQuAD datasets ✔ BLEU-n and ROUGE-L were used as evaluation metrics
Improving neural question generation using answer separation [30]	✔ Proposed an answer-separated sequence-to-sequence model ✔ The model learns to identify which interrogative word should be used ✔ Also proposed a new module keyword net ✔ Reduces the number of improper questions

Continued

Table 6.3 Machine learning techniques for online examination system.—cont'd

Paper	Keypoints
Neural question generation with semantics of question type [31]	✔ Has strong ability to generate right questions ✔ BLEU-4, Meteor, and ROUGE-L were used as evaluation metrics ✔ Uses CNN for predicting question type of the answer phases ✔ Classify the question type to incorporate the question type semantics into the generating model ✔ Uses Bi-LSTM to construct the question-generating model ✔ Experiments were conducted on the SQuAD ✔ The results show an improvement of 1.7% on BLEU-4 score
A real-time multiple-choice question generation for language testing: a preliminary study [32]	✔ Using basic machine learning algorithms like naïve Bayes and K-nearest neighbors, we have developed a real-time system that generates questions on English grammar and vocabulary from online news articles ✔ They have found KNN algorithm to give more useful output than the latter due the mixed nature of the training data

Table 6.3 Machine learning techniques for online examination system.—cont'd

Paper	Keypoints
Question generator system of sentence completion in TOEFL using NLP and K-nearest neighbor [33]	✔ Gathered data set from various TOEFL question and answer books ✔ Preprocessing was done on two types of datasets (i.e., data training and data testing). The first stage was removal of punctuation (regex). The removed punctuation marks were other than dots and underscores. A dot is used for a marker or separator between sentences
Automatic gap-fill question generation from textbooks [34]	✔ Fill in the blanks and multiple choice questions are taken ✔ Weighted sum of extracted feature is generated
Automatic evaluation of descriptive answer using pattern-matching algorithm [35]	✔ Descriptive answer correction method is discussed here ✔ Pattern-matching algorithm-based method is used for evaluation of answers

6.3.2.2 Subjective answer evaluation

The answer for the subjective type of question is generated along with the process of question generation. The evaluation technique uses both the answer given by the user and the answer generated during the question generation. The user answer is then divided into tokens, and the generated answer is generated into tokens. Both tokens are combined, and a list containing all tokens is created. A vector is created for both the user answer and the generated answer. The sentence is tokenized on a word level. A one-hot encoded vector is then created by creating a vector with zeros and ones with one representing a word present in the user's answer as well as the generated answer and zero representing a word not present in the user's answer but being present in the generated answer and vice versa. The final score is calculated by using the resulting two vectors using cosine similarity score with Euclidian

 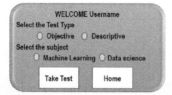 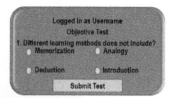

FIGURE 6.12

Intelligent interface for online examination.

distance. The final score is then displayed, and if the score is greater than 50, then the user is declared to "PASS," or else the user is declared to "FAIL". Machine learning techniques for online examination system are dicussed in Table 6.5.

6.3.3 Intelligent interface for online music genre classification system using machine learning techniques

See Table 6.5.

The UI of the intelligent interface for an online music genre classification system using machine learning techniques is visualized using three web interfaces, namely, homepage interface, shown in Fig. 6.13, check genre page interface, shown in Fig. 6.14, and statistics page interface, as shown in Fig. 6.15. The first webpage (home page) is designed to implement the user authentication module to authenticate the users who need to access the resources available. The second webpage (check genre) extracts the audio file from the user as the input, classifies the genre of the music at the back end, and displays the genre as a text message or in an alert dialog. The final webpage (statistics) displays the details of the dataset count, training, and testing data count and the accuracy of the system.

Feature extraction is a process of dimensionality reduction by which an initial set of raw data is reduced to more manageable groups for processing. In the GTZAN dataset, a total of nine features can be extracted, which are tempo, beats, chroma STFT, root mean square energy, spectral centroid, spectral bandwidth, spectral roll-off, zero crossing rate, and mel frequency cepstral coefficients. The audio file to be classified is obtained from the user through the check genre webpage build. The user will be able to upload any file into the webpage. It is the role of the webpage to check if it is a valid audio file or not.

i. If the file is not of the .wav format, an error pops up as a text message stating that the file is invalid.

Table 6.4 Testing the user interface of an online examination system.

Module name	Webpage	Test scenario	Expected result	Actual result	Pass/fail
Testing the user interface	Page 1: login page (Role: user authentication)	Get details	Get the username of type varchar and password of type varchar from the student	The system accepts the inputs for the username and password fields Example username is Suriya Password is 12345	Pass
		Validate details	Validate the students' details thus collected	The system checks the username and password with the entries present in the database and thus authenticates the user and directs the user to the next page	Pass
	Page 2: select test type and subject	Get details	Get the details for the test type and subject from the student	The system gets the test type and the subject by checking the option that is enabled in the checkbox and then directs the user to the next page	Pass
	Page 3: test	Display questions	Display the questions based on the type and subject chosen by the student	The system properly displays the question per the options selected	Pass

ii. If the user uploads, a valid .wav file, the file gets uploaded and commences the classification process.

   The audio file to be classified is extracted from the UI where the user has uploaded the file. The features are extracted from the audio file and the same process for creation of dataset sticks to this as well. The model created is then loaded, and the features thus generated are used to classify the audio file to its proper genre (Table 6.6).

Table 6.5 Machine learning techniques for music genre classification.

Paper	Key points

A double-weighted KNN algorithm and its application in the music genre classification [1]	✔ Dataset collection: 1000 pieces in all (100 from each genre)
	✔ Data preprocessing
	  1. Generating characteristic matrix, extracting 59-dimensional characteristic of each song
	  2. The entire dataset is divided into training (3/4) and testing (1/4) data
	✔ Data normalization into the range $[-1,1]$
	✔ Evaluation criteria and validation methods
	  1. Evaluation criteria: accuracy rate
	  2. Validation methods: cross-validation method, sample is divided into k collections $(k-1$ for training and 1 for testing); this is repeated k times
	✔ Experimental results and analysis: select a proper value of k and perform k-NN
	✔ Algorithm is simple and symmetrical and has better accuracy rate

Table 6.5 Machine learning techniques for music genre classification.—cont'd

Paper	Key points
Music genre classification using transfer learning [2]	✓ Dataset collection: 1100 pieces in all (11 genres, 100 from each) 75% training, 25% testing ✓ Transfer learning: source task and target task ✓ Feature extraction: 50-dimensional output ✓ Baseline machine learning classifier used is k-NN ✓ Future works: fine tuning the system to classify pop genre
Novel approach to music genre classification using clustering augmented learning method [3]	✓ Dataset collection: GTZAN dataset, 10 genres (100 in each), 1000 in all, training: testing: validation = 8:1:1 ✓ The model consists of four-layer CNN of 64 features map; output is a sequence in which every timestamp relies on immediate predecessor and long-term structure ✓ Feature extraction: the sequence is fed to LSTM sequence-to-sequence autoencoder to capture the characteristics ✓ CALM (clustering augmented learning method) classifier is used ✓ Accuracy: 90% ✓ Future work: improvising new

Continued

Table 6.5 Machine learning techniques for music genre classification.—cont'd

Paper	Key points
	distance metric methods to compute the similarity between genres
Automatic music genre classification using convolution neural network [4]	✔ Dataset collection: 1000 pieces in all (10 genres, 100 from each genre)
	✔ Feature extraction: the features are extracted from the waveforms by applying Fourier transforms followed by logarithmic of the power values, and finally applying cosine transforms; these features are called mel frequency cepstral coefficients (MFCC)
	✔ Model: extracted features act as inputs to the neurons in CNN for training
	✔ Accuracy: 76%
	✔ Future work: fine tuning the system to classify the songs based on mood, so it could be helpful in music therapy systems
Music genre classification using deep neural networks [5]	✔ Data collection: 400 audio formats (four genres, 100 in each); the dataset is divided into three sections: 60% for training, 20% for validation, and 20% for testing
	✔ Feature extraction: process that converts the audio signals into a sequence of

Table 6.5 Machine learning techniques for music genre classification.—cont'd

Paper	Key points
	feature vectors, where MFCC is used
	✔ Classification: where a particular label is assigned to a particular music format
	✔ Multilabel feed-forward deep neural network to recognize the genres, with one input, one output, and several hidden layers
	✔ Accuracy: 97.8%
	✔ Future work: increasing dataset and using other feature techniques to classify all genres
Jazz music subgenre classification using deep learning [6]	✔ Dataset collection: 3800 segments of subgenres of jazz (245 min. of acid jazz, 141 min. of bebop, 245 min. of swing, split up to 10 sec)
	✔ Data preprocessing: MFCC
	✔ Training: testing = 60:40
	✔ Several classifiers were tested: SVM tests were conducted with varying kernel functions; KNN different values of k were tested; for MLP the number of layers and hidden units per layer were varied and tested
	✔ Accuracy: 90%

Continued

Table 6.5 Machine learning techniques for music genre classification.—cont'd

Paper	Key points
Improved music genre classification with convolutional neural networks [7]	✔ Future work: training the system to classify up to 10 genres from GTZAN dataset ✔ Dataset collection: GTZAN dataset, 1000 in all (10 genres, 100 in each) ✔ Data preprocessing: applying Fourier transform to audio files ✔ Classification: the output from Fourier transform is fed to CNN ✔ The output of CNN is fed into a deep neural network ✔ Two ways are ✔ Combining max pooling and average pooling to provide more statistical information to higher level neural networks ✔ Using shortcut connections to skip one or more layers, a method inspired by residual learning method ✔ Method 2 provides a good accuracy ✔ Future work: to fuse new methods such as multiscale convolution and pooling with residual learning
Learning temporal features using a deep neural network and its	✔ Dataset collection: GTZAN dataset, 1000 files in all

Table 6.5 Machine learning techniques for music genre classification.—cont'd

Paper	Key points
application to music genre classification [8]	(10 genres, 100 from each) ✔ Dataset partitioning: two ways ✔ Dividing the dataset in ratio 50:25:25 and performing the experiments four times to present the averaged results ✔ "Fault-filtered" partitioning: the dataset is divided into 443/197/290 to avoid repetition of artist ✔ Classification: random forest with 500 trees ads a classifier ✔ Each music clip of 30 s was divided into 5-s-long segments, and classification was performed on each 5 sec and used majority voting to classify the whole 30-s music clip ✔ Both training and validation were used to train RF as it does not require additional data for validation ✔ Accuracy: 85% ✔ Future work: apply the proposed method to various MIR related tasks, classification, and instrument identification

Continued

Table 6.5 Machine learning techniques for music genre classification.—cont'd

Paper	Key points
Deep neural networks: a case study for music genre classification [9]	✔ Dataset collection: raw audio signals in .wav format ✔ Data preprocessing includes three steps ✔ Data manipulation: augmentation, normalization, and subsampling ✔ Power spectrogram ✔ Feature extraction ✔ Dimensionality reduction: manifold learning is a non-linear method that is applied on large datasets to reduce the curse of dimensionality and reduce the time complexity of learning models ✔ Two classifiers were tested ✔ DNN: architecture is two-hidden-layered feed-forward neural network ✔ SVM: 1-SVM, logistic regression, and 1-regression were adopted as baseline classifiers ✔ The accuracy rate obtained was compared ✔ Future work: explore different signal preprocessing and representations to measure the network sensitivity for classification
Music genre classification [10]	✔ Dataset collection: GTZAN genre collection, 400 in all

Table 6.5 Machine learning techniques for music genre classification.—cont'd

Paper	Key points
	(four genres, 100 in each) 70% training, 30% testing
	✔ Data preprocessing: MFCC
	✔ Several classifies were used
	✔ KNN: calculating the distance between two songs is computed using Kullback—Leibler divergence
	✔ K-means: represent cluster centroids and update centroids
	✔ SVM: DAG of two class SVMs are trained on each pair of classes to avoid data falling into multiple classes
	✔ Neural networks: the data is split into 70:15:15; after multiple tests runs, the feed-forward model with 10 layers gives best results
	✔ Accuracy of KNN and SVM are 80% and 87%
	✔ Future work: adding validation step to DAG SVM and also including additional metadata text features
Audio music genre classification using different classifiers and feature selection methods [11]	✔ Experimented with 10 different classifiers like KNN, Naïve bayes classifier, etc.
	✔ Forward and backward selection

Continued

Table 6.5 Machine learning techniques for music genre classification.—cont'd

Paper	Key points
	algorithm to select best feature
	✔ 80% classification performance is achieved
Combination of homogeneous classifiers for musical genre classification [12]	✔ The classifiers are based on neural networks
	✔ A validation set with 246 feature vectors was used during the training of the MLP classifiers to look over the generalization and to avoid overfitting
Improving music genre classification by short time feature integration [13]	✔ A new feature integration technique, the AR model, has been proposed as an alternative to the dominating mean variance feature integration
A comparative study on content-based music genre classification [14]	✔ A comparative study of various feature extraction and classification methods that investigates the classification performance of various classification methods on different feature sets
	✔ For classical genre, the accuracy was 98.89%, which was highest of all genres
Musical genre classification of audio signals [15]	✔ More specifically, three feature sets for representing timbral texture, rhythmic

Table 6.5 Machine learning techniques for music genre classification.—cont'd

Paper	Key points
	content, and pitch content are proposed
	✔ Using the proposed feature sets, classification of 61% for 10 musical genres is achieved
Music genre classification using machine learning techniques [16]	✔ To improve signal-to-noise ratio, a preemphasis filter is used
	✔ $y(t) = x(t) - \alpha *$ (t-1) x(t) - > original signal y(t) - > filtered signal α - > filter constant
	✔ The audio is converted into a three-channel (RGB) matrix representation and fed into CNN
	✔ Sound waves are treated as histograms
	✔ VGG-16 architecture is used
	✔ Evaluation metrics
	✔ Accuracy is 0.63, and F-score is 0.61
Automatic musical pattern feature extraction using convolutional neural network [17]	✔ Uses CNN with five layers to extract musical pattern feature
	✔ The classification systems are generic classifiers and majority voting
	✔ MFCC extraction from audio signals
	✔ These features are passed into CNN along with labels
	✔ Various multiclass classifiers like

Continued

Table 6.5 Machine learning techniques for music genre classification.—cont'd

Paper	Key points
	decision tree, SVM, etc., are used to classify, and the final result is selected by majority voting
	✔ Provides an accuracy of 84% for GTZAN dataset
Multiexpert system for automatic music genre classification [18]	✔ Uses a multiExpert system where each individual expert is specific to one type of characteristic
	✔ Acoustic expert uses acoustic features
	✔ Rhythmic expert uses beat-related features
	✔ Timbre expert used timbre features
	✔ Based on probability: uses probabilistic graphical models and multilayer perceptron classifier
Music genre classification using novel features and a weighted voting method [19]	✔ Classification system based on two novel features and a weighted voting method
	✔ The proposed features are modulation spectral flatness measure (MSFF):
	✔ A measure used in digital signal processing to characterize an audio spectrum, where spectral flatness is typically measured in

Table 6.5 Machine learning techniques for music genre classification.—cont'd

Paper	Key points
	decibels and provides a way to quantify how a tone like a sound is as opposed to being noise-like
	Modulation spectral crest measure (MSCM):
	✔ Crest factor is a parameter of a waveform, such as alternating current or sound, showing the ratio of peak values to the effective value
	✔ In other words, crest factor indicates how extreme the peaks are in a waveform
	✔ The proposed weighted voting method determines a music genre by summarizing the classification results of consecutive time windows
	✔ Provides an accuracy of 76% for GTZAN dataset
Content analysis for audio classification and segmentation [20]	✔ They dealt with conversion of audio files into comma-separated values format for processing
	✔ They classified a sound into one of the three categories of speech, music, and environment sound
	✔ The classification is a two-step process

Continued

Table 6.5 Machine learning techniques for music genre classification.—cont'd	
Paper	**Key points**
	✔ A novel algorithm that is based on KNN and linear spectral pairs-vector quantization (LSP-VQ) has been developed ✔ The second step is to divide the non-speech class into music, environmental sounds, and silence with a rule-based classification method

FIGURE 6.13

Homepage: intelligent interface for online music genre classification.

FIGURE 6.14

Check genre page: intelligent interface for online music genre classification.

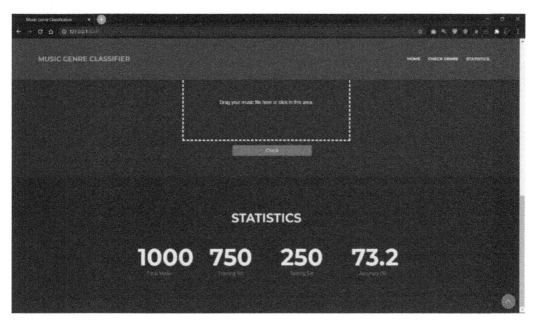

FIGURE 6.15

Statistics page: intelligent interface for online music genre classification.

Table 6.6 Testing the user interface of online music genre classification system.

Module name	Webpage	Test scenario	Expected result	Actual result	Pass/fail
Testing the user interface	Page 1: home page	Tab switching	The button when clicked will lead to the check genre page	The page then switches to the check genre page where the user would be able to classify the audio	Pass
	Page 2: check genre	Get audio	If user uploads a valid audio file, the webpage accepts the audio file	The webpage accepts a valid .wav audio file and the system extracts the file for classification	Pass
			If the user uploads an invalid file, the system should not accept the file	The webpage identifies the file format, rejects the file, and notifies the user that only .wav file type is allowed	Pass
		Displays result	Once the user has uploaded the valid audio file, the classification result, the genre of the audio clip, must be displayed	The file is extracted by the system, the features are then extracted that are used in classification, and the result is displayed to the user	Pass
	Page 3: statistics	Display statistics	Display the statistics to the user	Once the audio is classified, the details of the total dataset count, training and testing data, and the accuracy of the system are displayed to the user	Pass

6.4 Conclusions and future work

Intelligent interfaces play a vital role in recent innovations. The three different intelligent interfaces discussed in this chapter, namely, Tamil character recognition, online examination system, and online music genre classification gave a very clear insight of how ML techniques get integrated with the UI to efficiently handle tasks.

A lot of research works exist in the survey for handwritten Tamil character recognition. However, there is standard solution to identify all Tamil characters with reasonable accuracy. Various methods have been used in each phase of the recognition process. Challenges still prevail in the recognition of normal as well as abnormal writing, slanting characters, similar shaped characters, joined characters, curves, and so on during recognition process. The proposed system has projected various aspects of each phase of the Tamil character recognition process. This project mainly focuses on a particular part of Tamil characters (i.e., uyir eluthukkal). Coverage is not given for different writing styles and font size issues. The following key challenges can be further explored in the future. As a result, the proposed system has been found to yield the highest recognition accuracy of 95.3%. The handwritten Tamil character recognition system described in this paper will find potential applications in handwritten character recognition. The proposed architecture has shown enhanced performance in recognizing the Tamil character.

The proposed system (online examination system) reduces laborious manual work and automates the task. Various NLP techniques and methods have been used in each phase in this system. Challenges still prevail in the system like taking up a challenging question from a given document and evaluating the answer if the user has referred from another document rather than the given document. In this chapter, various aspects of each phase of the question and answer evaluation process are given. Understanding the given context conceptually by the system and taking up analytical questions based on the concept is the hardest task of NLP, and it is not covered in the proposed system. The proposed system has shown enhanced performance in making the question and answer evaluation.

The exponential growth in the internet and multimedia systems applications that categorize music based on genre has led us to develop a system for the task. The proposed system (online music genre classification) can help apps that organize and classify songs, albums, and artists into broader groups that share similar musical characteristics. Automatic analysis and classification of the music is one of the required components of such music information retrieval systems. The proposed system to classify music reduces laborious manual work and automates the task of classifying music. Hence, we have proposed a system covering the stated functionality with optimal accuracy. Various techniques have been employed in each phase in this system to classify the music. Challenges still prevail in the system like classifying a music genre that is new to the system and input file with more noise. The proposed system has shown enhanced performance in classifying music genres.

References

[1] Ian Sommerville, Software Engineering, ninth ed., Addison-Wesley, 2011.

[2] T. Mandel, The Elements of User Interface design, John Wiley & Sons, 1997.

[3] R. Pressman, B.R. Maxin, Software Engineering - A Practitioner's Approach, McGraw-Hill Education, 2014.

[4] H. Lieberman, User interface goals, AI opportunities, AI Mag. 30 (4) (2009).

[5] V. Bader, S. Kaiser, Algorithmic decision-making? The user interface and its role for human involvement in decisions supported by artificial intelligence, Special Issue Article Organization, SAGE publications 26 (5) (2019) 655–672.

[6] J.J. Dudley, P. Ola Kristensson, A review of user interface design for interactive machine learning, ACM Trans. Interac. Intell. Syst. 8 (2) (2018) 1–37.

[7] T.M. Mitchell, Machine Learning, first ed., McGraw-Hill International Editions Computer Science Series, 1997.

[8] B.R. Kavitha, C. Srimathi, Benchmarking on Offline Handwritten Tamil Character Recognition Using Convolutional Neural Networks", Journal of King Saud University-Computer and Information Sciences, 2019.

[9] M.A.R. Raj, S. Abirami, Structural representation-based off-line Tamil handwritten character recognition, Soft Comput. (2019) 1−26.

[10] V. Elakkiya, I. Muthumani, M. Jegajothi, Tamil text recognition using KNN classifier, Adv. Natural Appl. Sci. 11 (7) (2017) 41−46.

[11] S. Manisha, T.S. Sharmila, Effective Printed Tamil Text Segmentation and Recognition Using Bayesian Classifier, Computational Intelligence in Data Mining Springer, Singapore, 2017, pp. 729−738.

[12] M. Ramanan, A. Ramanan, E.Y.A. Charles, A hybrid decision tree for printed Tamil character recognition using SVMs, Fifteenth IEEE Int. Conf. Adv. ICT Emerg. Regions (ICTer) (2015) 176−181.

[13] P. Stephen, S. Jaganathan, March. Linear regression for pattern recognition, IEEE Int. Conf. Green Comput. Commun. Electrical Eng. (ICGCCEE) (2014) 1−6.

[14] R.M. Suresh, S. Arumugam, Fuzzy technique based recognition of handwritten characters, Image Vis Comput. 25 (2) (2007) 230−239.

[15] R.I. Gandhi, K. Iyakutti, An attempt to recognize handwritten Tamil character using Kohonen SOM, Int. J. Adv. Netw. Appl. 1 (3) (2009) 188−192.

[16] I. Das, B. Sharma, S.S. Rautaray, M. Pandey, An examination system automation using Natural Language processing, IEEE Int. Conf. Commun. Electr. Syst. (ICCES) (2019) 1064−1069.

[17] T.M. Tashu, J.P. Esclamado, T. Horvath, Intelligent On-Line Exam Management and Evaluation System, Springer International Conference on Intelligent Tutoring Systems, 2019, pp. 105−111.

[18] T. Patil, Automatic assessment of descriptive answers for online examination using semantic analysis, J. Gujarat Res. Soc. 21 (5) (2019) 413−419.

[19] Y. Kim, H. Lee, J. Shin, K. Jung, Improving neural question generation using answer separation, AAAI Conf. Artificial Intell. 33 (2019) 6602−6609.

[20] L.S. Riza, A.D. Pertiwi, E.F. Rahman, M. Munir, C.U. Abdullah, Question generator system of sentence completion in TOEFL using NLP and K-nearest neighbor, Indonesian J. Sci. Technol. 4 (2) (2019) 294−311.

[21] X. Lu, Learning to Generate Questions with Adaptive Copying Neural Networks, International Conference on Management of Data, 2019, pp. 1838−1840.

[22] V. Harrison, M. Walker, Neural Generation of Diverse Questions Using Answer Focus, Contextual and Linguistic Features, 2018 arXiv preprint arXiv:1809.02637.

[23] X. Dong, Y. Hong, X. Chen, W. Li, M. Zhang, Q. Zhu, Neural Question Generation with Semantics of Question Type, Springer International Conference on Natural Language Processing and Chinese Computing, 2018, pp. 213−223.

[24] S. Upadhyay, C. Nehete, V. Powar, J. Wadhwani, Checkpoint-an online descriptive answers grading tool, Int. J. Adv. Res. Comput. Sci. 8 (3) (2017).

[25] S. Subramanian, T. Wang, X. Yuan, S. Zhang, Y. Bengio, A. Trischler, Neural Models for Key Phrase Detection and Question Generation, 2017 arXiv preprint arXiv:1706.04560.

[26] P. Nikam, M. Shinde, R. Mahajan, S. Kadam, Automatic evaluation of descriptive answer using pattern matching algorithm, Int. J. Comput. Sci. Eng. 3 (1) (2015) 69−70.

[27] B. Kaiche, S. Kalan, S. More, L. Shelukar, Online descriptive examination and assessment system, Int. J. Emerg. Technol. Adv. Eng. 4 (3) (2014) 660−664.

[28] D.V. Paul, J.D. Pawar, Use of Syntactic Similarity Based Similarity Matrix for Evaluating Descriptive Answer, IEEE Sixth International Conference on Technology for Education, 2014.

[29] K. Meena, L. Raj, Evaluation of the Descriptive Type Answers Using Hyperspace Analog to Language and Self-Organizing Map, IEEE International Conference on Computational Intelligence and Computing Research, 2014, pp. 1−5.

[30] P. Kudi, A. Manekar, K. Daware, T. Dhatrak, Online Examination with short text matching, IEEE Global Conf. Wireless Comput. Networking (GCWCN) (2014) 56−60.

[31] A. Kaur, M. Sasikumar, S. Nema, S. Pawar, Algorithm for Automatic evaluation of single sentence descriptive answer, Int. J. Inventive Eng. Sci. 19 (2013) 112−121.

[32] M. Agarwal, P. Mannem, Automatic gap-fill question generation from text books, in: Proceedings of the Sixth Workshop on Innovative Use of NLP for Building Educational Applications, 2011, pp. 56−64.

[33] A. Hoshino, H. Nakagawa, A real-time multiple-choice question generation for language testing: a preliminary study, in: Second Workshop on Building Educational Applications Using NLP, 2005, pp. 17−20.

[34] R. Dubey, R.R.S. Makwana, Comparative analysis of computer assisted valuation of descriptive answers using WEKA with different classification algorithms, Int. J. Comput. Sci. Eng. 4 (2017) 5−10.

[35] A.K. Ghavat, B.G. Tekade, V.S. Bhute, M.D. Chikhalkar, P. Vijaykar, AI based symmetric answer evaluation system for descriptive answering, Int. Res. J. Modernization Eng. Technol. Sci. 2 (3) (2020) 449−455.

Further reading

[1] M. Wu, X. Liu, A Double Weighted KNN Algorithm and its Application in the Music Genre Classification, in: 6th IEEE International Conference on Dependable Systems and Their Applications (DSA), 2020, pp. 335−340.

[2] B. Liang, M. Gu, Music genre classification using transfer learning, in: IEEE Conference on Multimedia Information Processing and Retrieval (MIPR), 2020, pp. 392−393.

[3] S.S. Ghosal, I. Sarkar, Novel approach to music genre classification using clustering augmented learning method (CALM), AAAI Spring Symposium: Combining Machine Learning Knowledge Eng. 1 (2020).

[4] S. Vishnupriya, K. Meenakshi, Automatic music genre classification using convolution neural network, in: IEEE International Conference on Computer Communication and Informatics (ICCCI), 2018, pp. 1−4.

[5] G. Jawaherlalnehru, S. Jothilakshmi, Music genre classification using deep neural networks, Int. J. Scientific Res. Sci. Eng. Technol. 4 (4) (2018) 935.

[6] R.J.M. Quinto, R.O. Atienza, N.M.C. Tiglao, Jazz music sub- genre classification using deep learning, in: IEEE TENCON Region 10 Conference, 2017, pp. 3111−3116.

[7] W. Zhang, W. Lei, X. Xu, X. Xing, Improved Music Genre Classification with Convolutional Neural Networks, Interspeech, 2016, pp. 3304−3308.

[8] I.Y. Jeong, K. Lee, Learning Temporal Features Using a Deep Neural Network and its Application to Music Genre Classification, Ismir, 2016, pp. 434−440.

[9] A.R. Rajanna, K. Aryafar, A. Shokoufandeh, R. Ptucha, Deep neural networks: a case study for music genre classification, in: IEEE 14th International Conference on Machine Learning and Applications (ICMLA), 2015, pp. 655−660.

[10] M. Haggblade, Y. Hong, K. Kao, Music Genre Classification. Department of Computer Science, vol 131, Stanford University, 2011, p. 132.

[11] Y. Yaslan, Z. Cataltepe, Audio music genre classification using different classifiers and feature selection methods, in: IEEE 18th International Conference on Pattern Recognition (ICPR'06), vol 2, 2006, pp. 573−576.

[12] A.L. Koerich, C. Poitevin, Combination of homogeneous classifiers for musical genre classification, in: IEEE International Conference on Systems, Man and Cybernetics, vol 1, 2005, pp. 554−559.

[13] A. Meng, P. Ahrendt, J. Larsen, Improving music genre classification by short time feature integration, in: (ICASSP'05) IEEE International Conference on Acoustics, Speech, and Signal Processing, vol 5, 2005, pp. v−497.

[14] T. Li, M. Ogihara, Q. Li, A comparative study on content-based music genre classification, in: 26th Annual International ACM SIGIR Conference on Research and Development in Information Retrieval, 2003, pp. 282–289.

[15] G. Tzanetakis, P. Cook, Musical genre classification of audio signals, IEEE Trans. Speech Audio Process. 10 (5) (2002) 293–302.

[16] H. Bahuleyan, Music Genre Classification Using Machine Learning Techniques, 2018 arXiv preprint arXiv: 1804.01149.

[17] T.L. Li, A.B. Chan, A.H. Chun, Automatic musical pattern feature extraction using convolutional neural network, Genre 10 (2010).

[18] A. Paradzinets, H. Harb, L. Chen, Multiexpert System for Automatic Music Genre Classification, Teknik Rapor, Ecole Centrale de Lyon, Departement MathInfo, 2009.

[19] D. Jang, M. Jin, C.D. Yoo, Music genre classification using novel features and a weighted voting method, in: IEEE International Conference on Multimedia and Expo, 2008, pp. 1377–1380.

[20] L. Lu, H.J. Zhang, H. Jiang, Content analysis for audio classification and segmentation, IEEE Trans. Speech Audio Process. 10 (7) (2002) 504–516.

Uses of artificial intelligence with human-computer interaction in psychology

Achyut Tiwari[a], Aryan Chugh[a] and Aman Sharma

Department of Computer Science & Engineering and Information Technology, Jaypee University of Information Technology, Solan, Himachal Pradesh, India

7.1 Introduction

Human history is an interesting tale of how technologies have evolved and enhanced our abilities and capacities of how we conduct ourselves. The introduction of the wheel has transformed our ability to carry things; changes in record keeping and writing tools have significantly affected the human ability to recall things. We may think of artificial intelligence (AI) and machine learning (ML) as a new technical foundation that can be used to create new tools, and this transforms the kind of tools that can be created [1]. The tools like human—computer interaction (HCI) and AI can be seen in our surroundings, and it is prevalent that they have changed a massive part of how humans function. The innovation of these tools is seen across all the disciplines. User interfaces are the portal through which we interact with technology, be it something as simple as a phone or as complicated as a supercomputer. Building used-centered systems is a priority so that technology can be used by any person. We have also discussed various avenues on how the internet has evolved through all these years, from a military defense system to civilian pockets [2].

7.1.1 Motivation

Social media is affecting our decision-making abilities during this pandemic in terms of how human and computers interact. Various human decisions are driven by AI-run programs, e.g., the repetitive ads that drive our decisions. This model is one of the most used advertising business models around the world. These factors motivated us to write about the application of AI and HCI. Also, we have shown how AI algorithms shape human consciousness. As web 3.0 is arriving, that motivated us to discuss Web 1.0 and Web 2.0 and how they evolved with time.

7.1.2 Contribution

Effects of advanced technologies in human psychology are discussed.

---

[a]These authors contributed equally to the work.

Innovations in Artificial Intelligence and Human-Computer Interaction in the Digital Era. https://doi.org/10.1016/B978-0-323-99891-8.00003-6

Contribution of AI and HCI in democratization of information technology and consideration of AI and human rights.

Discussion pertaining the importance of HCI and design by making a case of the Three Mile Island accident in which its design contributed in a major way to near nuclear catastrophe.

Discussed how HCI as a field contributed in developing a major industry standard practice: A/B testing and HCI.

Elaborated about how intelligence amplification (IA) can complement AI and HCI to decrease the gap of decision-making by machines in comparison to humans.

7.2 Preliminaries

In the first section of the chapter, we have discussed how HCI and AI shape our human behavior. We have also explained it through the lens of psychology. In the latter part of the first section, we have discussed how AI will affect human rights and how we can regulate and shape it so that it can only be used for human transcendence. In the second section of the chapter, we have discussed how we can build technologies using used-centered design development (UCDD). In the third section of the chapter, we have discussed all the tools of usability engineering and verification. We have also discussed the rigorous processes of how designs are developed. In the latter part of the third section, we have discussed why design is important and how it almost caused a nuclear holocaust. In the last section of the chapter, we have discussed the democratization of information technology and the rise of technology. We have also addressed the implications of Web 2.0 and how social media shapes behavior.

7.3 Role of HCI and AI in psychology

HCI is a multidisciplinary field concerned with the theory, design, implementation, and assessment of how people use and interact with computer devices and interfaces. HCI has gained prominence in recent years as embedded devices, computers, and technology have become frequent features of our lives and are being used in almost every field, e.g., economics and human factors, sociology, ethnography, etc.

The field of psychology, similar to the scope of other areas, has been affected by the insurgency in advanced innovation in HCI and AI, with the field of psychology presently immovably settled just as proceeded and arising work on AI drives answers for emotional wellness. AI and HCI are broad terms, including a range of techniques and ways to deal with the creation of computational frameworks that perform psychological cycles generally for people, like learning, interacting with machines, problem-solving and the capacity to reason, design acknowledgment, generalization, and pattern recognition [3,4].

So, the prospect that psychology cannot be computerized is out of date. Psychologists dread that these HCI and AI-based master frameworks will supplant them [4,5]. The indistinguishable responses have been experienced in the past among medical experts when the principal robotized examined system was attempted. Although now human behavior-based models have not yet arrived at that period of execution successfully, the analysts are on the right track to show up.

The HCI and AI techniques used to treat psychological instability mainly involve the use of computer processing technologies, such as data mining for significant diseases, facial and body language processing, and deep learning algorithms [6]. AI can utilize extensive quantitative information to break down and clarify individuals' physical and mental aspects and reclassify the comprehension of psychological sickness. What is more, the advancing technologies of HCI and AI can make foresight models and tools to distinguish and forestall the danger of psychological instability [6]. Further, we will be focusing on one of the main ways AI and HCI are being applied in psychology.

7.3.1 Chatbots

A chatbot is an HCI and AI program that can imitate a discussion with humans in natural language through voice orders or text visits or both [7]. They are also known as virtual assistants that understand human capabilities. Chatbots in psychology give steady support to humans, engaging them with discussion on occasion when they feel low or depressed.

7.3.1.1 History of chatbots

The origins of chatbots are fundamentally connected to psychology. The first-ever human—computer interface chatbot was developed by the Massachusetts Institute of Technology's computer scientist Joseph Weizenbaum in the year 1966 [3,7—9], and it was called ELIZA. Although the appropriate responses are predefined, this robot passes on the inclination that it is fit for understanding the client.

Parry, the second chatbot, was made at Stanford University by the psychiatrist Kenneth Colby in the year 1972. It was a chatbot intended to mimic a paranoid schizophrenic [7,9,10]. In the year 1988, Jabberwacky was acquainted as the first chatbot imitating the human voice [7]. Following Jabberwacky's strides, another chatbot was created in 1992 called "Dr. Sbaitso." The chatbot had a user interface where Dr. Sbaitso reenacted the reactions of a psychologist.

ALICE (artificial linguistic internet computer entity), the most famous chatbot of the 20th century, was created in 1995 by Richard Wallace. ALICE [7,9] is an open-source natural language AI chatbot [10]. It was a three times winner of the Loebner Prize, an honor given to the most human-like artificial intelligence. Inspired by ALICE, different chatbots were made including Apple's Siri, Woebot, and many more.

Chatbots are used for psychological treatment.

7.3.1.2 Woebot

Woebot is a chat interface founded in the year 2017 by Dr. Alison Darcy. Woebot screens the perspectives of users and gives a setting wherein users can impart their insights, musings, and sentiments through supportive and helpful conversations [11]. It additionally gives projects of psychoeducation for coping with stress.

It is based on a foundation of CBT (cognitive behavioral therapy), a process of psychotherapy that can help users with administering emotional conditions by altering the way in which they meditate and behave by empowering patients to reevaluate their pessimistic musings into optimistic ones [11].

The app utilizes a blend of natural language processing, a sense of humor, painstakingly developed composition, and psychological expertise. Woebot communicates with users about their mindset and thoughts and sends audios and other significant apparatuses depending upon the user's current state of mind, relevance, and mood. The Woebot study shows the present chatbots can enhance similar standards patients learn in psychologists' workplaces.

7.3.1.3 Wysa

Jo Aggarwal and Ramakant Vempati founded Wysa in the year 2015. Wysa is an AI-based chatbot that is emotionally intelligent. Wysa professes to assist users in dealing with their feelings and contemplations through various apparatuses and procedures, like proof-based CBT and dialectical behavior therapy, with instructions for meditation, yoga, and breathing [12]. It includes a mood tracker and can instantiate if you are feeling down.

Wysa prompts you to take a depression test and may suggest looking for proficient assistance, contingent upon the outcomes. Individuals regularly do not understand how widely inclusive and dependable their emotional wellness side effects are; however, Wysa could feature that information and cause people to understand it is an ideal opportunity to make a conclusive move.

7.3.1.4 Pacifica

The Pacifica application was founded in 2014, as asserted by maker Pacifica Labs. Pacifica is an application that can help address tension issues dependent on CBT-based standards. Instruments and exercises include relaxation, unwinding, state of mind, and health-tracking tools [13].

Pacifica's mediation tool incorporates over 30 sound activities, including profound breathing and muscle unwinding. The sound and text diaries guarantee to assist clients with comprehension, challenge their deduction examples, and direct them toward more uplifting outlooks. The well-being tracker screens propensities that trigger tension like rest, caffeine, exercise, liquor, and so on; in light of these, it assists clients with laying out objectives that can uplift their mood [13].

It gives the patients admittance to their community of companions to share stories, tips, and backing. Patients could likewise survey information from those activities together and use it to change their treatment plan. This incorporated methodology is one way Pacifica wants to differentiate from the increasingly long list of emotional well-being engaged applications that have dispatched in recent years, including Talkspace, Happify, Lantern, Joyable, and Ginger.io [7].

7.3.1.5 Advantages and limitations

One of the most significant benefits is that while communicating with bots, individuals hope to have more power than the opposite side, to feel they can handle the conversation and lead the discussion to whatever topics they feel like. Unwittingly this makes them have a positive outlook toward themselves and have a sense of control over their lives. At the end of the day, we have a hidden desire to hold at least one power-driven relationship in our life to support our self-esteem. Chatbots are the best contender for this relationship.

To launch a propensity change, in any case, chatbots feel more accessible than cooperating with psychologists, as there is more control in the beginning and halting of a discussion. Eventually, this equivalent benefit is additionally their ruin since being in charge consistently can make genuinely moving your mentality somewhat harder.

The internet inventions have often been assessed and are viewed as a medium liberated from spot and time. Subsequently, people can access bots irrespective of place and time. They could help decrease treatment boundaries and grow the accessibility of care. Various studies have shown that these inventions, frequently utilizing cognitive behavioral strategies, are tantamount to their viability to traditional in-person psychotherapy. Psychological problems, for example, anxiety, uneasiness, and depression, are now being diagnosed, treated, and addressed to the masses through this method [14].

A 24/7 response system maintained by chatbots brings consistent correspondence as you need support at any second [14]. Additionally, chatbots can address countless requests or inquiries simultaneously with instant responses though a psychologist that can focus on each client in turn and answer one query at a second. Another advantage of a chatbot is that it maintains the record of the conversation, and a patient can return to that conversation at whatever point they prefer; responses given by the chatbot can be challenged by the user.

In particular, chatbots may support the association by the individuals who have generally been hesitant to look for mental health advice due to stigmatization or bad experiences with professionals, negative mentalities toward psychotherapeutic and pharmacologic treatment choices, or maybe the absence of understanding of their sickness [16]. In addition, chatbots are intended to be non-judgmental and subsequently more merciful toward patient concerns. This could motivate people to unhesitatingly open up.

Some concerns regarding chatbots include universality of application, absence of normalization and monitoring, overdependence on the chatbots, and absence of genuine mental problems. Numerous specialists said that chatbots could not effectively deal with each one of the requirements of patients or show human feelings [15]. A few professionals additionally said that chatbots for medical care may represent a danger to patients in the event that they diagnose themselves too often and if something goes wrong with diagnoses.

Bots that cannot serve simple client queries fail to add esteem regardless of whether they are 24/7 accessible. The principal issue is the manner by which and how well chatbots can comprehend and tackle client issues. At last, featuring all-day accessibility can have kickback when due to maintenance or security issues, bots are not working. To communicate with a chatbot, you need to have a computer or cell phone and also an active internet connection. Along these lines, utilizing a chatbot for certain areas of the populace may not be an ideal alternative [15]. Additionally and comparable to that, one should be associated with the internet, and cooperation with the device is dependent upon potential association issues, which can contrarily influence the client experience.

Chatbots cannot distinguish between the good and the bad as they lack decision-making abilities and have no feelings, and they cannot identify with any low circumstance. Having no feelings implies a chatbot can never establish a connection with the client [17]. Chatbots without notion investigation or analysis information will manage the clients with a certain goal in mind independent of the talk stream. Thus, a few clients like to close the bot!

Despite all the advantages and limitations, several psychologists have predicted that chatbots might soon take over a considerable portion of the work of human healthcare providers [18]. Regardless, the best way chatbots can be applied is to assist specialists rather than supersede them. Chatbots are practical to run and can mechanize dreary authoritative undertakings, accordingly liberating time for psychologists to give better caliber, personalized, and sympathetic consideration to their patients. This exploration establishes the framework for future examinations on the components affecting psychologists' and physicians' reception of chatbots. Furnishing doctors with proof by putting together examinations with respect to the benefits and limitations of this arising technology will assist with educating them on the most appropriate use to supplement their training instead of hindering their work.

Numerous organizations' research and development centers are focusing on instructing chatbots to act as humans do. They are acquiring the skills and stuff of humans, and this will expand the pace of fulfillment. Chatbots will want to investigate data, settle on their own choices, and give suggestions in the coming years. This will empower individuals to resolve their problems and issues efficiently, viably, and productively.

7.3.2 Cyberpsychology

As technology progresses and increasingly keeps on influencing our methods of thinking and reasoning, psychologists have chosen to center their endeavors in a new field called cyberpsychology. The term "cyber" is derived from the phrase "cyberspace," which is the study of the operation of control and communication, whereas psychology is the study of the mind and behavior [19,20].

Cyberpsychology, also called internet psychology, digital psychology, or web psychology, is a creative field that incorporates all mental marvels related to or influenced by arising technology [19]. Also, cyberpsychology contemplates and studies the character advancement, addictions of technology, the connections we create over the internet, and personality developed through these technologies.

How has the interaction process changed over time due to technology?

The internet has conceivably affected numerous parts of our lives, for example, our relationships with loved ones, the manner by which we lead our connections, schoolwork, or career, the ways in which we act in gatherings and socialize, the development and appearance of generalizations, and our thought process and emotions among many other things [21].

As the internet has become a significant part of one's life, numerous individuals have started looking up to these technologies as a rescuer, a companion, and wellspring of coping pressure. Due to this, there is a lot of change in the daily routine and the activities in which one participates [22]. Interpersonal interaction sites like Facebook, Twitter, Instagram, or Snapchat have taken over the communication process with messages or video chats that were done in person and the conveyance of emotions was face to face. Rather than holding a book to read it, one now prefers to read a digital book on phones or PCs [23]. Indeed, the learning process has been changed, and education is becoming increasingly dependent on innovations and with instruction being given on modern technologies to disseminate information.

The cyberspace in which humans are engaging themselves derives a lot of pleasure from them as it gives a platform to express their thoughts and feelings, whether they are sad or happy, and they receive reactions, appreciations, and comments and feel satisfied. Since the youngsters have a perceptible presence on several social networks and want to maintain their privacy, they try not to get connected with the older generation via online media as they feel that getting associated with them will offer the older generation a chance to observe what is happening and welcome pointless interruption from them [22].

The internet is crowded by all ages as its simplicity of utilization and navigation make it a virtual domain. The simplicity of utilization and navigation makes the web a virtual area crowded by individuals, all things considered. There are numerous social networking sites and technologies to which individuals are continually snared and hooked up. Individuals also likewise utilize the technology and internet to benefit different facilities. From reading online books to online shopping, buying tickets on the internet is possible as it helps them in settling on their choices while sitting at home [22].

7.3.2.1 Addiction to internet and technologies

Addiction to the internet and advanced technologies has been portrayed as "inordinate, poorly or ineffectively controlled distraction, desires or behaviors with respect to computer use and access that prompts debilitation, distress or trouble." Moreover, addiction to technologies and the internet is inversely identified with the quality of life [19]. The overuse of these technologies is quickly turning into a sensitive issue.

Needless to say, youths invest an enormous amount of time and energy on the web and the new technologies without doing anything specific, conveying this propensity and intimidation for them. Overuse of these webs and technologies is prompting a few issues like wretchedness, anxiety disorders, social detachment, lack of sleep, low self-esteem, dietary problems, and nervousness issues [24].

Individuals feel upset and inadequate in their lives after scrolling on social media and seeing the good happenings in the lives of others. Thus, this, in turn, affects an individual's mental health, and they continuously begin retreating from other social activities, consequently feeling segregated, isolated, and upset. Using the advanced AI- and HCI-based technologies, people start depending upon them, and when they are not available, they feel annoyed and powerless, craving for them, and thus it decreases their level of tolerance [19]. Furthermore, individuals start forming cocoons around themselves as a feeling of antagonism inundates them. Progressively, fixation of these sets in bringing forth a few issues like sleep problems or disorders and so on. Individuals using these technologies excessively start neglecting their personal life and appear to have mental preoccupation, mood-modifying experiences, or escapism.

In outrageous cases, it is not easy to tackle the situations of depression or social detachment, and one has to consult a cyberpsychologist to get rid of these issues [22]. The increasing frequency of such cases has expanded the interest of specialists related to mental problems or psychological disorders, consequently making the field of cyberpsychology exceptionally pertinent in the modern era.

7.3.2.2 Online behavior, identity, and comparison
People behave differently on the internet than they behave face to face or in physical realms, and it is seen pretty commonly nowadays. A few users attempt to conceal their genuine personality/identity behind the anonymity of an online stage, and cyberpsychology sees the virtual world as an augmentation of the person's mystic world. Hence, it endeavors to distinguish the explanations for online ways of life just as online connections.

These days, people start comparing their life with others as they go through the posts and stories of others on Twitter, Instagram, and so on; this brings down their confidence and feelings of self-worth, especially when they see others glad, cheerful, and doing unique activities in their life. This comparison builds fretfulness continuously, and consequently, these social media identifications seem to misuse an Achilles' heel of human nature [19]. It is relatively seen that individuals may have thousands of friends in the virtual world, but in real life, it is improbable for an individual to have that many strong connections, and this creates a social detachment for them. At times the virtual environment creates social isolation and disconnect instead of creating a social connectedness [19].

7.3.2.3 Negative relationships and online vulnerability
Excess use of social media results in adverse relationship outcomes, and these connections are, in fact, interceded by social media—related clashes. Moreover, increasing rates of break-ups and divorces have been connected with social networking sites when jealousy comes in when their partner gets more popular on social media than him/her and also due to the comments, likes, or reactions to the opposite gender's posts or stories on social networking sites [19]. There is an increment in the number of cases identified with accomplice's monitoring and surveillance on social media to cope and adapt to the vulnerability of speculated delightful relations.

Online vulnerability is characterized as inconvenient activities, for example, cyberbullying, abuse of individuals and burglary and misuse of their information, and openness to improper information and content that can seriously affect a person's psychological, physical, and emotional well-being. Individuals are unintentionally becoming susceptible to online threats by sharing personal photos, information, locations, and videos on online platforms [25].

7.3.2.4 Phubbing

The omnipresence of phones and people using them in between real-time conversations and ignoring their companions is known as phubbing [26]. Phubbing is derived from two words: phone and snubbing [25]. Phubbing has become a standard among the younger generation, although its results are inimical to perceived communication quality and relationship satisfaction due to inducing excessive, uncontrolled internet and technologies use. It is also seen as aggravating and impolite behavior and can cause serious emotional, psychological, and behavioral debilitations in communications.

7.3.2.5 Fear of missing out

Adolescence is a critical time of advancement and development, wherein the adolescent embarks on the journey toward adulthood amidst physical and cognitive development. Rightly called the period of "storm and stress" [25], youths experience an increased sense of belongingness, endorsement, and appreciation, particularly from their companions. Also, they will, in general, separate away from their folks, getting into successive struggles, and these conflicts should be handled reasonably and sensibly as it is a significant piece of parent–child relationships. Contrarily, floating toward their companions is common, looking for acknowledgment in the group of friends, peer affiliations, prominence, popularity, and so on. Conversely, the dread of being forgotten about or the fear of missing out (FOMO) develops anxiety, misery, and depression among young people. This decreases self-esteem, and the main cause is the overuse of technology and social media.

This dread includes a fanatical need to give steady status updates on social media accounts and not access the trending technology. Also, this dread creates a habit of repetitively checking the messages even though they have not received any and obsessively checking the sites to get an update about others' status and posts, imagining that others inside their group of friends are archiving rewarding encounters and experiences in their lives, while one is being left out [19]. FOMO has additionally been demonstrated to be a mediator between mental requirements and social media engagement, as an indicator of internet and technology habits.

For most FOMO-prone humans, their life spins around comments and likes, the latest technologies, and following news feeds, which evidently influences their emotional wellness and mental health. Individuals get into serious depression or a state of distress if they receive negative remarks/responses from their companions or have the experience of being ignored. Additionally, spending too much energy and time on social media and technologies deviates their psyches from their actual duties and responsibilities, such as scholastic involvements, investing in interpersonal social relationships, co-curricular cooperation, and so on [25]. Various studies have uncovered that people who experience shortfalls in fundamental psychological necessities like less self-viability, low satisfaction, and diminished self-rule and relatedness exhibit a more significant level of FOMO.

Even during bedtime, most people keep their phones and gadgets by their bedsides, so they can immediately reach and use them due to FOMO and to stay connected with their virtual friends and groups. This prompts deficient and upset sleeping hours, delayed sleep onset, and in outrageous cases, sleep deprivation [25]. Behaviorally, FOMO prompts investing more time in technologies, which defers sleep schedule, while hidden psychological worries before rest further defer sleep onset.

Nowadays people are in a constant state of the cyber matrix and have manifested behavioral traits of anonymity, online disinhibition, and immersion in a virtual context. Online disinhibition means that people do a lot of stuff under the context of online anonymity that they will not do in the real world. As seen, today's generation is overly immersed in cyber entities at the moment in terms of turning up at the dining table, during lectures, walking, before sleep, or after they wake up with the mobile phones and advanced technologies; then wait till the day when the next generation of kids will turn with full helmets (hmd: head mounted display) where they will not only be psychologically immersed in the space but also physically immersed in the space. So, it is important to use the principles of a discipline like cyberpsychology to extrapolate learnings and figure out as humans that how humans are going to engage will be all things cyber going forward.

7.3.3 Intelligence amplification

Before the introduction of AI in the 1950s and 1960s, computer pioneers and cybernetics proposed the idea of IA [27,28]. The effective utilization of technology and its innovation in expanding human insight is referred to as IA [27,29,30].

IA is often cited alongside AI, but both concepts are considerably and quite different from each other.

The sole purpose of building AI is to make a standalone system capable of processing information and data with human-like intelligence as a self-ruling, autonomous, and innovative framework [27,29,30].

Whereas, IA is intended to complement and enhance human insight and to broaden the data-handling capacities of the human psyche or ability in some way. IA has one major edge over AI. AI endeavors to assemble intelligence and insight from scratch, while IA expands on human knowledge, which has advanced for a long period [29]. Many experts view that IA has been around from the time people initially started to communicate.

IA is also called enhanced intelligence, cognitive augmentation, assistive intelligence, or machine-augmented intelligence [30]. IA empowers us to upgrade our efficiency, imagination, knowledge, intelligence, proficiency, and understanding.

IA focuses on assisting ML technologies. IA works with both ML and the human brain in tandem. IA intends to make the working environment more effective, productive, and useful in association with humans to help with new disclosures and critical thinking. AI, on the other hand, is unique in itself because it looks to sidestep humans inside and out [27].

William Ross Ashby was the one who referred to amplifying intelligence in 1956 in his book *Introduction to Cybernetics* [29,31]. He claims that the intelligential power is comparable to the force of appropriate choice, i.e., the insight of critical thinking is refined by augmenting and enlarging the power of choice.

Another great thinker in cyberpsychology is a professor called J. C. R. Licklider who wrote a brilliant paper called "Man-computer symbiosis" and discussed the symbiotic relationship between man and technology. He claims that the essence of cyberpsychology is tech and humans coming together. He contends that choices ought to be made under the collaboration of humans and machines rather than relying upon the foreordained programs, particularly concerning complex circumstances. Because of the way that either computers or humans, two unique entities, play out certain errands better than the other, J. C. R. Licklider recommends framing the elements of computers and humans in a harmonious association and symbiotic partnership [31]. All in all, the symbiotic relationship is to permit the two computers and humans to zero in on the undertakings that they are unrivaled in as humans are predominant in laying out objectives, deciding models, calculating speculations, performing assessments, and taking care of vulnerabilities. Anyhow, human capacities are restricted in adapting to issues at scale, volume, and computation. Henceforth, computers are needed to help humans with formed, ongoing reasoning and real-time thinking as far as proficient.

IA has not been a broadly perceived subject even though it has been around for a long time. With frameworks like HoloLens using AI to boost IA, IA will now be able to be unequivocally evolve to be quicker than was conceivable before [27,28].

One of IA's characteristics is that IA enhances human knowledge in managing exceptional and extraordinary situations and insights to make conclusive resolutions. By implementing the IA with the ongoing technologies, AI, in particular, the gap of understanding and decision-making between humans and machines will be closed. Also, HCI has still not taken a definite shape and is still malleable, and the repercussions of these changes are affecting the uses of AI and IA respectively.

IA permits innovation to address standard principles that can be arranged, executed, and codified autonomously. IA will empower machines not only to think like humans but also to understand their emotions and process feelings. Implementation of this technology will, essentially, provide everyone with a personal therapist as well as a close friend in which to confide. During the age of technology, where humans have grown apart, everyone will actually have a virtual companion with whom they would be able to share their thoughts and emotions, which would be understood, accepted, and reciprocated.

Also, thinking about usability interface design, it is designed to be rewarding, engaging, and seductive for normal populations, but nobody thought about deviant abnormal and vulnerable populations. As the technology is propelling, the day is not that far that we can see IA assisting with enhancing the innovation for those who are have underlying conditions.

7.3.4 Physiological impacts of COVID-19

Due to pandemics like COVID-19, there are many physiologic impacts on the human body [32,33]. We have seen various research works pertaining to the physiologic aspects of pandemics like COVID-19 and Middle East respiratory syndrome outbreak [34]. Highly distressed people's mental health risks are heightened when they have a low overall stress resilience and other risk factors, such as a general proclivity for psychological discomfort and poor self-control [35,36]. Early identification of these mental disorders can help the individual and prevent the development of serious illnesses such as PTSD and suicidal behavior. Meanwhile, the ability to predict mental disorders is difficult because of the inherent nature of human subjectivity. In the present times, we have a great impact of digital psychiatry, ML algorithms and applied AI [37–40]. In Ćosić et al. [41], we see a methodology by which the researchers determine mental health disorders induced by COVID-19 among healthcare workers. The researchers have used a five-phased method that includes objective assessment of the intensity of healthcare workers' stress exposure during COVID pandemic in Phase 1, subjective assessment through a custom questionnaire in Phase 2, Phase 3 involved in designing and developing unique stimulation paradigms, Phase 4 involved with computing neurophysiological features based on stimulation responses, and Phase 5 involved with statistical and ML data analysis.

The data used to train the models can only be as good as the AI and ML technology, which is significantly vital in mental health diagnosis. For most classification or prediction problems arising from the field of mental health, labels are most likely still not well described enough to successfully train an algorithm. Data-driven AI technology supporting mental health practitioners in more objectively characterizing mental diseases is one possible outcome of this labeling issue [41]. When it comes to identifying persons who are especially vulnerable, including neurophysiologic characteristics is likely to provide more information and improve dependability. Such attempts are consistent with the growing literature on the use of AI techniques to the prognosis of chronic mental diseases, which began with self-report predictor factors [42,43] but has since expanded to include speech features and other biomarkers [44,45]. These initiatives should make it easier for mental health providers to make more objective diagnoses than the DSM-5 currently allows.

7.3.5 AI and human rights

Throughout history, we as a civilization and now nation-states have come across many problems, and as the species of problem solvers, we have found suitable solutions by experimenting across various fields. Over the course of the past 80 years, we have been working on AI, and we have seen how AI can be used in different fields and can impact humans in a positive way and vice versa.

We as stakeholders, users, and developers possess a moral responsibility to make sure that technology like AI should be used for the welfare of human society.

In United Nations policy documents, there is evidence of international coverage of legal and human rights concerns [46]. There are many issues of consideration for AI and human rights, and some are as follows.

7.3.5.1 Lack of algorithmic transparency

There have been cases of people being denied employment, loans, being placed on no-fly lists, or being denied benefits without their knowledge "why that happened other than the decision was processed through some software" [47]. Large multinational companies process resumes and work feedback through which an AI software decides which employee company should drop to facilitate monetary and efficiency benefits, and the question arises at times, "is it fair to have decisions of this magnitude made by a software?" There are several proposed solutions that can be followed to solve this problem around the globe. Each option will address a different aspect of algorithmic transparency and accountability.

1. Awareness raising in education, promoting watchdogs and whistleblowers,
2. Accountability in public sector use of algorithmic decision-making,
3. Legal liability and regulatory oversights by governing bodies,
4. Global coordination for algorithmic governance.

AI is a tool for humanity. It is a universal tool that can be used in both human-centric or in destructive ways. We will discuss what sort of threats AI poses to humans and how we can build and regulate a better human-centered AI.

7.3.5.2 Cybersecurity vulnerabilities

Cybersecurity vulnerabilities pose a greater threat than others because they often come to light when the damage has been done. Working on better cybersecurity is a big issue; we often see big bounties to crack into an multinational company's system so that the corporates can build a robust system. Building robust security should be a priority for every organization; the organization can set up red teams so that they can encounter real-time threats.

7.3.5.3 Unfairness, bias, and discrimination

The EU Agency for Fundamental Rights published a focused report that illustrates the risk for algorithmic discrimination against persons and states that "the principle of non-discrimination, as enshrined in Article 21 of the Charter of Fundamental Rights of the European Union, needs to be taken into account when applying algorithms to everyday life" (FRA, 2018). Similarly, we have seen at times, AI is used in image processing and marks people with non-White color as monkeys. Linking biases in social datasets can be exacerbated by how data is gathered and sampled, as well as how links are defined, influencing the reported features of a number of network-based user variables, such as their correspondence within a social network [46]. Instances of occurring biases are prevalent in nature as AI and ML algorithms are trained on small data sets.

Various proposals have been made around the world in order to address these threats and issues. One Institute of Electrical and Electronics Engineers ethics-related standard (under development as part of the IEEE Global Initiative on Ethics of Autonomous and Intelligent Systems) is the IEEE P7003 Standard for Algorithmic Bias Considerations, which focuses on providing individuals or organizations creating algorithmic systems with a development framework to avoid unjustified, unintended, and inappropriately differential outcomes for users [48].

7.3.5.4 Lack of contestability

"A satisfactory standard of contestability will be imperative in case of threat to individual dignity and fundamental rights" and "the 'human element' of judgment is, at least for some types of decisions, an irreducible aspect of legitimacy in that reviewability and contestability are seen as the concomitant of the rule of law and thus, crucial prerequisites of democratic governance" [49].

Contestability by design is to make sure that rights of the decision are based totally on automated processing as a necessity at each level of an AI system's life cycle.

7.3.5.5 Intellectual property issues

Intellectual property rights are part of the Universal Declaration of Human Rights (UDHR, Article 27). AI raises various intellectual property prospects: for example, who owns AI-generated work or inventions? Who owns the dataset from which AI learns? Who should be liable for creativity and innovation generated by AI?

There is no universal precedent for computer-generated works. There are issues that are not addressed yet, and it will be too late to set a precedent because of the basic nature of technology, which is exponential in terms of growth.

7.3.5.6 Privacy and data protection issues

AI poses a great threat to the data protection rights of individuals such as the right of access to personal data. Individuals are granted very little access to how their data will be used; every day, individuals accept hundreds of terms and conditions and cookies. Privacy and data protection laws do not address all AI issues. In the speedily changing AI, it is difficult to understand the scope of data protection laws. Anticipating the future impact of a growing technology is out of scope for the majority of lawmakers; dealing with randomness in this aspect of regulation is what makes it a difficult task [51].

7.3.5.7 Liability for damage

The deployment of AI technologies may cause damage in and around the surroundings; for example, what if an automatic car runs over a pedestrian, crashing and damage caused by an automated drone, or wrongful medical treatment by an AI medical software. There are many countries that put the liability on the developer of the AI, but the problem arises when the developer themselves are not able to anticipate the scope of the problem and its adverse effects. There really is no ideal answer to AI accountability. One of the most serious hazards associated with the plan to hold developers accountable is a negative influence on AI development. After all, AI engineers are frequently insignificant contributions for individuals or small businesses. Whether or if they are the most to blame when their inventions do harm, the practical nightmare of facing litigation every time their AI produces harm should make AI developers extremely cautious about putting their products into the world [50]. In problems like this one where we are unable to find a universal solution, all we need to find is the right balance.

In the past, we have names eras by the underlying material (for example, "stone age," "bronze age," or "iron age") rather than the instruments that were made [1]. As a result, AI might be a new substance that promotes humanity. What the tools are that we construct out of it (how we regulate and build AI): an iron shovel for digging enormous irrigation canals or a deadly combat ax. It is up to us to determine how we will mold this instrument for human progress.

Pertaining to AI and various privacy considerations, General Data Protection Regulation (GDPR) has been passed by the European Union [77].

The right to privacy has been part of the European convention on human rights since 1950. As technologic progress has continued with time, the factors pertaining to privacy have also changed. The internet became a major contributor in human progress, and fault lines started to show up. Various court cases were filed in European courts. After a while, Europe's data protection authority declared the need for a comprehensive policy on personal data protection [77].

In the year 2016, GDPR was passed in the European Parliament [77]. As of May of 2018, all concerned organizations were required to be compliant.

GDPR is a legal document with its scope pertaining to personal data, data processing, data subjects, data controllers, and data processors.

There are various data protection principles listed in GDPR, which are as follows:

1. Lawfulness, fairness, and transparency
2. Purpose limitation
3. Data minimization
4. Accuracy
5. Storage limitation
6. Integrity and confidentiality
7. Accountability

The regulation lists all the directives that are to be followed. GDPR is the guiding document on internet and human right protection. The regulation is more than 88 pages long [77], so we have just covered varied aspects of GDPR.

7.4 User-centered system development

UCD is a group of design philosophies and methodologies focused on building technology to serve users. It is also an interactive process in which the developers and designers completely focus on the user and iterate the product according to the user feedback [52].

UCDD focuses on various aspects of design, where a team conducts various surveys on how people want the product to look, how they want to consume the product, and the usability. There are many aspects that the designers take into account such as domain experts, stakeholders, engineers, researchers, marketers, etc.

Let us suppose an organization is given a task to build an AI that predicts the weather conditions and suggests which crop will give the maximum return in terms of monetary benefits. In terms of the variety of departments, the organization has to take into account all the diverse departments. There are farmers who need this specific information to increase their outputs, and there are different government organizations that need this information to provide subsidies on those different seeds that have a better chance of growing in the respective season. There are regulatory and export bodies of the government that need this information to maximize their efficiency and predict the outcomes. In the same case, there are risk management departments that need this specific info to build an infrastructure to fight the odds if the intuitive outcomes do not perform as anticipated (Fig. 7.1).

Therefore, we can majorly divide the whole UCDD process into the following parts.

7.4.1 Key elements of UCDD

UCDD can be considered a part of the socio-technical approach. UCDD and the socio-technologic perspective are guiding ideas and thought processes, not specific methods or processes for design. The idea is to approach design with knowledge and the will to utilize social, heuristic, and cognitive exploration and research of human activities. These are the basic fundamentals that guide the whole

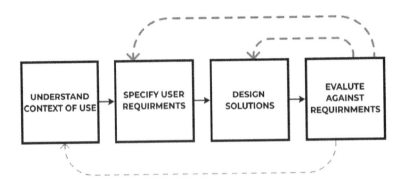

FIGURE 7.1

System model of the proposed scheme [52].

process. This method also focuses on developing user-oriented technologies that must be tested for usability. Users should be actively involved in the entire design process, not just consulted at the beginning or during the testing stages of a product, as is the case with UCDD design [53].

7.4.1.1 Levels of user participation

	Weak participation	Strong participation
Interaction	Indirect	Direct
Length	Short	Long
Scope	Small	Large
Control	Very limited	Very broad

7.4.2 Context analysis

Another important aspect of UCDD is taking into account the user's work needs in context. Users' participation in design activities is influenced by a variety of environmental circumstances. Environment, knowledge, skills, and security are among them.

- A participatory design activity will be influenced by the cultural and physical setting in which it takes place [53].
- Each participant will bring his or her own general, subject, and tech knowledge to the design activity [53].
- Cognitive, motor, and articulatory skills will all have an impact on an individual's capacity to participate in a participatory design exercise. Diverse participants will bring different perspective to any project, and the skill balance within a group is likely to have an impact on its functionality [53].
- People's comfort levels, emotional stability, and stress levels all influence how they contribute to a group activity. Environment, knowledge, and skills all have an impact on a group's sense of security [53].

7.4.3 Iterative design

After user research the designers are required to build a design space specific to a particular design problem. The ultimate goal of the designers is to build and design a solution that is best for the end users.

7.4.4 Process approach within UCDD

Under UCDD, we place multiple process perspectives. These include participatory design (PD), rapid prototyping, user-friendly design, pluralistic walk through, contextual design, cooperative inquiry, situated design, the user design approach, ID two transactional tests, R2D2 model, emancipatory design, and user design.

7.5 Usability engineering and verification

Usability engineering is the discipline that deals with HCI and with developing human–computer interfaces that have high usability and user-friendliness. There are several broad disciplines that subsume usability and engineering including psychology, human factors, cognitive science, and AI [57].

The ultimate goal of usability engineering is the creation of more useable or user-friendly products that are designed and built to the actual needs of target end users.

Usability engineering has become more and more prevalent as we observe the exponential rise in the average screen time, hence the rise in computer interfaces; from our alarm clocks to work to social interaction, we use computer interfaces in the form of mobile applications, websites, and the list goes on.

7.5.1 Usability

Usability is a measure of the capacity of a system to provide a specific solution for its user to perform the task safely, effectively, and efficiently while enjoying the experience [54].

The key points in usability are as follows [54].

1. Learnability

   The system should be easy so that users can learn to use it right away.

2. Efficiency of use

   Once the user has learned how to use the system, then it should be easy to use to achieve any specific task.

3. Memorability

   When the system is not used for some time, it should be easy to return to it without learning it again.

4. Few and non-catastrophic errors

   There should be minimal errors, and if errors occur, they should be easy to recover.

5. Subjective satisfaction

   The user should be satisfied when using the system.

7.5.2 The usability engineering lifecycle

The first step for any usability engineering on the project is to lay out the usability engineering proposition for it [55]. Let us suppose an application is made for crop prediction, and we will use feedback-looped AI software, which will predict the tentative crop for the next quarter. The first step is to identify the requirements; our software will identify the terrain according to the respective geography of the place. The second step is to build an interaction design for the application considering it will be used by multiple potential stakeholders (farmers, local government bodies, federal/central government). Following with the interaction is a prototype. The third step is to build a user interface specification following up with its software implementation.

7.5.2.1 *Know the user*

The primary step is to recognize the target audience to perform a successful usability process. No universal solutions exist in the real world. The organization needs to invest a large chunk of time and money into understanding the user.

These are some specific key points that need to be taken under consideration:

a) Individual user characteristics
b) The user's current and desired tasks
c) Functional analysis
d) The evolution of the user and the job

7.5.2.2 *Competitive analysis*

Prototyping is an essential part of the usability process and as we know that competing products are the best prototype for obvious reasons. A competing product is already fully implemented and therefore can be tested very easily.

This phenomenon is easily visible in today's world, where we have hundreds of substitutes for any given service. Suppose if we are to build an email service, we can look around us and find any number of services. We can develop competitive analysis, subsequently developing a framework for our own email service. One can understand and learn more from a preexisting piece of tech simply because it has been tested and used by hundreds of real-time users.

Competitive analysis implies building a better design by analyzing previous products' strengths and weaknesses. It in no way suggests stealing other people's copyrighted or patented ideas and intellectual property.

7.5.2.3 *Setting usability goals*

Usability is not a one-dimensional attribute of a system [56]. Typically, all attributes of usability cannot be given the same weight, so one needs to prioritize according to the user research and the target audience. For instance, learnability is especially important in any piece of tech or software built for interns because interns are brought on a temporary basis. The ability of irregular users to return to the system is essential for a reconfiguration utility that is supposed to be used once every 3 to 4 months.

7.5.2.4 *Parallel design*

"The main goal of parallel design is to explore things differently before one settles on a single approach that can then be developed in further detail and subjected to more detailed usability activities" (Fig. 7.2) [57].

It is better to start five different product designs with their selective leads because our ultimate goal is to build a design that is collaborative in nature. When we get five different inputs from various teams, it is possible to create a new combined design after having compared, discussed, and extrapolated the set of initial designs and then incorporating the best of ideas from each design into the final one. A variant of parallel design is known as diversified parallel design. The main advantage of parallel design is that when a number of designers are allocated with different goals, as in one is building for an expert user while one is building for a novice user, one is building a nonverbal interface. By guiding each designer to a specific design approach, diversified parallel designs will emerge. This will drive each approach to its limits, leading to diverse design ideas that might never have emerged in a collaborative design process.

FIGURE 7.2

Conceptual illustration of the relation between parallel and iterative design. Normally, the first prototype would be based on ideas from several of the parallel design sketches [64].

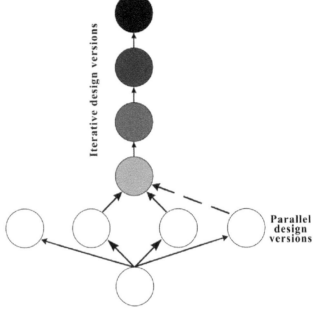

7.5.2.5 Participatory design

One can follow "know your user" as much as they can, but still, they will be unable to answer all the issues that might come up when the product is used in real time. It is our human tendency to be biased toward certain things, and here comes hindsight bias where we start seeing things differently when we are involved in the same thing for too long. In the case of PD, the designers cannot rely on the users who are involved in the process from the start, as they will be biased toward the design because they know the whole story behind the design and might end up giving silly feedback. PD solves this problem by introducing the project to new users and taking feedback accordingly.

7.5.2.6 Prototyping

The purpose of prototyping is to reduce the cost and time required to develop something that can be tested by users themselves in real time. The usability engineering cycle contains various other factors including empirical testing, iterative design, etc.

7.5.3 Usability heuristics

Humans share some fundamental biases in how they learn from their surroundings. In the case of modern computer interfaces, it is how we scroll down a webpage not upward and how a notification bar is always upward in mainstream operating systems [58]. Usability heuristics is closely related to how human psychology shapes building technology. Usability heuristics is the fundamental part of understanding and building technology around us.

Jakob Nielsen, a guru of web page usability, calls heuristics for design "discount usability engineering methods". There are 10 different usability heuristics for user interface design [55].

7.5.4 Usability testing

Testing with real users is a rudimentary method and is unique in a sense since it provides real-time data about how people operate computers and what their issues are with the palpable interface being tested [58]. In all kinds of testing, the organization focuses on issues of reliability and validity.

7.5.4.1 Test goals and test plans

Testing is an integral part of the process. The organization needs to define what sort of testing is required and then proceed with the same. This is where AI comes into play. In the past decades, we have seen multiple APIs that are helpful and more reliable than the conventional methods. One of the examples of that is AI spidering. More than 40% of work can be automated by using AI. Testing engineers can use ML to teach various systems to make decisions based on previous actions and catch errors that might have been left otherwise. Categorization of various fields helps us in understanding and developing test plans as well.

By integrating AI in testing procedures, one can see more efficient and accurate results. Understanding data is critical to building a powerful ML system. Google Facets is one of the examples that shows how AI and ML helps us in the visualization of any sort of data [58].

7.5.5 A/B testing

A user experience research methodology is known as AB testing [59]. A/B is a randomized content system with two variations, A and B [59]. It is a method of comparing two variations of a single variable, usually by comparing a subject's (customer's) response to variant A with variant B and determining which of the two variants is more effective [60].

A/B testing is also used in understanding how users engage in offline and online modes, how user action is affected, and how users influence one another [61].

Large social media sites like Instagram, Facebook, and LinkedIn use A/B testing to make a better user experience, and it also helps in streamlining their services. We have seen how social media website Twitter has changed its homepage in recent years and how they take continuous feedback from users.

As we can see in Fig. 7.3, we have two diverse colors. We can test both colors when put into a software and compare the same for more efficient results [61].

7.5.6 Test budget

There are multiple factors that are involved in testing budgets, but here are a few for developing a basic understanding of how testing budgets should be set. One major factor that one must take into consideration is the uncertainty of how one major change can impact the whole usability and engineering process.

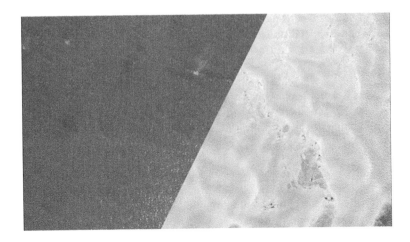

FIGURE 7.3

A/B testing via two versions.

7.5.7 Importance of user-centered design

The Three Mile Island accident happened on March 28, 1979, when reactor number 2 of the Three Mile Island Nuclear Generating Station (TMI-2) in the United States of America partially melted down, resulting in a radioactive release. It is the most serious accident in the history of commercial nuclear power plants in the United States. After the accident, President Carter signed an executive order and formed a presidential commission and directed them to study the accident and produce a report so that future accidents can be prevented.

In the report of the president's commission on the accident at Three Mile Island, multiple findings and recommendations were made. Some of the findings and recommendations pertaining to design are discussed next.

It was found in the investigation of the reactor control system's user interface that even though a valve was stuck open, a light on the control panel indicated that the valve was closed. The light did not even indicate the position of the valve, only the status of the solenoid being powered or not, thus giving false evidence of a closed value. As a result, operators were not able to correctly diagnose the problem for several hours.

The presidential commission findings clearly mention the following [62]:

1. "The control room was not adequately designed with the management of an accident in mind."

For example, Burns and Roe, the TMI-2 architect-engineer, had never systematically evaluated control room design in the context of a serious accident to see how well it would serve in emergency conditions.

The information was presented in a manner that could confuse operators.

(i) Over 100 alarms went off in the early stages of the accident with no way of suppressing the unimportant ones and identifying the important ones. The danger of having too many alarms was recognized by Burns and Roe during the design stage but the problem was never resolved.

(ii) The computer printer registering alarms was running more than 2000 hours behind the events and at one point jammed, thereby losing valuable information.

(iii) The arrangement of controls and indicators was not well thought out. Some key indicators relevant to the accident were on the back of the control panel.

(iv) Several instruments went off-scale during the course of the accident, depriving the operators of highly significant diagnostic information. These instruments were not designed to follow the course of an accident.

2. Regarding the designed channel of communication and specific responsibilities assigned for other contributing federal agencies responding to radiological emergency at TMI, the mere existence of channels was unknown to many high-level federal officials.

3. The official involved in designing the control panel and the people involved in operating it were completely different. There was inadequate training for the operators: even the training module was different.

4. The design of the pilot-operated relief valve indicator light was fundamentally flawed.

The presidential commission [62] recommended the following directives pertaining to design:

1. A system engineering examination of overall plant design and performance, including interaction among major systems and increased attention to the possibility of multiple failures;

2. Review and approval of control room design; the agency should consider the need for additional instrumentation and for changes in overall design to aid understanding of the plant station, particularly for response of emergencies;

3. A central authority deemed accountable for design, construction, operations, and emergency response and organizational entities to be formed;

4. Equipment design and maintenance inadequacies noted at TMI should be reviewed from the point of view of mitigating the consequences of an accident.

The report on the accident is nuanced, and parts of the commission findings are classified. Detailed views on the accident can only be viewed by nuanced perspectives of the full report. We have only discussed the design issues pertaining to the accident. As we can see, a small design problem ended up contributing to a partial nuclear meltdown, which in the aftermath turned out to be one of the factors cited for the decline of new reactor construction. UCD should be the priority of any industry across all the fields.

7.5.8 Google homepage over 20 years

Throughout the book chapter, we have learned about how humans interact with computer interfaces and how we develop and design technology by various methods. For understanding it in a better way, let's look at the most visited website of 2020, i.e., Google.com[63].

Google.com used to be a holding page. Google had the "I am feeling lucky" button from the start.

In 1999, Google went for a minimalistic view, and this table-based design was all over the web. If we compare this design with the design of the present homepage, they look similar.

Google made multiple iterations throughout 2018. HCI and design problems in the industry are mainly solved with the trial and error method.

Till 2019, the homepage went under minimal changes; Google packaged all the other Google products and bundled them into a square and placed it right after the sign-in button.

As shown in Figs. 7.4 and 7.5, we can see in hindsight how iterations have turned Google homepage into a refined webpage.

After 20 years, Google kept making small changes in order to facilitate other products, but one thing that remains constant is the code size of the page. There are many conclusions we can draw in hindsight. Google kept a theme that is quite similar in nature; the learnability and usability remained

FIGURE 7.4

Google homepage in 1998.

FIGURE 7.5

Google.com homepage in 2019.

the same. Google launched many different products, but they kept the search at the same position no matter the iteration. One can draw many conclusions on why Google search became this successful, but their design has been a benchmark for the Web 2.0 industry. This section is simply a conjecture for understanding design iterations in the industry.

7.6 Democratization of information technology

We as a civilization have seen massive breakthroughs/advancements throughout the history of our time, be it fire, metal weapons, guns, or nukes. One of the biggest breakthroughs of the 21st century was the dot-com boom. We saw the immense power of capitalism combined with tech, and the rest is history. If we look throughout the history of our time, whenever we have combined the tremendous power of capitalism and technology, it has produced outstanding results and collaborated in significant human progress.

One of the most significant breakthroughs of the 21st century was the introduction of the internet to civilians. Earlier the internet was only used by the military and academia. From military to academia, the internet paved its way and proved its value throughout diverse fields. Later we saw the enormous power of capitalism combined with technology, and the rest is history. The coupled power of capitalism and technology resulted in affordable computers. We saw the dot-com boom in the 1990s. Later we saw mobile tech. Now we carry computers in our pockets and wear the same on our wrists. Throughout the day, we interact with computers of different shapes and sizes.

Let's look at what Moore's law says "Moore's Law is the observation that the number of transistors in a dense integrated circuit (IC) doubles about every 2 years"[64].

Conventional concepts like Moore's law prove how technologic progress is and has been exponential in nature. Rising computational power and storage capacity leaves us with big data (we will discuss big data and its possible implications in the next topic) (Fig. 7.6).

Let's see how we have surpassed Moore's imagination and hit peak centralization. We have an immense amount of processing power, but look at the figure where the expensive bottleneck lies: network and storage. If we look counterintuitively, we see how companies like Amazon Web Services, Google Cloud, and Microsoft Cloud Business have shown exponential progress (Fig. 7.7).

One of many amazing things big data and AI has created is a conversational chatbot for a specific person. Social data may be used to create or modify a special index in the theme of the specific person's personality. The special index may be used to train a chat bot to converse in the personality of the specific person [65].

7.6.1 Distribution of information

The internet has been around for some decades now. Email has been with us since the 1960s, file sharing since at least the 1970s, and TCP/IP was standardized in 1982. Earlier in the 1980s, the internet was only used by academia and the military.

7.6.1.1 Web 1.0

Later in 1993, computer scientist Tim Berners-Lee released the source code for the world's first web browser and editor, which led to the first stage of the World Wide Web evolution known as Web 1.0.

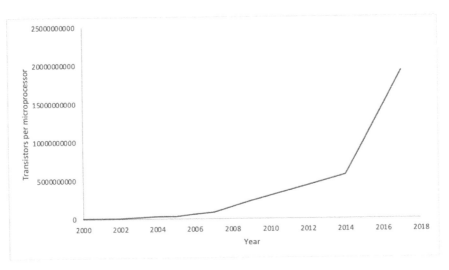

FIGURE 7.6

A semi-plot of microprocessor transistor counts versus introduction dates, roughly tripling every 2 years [66].

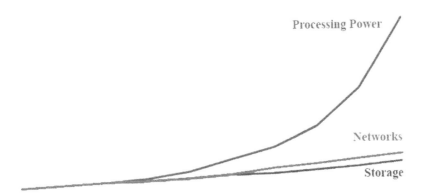

FIGURE 7.7

Growth of processing power with respect to networks and storage.

7.6.1.2 Web 2.0

In 2004, Web 2.0 emerged as a massive change throughout the internet because of its participatory nature. Examples of Web 2.0 websites are Facebook, Reddit, YouTube, etc.

The key features of Web 2.0 are as follows:

1. Freely available and indexable information helps users to retrieve data in a systematic and user-friendly manner.
2. There is real-time user interaction.

Social media and podcasting are part of Web 2.0.

As of January 2021, there were 4.66 billion active internet users worldwide: 59.5% of the global population [69]. The distribution and reach of the internet are recorded across many countries and have introduced many new avenues including cyberwarfare (Fig. 7.8).

Nowadays, narratives are built and destroyed on the internet. The majority of the news is generated on social media applications. By clicking one button, one can send a point of view. Earlier we never had a standardized system for mailing. Every country around the globe follows a different standard for addresses. The internet solved this with MX records, and now one can send an email at any address around the world at name@domain name. The flow of information has been built so that one can access any information around the world within seconds. Increasing internet speeds will make video content more and more prevalent.

7.6.1.3 Social media

Social media is a product of Web 2.0, and it has become an integral part of our daily lives. Social media shapes how we think of our surroundings as we know them. Social media has come to be a technology that facilitates the free flow of ideas and collaboration in the true democratization of data (Fig. 7.9). Earlier only a few people had the influence to publish any sort of data or news. In today's world of citizen journalism, anyone with a smartphone can publish ideas with one click. Social media platforms being so interactive has proved why the growth of these platforms has been exponential. In the next section, we will discuss how social media and AI work hand in hand.

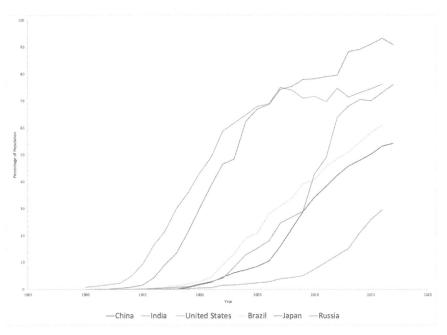

FIGURE 7.8

Graph shows the rise of the internet in India, China, the United States, Brazil, Japan, and Russia [69].

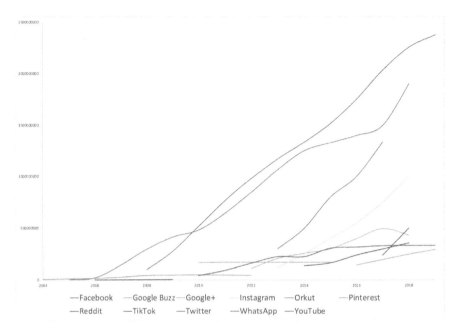

FIGURE 7.9

Growth of social media from 2004 to 2020 [70].

7.6.1.4 Social media and big data

In this section, we will discuss how social media companies drive growth and products using big data.

7.6.1.5 Target advertising

Assessing the search preferences and engagement insights from the users, companies target advertisements to the target audience. They sell their targeted distribution to the businesses. Imagine we need to sell a particular book, perhaps a computer science book. In a conventional sense, one has to advertise the book through the bookstores even though we know the majority of the audience will not be interested in our book. In case we have a set of insights gathered from an enormous pool of people and by using AI and our effective computing power, we can generate a pool of people who are interested in computer science. It is likely people who are interested in the subject might consider buying the book.

7.6.1.6 Enhance user experience

To ensure users spend maximum time on the platform, it is important for social media companies to make sure they show what users like. Platforms build various ML algorithms for recommending all sorts of data and train accordingly. This practice of pushing the most relevant and favorable content leads to major problems, which are visible in the social fabric. Personalized content that is linear in nature creates polarization [65].

7.6.1.7 *Study the human condition*

One hundred million Instagram photos were used to learn global clothing patterns [67,68]. The immense potential of big data and ML has achieved what is impossible to do manually. We possess a humongous amount of data on the internet, and that leaves us with a window to understand human behavior and psychology at a scale that could not have been imagined before.

There are many research works that can help understanding AI with respect to HCI [71–76].

7.7 Challenges

As technology has advanced, the relation between humans and machines has changed, from humans adopting machines before World War II to machines adopting humans after that conflict. Following the introduction of HCI and AI in the computer era and after that the two technologies HCI and AI were combined in the current AI era [78]. HCI and AI also face issues with regard to psychology as a result of the increasing complexity of technology. One of the challenges is that psychologists fear that the day will come when these technology-based bots will replace them. But since no technology can function and think like a human brain, technology creators should grasp that the bots are meant to support psychologists rather than to replace them and act appropriately.

Kurzweil made the following prediction in 2005: in the years to come, powerful AI and HCI technologies will exceed humans [4]. However, the concern arises as to what humans would do if these technologies surpass and begin harming or threatening humans and the technologies take over the globe. As a result, specialists are required to concentrate on how to create these technologies while keeping the user/human in mind while building AI and HCI-based technologies as a peer to humans. The goal now is to develop AI and HCI-based solutions that are human controllable rather than AI controllable [78].

The challenges that AI and HCI-based chatbots confront include determining who is liable if the bot does harm to humans or makes wrong decisions. How reliable is the bot? Or, is it biased toward one group?

One such example happened in 2019, when researchers discovered that a prediction algorithm utilized by UnitedHealth Group was biased toward Black patients [79]. Another challenge is how well one can trust the chatbot that one has knowledge and experience as a human and establish a bond as a human can. Also, what happens if the app doesn't operate due to technical reasons and a patient is in need of psychological assistance? These problems must yet be addressed [4]. With this, there are also challenges that are being addressed, yet flaws remain, such as chatbots unable to grasp human commands, hackability, cybersecurity issues, and privacy concerns. Also, there is also a challenge for specialists to determine how IA might accompany AI and HCI to increase the intelligence of machines that complement humans. Another challenge for humans is to use discipline principles such as cyberpsychology when the world is progressing into cyberspace.

Challenges related to AI are hard because deciding the scope of the problem is the major issue. When the scope of the problem is defined, it is easy to map things and resolve step by step. There is uncertainty involved in ever growing fields like AI and HCI. Related to Web 2.0, there are various challenges that are static in nature such as testing, frequent changes, etc. As we move toward the democratization of information technology, we see various technologies coming up like blockchain,

Ethereum-based tech, and others. There are fundamental challenges involved here such as account-ability and organizational structure. There are no static solutions available that are widely accepted throughout the industry.

7.8 Conclusion and future scope

At present, HCI and AI technologies are broadly used with the designing objective of working on the ease of use of computer frameworks and applications. In this chapter, from a psychological point of view, we discuss how advances in technology will empower tackling problems and difficulties in a more efficient, viable, and productive manner. But in the foreseeable future, where everything, including physical and non-physical aspects, will be cyber, it is necessary to map out preventive measure and restrictions before this turns into a hitch. It is important to utilize the principle of disciplines like cyberpsychology and extrapolate learning in formulating these restrictions.

The Three Mile Island accident was a major accident in the history of the United States of America due to a minor design fault. So, UCDs should be prioritized in any sector/field, as a small defect in design might result in significant mishaps. To build effective UCDs, designers should design with the basic principles in mind, including social, heuristics, and cognitive investigation and research of human behaviors. To develop more user-centered systems and technology that protect privacy, designers should grasp the context, include more users in identifying and specifying the users' requirements, and conduct an evaluation process. The rise in computer interfaces is directly proportional to the usage and demand of the latest technologies that have high usability with learnability, memorability, and efficiency. To create highly useable human computer interfaces, one must first understand the characteristics of the users and then develop products after studying and assessing past versions and setting objectives for better and newer versions. A parallel design strategy must be used, which will result in varied design ideas, followed by a PD approach, which will involve gathering input from new users and then making adjustments based on reviews and prototyping. Usability heuristics are an essential aspect of understanding and designing technology for humans. One important factor to consider is the uncertainty of how a single massive change might affect the whole usability and engineering process. As a result, a testing budget should be set aside, and usability testing should be done with real users. After a detailed discussion both from a technical and psychological standpoint, we conclude that newer technologies should be innovated while keeping the user in mind to have a great user experience and user–client interaction. The future is one where a user-centric interface will be a legitimate paradigm to gauge/appraise technology.

7.9 Discussion

In the chapter, we have discussed how technology, especially HCI, has shaped human behavior and how human decision-making is evolving with time. To ensure the integrity of human thought, we need certain rules of how these marketing algorithms used by social media brands should be used. We have also briefed on how design and user design development has evolved with time and how its different methodologies shape today's design including the one of the Google homepage. We have shown how design is integral to today's life and how it shapes everything.

References

[1] A.S.L.-M.-U.M. München, A. Schmidt, L.-M.-U.M. München, *Interactive human centered artificial intelligence: a definition and research challenges.* Interactive human-centered artificial intelligence, Contributor MetricsExpand All ALBRECHT SCHMIDT University of Stuttgart Publication Years 1999 - 2021Publicat, in: Proceedings of the International Conference on Advanced Visual Interfaces, 2020, https://dl.acm.org/doi/10.1145/3399715.3400873.

[2] M. Caleffi, D. Chandra, D. Cuomo, S. Hassanpour, A.S. Cacciapuoti, The rise of the quantum internet, Computer 53 (6) (2020) 67–72.

[3] S. D'Alfonso, Ai in mental health, Curr. Opin. Psychol. 36 (2020) 112–117, https://doi.org/10.1016/j.copsyc.2020.04.005.

[4] D.D. Luxton, Artificial intelligence in psychological practice: current and future applications and implications, Prof. Psychol. Res. Pract. 45 (5) (2014) 332–339, https://doi.org/10.1037/a0034559.

[5] M. Tahan, P. Zygoulis, Artificial intelligence and clinical psychology, current trends, J. Clinical Develop. Psychol. 2 (1) (2019), https://doi.org/10.6092/2612-4033/0110-2184.

[6] F. Yang, T. Han, K. Deng, Y. Han, The application of artificial intelligence in the mental diseases, in: Proceedings of the 2020 Conference on Artificial Intelligence and Healthcare, 2020, https://doi.org/10.1145/3433996.3434004.

[7] M. Vijayarani, G. Balamurugan, Chatbot in mental health care, Chatbot Mental Health Care Vijayarani M, Balamurugan G - Indian J PsyNsg 16 (2) (2020) 126–128. https://www.ijpn.in/text.asp?2019/16/2/126/276355.

[8] M. Romero, C. Casadevante, H. Montoro, HOW to create a psychologist-chatbot, Papeles Del Psicólogo - Psychologist Papers 41 (1) (2020) 27–34, https://doi.org/10.23923/pap.psicol2020.2920.

[9] M.T. ZEMČÍK, A brief history of chatbots, DEStech Trans. Comput. Sci. Eng. 10 (2019).

[10] F.O. Adibe, E.C. Nwokorie, J.N. Odii, Chatbot technology and human deception, Rev. Art Social Sci 5 (2016). ISSN 1119-961 X.

[11] K.K. Fitzpatrick, A. Darcy, Vierhile M delivering cognitive behavior Therapy to young adults with symptoms of depression and anxiety using a fully automated conversational agent (Woebot), A Randomized Controlled Trial JMIR Ment Health 4 (2) (2017) e19.

[12] M. Gupta, T. Malik, C. Sinha, Delivery of a mental health intervention for chronic pain through an artificial intelligence–enabled app (Wysa): protocol for a prospective pilot study, JMIR Res Protoc 11 (3) (2022) e36910.

[13] C. Moberg, A. Niles, D. Beermann, Guided self-help works: randomized waitlist controlled trial of Pacifica, a mobile app integrating cognitive behavioral Therapy and mindfulness for stress, anxiety, and depression, J. Med. Internet Res. 21 (6) (2019) e12556.

[14] K. Kretzschmar, H. Tyroll, G. Pavarini, A. Manzini, I. Singh, NeurOx Young People's Advisory Group, Can your phone be your therapist? Young people's ethical perspectives on the use of fully automated conversational agents (chatbots) in mental health support, Biomed. Inf. Insights 11 (2019) 1–9.

[15] K. Denecke, A. Abd-Alrazaq, M. Househ, Artificial intelligence for chatbots in mental health: opportunities and challenges, Multiple Perspec. Artific. Intell. Healthcare (2021) 115–128.

[16] C. Sweeney, C. Potts, E. Ennis, R. Bond, M.D. Mulvenna, S. O'neill, M.F. Mctear, Can Chatbots help support a person's mental health? Perceptions and views from mental healthcare professionals and experts, ACM Transac. Comput. Healthcare 2 (3) (2021) 1–15.

[17] L. Xu, L. Sanders, K. Li, J.C. Chow, Chatbot for health care and oncology applications using artificial intelligence and machine learning: systematic review, JMIR cancer 7 (4) (2021) e27850.

[18] A. Palanica1, P. Flaschner2, A. Thommandram1, M. Li1, Y. Fossat1, 1L. Department, C.A.A. Palanica, Physicians' perceptions of chatbots in health care: Cross-sectional web-based survey, J. Med. Internet Res. 21 (4) (2019). https://www.jmir.org/2019/4/e12887/.

[19] Wikimedia Foundation, Cyberpsychology, Wikipedia, 2021. https://en.wikipedia.org/wiki/Cyberpsychology.

[20] Z. Mihai, Ai applications in psychology, Expert Syst. Human, Mater. Automation (2011) 75–81, https://doi.org/10.5772/16620.

[21] J. Meredith, Conversation analysis, cyberpsychology and online interaction, Social Personality Psychol. Compass 14 (5) (2020) 285–294, https://doi.org/10.1111/spc3.12529.

[22] V. Ahuja, S. Alavi, Cyber psychology and cyber behaviour of adolescents-the need of the contemporary era, Procedia Comput. Sci. 122 (2017) 671–676, https://doi.org/10.1016/j.procs.2017.11.422.

[23] Cyberpsychologist career guide. Cyberpsychologist | Duties and Career Opportunities | PsychologySchoolGuide. net. (n.d.). https://www.psychologyschoolguide.net/psychology-careers/cyberpsychologist/.

[24] J.R. Ancis, The age of cyberpsychology: an overview, Technol. Mind Behavior 1 (1) (2020), https://doi.org/10.1037/tmb0000009.

[25] N. Gogoi, Impact of fear-of-missing-out (FOMO) on the well-being of adolescents, in: Cyberpsychology in the Tech-Fed Virtual World, essay, Lulu Publication, 1998, pp. 175–207.

[26] T.R. Nuñez, T. Radtke, S.C. Eimler, A Third-Person Perspective on Phubbing: OBSERVING Smartphone-Induced Social Exclusion Generates Negative Affect, Stress, and Derogatory Attitudes, Cyberpsychology, August 10, 2020. https://cyberpsychology.eu/article/view/12590/11560.

[27] Analytics Insight, How does intelligence amplification make smarter ai? Artificial Intell. Big Data Analyt. Insight (2021). https://www.analyticsinsight.net/how-does-intelligence-amplification-make-smarter-ai/.

[28] Alvin DMello PhD Candidate, Rise of the humans: intelligence amplification will make us as smart as the machines, The Conversation (October 21, 2019). https://theconversation.com/rise-of-the-humans-intelligence-amplification-will-make-us-as-smart-as-the-machines-44767.

[29] Wikimedia Foundation, Intelligence Amplification, Wikipedia, 2021. https://en.wikipedia.org/wiki/Intelligence_amplification.

[30] Techopedia, What Is Intelligence Amplification (Ia)? - Definition from Techopedia, Techopedia.com, 2017. https://www.techopedia.com/definition/32577/intelligence-amplification-ia.

[31] L. Liu, Applying Intelligence Amplification in Decision Making, 2016. https://essay.utwente.nl/69712/1/Liu_MA_EEMCS.pdf.

[32] y huang, N. Zhao, Generalized anxiety disorder, depressive symptoms and sleep quality during COVID-19 outbreak in China: a web-based cross-sectional survey, Psychiatry res (2020) 112954, https://doi.org/10.1016/j.psychres.2020.112954.

[33] J. lai, S. Ma, y Wang, Z. Cai, J. hu, N. Wei, et al., Factors associated with mental health outcomes among health care workers exposed to Coronavirus disease 2019, JAMA Netw. Open 3 (2020) e203976, https://doi.org/10.1001/jamanetworkopen.2020.3976.

[34] S.M. lee, W.S. Kang, A. Cho, T. Kim, J.K. Park, Psychological impact of the 2015 MerS outbreak on hospital workers and quarantine hemodialysis patients, Compr Psychiatry 87 (2018) 123–127, https://doi.org/10.1016/j.comppsych.2018.10.003.

[35] J. denollet, A.A. Schiffer, V. Spek, A general propensity to psychological distress affects cardiovascular outcomes: evidence from research on the type d (distressed) personality profile, Circ Cardiovasc Qual outcomes 3 (2010) 546–557, https://doi.org/10.1161/CIrCouTCoMeS.109.934406.

[36] J.B. li, A. yang, K. dou, ry Cheung, Self-control Moderates the Association between Perceived Severity of the Coronavirus Disease 2019 (COVID-19) and Mental Health Problems Among the Chinese Public, Psy-ArXiv, 2020. https://psyarxiv.com/2xadq/.

[37] K. Ćosić, S. Popović, M. Šarlija, I. Kesedžić, Impact of human disasters and COVID-19 pandemic on mental health: potential of digital psychiatry, Psychiatr. Danub. 32 (2020) 25−31, https://doi.org/10.24869/psyd.2020.25.

[38] S. graham, C. depp, ee lee, C. Nebeker, X. Tu, hC. Kim, et al., Artificial intelligence for mental health and mental illnesses: an overview, Curr Psychiatry rep 21 (2019) 116, https://doi.org/10.1007/s11920-019-1094-0.

[39] K. hariman, A. Ventriglio, d Bhugra, The future of digital psychiatry, Curr Psychiatry rep 21 (2019) 88, https://doi.org/10.1007/s11920-019-1074-4.

[40] A.B. Shatte, hutchinsondM, S.J. Teague, Machine learning in mental health: a scoping review of methods and applications, Psychol. Med. 49 (2019) 1426−1448, https://doi.org/10.1017/S0033291719000151.

[41] K. Ćosić, S. Popović, M. Šarlija, I. Kesedžić, T. Jovanovic, Artificial intelligence in prediction of mental health disorders induced by the COVID-19 pandemic among health care workers, Croat. Med. J. 61 (3) (2020) 279−288, https://doi.org/10.3325/cmj.2020.61.279.

[42] I. galatzer-levy, K.I. Karstoft, A. Statnikov, S. Ay, Quantitative forecasting of PTSd from early trauma responses: a machine learning application, J. Psychiatr. Res. 59 (2014) 68−76, https://doi.org/10.1016/j.jpsychires.2014.08.017.

[43] K.I. Karstoft, I. galatzer-levy, A. Statnikov, Z. li, S. Ay, Bridging a translational gap: using machine learning to improve the prediction of PTSd, BMC Psychiatr. 15 (2015) 30, https://doi.org/10.1186/s12888-015-0399-8.

[44] I. galatzer-levy, S. Ma, A. Statnikov, r yehuda, S. Ay, Utilization of machine learning for prediction of post-traumatic stress: a re-examination of cortisol in the prediction and pathways to non-remitting PTSd, Transl. Psychiatry 7 (2017) e0−e1070, https://doi.org/10.1038/tp.2017.38.

[45] K. Schultebraucks, A. Shalev, V. Michopoulos, J. Stevens, JovanovicT, g Bonanno, et al., A generalized predictive algorithm of posttraumatic stress development following emergency department admission using biological markers routinely collected from electronic medical records, Biol Psychiatry 87 (2020) S101−S102, https://doi.org/10.1016/j.biopsych.2020.02.279.

[46] R. Rodrigues, Legal and human rights issues of ai: gaps, challenges and vulnerabilities, J. Responsible Technol. 4 (2020) 100005. https://www.sciencedirect.com/science/article/pii/S2666659620300056.

[47] S. Wachter, B.D. Mittelstadt, A right to reasonable inferences: Re-thinking data protection law in the age of Big Data and AI, Columbia Bus. Law Rev. (2019) 494. https://heinonline.org/HOL/LandingPage?handle=hein.journals/colb2019&div=15&id=&page=.

[48] P7003 - Algorithmic Bias Considerations. IEEE SA - The IEEE Standards Association - Home. (n.d.). https://standards.ieee.org/project/7003.html.

[49] E. Bayamlioglu, Contesting automated decisions, European Data Protec. Law Rev. 4 (4) (1970) 433−446, https://doi.org/10.21552/edpl/2018/4/6.

[50] M. Bartlett, Solving the ai accountability gap, Medium (2019). https://towardsdatascience.com/solving-the-ai-accountability-gap-dd35698249fe.

[51] S. Counts, M. De Choudhury, J. Diesner, E. Gilbert, M. Gonzalez, B. Keegan, et al., Computational social science: Cscw in the social media era, in: Proceedings of the Companion Publication of the 17th ACM Conference on Computer Supported Cooperative Work and Social Computing, CSCW Companion '14, ACM), New York, NY, 2014, pp. 105−108.

[52] What is user Centered Design. The Interaction Design Foundation. (n.d.). https://www.interaction-design.org/literature/topics/user-centered-design.

[53] Wikimedia Foundation, User-centered Design, 2021. Wikipedia, https://en.wikipedia.org/wiki/User-centered_design.

[54] Theodore Frick, Kursat Kursat, User-Centered Design and Development, Routledge (2007), https://doi.org/10.4324/9780203880869.ch49.

[55] J. Nielsen, Usability Engineering, Academic Press, 1993.

[56] J. Nielsen, The usability engineering life cycle, Computer 25 (3) (1992) 12−22, https://doi.org/10.1109/2.121503.

[57] J. Nielsen, The usability engineering life cycle, Computer 25 (3) (1992) 70−85, https://doi.org/10.1109/2.121503.

[58] J. Nielsen, The usability engineering life cycle, Computer 25 (3) (1992) 90−110, https://doi.org/10.1109/2.121503.

[59] J. Nielsen, The usability engineering life cycle, Computer 25 (3) (1992) 120−180, https://doi.org/10.1109/2.121503.

[60] S.W.H. Young, Improving library user experience with A/B testing: principles and process, Weave: J. Library User Exp. 1 (1) (2014), https://doi.org/10.3998/weave.12535642.0001.101 hdl:2027/spo.12535642.0001.101.

[61] The ABCs of A/B Testing - Pardot". Pardot. Retrieved 2016-02-21.

[62] The President's Commission on the Accident at Three Mile Island. https://www.hsdl.org/?viewanddid=769775, 1979.

[63] C. Godden-Payne, How Google's homepage has changed over the last 20 years, Medium (2020). https://uxdesign.cc/google-how-the-biggest-search-engines-homepage-has-changed-over-the-last-20-years-3b59db931a0d.

[64] Wikimedia Foundation, Moore's Law, Wikipedia, 2021. https://en.wikipedia.org/wiki/Moore%27s_law.

[65] D.I. Abramson, J. Johnson Jr., Creating A Conversational Chatbot of A Specific Person, 2020. US Patent 10,853,717 B2, Apr. 11 , 2017, and issued Dec. 1 , 2020.

[66] Moore's law: Transistors Per microprocessor. Our World in Data. (n.d.). https://ourworldindata.org/grapher/transistors-per-microprocessor.

[67] B. Marr, The Amazing Ways Instagram Uses Big Data and Artificial Intelligence, Forbes, 2018. https://www.forbes.com/sites/bernardmarr/2018/03/16/the-amazing-ways-instagram-uses-big-data-and-artificial-intelligence/?sh=6cb755545ca6.

[68] K. Matzen, K. Bala, N. Snavely, StreetStyle: Exploring World-Wide Clothing Styles from Millions of Photos, arXiv.org, June 6, 2017. https://arxiv.org/abs/1706.01869.

[69] World development indicators, World Development Indicators (WDI) | Data Catalog, 2010. https://datacatalog.worldbank.org/dataset/world-development-indicators.

[70] C. Booth, [Best of 2019] the Most Popular Social Media Networks Each Year, Gloriously ANIMATED, TNW | Tech, 2021. https://thenextweb.com/news/most-popular-social-media-networks-year-animated.

[71] S. Swati, M. Kumar, S. Namasudra, Early prediction of cognitive impairments using physiological signal for enhanced socioeconomic status, Inf. Process. Manag. 59 (2) (2022), https://doi.org/10.1016/j.ipm.2021.102845.

[72] S. Namasudra, S. Dhamodharavadhani, R. Rathipriya, Nonlinear neural network based forecasting model for predicting COVID-19 cases, Neural Process. Lett. (2021), https://doi.org/10.1007/s11063-021-10495-w.

[73] S. Bhatia, M. Alojail, A Novel Technique for Behavioral Analytics Using Ensemble Learning Algorithms in E-Commerce, IEEE Access, 2020, pp. 1−9. ISSN: 2169-3536SCIE.

[74] S. Bhatia, A. Tyagi, Twitter Trends reveals: focus of interest in the sleep trend analytics on response to COVID-19 outbreak, Curr. Psychiatry Res. Rev. 16 (2020) 1, https://doi.org/10.2174/2666082216999201228143243, 2020.

[75] S. Chandna, D. Tonne, T. Jejkal, R. Stotzka, C. Krause, P. Vanscheidt, A. Prabhune, Software workflow for the automatic tagging of medieval manuscript images (SWATI), in: Document Recognition and Retrieval XXII, vol 9402, International Society for Optics and Photonics, February 2015, p. 940206.

[76] N. Salankar, D. Koundal, S. Mian Qaisar, Stress classification by multimodal physiological signals using variational mode decomposition and machine learning, J. Healthcare Eng. 2021 (2021).

[77] Official Legal Text of GDPR, General Data Protection Regulation (GDPR), 2022. Retrieved September 29, 2022, from, https://gdpr-info.eu/.

[78] W. Xu, M.J. Dainoff, L. Ge, Z. Gao, From Human-Computer Interaction to Human-AI Interaction: New Challenges and Opportunities for Enabling Human-Centered AI, 2021 arXiv preprint arXiv:2105.05424, 5.

[79] Z. Obermeyer, B. Powers, C. Vogeli, S. Mullainathan, Dissecting Racial Bias in an Algorithm Used to Manage the ... - Science, 2019. From, https://www.science.org/doi/10.1126/science.aax2342.

Managing postpandemic effects using artificial intelligence with human-computer interaction

V. Kakulapati[1], Sheri Mahender Reddy[2] and A. Paramasivam[3]

[1]*Department of IT, Sreenidhi Institute of Science and Technology, Hyderabad, Telangana, India;* [2]*Otto-Friedrich University of Bamberg, Bamberg, Germany;* [3]*Department of Mechanical Engineer, Rajalakshmi Engineering College, Chennai, Tamil Nadu, India*

8.1 Introduction

With the COVID-19 epidemic, companies have suffered enormous pressure. The automation of the working environment has been considerably increasing. The possibility exists to build an optimized and efficient business model through operational reinvention and the use of intelligent information and digitization [1].

A large percentage of users reported that AI (artificial intelligence) and DL (deep learning) could improve the information that aids clinical trials, pharmaceutical discovery, disease X-rays, and computerized treatments and healthcare apps. Also, technology is making it possible for business and finance to change in the coming years. This includes inventory control, marketing, and making more money.

Investment in AI has an immediate impact, but it has the long-term potential to explore new value streams and drive development. Currently, several AI applications include initializing current practices for increased profitability. Presently, AI can be used to reproduce system design and corporate strategies completely and invent different factors that affect and provide monetary value.

HCI (human—computer interaction) theoretical progress is being made on numerous fronts. Modeling the convergence of perceptive-cognitive-engine operations has become increasingly comprehensive to shed light on internet users' behavior millisecond by milliseconds. At a systemic level, decentralized intelligence develops with awareness of interacting with colleagues and personal treasures. HCI investigators are also concerned with certain other activities, like knowledge discovery. There seems to be no comprehensive peer interaction method, along with some of the significant implications of technology acceptance. This produces better results to be analyzed to ensure abstraction about using computing as an invention, as computer artifacts develop in several ways [2].

Someone is a valuable asset in the postpandemic financial system who combines corporate expertise with exceptional achievement. It will not simply help people to comprehend but will also enable the significant resources of AI. The competencies are continuous: service provider purchasing, retention/borrowing methodologies, financial management, market expansion, user interface design

Innovations in Artificial Intelligence and Human-Computer Interaction in the Digital Era. https://doi.org/10.1016/B978-0-323-99891-8.00008-5

thinking, the concept of multilinkages such as product, manufacturing, business intelligence, innovation, brand management, organizational structure, news channels, advertisers, agencies, and ensuring effectiveness.

Such competencies continue to go further than the capacity of a computer. Several responsibilities involve perception, creativity, administration, information exchange, awareness, criticism, and human-led abilities in risk monitoring. However, it is more significant to realize that individuals and machines rely on one another to operate in the coming automation development approach. Humans must create external strategic factors to encourage AI transformation across industries, as well as to prioritize the necessary inputs for major contributions [3].

The rest of the chapter is organized as follows: Section 8.1 discusses research motivation, pandemic effects, and consequences. In Section 8.2, the background on post-COVID-19 impact is explained. In Section 8.3, work from home (WFH) is briefly discussed. Section 8.4 describes blended learning, and Section 8.5 discusses the post-COVID-19 effects further discussed in Section 8.6. Finally, conclusions and directions for future work are presented in Section 8.7.

8.2 Background studies

According to historical records, the world has difficulties in addressing the apparent risk of infectious epidemics. The 1918 epidemic had an impact on around a million people worldwide [4]. As well, numerous threatening infectious disease epidemics have occurred during previous decades, including SARS-CoV in 2002, H1N1 in 2009, MARS (Middle East respiratory coronavirus) in 2012, Ebola in 2014, and Zika in 2015 [5].

By July 2021, COVID-19 had spread to nearly every nation and had affected more than 195,060,907 people worldwide. Because of health, money, and cultural problems, countries worked in a very unpredictable environment and had to deal with difficult exchanges. More than the majority of the world's population had strong facilitation.

However, many patients are recovering from chronic disease stages. But for weeks beyond the recovery, called extended COVID, several individuals persist in having a spectrum of symptoms, and genetic defects have been observed. Multistage research on the long-term consequences of the ailment has been ongoing.

The COVID-19 problem is about nutrition, health policy, jobs, and the workforce, especially the health of employees. The problem's longevity is important for putting in place employee security and healthcare providers, securing enough jobs, and keeping workers' rights in all sectors. The immediate and targeted response needs to include increasing worker security for the well-being of people who are severely affected so that they can get affordable healthcare and other help. These people include workers with weak and uncertain jobs, like young people, the elderly, and immigrants. The status of females, who are disproportionately represented in lower employment and medical care responsibilities, should be addressed immediately. Various types of assistance are necessary. These encompass transaction payments, children's subsidies and nutrition benefits for adolescents, housing and humanitarian assistance efforts, job security and healing process help, and financial support for industries such as micro- and small and medium enterprise (SME) businesses. Administrations must interact extensively with employers and employees in the design and implementation of these policies.

COVID-19 has the greatest impact on countries that are still dealing with natural disasters or other disasters. It is important to spread the word quickly about the epidemic and offer social and recovery help to meet needs [6].

8.2.1 Effect of COVID-19 outbreak

The current pandemic has affected people's daily lives and impacted the financial system. This epidemic has also affected individuals throughout the world socially. Illness is propagating in 213 nations around the world. The statistics are from World Health Organization (WHO) data, which show severe consequences for economic and healthcare sector locations [7,8]. To avoid the transmission of these illnesses, several nations have shut down centers, services, education, manufacturing companies, stock markets, and others [9,10]. This virus has dramatically affected various commerce and commercial sectors. In addition, several important implications and issues have been raised about medical providers, economics, and socioeconomic life.

Investigators from Oxford University in the United Kingdom found that the use of AI to better comprehend the COVID-19 virus facilitated both accurate diagnoses and the rapid advancement of medical interventions. Using linguistic and data analysis technologies, we can learn about the evolution of the virus, how it spreads, how to diagnose it, how to control it, and what we may learn from past outbreaks. AI may also be used to help find the infection, determine its cause, and stop its spread. Complementing congenital monitoring and other clinical systems and information transfers, intelligence detection systems may help discover epidemiological trends by analyzing current events, web material, and other communication platforms in several languages to generate warning signals [11].

Infervision's use of AI might be useful. Using a computed tomography scan of the lungs, the AI is trained to quickly identify injuries consistent with COVID-19 pneumonia, quantifying their extent, shape, and thickness; it also analyses the evolution of numerous lung sores in the images and provides a comprehensive report to assist physicians in making an accurate diagnosis. This new feature in COVID-19 has not yet been released into a corresponding inspection diary. AI is a valuable tool for detecting coronavirus-related disorders in their earliest stages and monitoring the health of infected people. However, disparities in care exist as a result of barriers such as a lack of knowledge and experience with digital mental healthcare, unsafe digital platforms, and a lack of a graduated approach to treatment [12]. People have suggested fixing these problems and putting money into AI-based apps for real-time monitoring and therapy that are easy to use and interesting.

Every part of life now involves some kind of computer interface, which is made possible by the fact that data processing is everywhere. As the amount of HCI increases, so does the operational error rate and the cognitive load of interacting with computers. Experts in HCI analyze and design interfaces for many types of technology. They investigate, improve, and create novel technical applications while evaluating existing ones. The field of HCI has converged its scholarly objectives to improve the accessibility and usability of computer systems. HCI challenges grounded in AI are proposed as a means of illuminating the connection between cognitive knowledge and the ability to understand both natural and artificial intelligence. HCI models explain how researchers think about how people and machines work together. Recent developments in HCI are explored, from user-friendly interfaces to direct brain–computer interfacing. Since interactions are based on multimodal architecture, proper harmonization in various areas will minimize computer issues.

8.2.1.1 Monetary effect

COVID-19 has had an immediate effect on people's daily lives, businesses, and the way people move around the world and do business. Early diagnosis is crucial for containing the outbreak due to the quick speed with which the virus may travel from human to human. The supply chain has decreased significantly across the board. Medicines, the renewable energy sector, the tourist industry, and the information and technologic businesses are just a few of the many that are impacted by this virus [13,14]. This infection has far-reaching repercussions for people's everyday lives and the global financial system.

The outbreak of COVID-19 has had a significant influence on the financial system. It was the worst financial crisis in a century, resulting in massive wage cuts and earnings for young people. In the different variants of COVID-19 infectious diseases, the gross domestic product (GDP) is expected to decrease [15]. In April 2020, the share market decreased by 35% in lockdown as e-commerce usage significantly decreased. The international number of aircraft has fallen considerably, with existing terminals being shut down in more than 100 countries [16]. Low-wage workers kept working to meet their basic needs during setbacks and failures [17]. Financial difficulties may enhance the exposure of minimum-wage employees to the virus. With the fear of disease and the uncertainty of providing for their dependents, such low-wage workers have struggled.

The financial disruptions caused by the COVID-19 epidemic were particularly bad for urbanization. The effects are complicated and may be accomplished at a wide variety of levels using different methods. Earlier than expected results demonstrate that the epidemic seems to have had a significant effect on taxes, people's incomes, travel and commerce, microfinance, metropolitan production lines, and the mobile workforce, and investigations on such issues are continuing. Furthermore, the inconsistent and imbalanced economic and spatial organization of the virus impacts was addressed in a developing investigation topic.

The virus is becoming not just a catastrophe for population wellness but also for the country's financial system. The tourism sector encountered a significant economic effect last year as a result of lower profitability, lost lives, business losses, and commerce disruption. Due to COVID-19, world leaders would be called on to increase collaboration to prepare for the pandemic and provide the funds needed for multinationally coordinated efforts. Although the predicted socioeconomic consequences of respiratory infections have been repeatedly confirmed [18,19], the community has not funded adequate prevention and readiness efforts to reduce large-scale vulnerabilities.

The global epidemic is developing steadily with no chance of control, and it certainly has had a significant unfavourable influence on the economy's prosperity. The United Nations has warned of the significant negative effects of coronaviral infection on the financial system, and economic growth in the modern economy is expected to fall to 4.8% [20]. Similarly, 2020 will demonstrate that in the hospitality and tourism sectors, monetary policy, and monetary links, COVID-19 will have substantial racial implications for the regions.

Financial experts have anticipated different socioeconomic possibilities of the emergence of viruses and measures to prevent these diseases via modeling techniques. The most simple scenario is that viruses are eradicated by May 2020 and the financial system recovers quickly in the third quarter. The second possibility is that viral deterrence has spread across society and that the financial catastrophe is not expected to occur until September 2020. The second scenario is that viral deterrence is spreading throughout the population and that the financial crisis will not occur until September. A lack of essential items is leading to rising consumption and pricing in the former instance. A prolonged downtime influences delivery and eliminates income for the year for firms.

There may be additional expenses for the medical care firm and intensification methods. A possible interpretation is that there is a pandemic all year, and all containment measures are successful. So, there is a severe contraction in the financial system, a pretty intense level of economic hardship, massive death losses, and thousands of citizens obligated into poverty.

Intelligence can have a wide variety of applications in a variety of contexts. Their capacity to offer intelligence technologies may be enhanced by industrialization, quality assurance transformations, manufacturing processes, product development, and facilities that produce customized marketing strategies and better quality brand awareness. These are common in industries such as farming, which took a back seat in the prehistoric period of technologic advancements. AI can answer sustainability goals by addressing emergency medicine, learning, and growing accessibility to society's financial and financial services demands. The analysis shows a beneficial and essential relationship between AI-utilizing companies and the overall increase in production. However, since the company makes a system that makes AI, incremental technologic progress improves with AI severity. According to the findings, intelligence effectiveness is increasing.

The life and financial disruption of the epidemic are horrifying; significant unease surrounds predictions only at the moment of the drafting of how astonishing as well as how effective non-pharmacological and pharmaceutical solutions can be. Enhancing AI is advantageous for reducing such insecurities, some of the probable predictive analytics technologies created over the previous generation, and more. Data analysts have recognized the importance of encouragement.

DL can be important because the outbreak needs to be found, researched, predicted, described, and kept track of, all of which have economic effects. As an epidemic has spread, chatbots and other data-examining tools have scrambled for use and investigation [21]. DL aims to quickly predict a rapid, intense analysis and generate an enormous information repository for investigation, diagnostic procedures, and clinical examinations. To lower these risks, it is very important to improve AI and make it one of the most promising data tools.

8.2.1.2 Stay-at-home orders

Cognitive science is now one of the significant neurosciences to investigate emotional relationships and technologic advancements during this century, characterized by an increase in healthy behavior. "People are increasingly living in a society of man-machines. Whoever recognizes or does not suffer as a result of the changing environment. Rapid change in the workplace, virtual reality environment is one of the periods' major problems, which applies to education" [22].

Addressing the impact of particular relations associated with electronic systems includes the development of new interorganizational and interpersonal communication, the implementation of novel analysis techniques, mental health intervention, the reproduction of multisensorial experiences of virtual and augmented realities, and thoughtful games.

Many individuals recommend remaining in their homes and working from there for a long time apart from persons with meaningful occupations, including foodstuffs, pharmaceuticals, universal healthcare services, and fundamental social connectivity tasks. The result was lower regular exercise and adverse consequences in the population for psychological wellness, as exercise usually reduces negative emotions [23]. This also impairs the inherent moral responsibility of the inner mentality. Therefore, in catastrophes, fair values are varied. In these instances, several sufferers, as probable, are excluded, even though it compromises social justice, which seems to be a moral condition that the doctors in intensive psychiatric practice experience. It is an interesting concern for the prioritization of inpatient psychiatric doctors.

Regarding the impact on medical employees, during the current COVID-19 epidemic, hospital staff have faced enormous emotional exhaustion as they battle COVID-19 [24] on the front lines. A severe diagnosis may be influenced by healthcare professionals. Because of the absence of ventilation systems, it might be necessary to refer to themselves to discontinue assistance to rescue patients who are afraid of infection. A few of them have little personalized protective equipment (PPE). According to the most recent investigation, protecting physicians from COVID-19 contamination in most hospitals is more expensive than WHO guidelines.

In contrast, improved PPE has already been used in fewer clinics for all treatments [9]. A combination of stress and liability in inexperienced medical professionals may impair functioning individual sensitivity. It may create long-lasting ethical damage; others may have indications of exhaustion.

Such a "showdown" can be powered by robotics exceptionally effectively. The computerization humans are dealing with now, though, is founded on artificially intelligent systems. Ultimately, these two manufacturing variables may be combined into one, rendering work obsolete. When industries worldwide begin to grow again after COVID-19, it will be difficult for laborers to deal with both the scarcity in the whole range of the production process and interpersonal distances due to the anxieties of the postpandemic wave and the worldwide medical issues of employees at work. This combination may destroy automated processes, resulting in significant shortages and the possibility of staff relocation and recovery.

Each type of business finds innovative methods to function efficiently and satisfy the requirements of its clients and staff, either small or large, business or government, as social distance and quarantine measures stay in place. AI performance is a significant factor in allowing this change by offering information transfer, healthcare, and food standard protection [25].

Employers need to use predictive analytics to develop novel organizational structures and improve performance while guaranteeing standards and safety. AI-powered systems play an important role in enabling customers to optimize decisions, allowing digital transformation to protect innovations and expanding programs to provide tangible outcomes to advance a value chain status [26].

The topic of catastrophic redundancy has been computational modeling and forecast estimation of anticipated skill shortages resulting from AI advances. The deterioration of the effect of partial or total economic losses on industries has occurred dramatically, and administrations and decision-makers have yet to deal with it. From such a unique "human versus machine" perspective, the pandemic's impact prompted organizations to change the approach of automated policies from a context of risk and security toward ongoing and prospective crises. Further building assures a healthy link between computerization and workers, helping to safeguard individuals and companies. In light of the appropriate policy push, the novel strategy assists in redefining marketing objectives to enhance appropriate automation, in which people have a vital role and, rather than becoming automated, operate actively or passively.

Numerous small companies refocused and incorporated operational strategies to cope with the uncertainties and complexity of the global epidemic, such as switching to noncontact delivery orders to keep their facilities accessible, requiring workers to acquire new skills to support the different business strategies, incorporating innovative technical processes into their operations, etc. Some examples of how new technology may help organizations include the automation of tasks, the prediction of sales, and the detection of fraud. Even small businesses and new businesses are using AI and machine learning to stay afloat during the epidemic.

These are the key points:

- Intelligent interactive systems are networks substituting for more expensive and inefficient channels of dealing with customers.
- Because of the epidemic, businesses are using AI in their logistical operations to deal with changing demand, with more people wanting the same resources, and with prices going up.
- AI-powered insights are letting small businesses make decisions based on data, automating and streamlining their operations and cutting their overhead costs.
- In using AI for talent acquisition, optimization techniques play a significant role in the powerful strategy for the intended audience, allowing businesses of all sizes to reap more commercial benefits. By performing sentiment analysis on job postings to spot biased wording and automating the screening of applicants, AI systems help streamline the recruitment process.

To make it through the COVID-19 crisis and back to normalcy, small firms throughout the economy will need to adopt new ways of doing business. AI and HCI may help businesses find hidden managerial accounting opportunities in their large amounts of structured and unstructured data. Since these technologies are changing so quickly, businesses do not have to spend as much on research and development to come up with their unique technologic solutions.

8.2.1.3 Human services (healthcare) impacts

With severe acute respiratory CoV-2's propagation and its spread to hospital staff, medical workers are under significant vulnerability, which constitutes probable transmitters of the illness, with such environmental effects including physical assessment, surgery, and contact with the clinician. The outpatient and operation departments may predispose people and medical personnel to be contaminated if appropriate measures are not implemented. The pandemic has had a terrible effect on health workers worldwide. The front-line hospital staff has a higher fatality rate.

However, this percentage of fatalities increased in different nations, and many of these deaths were attributable to increased susceptibility to the virus. Such a problem still impacts medical staff. Hospital staff confront several problems: pathogenic problems, work schedules, emotional anguish, tiredness, stress burning, stereotyping, and psychosocial abuse. In Ref. [14], the author describes the numerous dangers and problems that health professionals, in particular, confront as medical staff on the front line.

There were many significant risk indicators: durations of service, work in the intensive care units (ICUs), absence of PPE, relatives affected, unskilled cleaning of hands, and inappropriate treatment of infections. In addition, continuous use of the PPEs resulted in inflammation, the far more prevalent location becoming the nostril canal, and tackling COVID-19 on the front lines resulted in emotional difficulties for healthcare workers (HCWs). Severe melancholy, panic, nervousness, discomfort, wrath, worry, dread, sleeplessness, and after-traumatic psychiatric disorders in HCWs can be initiated. Psychological effects have been distributed unevenly to women and carers. Women front-line carers closely operate with sufferers because of a heavy workload that might lead to tiredness, tension, and anxiety [27].

While servicing COVID-19 victims and sacrificing their lives, how were they very badly treated? According to sources, physicians were spit on and driven out. Several doctors and their families were also humiliated by respective neighbors and homeowners for exposing COVID-19 victims.

The reasons behind the risk of HCWs are the following:

- shortage of PPE kits
- absence of medical amplification methods
- workload, stress at work, and not getting enough sleep have all made it more likely for healthcare workers to get sick
- prolonged identification of COVID-19 indications and absence of pulmonary infection awareness

Due to regular and personal visits with individuals in isolation, physicians, caretakers, and hospital staff were at that moment particularly useful in the battle with COVID-19. Shelves drive trolleys/smart trolleys to transport critical goods from ICUs to appropriate areas. They are controlled by human intervention through the use of webcam input. Supplies, medication, and clothing from isolation units comprise any of these experiences. Given the option of using unknown devices or robotic robots to fill insulating racks with vital elements while protecting qualified healthcare staff from COVID-19, they chose "human-enabling robots in hazardous environments" [28].

8.2.1.4 Social impacts

Social impact is any influence on individuals' feelings, motives, behavior, or thoughts from receiving others' real, implied, or imagined presence or actions. Considering this definition, social impact theory (SIT) aims to explain how the impact is reciprocal for either a majority or a minority. Latané supports SIT as an avenue for analyzing social impact resulting from forces working in a social force field, suggesting that impact "by either a majority or a minority is a multiplicative function of the strength, immediacy, and number of its sources." Resilience denotes the public's ability to interact with factors that have an effect that varies with adverse effect sources depending on authorization and situation. The more powerful the resource is, the greater is the societal influence. Urgency relates to the proximity between data or actions sent to the sender and the beneficiaries.

Further direct sources have a more significant societal effect. Furthermore, the number of organizations comprises the possible providers; the more resources there are, the more significant is the socioeconomic effect [20,29].

After COVID-19, there was a surge of human beings into crowded locations and entertainment venues to interact after months of the shutdown. That could lead to a second phase, though, if the situation is not controlled very carefully. The unwillingness of specific individuals to connect only with the external realm at first, despite the risk of contamination and community hearings, or just a novel and enduring method to be with another family and peer map that may function better to discard, is rather acknowledged. As a result, we saw a decrease in activity in many other categories and ran the risk of seeing some organizations and relief organizations not available for intelligent marketing programs, not begining to recover or regenerate [30].

Monitoring technologies, on the other hand, have legal consequences for underprivileged groups. Using AI to determine who loses their homes can result in a sort of COVID-19 affirmative action, with specific populations targeted for more stringent policing, reminiscent of another AI paradigm, anticipatory monitoring, which leads to more observation of racial disparities. The disproportionality of African Americans in the statistics leads to racialized enforcement consequences. Furthermore, populations affected by anticipated monitoring systems are probably weaker in areas of color that are more vulnerable to COVID-19 for a range of factors related to past injustices and prejudice [31].

AI's capabilities will be seen in the coming years, and its applications are growing concurrently. AI has indeed proven helpful in a variety of settings, including workplace settings and production processes. Technologic advancements are aiding the COVID-19 epidemic in a variety of ways. AI innovations that benefit the community may not assist every person individually [32]. An underlying contradiction of community versus personal advantage is essential in data analytics, but it is not something that AI can resolve. It is constantly considered a problem that affects humans, but it cannot be controlled because it requires engagement among all parties. Because of the dynamism and granularity of the environment in which moral behavior is represented, neither decision analogy predicts each point [33]. As a result, given the complex nature of contemporary communities, a consistent pattern of pragmatic standards of ethics integrating AI may not be recommended [34]. It is imperative to be conscious of the possibility of complications in human—AI interactions and the growing requirement for integrity regulation and validation processes for AI systems.

8.2.1.5 Fake news and misrepresentation

Misinformation can cause a lot of stress, but most of the time, it changes the way people think and feel. It becomes significantly more crucial than many other outbreaks. It warns the public about being safe and cautious about COVID-19 only through digital networking. The study aims to provide insights, including how to forecast propaganda intentions and design a technology that encourages the evaluation of news interests and various information values. Patients are increasing their awareness of the challenging words and anticipate taking precautions for their protection and to reduce fatalities. Resistance intensifies into resilience if they can analyze the genuineness of media channels in the event of a catastrophe. Support vector machine, gradient descent, stochastic gradient descent, binary decision tree, and random forest are research findings. With dependable functionality, a multimodal system is adequate. Evaluating how fake news dissemination connects to behavioral factors using different online media networks to present various insights to a specific supporter. The outcomes suggest beneficial optimal protection, such as strengthening public assurance and lowering dissatisfaction, to reduce the harmful effects of online media channels [35].

Possessing learning, perception, and culture regarding COVID-19 may contribute to developing a strategic plan for accurate and timely communication to mitigate the impacts of COVID-19 by using data on social networking sites such as Twitter, Facebook, etc. Methods in use for machine learning utilize detecting patterns and emotional assessment, offering knowledge about the structure of misleading data and reducing misinformation and rumors [36]. AI techniques are used to create an overview of treatment effectiveness and budget and to identify healthcare facilities and inadequacies. In this constantly evolving state, AI can provide the most recent information about developing research in diagnoses, therapy, a range of signs, and treatment results, assisting physicians in real-world situations to overcome dread and anxiety and to assist the population [37].

8.2.1.6 Imbalance of social discrepancies

Females have constantly combined employment and family commitments. Females throughout these communities have traditionally become the predominant protectors. Although most females are already out there contributing significantly to average earnings, this is not realized. Salaried mothers spend half as much time per day caring for their children as fathers. However, such responsibility has also been multiplied by COVID-19 and the uncertainties surrounding kids with special educational needs in school. Without additional involvement, many daycare places might be abandoned ultimately. The opening date of education at the state level utilizing various techniques and variable professional goals is primarily decided by institutions. In addition, one-on-one training for kids and the restoration of daycares are not offered. While a short respite may be obtained for mothers, who acquired more throughout the epidemic, occurrences may lead the kids and the parents into isolation, with institutions or daycare centers being shut down for a while and needing to learn online longer [38].

So as the high number and variety of opportunities for internet users increased during the 1980 and 1990s, HCI experts took on different social issues brought by such novel apps. Investigations on affordability to make computer systems useful for disabled individuals and integrations for particular population subgroups, including kids and elderly persons, and the participation of computer systems in different situations have been (and are) practical aspects of the HCI task. Innovative ideas were mainly analyzed as investigators explored the social consequences of instruments for remote collaborative working. Furthermore, HCI knowledge has influenced historical and political discussions on the right environment for technology in problems including elections and confidentiality.

In the same way, AI's beneficial societal consequences can only be achieved by coincidence, for instance, by misapplying an AI strategy to a diverse viewpoint. It was the situation with IBM's intellectual structure using a comparable model. The Watson method was first developed to discover physiologic systems, which encouraged engineers to address design issues in a traditional classroom [39]. AI provides a comprehensive form of schooling in this scenario. However, a lack of extensive knowledge of AI for social good results in unintentional achievement, and it can be methodically repeated. Numerous instances of lost potential to leverage AI's strengths to promote generally positive results in diverse contexts accompany every "unexpected accomplishment."

8.2.1.7 Sociological relevance
The impact of COVID-19 and the "shutdown" on everyday activities take different forms.

- Some acts that are no longer necessary or forbidden are restrained by production tactics.
- People postpone enjoying a music concert, studying in laboratories, and traveling from house to house.
- Regarding technique's replacement and adaptation, several practices can be modified or eliminated by similar activities: beverage at coffee shops is shifting to tea or coffee; exercise is done at home rather than in the fitness center; the organizational task is performed at home rather than in the workplace; cooking at home rather than eating out; internet purchasing is performed only with living rather than traveling to stores. Things alter the size and share of economics.
- Understanding new methods and staying at home necessitates learning new activities. An instance of a procedure one can use to organize interactive sessions has attracted much traction, and it has been the theme of numerous websites and comments. Nevertheless, education may also include cooking, maintenance, and increased horticulture usage to produce crops. Education has been applied to certain different things.
- Regarding rehabilitation and routine readjustment, in addition to these effects, people who share a busy house or apartment require people to engage in coordination techniques. In several ways, it is indeed probably essential to share daycare, education, paid positions, and everyday work in homes, mainly when something is unequaled. One critical point to consider is how these effects translate into shifting social implications for ordinary people.

To some extent, these changes are straightforward: avoiding traffic reduces it significantly. This impact is only compensated somewhat by extra emissions from online orders and the replacement of individual automobiles in public transportation. In some cases, the effects of products, facilities, and systems that simultaneously provide humans are much more complex [40].

8.2.1.8 Psychological impacts

Despite the fact that COVID-19 is in impose, several people are still afraid of contamination. Dr. Richard Branson says, "One cannot be certain if they ever return to former social expectations or if they recognize others are still engaging in public discrimination."

Contagious illness was one of several major threats to survival throughout the stages of evolutionary development. Dr. David Attenborough points out that the pictures seen on COVID-19 television and the fatalities have made us highly conscious of the risks of an infectious virus outbreak.

Even though HCI's human requirements first showed up in the 1950s, its psychological aspects did not become clear until the 1970s, when cognitive engineering and technologic advances in computer science began to work together [41]. During the 1980s, HCI grew in popularity, becoming a critical component for software developers to consider when creating user-friendly interfaces. HCI's focus on human needs was pushed to the side during the mid-1980s as breakthroughs in "harder" (more technical) sciences took center stage. In the late 1980s, creative computer system design tried to solve problems in areas like cognition, society, and government [42].

Human factors seem to have been a point of contention for scholars throughout the current era of HCI development. Due mostly to usability and adoption concerns, few computer services are employed in routine mental health treatment. Randomized control trials have shown that computer-based screening and monitoring for phobic, anxious, fearful, and intense syndromes can be done at a desk or on a laptop. This can be used for self-help and therapy.

The thorough analysis showed that technology for mental healthcare has needed better HCI integration for a long time. Users and mental health professionals may work together to increase the success rates of digital mental health products by code-signing HCI. Telemedicine, (self-) guided electronic therapies, AI, interactive solutions, and electronic morphologic properties are just a few of the numerous applications for web-based or mobile technologic products and services.

8.3 Managing effects of work from home

As the coronavirus spread worldwide, certain government agencies have enforced tight shutdowns and reinforced them with the shutdown of nonessential companies. Most peers advised the population to stay in the house and adopt societal isolation [43] as often as needed.

Deadly outbreaks have an inappropriate impact on specific working sectors, such as females and parents. Institutions must analyze potential losses, reconstitute, and rely on the accomplishments of the prepandemic time. Performance, professional contentment, tolerance, cooperation, and community involvement emphasize employment conditions and their influence.

Corporate executives failed to comprehend the role that AI might perform well before the COVID-19 epidemic. Several did not wholly understand AI's multiple benefits and usefulness. McKinsey reported that more than 50% of companies claimed that AI had been integrated into a single service or system [44].

WFH was investigated for most professionals examined during the second wave of Hong Kong disease for at least 1 day per week. The first firm in the country to completely migrate into the WFH seems to be 9GAG, a Hong Kong-located leading online network [45]. This hypothesis is that WFH persists for at least 1−2 days a week beyond the pandemic.

For management and workers, WFH has significant consequences. The benefits tend to involve and are not limited to lowered travel time, and internal politics are avoided. Workplaces achieve greater productivity and better relationship diversification and have good levels of absenteeism for healthy workers, good employee retention, good work performance, and better productivity [46,47]. An investigation in the Greater Dublin Area has revealed [48] that studies have shown that workers save commute time and travel expenses. E-work can also boost effectiveness, adaptability, and career progression and reduce conflicts between time management and trips [49].

The disadvantages of WFH include blurring of career and home life, diversions, a lack of social support, and the expense of workers in regard to WFH. There are many other limitations to WFH [50], including the utility payment of workers at their residences and the net expense oneself. Employees have been separating, and bosses are worried about production losses when at a place. Furthermore, colleague interactions may be impacted. The slight variation between friends or relatives, friends, and residence [51,52], and the unclear barriers between professional and shelter life can divert workers.

There have been changes to the talent balance between employees who desire to switch careers. German employees, for example, can pay less attention to fundamental intellectual capacity while spending more time socially and emotionally. In India, the percentage of overall time spent on physical and technical talents decreases, while essential capabilities increase. Employees in low-wage jobs have elementary neuropsychological and technical abilities, whereas such skills are less common in the intermediate salary band. These talents reflect the same or less than 20% of such time spent in the top two categories of COVID-19. The least-desired employees can get the most significant transfers to employment in the future. Employees with only a graduate degree appear to be more likely to change professional positions in Europe and the United States. Employees from racial and ethnic groups are 1.1 times more likely to change jobs. In other countries, females are higher than males due to the rise in employment transfers necessary due to COVID-19 trends. Further, senior managers are affected by the demand for a professional transformation, and those who have not adopted it have far fewer employees in the EU countries [53].

8.3.1 WFH benefits [54]

WFH is an enormous advantage for all individuals and highlights the best ability to work effectively at the house. Those are a few of the advantages that probably already are known, and others can potentially open minds to the effects of working remotely on organizations, workers, businesses, and the world.

8.3.1.1 Balance of work and life

Many remote service jobs have flexible hours, which means that the employee can start and end the job whenever they want. It may be important to be able to make work commitments if a person has a family. Suppose someone takes children out of school, makes a couple of orders, or does a daytime virtual workout. In that case, it would be easier for an employee to handle these tasks while working from home.

8.3.1.2 A reduced amount of travel trauma

Approximately "exceptional" passengers experience longer than average journey durations of 90 min or above. However, momentary loss from travel is one of the drawbacks of working. There are significant sources of stress and concern in addition to 30 min of single-lane traffic. Chronic diseases, including hypertension, diabetes, and depression, have all been related to daily 10-kilometre walks to and from work. A person who conserves energy may be able to devote that time and effort to other activities, such as obtaining a better night's sleep or spending more quality time with friends and family. Scrapping the route assists in promoting employee physical and emotional wellness.

8.3.1.3 Autonomy of location

Virtual employment is an excellent method to escape costly rental costs and increased financing locations, particularly for professions (such as technology) utilized in towns. Working remotely means one never has to reside in the vicinity of a large city for a profession one likes. Workers, including armed spouses, who must travel frequently can take advantage of job opportunities from all over the world.

8.3.1.4 More tolerance and diversity

Employees who work remotely can achieve their professional goals without having to commute to a workplace. Organizations prefer to promote diversity, culture, and society by recruiting from within, in places where people are often confident and empowered. Working remotely also offers an opportunity to restart the profession for someone who might find it challenging to secure permanent jobs.

8.3.1.5 Investments in wealth

Fifty percent of WFH households may save almost $4000 annually. Fuel, vehicle servicing, transit, parking, a corporate outfit, purchased meals, etc., are all expenses that can be cut entirely or reduced. The significant socioeconomic benefit of remote working may continue as firms become a longer possibility. With every person that WFH, the ability to remain might even save approximately $11,000 annually. Adjustable employment saved over $5 million on expenses and property investment expenditures from distant employment. US companies saved more than $30 billion a day during the COVID-19 epidemic, enabling workers to perform their jobs from their homes.

8.3.1.6 Significant influence of nature

According to the US Environmental Protection Agency, WFH at least partially conserves 7.8 billion car kilometers and three billion metric tonnes of ecologic emissions annually. The possible effect on pollution levels is equivalent to establishing a forest full of 91 million plants. Distant employees also avoid $980 million in annual fuel expenditures by adopting ecologic practices quickly and reliably.

8.3.1.7 Environment effects

Virtual employment helps several projects for ecology, including prosperity and decreased disparities, the viability of municipalities, global warming, and conscious consumerism. One of the easiest and simplest ways to decrease the ecologic effect and climate variability for organizations and staff is to cut back on commuting. Indeed, worldwide contamination, overcrowding, and transport during the epidemic crisis are diminishing, and everybody can enjoy the benefits of a distant activity.

8.3.1.8 Personalized organizations

Creating a pleasant workspace is an excellent advantage of working remotely. An employee can arrange their personal space and customize anything they want, whether they want much more comfortable seating or specific office supplies for healthcare problems.

8.3.1.9 Improve efficiency and throughput

WFH generally results in fewer minor distractions, smaller agenda items, lower loudness intensity, and far fewer and more effective conversations. Furthermore, the remote staff seems to have additional leisure and fewer interruptions, leading to higher productivity, which is a great advantage of WFH for individuals and companies alike. If performed correctly, remote working enables people and businesses to concentrate on what counts: effectiveness. And Flex Jobs' 2020 poll revealed that the employees who considered themselves to be more efficient WFH were far more successful in working remotely. As the explanation for the greater productivity, several mentioned fewer disruptions and peaceful working conditions.

8.3.1.10 Secure work life

WFH can result in improved wellness, longer passions and activities, and healthier interpersonal friendships. Talent turnover from job listings also has a significant influence, as 72% believe that remotes are beneficial for the staff. The ability to build a pleasant and flexible workplace motivates WFH.

8.3.2 Drawbacks of WFH

There is a considerable inconvenience of WFH. The majority of employees are facing a portion of the weekly sessions, which are the same for everyone at the house:

- WFH is not for everyone and may not be appropriate for everyone's attitude or abilities. A few staff may enjoy the regularity and organization present in a workplace. A few people may like to communicate with colleagues directly. Managers are likely useful in assisting employees in understanding their roles and responsibilities and achieving their respective objectives. WFH might harm productivity. WFH may not suit everybody's family. For example, a few people may have small children who are unaware of time constraints and may disrupt work hours.
- WFH employees may believe that they are not connecting with their peers or the company. Organizations might guarantee that videoconferencing is too often available for collaboration. Increasingly complex interpersonal inventories might also contribute to counteracting isolation, in line with the WFH strategy of the BBC.
- Management and maintenance of their functioning might be challenging. Different mindsets might also react with diverse attitudes to surveillance. Having employees who correctly guide one may explore creating goals to determine whether employees fulfill goals, accept them, or reject them.
- WFH may make it challenging until they maintain a designated workspace at the house to focus on their respective responsibilities. People may readily divert themselves from the sounds of their conversations by home disturbances or by residents of the family, including TV or radio.

- WFH might make employees neglect to distinguish between duty and family at the house. It might make it challenging for individuals to decide to then exit the job. Organizations can urge their employees to have break time and inform employees of the necessity of leaving.
- WFH costs include initial learning expenses as well as the availability of appropriate technology such as computers, mobile phones, and other technologic devices. If a person is a teacher or works in the community, they may need to make some changes to meet safety requirements for sitting at home or work.
- Organizations may struggle to sustain training programs and skill development because workers may not be nearby. Nevertheless, in many ways—for instance, through promotion—companies may push workers to acquire relevant talents via online events and training.
- WFH employees are even more susceptible to experiencing cybersecurity risks. The possibility of procuring computers and the requirement for workers to connect to the network is growing. Organizations can verify that corporate data protection procedures are in effect. In addition, networks protect personal privacy and offer a safe internet connection to a remote host.
- Create a designated workplace and impose limits for all the children in the family. Add additional possibilities for workers to keep up with conversations and teamwork meetings on a consistent schedule. Good nutrition and physical fitness can also improve psychological health, mainly if specialists recommend regular instruction.
- Regarding reduced morale for personnel, it might be more challenging to work together while employees work alone at home.
- Not all occupations are suitable for WFH; it is preferable for some businesses. WFH also matches certain kinds of behaviors, but not all. A few individuals may desire interaction with their colleagues through personal conversation.
- One might have to find out if company workers in different parts of the United Kingdom can connect to the internet so they can do their jobs well.

Because of the epidemic, businesses now know how WFH affects the company and its employees. It has allowed firms to realize the benefits and challenges of WFH in a first-hand way. Such practices can greatly benefit from a new strategy for the employment conditions of employees [55].

AI certainly offers superiority over interpretive approaches and therapeutic choice methodologies in the healthcare sector. ML algorithms can help analyze enormously complex data to be more precise when interacting with training examples. This might allow people to obtain an unparalleled understanding of the fundamental identification of illnesses, pharmaceutical development, diagnosis, public medical procedures, diversity in therapy, and treatment outcomes [56].

The goal of our everyday work is to improve people's lives through technology. HCI is a broad field, though, and improving lives can mean various things as we combine our expertise in the interdisciplinary research areas of computer science, cognitive sciences, and design.

The most recent regulatory reform necessitates the formation of medical associations.

Clinics, professional medical centers, and inpatient treatment providers may be able to assist patients rather than through lengthy procedures.

They need information. The good news is that, whether data collection is computerized or not, unique and confidential information is available to users with little or no participation. Using such technologic applications for automation is highly repetitive. Regular activities usually done by skilled employees are robotic process automation. Working remotely has prompted a rethinking of the company's work methods. The input of facts and other conventional processes is digitized, decreasing the repeated workflow duration by up to 90%. The outcome is rapid, with enormous expenses and improved collaboration between the hospital and the patients involved.

WFH offers greater effectiveness and talent retention, which subsequently increases production and increases the sustainability of organizations. Reduced workplaces, lows in payment, and adequate staff emboldened by local freedom are a few bells and flourishes companies may acquire. They are not required to make concessions for unsatisfactory situations.

According to a recent Glassdoor opinion poll, more than 65% of employees support the manager's decision to assign a team to work entirely from home due to the emergence of the coronavirus. WFH for people and businesses is very profitable. In reality, firms are gradually starting to give WFH to their staff, therefore dramatically changing the post-COVID period compared with the pre-COVID age [57].

8.4 Managing effects of blended learning

Blended learning is an approach that integrates eLearning (or combinations thereof) with conventional classroom-based techniques. It entails an instructor and student's academic interaction, with certain aspects of learner discretion regarding schedule, location, method, or speed [58]. Though institutions with instructor attendance indeed require learners, face-to-face instruction is blended with machine information and presentation methods [59].

The majority of us are afraid that the rapid transformation to eLearning damages the perception of electronic learning. Enhanced transactions demand both innovation and considerable costs, as well as excellent online educational programs. Remote tutoring, which all the instructors and students are presently undertaking, does not appear as we have seen in traditional eLearning [60].

Nevertheless, it is commendable that corporate training organizations and public organizations were quick to provide services for the development of students, regardless of the extent and severity of this epidemic. In India, there are various government schemes such as the National Online Education Platform SWAYAM, the National Digital Infrastructure for Teachers Diksha, and the Performance Assessment, Review, and Analysis of Knowledge in Holistic Development Program PARAKH. These address instructors' and pupils' training requirements in all of these sectors, in addition to the ongoing efforts of all essential educational information and services providers. Since these measures have ensured that many people continue to teach and learn, a more comprehensive and complex "technologic gap" scenario has emerged [61].

Blended or merged instructional strategies seamlessly combine printed and electronic materials, resulting in an appropriate ability to learn the context for students, instructors, and parents. Students view a printing manual for a virtual whiteboard matched with digital components and a structure that ensures efficiency and regularly provides performance metrics to parents. Such services provide teaching materials for the continuous and adaptive analysis of specific students to find knowledge gaps that allow them to give learner-specific correctional information. Strategies like these help put the student at the center of a learning system.

The classroom evaluation process and automatic parental notifications available via smartphones are practical tools that combine technology solutions, print books and practice manuals, and assessment tools with question banks related to different stages of education and the challenges of eLearning tools. A digital setup from a teaching viewpoint gives a wide range of traditional and digital materials through such a blending of training technologies, enabling instructors to interact with learners in a more dynamic and engaging educational context. A qualitative methodology can also meet the notion of multidisciplinary education in both instruction and the learning process.

Some students, particularly those with intellectual disabilities or those who are more introverted, benefited from the online or personalized reverse-class approach. This strategy gave students a chance to look over new learning materials before the session started. This gave them more confidence in the information and helped them contribute more to the live discussion. One of the biggest problems is that some students have to rely on their classmates and teachers to "digest" their content, which means that they have to ask them to make connections or predict future links or trends. The flipped model places a greater emphasis on the student putting in more of their intellectual effort, leading to excellent retention of the material and a significant increase in confidence [62].

Rapid technology and related eLearning processes lack what is so essential and essential to superior educational experiences: the instructor. Massive online open courses (MOOCs) can provide opportunities and mentoring programs that transform individuals if they directly interact with faculty and colleagues. Neither can training courses offer the chances an expert trainer may provide for extended soft skill acquisition.

Competencies that include interaction, cooperation, and troubleshooting in an entirely virtual setting are difficult to nurture but are essential to a continually changing work market. Effective learning relies on three unique positive attributes:

- By getting to know their students, teachers lay the groundwork for more effective and powerful lessons.
- With input from training instruments, instructors can determine what learners accomplish and adjust the educational experiences—right now and throughout time—to enhance that.
- Regarding expertise in the field, by sharing their own experiences, instructors help students see the bigger picture and develop the ability and strength to be aware both inside and outside of the classroom.

While the internet provides excellent opportunities for improving educational potential, expert teachers must apply this directly to the forefront and the subject.

8.4.1 Advantages of blended learning [63]

- Customized training: The learners' learning and retention of material are distinct. A few people quickly understand things, but others are poor students. Another online teaching method assists students in learning at their own pace. They constantly make time outside of the classes for tough topics or regions that are not fully grasped. It is particularly essential for individuals who seem timid about raising their voices or asking classroom questions.
- Taking feedback immediately: Blended learning enables learners to do examinations electronically and receive a rapid response. It allows a considerable amount of time to aid poor learners by interacting with them.
- Different educational approaches: Learners can learn in various methods, and the learners require images, videos, audio, and activities on the eLearning systems that appeal to every aspect. Through such media, the education method is entertaining and appealing to students. They help develop and sustain the curiosity of pupils about the topics they study.

- Teamwork: The learners and the instructor are restricted inside the classroom setting. The technique allows students to collaborate with friends and other institutions while operating on a global scale. Users may actively communicate on initiatives and get a broader knowledge of international issues. Learners can also participate in writing challenges, which is a great motivator to learn. To promote the skill set, they can collaborate with colleagues at all levels of higher education.
- Parental responsibility: Students' access to digital communications must be monitored by carers. Another aspect of the classroom activities is the parents' involvement. Technology enables parents to participate in educational processes by providing house coaching and assistance. As a carer, one may interact instantly with instructors on the growth of their kid. Whatever impact on the house or institution might be discussed with parents and the professor to secure the well-being and advancement of the student.
- To achieve a good result: eLearning means that some lifelong talents are needed to make it succeed. Learners must understand the best avenues, the ability to work under pressure, and internet tagging. Students ought to be technologically knowledgeable to work remotely. The sending of e-mails and skills in presenting are encouraged by technologic utilization. All such abilities are necessary for the 21st century, and they equip pupils for employment prospects, regardless of vocation.

AI advancements have enabled instructors to diversify training and provide additional help and content for learners with experience and competencies that are either below or above grading standards. The new "intelligent" teaching technologies can evaluate the present faults and determine how some kids make particular mistakes [64]. Such techniques might support educators in approaching kids much beyond their classroom averages and assisting pupils with a lower education level. The realms of learning and machine learning have to a considerable degree merged into what is frequently known as mixed or customized learning approaches. Several intriguing national programs include prototypes that promote the next generation of technology teaching goals of the Gates Foundation and charters created to give each learner a genuinely individualized learning opportunity.

8.5 Managing effects of eLearning

The COVID-19 outbreak has provided an unexpected boost to online learning in K−12 classrooms. Nations, towns, and regions must benefit from the changing events encircling classrooms and build an electronic learning sector that is feasible in a timely fashion. Online learning depends on four basic requirements: government, society, pedagogy, facilities, and services (Fig. 8.1). The educational process improves students' learning effectiveness by establishing concrete initiatives in those four areas. It would also ensure continual progression and compatibility with the increasingly changing competencies necessary in the community, with a higher degree of inclusiveness.

However, virtual learning's efficacy differs between grade levels. The consensus on children, particularly young children, is that broad discipline is required because children are more easily distracted. To make proper use of digital training, there is a genuine effort to offer this discipline and, consequently, use various collaborative techniques and interaction approaches to replicate a physical class or reading [65,66].

Framework for enabling sustainable value in education

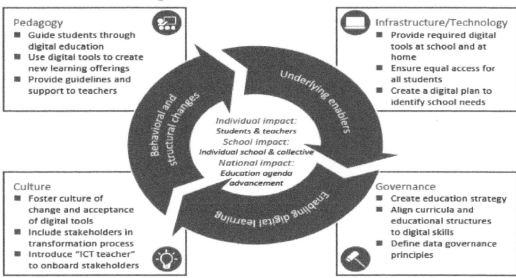

FIGURE 8.1

eLearning impacts [57].

eLearning fosters an improved and team-based educational prospect. Intelligent classes not only change instruction in educational institutions but also quickly break apart public institutions. Researchers, legislators, and academics are already technologically advanced and equipped with cutting-edge aging methods and strategies to aid in the reinvention of higher education. It enables learners to have more significant learning and lines of interaction and allows teachers to manage performance in real-time.

The epidemic that caused institutions to close has boosted innovation and growth throughout the nation. Institutions have moved to eLearning systems and have given families and students free sessions periodically throughout education budgets. The epidemic has generated an increase in the supply and prominence of eLearning [67], which is a significant disadvantage for several people.

Several places have looked into AI as a way to make it easier to find out what is wrong with someone. Tencent, for example, collaborated with Medopan in 2019 for AI diagnostics, while Merck signed a deal with Jansen in 2019 to build an AI capability to display techniques for enhancing the identification of "neglected tropical diseases." The cooperation with DeepMind and Google Health, among a variety of healthcare institutions, has allowed clinicians, since 2016, to utilize AI's strength to diagnose illnesses.

To educate instructors on new ways to focus on ideas, the COVID-19 epidemic provides a chance. While it has been involuntary and hasty to reassess teaching techniques, this practice provided a unique opportunity to review tactics that make the students more comfortable in the online environment. In addition, more diversity in training and learning tasks still disputes the need for "seat time." Lengthy zoom sessions are rarely essential in education and therefore do not match the behavioral science of how students learn. Learning requires interaction as well as mandatory study sessions [68].

8.5.1 eLearning benefits

- As learners go through higher education institutions, students would like more independence and academic mobility. eLearning can assist learners in taking highly customized training, potentially also at the university level. These can be highly advantageous to their development when paired with practical experience activities, real-world investigation, and comprehensive evaluations.
- It gives people a chance to try out basic ideas from different areas before getting into more specialized knowledge. Such pupils grow highly autonomous via eLearning approaches.
- Using minimal infrastructure allows eLearning to provide viewers with self-determination. The learners may customize their education. It makes it possible for learners to study training programs and study from practically everywhere.
- Everyone has a different and unique learning pace matched by the delivery of online learning. Online learners benefit from flexible learning schedules.
- eLearning gives an improved aspect for debate, generally in a chat group platform.
- Virtual classes do not want to be concerned with body language and facial expressions conflicting and compromising the messages, as interaction is visual. eLearning reduces reasonable conversations to physical opinions, which might be foggy.
- Communicating with an instructor even after class might be hard in established institutions. It is not the situation in the context of virtual training.
- eLearning promotes interactions between parents and teachers that are pleasant and accessible [69].
- A thorough assessment of pupil performance is permitted via digital platforms. It creates for every learner a customized learning path.
- One can talk to someone online and help them figure out their problems through discussion forums and conversations.
- The visual lessons for sound/visual training may be redressed and listened to repeatedly unless initially grasping the content.

8.5.2 eLearning drawbacks

eLearning does not have many inconveniences. The critical thing is that it has information on a scientific level, which may be slightly weird if it uses everything from that study. There is a scarcity of facial expression training, which may be required for certain aspects [70].

- Many digital evaluations are restricted to questionnaire items.
- The protection aspect of teaching methods is another problem.
- The genuineness of the activity of a particular learner is an issue, as virtually anybody may make a study instead of the natural learner.
- Evaluations that are mainly desktop in nature tend to be based on experience and understanding and are not particularly practical.

8.5.3 Inequalities in ethnicity

Fontichiaro explains that scientists discover that several African and minority ethnic victims believe the youngsters perform much better inside a family environment. She contends that the aspect of eLearning may influence it, resulting in fewer racial injustices and microaggressions [71].

o "Government learning wasn't just capable of giving its capabilities a powerful message once pupils go over to the classroom, but was also capable of restoring them [71]."

o Fontichiaro says that, despite its benefits, long-term eLearning could make things unfair for racial minorities after a pandemic.

o "There seems to be a need in eLearning for learners who are going beyond the epidemic," says Fontichiaro.

The comprehensive training tendency through online instructional methods has been beneficial for highly qualified industry experts but has affected several students. This tendency remains in the following years, according to research firms. AI has equipped online learning with novel, much more fascinating techniques than conventional ones. The rationale for this is that AI makes it possible to create customized opportunities for learners adapted to individual requirements [72]. This method of education is an advantage in university learning that fails to thrive with a one-sized technology and a customized learning approach. Adopting a personalized learning process would assist institutions and organizations in tackling prevalent challenges such as poor student performance, shortage of reflective teaching resources, etc. The strategy can also help instructors follow every learner's learning goal and make space for even more teaching methodologies.

8.6 Discussion

This chapter discussed the various effects of COVID-19, as well as the benefits and drawbacks. This study aims to comprehend the effects of the pandemic on the various categories observed, as well as discuss significant benefits and drawbacks that can be learned for post-COVID-19, with effective management of the results using AI and HCI technologies. As AI applications deduce human responsibilities, significant collaboration from research scientists is required. The COVID-19 pandemic has repercussions for all of society, but it has an especially negative impact on the most vulnerable populations. From what we know so far, it seems that the poor are paying a disproportionate amount of the health and economic costs of the virus. The pandemic is a consequence of various occurrences in both environments of those relationships and has possible implications for the community and public well-being.

In catastrophic events, social distance and other preventative precautions must be encouraged on an ongoing basis. The unexpected suddenness and intensity of COVID-19 disrupted the economy throughout the globe. This is the greatest forecasted loss in world GDP in 8 decades, at 5.2% in 2020, owing to pandemic impacts. As a result of the pandemic, emerging and developing nations will see their GDP fall by almost 6% by the end of 2024. Financial stability and progress in the economy are the goals of both conventional and unconventional monetary policy tools. We have shown that the economy is susceptible to several shocks and disturbances. COVID-19's effects will linger for quite some time, wreaking havoc on the already fragile economies of developing nations. The COVID-19 outbreak has had a significant negative impact on economic activity worldwide. Stopping the epidemic from spreading much further is crucial. Many countries have taken the extreme step of locking down due to this. The GDP of each country has likely been affected by the lockdown or shutdown. Comprehensive efforts to reduce inequality and improve the lives of exploited populations should be given priority. Slum upgrading should be given priority. Social distancing measures should be combined with direct aid systems.

Orders to stay at home as a preventative measure against the epidemic coronavirus illness in 2019 (COVID-19) have resulted in immediate adjustments to regular activities. The neuropsychological effects of the epidemic and the extended stay-at-home ordering time are still unclear. However, research into the effects of environmental interaction on psychological well-being and mental health in the postpandemic world has not yet been conducted.

There were negative effects on health, access to treatment, and care goal accomplishment for people with chronic diseases in India due to pandemic-related limitations. When lockdowns were in place, people with diabetes complications had more problems or could not control their blood pressure because there were fewer medical services available. Our research shows that the negative effects of the pandemic do not just affect health, but also the economy, how people interact with each other, how resilient they are, what they eat, and other things.

Genuine and geo-referenced information is publicly available and allows for improved reaction and rehabilitation from bad occurrences. Innovative initiatives need not compromise intrusions and cannot be used to strengthen relationships with authority. The global postepidemic scenario of the pandemic was badly influenced by misinformation, mostly through web-based networking media. New research methods are tapping into sociology to trace the dissemination of false information. Co-prejudice, showing reluctance, and corrections that include explanations of how something happened are all things that make it harder to fight disinformation. Human-driven techniques are best suited to empowering citizens; integrated methods are more suitable for epidemic containment, confidentiality, cooperation, communication of knowledge, and monitoring of false news.

Investigators of HCI are keen to establish novel design approaches, investigate appropriate communication patterns, establish interaction concepts and hypotheses, innovate solutions, and prototype new information technology processes. The age of human intellectual contact is becoming more frequent as self-sufficient and intelligent systems range from voices and commercial advisors to smart technology, intelligent automobiles, and socializing robotic systems. The new statement of AI is designing and examining sample techniques offering different design specifications. The senior generation is one of the most significant social transformations of the 21st century.

Computational issues that are difficult or impossible for current AI algorithms to tackle have prompted the investigation of human computation. As the internet has expanded, human computation systems have found a way to harness the skills of a huge pool of individuals to solve more difficult problems in computing. HCI needs to be studied in depth to figure out how to make AI systems with a human in the loop.

8.7 Conclusions and future works

AI is equipped for transformational and revolutionary advancements in medicine in the medical system. The need for intelligent, comprehensive medical insurance AI, which prepares, effectively controls, and eliminates any unexpected effects without resulting from media hype or commercial motivations, must be balanced with caution. AI's best solution is to start with actual medical issues and get the best response possible with the involvement of various authorities, front-line workers, patients, and families. AI has progressed rapidly, which may also be extremely helpful in mining employees' risk analysis, infection, and testing in the context of the COVID-19 epidemic. An AI real-time visual analysis system may be used for remote access and safety regulations in subterranean and mining contexts to evaluate personal health. AI can help to avoid and regulate COVID-19 propagation from many contemporary perspectives. Presumptive disease surveillance, extensive testing, surveillance, communication detection with investigational treatments, pneumonia screening, data collection and incorporation of online databases of perceptive factors, resource allocation management, forecasting development, and computation are some of these.

The new guidelines consist of revolutionary and profound digitization and have established new life rules that are closely interconnected, interacting, and cooperative communal systems that are compartmentalized, separated, and decentralized. In the future, shifting to a human—machine—robot online platform may be a better strategy. But this shift provides the chance to hide the deeper issue of communism in the connection between robots and humans, which needs the descriptive components of humanitarianism, principles, and morals encoded in such integrations. People as well as networking automation can monitor and support the actions. The COVID-19 issue has resulted in a severe concentration and communal effort to prevent the consequences of isolation, the death of family members, and remote working.

References

[1] Insurance Thought Leadership. https://www.insurancethoughtleadership.com/ai-in-a-post-pandemic-future.

[2] G.M. Olson, et al., Human-computer interaction psychological aspects of the human use of computing, Annu. Rev. Psychol. 54 (1) (February 2003) 491—516, https://doi.org/10.1146/annurev.psych. 54.101601.145044.

[3] Lomit Patel. https://www.lomitpatel.com/articles/ai-will-drive-post-pandemic-growth-and-change-the-nature-of-leadership/.

[4] D.M. Morens, G.K. Folkers, A.S. Fauci, The challenge of emerging and re-emerging infectious diseases, Nature 430 (6996) (2004) 242—249.

[5] Ao GF, From "A" IV to "Z" IKV: attacks from emerging and re-emerging pathogens, Cell 172 (6) (2018) 1157—1159.

[6] WHO. https://www.who.int/news/item/13-10-2020-impact-of-covid-19-on-people's-livelihoods-their-health-and-our-food-systems.

[7] C. Huang, Y., et al., Clinical features of patients infected with 2019 novel coronavirus in Wuhan, China, Lancet (2020) 497—506.

[8] M. Wang, et al., Remdesivir and chloroquine effectively inhibit the recently emerged novel coronavirus (2019-nCoV) in vitro, Cell Res. (2020) 269—271.

[9] M. Walton, et al., Mental health care for medical staff and affiliated healthcare workers during the COVID-19 pandemic. Version 2, Eur. Heart J. Acute Cardiovasc. Care 9 (3) (2020) 241—247.

[10] Y.H. Jin, et al., A rapid advice guideline for the diagnosis and treatment of 2019 novel coronavirus (2019-nCoV) infected pneumonia (standard version), Mil. Med. Res. (2020) 4.

[11] OECD. https://www.oecd.org/coronavirus/policy-responses/using-artificial-intelligence-to-help-combat-covid-19-ae4c5c21.

[12] D. Gratzer, J. Torous, R.W. Lam, S.B. Patten, S. Kutcher, S. Chan, L.N. Yatham, Our digital moment: innovations and opportunities in digital mental health care, Can. J. Psychiatr. 66 (2020) 5—8.

[13] Y.H. Jin, L. Cai, Z.S. Cheng, A rapid advice guideline for the diagnosis and treatment of 2019 novel coronavirus (2019-nCoV) infected pneumonia (standard version), Mil. Med. Res. 7 (1) (2020) 4.

[14] D. Campbell, C. Bannock, 'Unlike Anything Seen in Peacetime': NHS Prepares for a Surge in Covid-19, 2020, p. 128121128.

[15] Economic Co-operation and Development (OECD), The World Economy Is on a Tightrope, OECD Economic Outlook, June 2020. http://www.oecd.org/economic-outlook/June-2020/. (Accessed 10 June 2020).

[16] L. Jones, et al., Coronavirus: A Visual Guide to the Economic Impact, BBC News, April 30, 2020. https://www.bbc.com/news/business-51706225. (Accessed 9 June 2020).

[17] H. Jahromi, et al., Why African Americans are a potential target for COVID-19 infection in the United States (USA), J. Med. Internet Res. 22 (6) (2020) e19934, https://doi.org/10.2196/19934.

[18] G. Yamey, et al., Financing of international collective action for epidemic and pandemic preparedness, Lancet Global Health 5 (2017) e742−e744, https://doi.org/10.1016/S2214-109X(17)30203-6.

[19] Global Preparedness Monitoring Board, A World at Risk: Annual Report on Global Preparedness for Health Emergencies, World Health Organization, Geneva, 2019.

[20] United Nations, Economic and Social Survey of Asia and the Pacific, Economic and Social Commission for Asia and the Pacific Decade of Action (ESCAP), 2020.

[21] W. Naudé, Artificial Intelligence against COVID-19: An Early Review, 2020.

[22] M. Prensky, What is ISN'T technology good at? Empathy for one thing!, Educat. Technol. 52 (2012) 64.

[23] Y. Zhang, et al., Mental health problems during the COVID-19 pandemics and the mitigation effects of exercise: a longitudinal study of college students in China, Int. J. Environ. Res. Publ. Health 17 (2020) E3722.

[24] A. Patriti, et al., FACS on behalf of the AssociazioneChirurghiOspedalieriItaliani (ACOI). Emergency general surgery in Italy during the COVID-19 outbreak: the first survey from real life. Version 2, World J. Emerg. Surg. 15 (1) (2020) 36.

[25] https://www.weforum.org/agenda/2020/05/how-ai-and-machine-learning-are-helping-to-fight-covid-19/.

[26] Wipro. https://www.wipro.com/process-and-industrial-manufacturing/intelligent-manufacturing-post-covid-19-the-emergence-of-a-new-era/.

[27] JAPI. https://www.japi.org/x26474a4/corona-virus-covid-19-and-its-impact-on-health-care-workers.

[28] DRDO. https://www.drdo.gov.in/medidoot-medical-trolly.

[29] B. Latané, The psychology of social impact, Am. Psychol. 36 (4) (1981) 343−356.

[30] B. Latané, S. Wolf, The social impact of majorities and minorities, Psychol. Rev. 88 (5) (1981) 438−453, https://doi.org/10.1037/0033-295X.88.5.438.

[31] SSIR. https://ssir.org/articles/entry/the_problem_with_covid_19_artificial_intelligence_solutions_and_how_to_fix_them.

[32] J.-F. Bonnefon, A. Shariff, I. Rahwan, The social dilemma of autonomous vehicles, Science 352 (2016) 1573−1576.

[33] V. Dignum, Responsible Artificial Intelligence, Springer International Publishing, 2019.

[34] R. Scholz, et al., Unintended side effects of the digital transition: European scientists' messages from a proposition-based expert round table, Sustainability 10 (2018) 2001.

[35] Sunderland. https://www.sunderland.ac.uk/more/news/story/covid-19-the-economic-psychological-and-social-impact-of-post-pandemic-life-1301.

[36] R. Khan, P. Shrivastava, A. Kapoor, A. Tiwari, A. Mittal, Social media analysis with AI: sentiment analysis techniques for the analysis of Twitter covid-19 data, J. Critical Rev. 7 (9) (2020) 2761−2774.

[37] J. Samuel, G.G. Ali, M. Rahman, E. Esawi, Y. Samuel, Covid-19 public sentiment insights and machine learning for tweets classification, Information 11 (6) (2020) 314.

[38] V. Kakulapati, et al., Multimodal detection of COVID-19 fake news and public behavior analysis—machine learning perspective, in: S. Bhatia, A.K. Dubey, R. Chhikara, P. Chaudhary, A. Kumar (Eds.), Intelligent Healthcare. EAI/Springer Innovations in Communication and Computing, Springer, Cham, 2021, https://doi.org/10.1007/978-3-030-67051-1_14.

[39] A. Goel, B. Creeden, M. Kumble, S. Salunke, A. Shetty, B. Wiltgen, Using Watson for enhancing human-computer co-creativity, in: 2015 AAAI Fall Symposium Series, 2015.

[40] Brookings. https://www.brookings.edu/essay/why-has-covid-19-been-especially-harmful-for-working-women.

[41] S.K. Card, T.P. Moran, A. Newell, The Psychology of Human-Computer Interaction, CRC Press, Boca Raton, FL, USA, 2018.

[42] D. Morrison, The applications of cognitive theory and science to HCI: a psychological perspective, Int. J. Hum. Comput. Interact. (1992).

[43] F.A. Boons, et al., Covid-19, changing social practices and the transition to sustainable production and consumption. Version 1.0, Sustainable Consumption Institute, Manchester, 2020, https://doi.org/10.13140/RG.2.2.18506.59840 (May 2020).

[44] L. Vyas, et al., The impact of working from home during COVID-19 on work and life domains: an exploratory study on Hong Kong, Policy Design Practice 4 (1) (2021) 59–76, https://doi.org/10.1080/25741292.2020.1863560.

[45] CIO. https://www.cio.com/article/3602812/ai-and-automation-are-linchpins-for-post-pandemic-business-success.html.

[46] S. Chan, 9gag Announces Work from Home Forever, 2020. Accessed 25 May, https://www.humanresourcesonline.net/9gag-announces-work-from-home-forever.

[47] H. Wong, et al., Survey Findings on Working from Home under COVID19, Lingnan University, 2020. (Accessed 20 May 2020).

[48] J.A. Mello, Managing telework programs effectively, Empl. Responsib. Rights J. 19 (4) (2007) 247–261, https://doi.org/10.1007/s10672-007-9051-1.

[49] M. Robertson, et al., Telecommuting: managing the safety of workers in home office environments, Prof. Saf. 48 (4) (2003) 30–36.

[50] J.H. Collins, J.J. Moschler, The benefits and limitations of telecommuting, Defense AR J. 16 (1) (2009) 55–66.

[51] B. Caulfield, Does it pay to work from home? Examining the factors influencing working from home in the greater Dublin area, Case Stud. Transp. Policy 3 (2) (2015) 206–214, https://doi.org/10.1016/j.cstp.2015.04.004(remove).

[52] C. Grant, et al., Construction and initial validation of the e-work life scale to measure remote e-working, Employee Relat. 41 (1) (2019) 16–33, https://doi.org/10.1108/ER-09-2017-0229.

[53] K. Eddleston, et al., Toward understanding remote workers' management of work-family boundaries: the complexity of workplace embeddedness, Group Organ. Manag. 42 (3) (2017) 346–387, https://doi.org/10.1177/1059601115619548.

[54] McKinsey & Company. https://www.mckinsey.com/featured-insights/future-of-work/the-future-of-work-after-covid-19.

[55] FlexJobs. https://www.flexjobs.com/blog/post/benefits-of-remote-work/.

[56] nibusinessinfo. https://www.nibusinessinfo.co.uk/content/advantages-and-disadvantages-employees-working-home.

[57] F. Jiang, et al., Artificial intelligence in healthcare: past, present, and future, Stroke Vascular Neurol. 2 (2017) 230–243, https://doi.org/10.1136/svn-2017-000101.

[58] Michael Page. https://www.michaelpage.ae/advice/management-advice/development-and-retention/covid-19-and-its-ripple-effects-working.

[59] N. Friesen, Report Dening Blended Learning, 2012. https://www.normfriesen.info/papers/Dening_Blended_Learning_NF.pdf. Retrieved on 2020-07-02.

[60] V. Strauss, Three Fears about Blended Learning, The Washington Post, September 22, 2012. Retrieved 2020-07- 02.

[61] Inside Higher Ed. https://www.insidehighered.com/digital-learning/blogs/learning-innovation/teaching-and-learning-after-covid-19.

[62] BW People. http://bwpeople.businessworld.in/article/The-Growing-Significance-of-Blended-Learning-and-Teaching-in-the-Post-Pandemic-World/03-11-2020-338518/.

[63] Harvard Business Publishing. https://hbsp.harvard.edu/inspiring-minds/the-pandemic-hit-colleges-hard-but-surfaced-the-potential-of-blended-learning.

[64] Credo-tech. https://credo.stanford.edu/pdfs/Online%20Charter%20Study%20Final.pdf.

[65] eLearning Industry. https://elearningindustry.com/6-benefits-blended-learning-looking-beyond-covid.

[66] World Economic Forum. https://www.weforum.org/agenda/2020/04/coronavirus-education-global-covid19-online-digital-learning.

[67] Arthur D. Little. https://www.adlittle.com/en/insights/viewpoints/accelerating-post-pandemic-e-learning.

[68] YourStory. https://yourstory.com/2020/07/schooling-post-pandemic-reality-elearning-trends/amp.

[69] B.B. Lockee, Online education in the post-COVID era, Nat. Electron. 4 (2021) 5−6, https://doi.org/10.1038/s41928-020-00534-0.

[70] Higher Education Digest. https://www.highereducationdigest.com/the-importance-of-online-learning-in-the-times-of-covid-19-and-beyond.

[71] eLearning Industry. https://elearningindustry.com/advantages-and-disadvantages-of-elearning.

[72] eLearning Industry. https://elearningindustry.com/how-will-covid-19-impact-future-of-educational-learning-sectro.

Practical case studies on human-computer interaction

Sheela S.V.[1], Abhinand P.[2] and Radhika K.R.[1]

[1]*Department of Information Science and Engineering, BMS College of Engineering, Bangalore, Karnataka, India;*
[2]*Bosch Group, Bangalore, Karnataka, India*

9.1 Introduction

Human—computer interaction (HCI) has emerged as one of the prominent threads connecting computing-based research that involves advanced information and communication aspects [1]. In other words, HCI is an application-oriented tool associated with analysis, design, and implementation for human use and their interaction with computing devices. Interaction refers to a conceptual and hypothetical model through which users relate with computers for carrying out a specific task. The framework uses a collaborative system for communication and is technically realized using an application-specific hardware or software.

HCI has gained enormous impact as one of the embedded devices and has become an integral component of various applications such as automotive, healthcare, and virtual reality. The main motive behind the design of a user interface system is the necessity to develop an effective interaction and interfacing medium for human users and to increase adaptability of computing devices for accomplishing necessary tasks [2]. As shown in Fig. 9.1, the interaction system consists of different software and hardware modules along with a multimedia interface module for generating an interactive output in accordance to user requirements. Based on the information displayed on interface module, the user accepts the output for various tasks.

There are four major goals of HCI, namely, high usability, functionality, aesthetic appeal, and enthralling user experience, which plays an important role in the development of applications. High usability and functionality are major concerns in the design of HCI systems [3]. High usability refers to various factors of interactive platforms such as easy and simple implementation, efficient task accomplishment, and user safety. Functionality refers to actions or services provided to the users. These factors contribute to accurate completion of tasks, which in turn results in increased productivity. Apart from high usability and functionality, the ease and plain aesthetic look of the interface is another critical factor in the design of interactive modules, which adds to commercial success of applications and products. In this context, user experience has gained huge attention, which not only satisfies the functionalities of the application but also seamlessly integrates into one's lifestyle without any complexity [4].

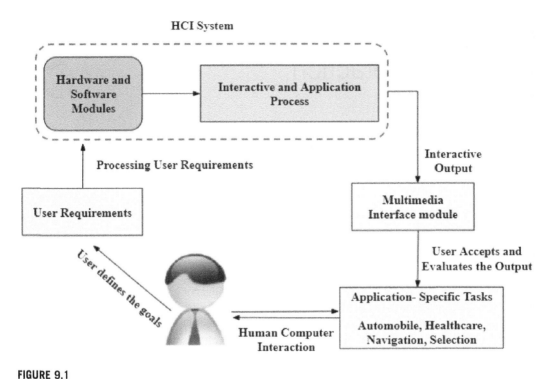

FIGURE 9.1

Concepts of HCI system with interaction and interface.

The evolution of the internet would not have been so successful without an effective web-browser interface. Touch-based, gesture-based, and audio-based interfaces are being adopted widely because of their alluring features and user convenience [5]. Communication-oriented applications use feature-based interfaces to increase corporate outlook. An example of a touch-based and voice command-based application is the design of modern smartphones that have replaced previous generation of telephones. Computerized video games that work on gesture-based and action-based commands have introduced innovative ways to play computer games. It is still compelling that HCI provides an effective way to develop creative and appealing displays that can be customized according to user needs and capabilities [6].

9.1.1 Principles of HCI

HCI has simplified human lives with its excellent features. It is challenging to design an effective interactive system because of its multiobjective functions, which involves simultaneous execution of multiple factors such as interaction with different users, analyzing the characteristics of tasks, differing technologies, cost of computing devices, lack of capabilities, and adapting to different quantitative evaluation metrics. In addition, substantial knowledge in various domains is required. Researchers have accumulated and discussed fundamental principles for design of user interface systems to achieve the desired goals. The principles of the HCI mentioned next are generic and can be applicable to various application-specific tasks.

- *User information-based principle:* The foremost affiliation in HCI is to control interaction and interface between users. The design is generally user centered, which is quite appropriate. The intent is that the interaction and interface must satisfy all requirements of users [7]. However, the process is difficult since requirements are inconsistent, and it requires a deep knowledge about user information. Primary details of a user such as age, gender, and qualification must be collected and analyzed to determine the capability and skill level. The information is used for interaction and aids in identifying a proper interface medium.

- *Understand the task:* An important principle is to design HCI systems based on the understanding of task. The "task" refers to activity or work that needs to be completed by using an interactive system. Understanding the task refers to an interaction model and precise evaluation of user requirements [2]. It identifies the context and information of tasks with respect to application guidelines. Users work on different tasks for the same application, and in such cases, tasks handled by individual users are evaluated. Information related to tasks is reflected in the interface model, thereby simplifying the interaction process.

- *Memory-based principle:* The design of an effective memory-oriented interface is one of the prominent requirements in HCI systems. The principle is based on the fact that the interaction and interface model must be designed with routine and familiarity that assist users to memorize [8]. The user gains a good understanding about the interface, so it can be used effectively. In addition, a theoretical concept states that humans are more efficient in accomplishing tasks that require less memory burden. A lighter memory load, especially for short-term memory, enhances the role of interference by providing relevant instructions and guidance in completing the tasks. Reduced memory burden will also improve erroneous behavior of the interaction system.

- *Consistency:* This principle in subtasks of an application benefits users to accurately carry out tasks. For example, it may be confusing during task execution if interaction steps and subtasks are inconsistent, resulting in erroneous outcome and restricted adaptability. Thus, an HCI principle based on consistency holds prominence and leads to high acceptability among users [9].

- *Feedback and reminders:* An interactive system provides continuous reminders of important data and refreshes the memory of users [2]. It is a well-known fact that the memory capacity of humans is limited, and it regularly dissipates information, especially in a multitasking environment. To overcome the glitches related to memory and to maintain the user's cognizance for accurate responses, it is essential to provide a continuous reminder or feedback that helps to refresh memory and assist users in completing tasks easily.

The rest of the chapter is structured as follows: Section 9.2 discusses the implementation of HCI for healthcare systems. Section 9.3 provides an outline on HCI for digital hearing. Section 9.4 explicates on digital humanities. Section 9.5 presents a description on business intelligence. Section 9.6 explores the different case studies on HCI, and Section 9.7 concludes the chapter with prominent observations.

9.2 Healthcare systems

The application of HCI has been a drifting topic of research. In the past few decades, various research works have presented several experimental and theoretical perceptions about user experience and interaction models to guide future healthcare applications. Theoretical perception based on empirical analysis is not sufficient to understand diversified healthcare systems. Constantly changing medical developments require an effective interaction and interface model to deal with modern and sophisticated healthcare applications [10]. Existing research works on medicine practice have suggested the need to develop a comprehensive model to understand the user experience and to provide accurate interpretation of requirements. HCI has expanded substantially as a disciplined area focused on various bilateral tasks in healthcare applications such as information retrieval, image quality enhancement, comprehensive analysis of medical data, and software programming [11].

Different ways of interacting range from smartphone-based medical applications to kiosks. Research based on HCI has focused on wide range of information technologies such as electronic health record systems and sensor-based wearable healthcare devices such as Fitbits and health tracker wrist watches. Sensors in wearable devices identify the abnormalities in a patient's health conditions by continuously observing physiologic parameters along with other symptoms. The health data is processed and is displayed on an adaptive user interface, as shown in Fig. 9.2.

However, it is not feasible for HCI alone to accomplish all tasks, so it is combined with cognitive theories that satisfy the distributed computing nature [12]. Fig. 9.3 shows an adaptive user interface—based HCI for healthcare systems. To serve several applications, a smart adaptive user interface has been proposed. The novel concept is handling of data collection, managing patient information and communication aspects by the controller, which in turn collaborates with visualization tools.

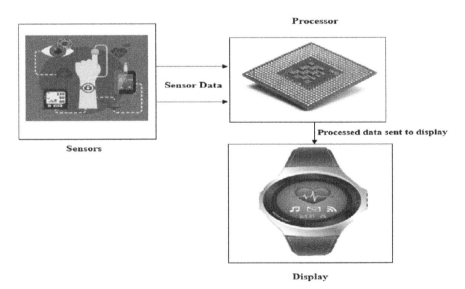

FIGURE 9.2

Illustration of smart wearable sensing device.

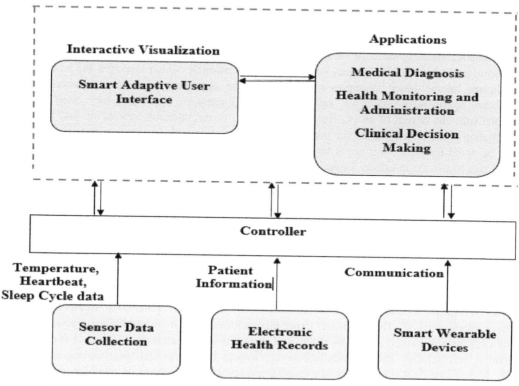

FIGURE 9.3

Adaptive user interface—based HCI for healthcare.

Design of an adaptive user interface based on HCI is one of the prominent aspects in healthcare applications [13]. It consists of a smart adaptive user interface for enabling interactive visualization between users and computer systems. The controller is responsible for coordinating different user interaction modules with an HCI system and acts as a communication interface. During initial design, user interface and requirements are calibrated to target a larger section of consumers along with potential individuals [14]. Most importantly, the user interfaces must adapt to constantly changing demands. It is also necessary to conduct hands-on remote usability testing using interface techniques, such as video conferencing in remote areas to conduct health workshops. It is observed that usage of pervasive and ubiquitous computing influences the design and development of consumer health systems with respect to user interface design and usability testing. Variations can be estimated and treated accordingly. Other changes are highly variable and quite difficult to predict. It is a well-known fact that the perception of an individual along with physical and cognitive characteristics deteriorates with aging [15]. The user interface must be capable of providing an effective interaction for older adults since it is difficult for them to perceive and understand different elements of user interfaces [16].

A user's access to the information related to health is likely to improve with exposure to the interface. Health information is well documented and can be obtained easily using the interface. For example, variations in fundamental health factors such as temperature, sleep cycle, and heart beat are recorded periodically, resulting in an optimized interface. Every user is categorized based on health characteristics and assigned to the most relevant interface. With the latest developments in commercial platforms, users can directly interact with medical professionals, which leverages the advantages of healthcare. Internet-based strategies have widened the opportunity for users to access desired healthcare applications and hence validate the effectiveness of HCI-based user interfaces [17]. Alternatively, the design of an interface must adapt to communication approaches and task-based information processing capacity, for instance, domain-based knowledge level of individual users. It must be noted that few users might be naive about their health problems and require fundamental knowledge to use the interface. To address these issues, modern HCI systems are incorporated with sophisticated sensors, networking, and interference software, which provides an opportunity to make effective usage of the interface.

Healthcare sectors have seen rapid expansion of sensors to measure various activities, track location of users, and monitor physiologic variations [18]. Based on the information collected by sensors, the interfacing medium is designed and programmed to collect routine physiologic data such as blood pressure, oxygen, and glucose levels. The sensors also enable the users to carry on a continuous and fluent monitoring for relevant information. Smartphones are used as an interfacing model that communicates with other systems via the internet [19]. Connecting the display of smart-phones in different locations with changing dimensions provides a sophisticated user experience and better convenience [20]. The techniques experiment with various circumstantial methods that provide a valuable insight into future designs in terms of system usability and related factors such as learning, adoption, and training. The methods incorporate various innovative and spearheading technologies such as computational ethnography to expand the scope of HCI systems in healthcare applications. Innovative applications simplify healthcare processes that were not perceived in the past.

HCI techniques continue to play an efficient and high-yielding role in the healthcare sector to satisfy the ever changing and growing demands of users, for example, mobile health (mhealth) applications. Further improvement in the design of a convenient and reliable healthcare environment preserves a patient's information. Advanced healthcare depends on connected, integrated, and sophisticated systems for communicating health records of patients. The role of HCI in creating such a transformation in system design and development is important. Latest developments adopt decision-making tasks for integration of unstructured information resulting in precision medicine [21]. Machine learning techniques such as text mining, search engines, neuro-fuzzy inference system, analytical hierarchy process, medical imaging, and interactive visualization improve healthcare workflows.

9.3 Digital hearing

Prior to the digital hearing devices, analog devices were commonly used for people who are hearing impaired. Different levels of sound were adapted without reduction in background noises. Lack of sophistication in analog devices led to inventing digital hearing that provides a natural sounding mechanism with enhanced audio variations. The main components are a microphone, amplifier, and battery. The amplifier acts upon nuances and natural sound to adapt personalized settings. Advances in digital signal processing provided reduction in noise, feedback cancellation, and self-adaptation directional inputs for acoustic amplification. Customized hearing enhances comfort for different types of hearing loss. The benefit of digital hearing devices is that they can pair up with smartphones or tablets and connect to stream calls through wireless communication.

The initial developments of hearing devices used an array processor for processing audio signals digitally in real time [22]. Analog input signals from three possibilities, microphone, tape player, or receiver, were provided to an antialiasing filter and analog-to-digital converter. The digitized signal was processed using an array processor. The controlling mechanism determines the type of processing such as linear/adaptive filtering, spectral shaping, and spectrum subtraction. The array processor output is fed to a digital-to-analog converter and anti-imaging filter. Hearing device receiver, headphone, or transmitter are some of the options for the resulting analog signal. Further, a wearable microprocessor hearing device was devised to extract frequency from speech signals and modulate the sine wave in accordance with a listener's hearing capability. High-speed digital signal processing (DSP) chips, programmable devices, and switched capacitors were the techniques adapted for manufacturing hearing devices. Commercial devices were introduced considering multichannel amplitude compression.

Interactive and user-centric design are essential concepts in HCI for people with special needs [23]. It is required to highlight usability values by matching task requirements with design. Special thematic sessions based on equipment and services for the hearing impaired help to improve communication [24]. Automatic captioning, internet techniques, and gesture-based approaches provide substantial support for users [25]. Sign language has been adapted as the most common means of communication for hearing impaired. A screen reader facilitates the deaf by providing visual translation of text to sign language animation using avatars [26]. Website contents are translated into sign language video sequences. Eye gaze can be measured through electrooculography (EOG) [27]. Eye gaze is estimated from EOG measures to select the desired audio stream, resulting in increased speech intelligibility.

An instance of HCI for digital hearing is represented using a sign language translation system. Exchange of information and conversation would significantly improve communication for the hearing impaired. Design of interfaces for speech to sign language conversion includes speech acquisition, speech to text conversion, generation of tokens, matching with sign language database, and display animation with relevant captions, as shown in Fig. 9.4 [28]. The novelty here is the display of a caption corresponding to animated or video output for a better receptive view. The sequence of steps is as follows:

- Speech input in the form of audio signals is captured using a microphone and stored as a repository. Input could also be any of the audio clips from internet sources.
- Feature extraction uses Cepstral coefficients, spectrum bands, and energy distribution specific to the vocal tract. A trained model is devised for speech to text conversion. The process identifies words based on pre-trained vocabulary by mapping every spoken word into text. A repository of word templates, phonemes, and recorded audio signals is used to obtain text corresponding to audio input.
- Text is parsed to generate tokens based on the grammar rules. A normalization process helps to remove less informative words.

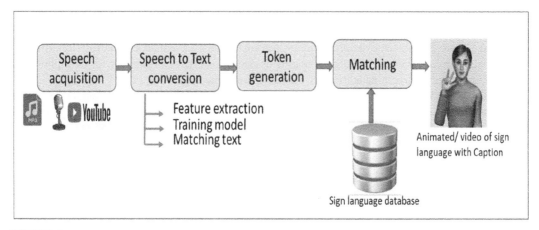

FIGURE 9.4

Interface for digital hearing considering speech to sign language conversion.

- A sign language database consists of visual images or videos with tags. Every character or word from processed text is matched based on the tags. The output can be amalgamated to obtain an animation or video of sign language. It is important to display captions for clear understanding.

Fusion of more than one feature coefficient can result in increased accuracy. Incorporating prediction in real time based on generative models, sign characteristics, and hand position leads to a natural means of communication.

9.4 Digital humanities

Digital humanities is an emerging field highlighting the technologic developments based on literature, philosophy, and history. Application of computational methods and tools to traditional disciplines provides a reflective analysis for modern evolving scenarios. Annotation of historical content, creating digital libraries, mapping of similar cultural areas, and data visualization are a few examples. The initial work was based on migration of material related to culture, classical literature, entertainment, and multimedia. With the advent of automation, several algorithms were devised to support collaborative cross-platform and cross-media works with the advantage of communication networks. Projects related to visualization, simulation, model representation, network analysis, and repository development evolved as a generative practice. A wide range of communicative tools, motion graphics, screen capture, and animation contribute to an interactive design. Cultural dimensions, interoperability, and compatibility are essential for sustainable solutions. A few examples are discussed here.

Journal Storage (JSTOR) is an example of digital humanities established in New York [29]. It encompasses a massive repository of journals in academics, humanities, and social science. Full text searches are possible in 8000 institutions across 160 countries in partnership with museums, libraries, and publishers. Access to 12 million academic journals, one lakh books, materials of 75 disciplines, and millions of images has been provided. HCI is designed with a simple user interface consisting of search sequence, choice of available volumes and transaction, listing, and indexing [30]. Search filters are based on articles, books, and research reports. Language options and discipline selection are available. Convenient information retrieval is enabled through image search.

Visual search of BBC news and paintings digital repositories have been developed by Visual Geometry Group, University of Oxford [31]. Data provided by BBC comprises prime time news broadcasts of over 5 years. Object, instance, and people are the different query type search options. A visual model is trained based on positive and negative samples using an image encoder. Objects in paintings are retrieved by searching the dataset of 2 lakh paintings. A classifier is trained based on a convolutional neural network model using photographs available on the internet. Other digital humanities projects developed are American Panorama based on American history, 1947 partition archive documenting Indian history, Cinemaazi featuring regional vintage cinema, and Bhakti virtual archive exploring devotional traditions in South Asia.

Development of research infrastructure in the field of humanities deals with usability of digital tools [32]. User-centered research aids in identifying requirements at initial stages of design process. Improved user experience is attained by switching between tools and devices. Research workflow comprises integration of images, using specialized applications relevant to devices, considering domain specific data and visualization of collections. Suitability of user experience is tested with prototypes and implementation iterations.

9.5 Business intelligence

Business intelligence encompasses technologies and strategies for information management and data analysis. Finance, sales, procurement, operations, human resources, manufacturing, media, and analytics are a few application areas. Operating and strategic decisions are made effectively with dashboards, charts, reports, and graphs. Processes involved are data visualization, querying, data mining, and statistical analysis. Intelligent practices in business provide increased efficiency, data clarity, and improved customer satisfaction. An online analytical processing engine facilitates business intelligence through analytic computations, data discovery, and predictive analysis. Consistent information improves processes, product features, and customer collaborations.

HCI for business intelligence presents usefulness of technology, look, and feel to end users. Initially, data is extracted, processed, and stored in the warehouse. Further, the data is structured for analysis. Dependencies and trends are determined using online analytical processing. Specialized indicators and informational dashboards display processed results in the required format. Companies like Oracle, IBM, Microsoft, and SAP provide software and business solutions. The functionalities and interfaces are assimilated in building the tools, such as Sisense, icCube, Domo, Gooddata, Clear analytics, QlikView, and Solver [33].

Several organizations benefit from business intelligence. A few of them are discussed here. Amazon, being a leading online retailer, applies intelligent solutions for targeted marketing, user recommendations, and pricing optimizations. Product grouping and route scheduling are best operated with predictive analysis. American Express has streamlined payment methods, market offers, and customer retention. Report processing has been utilized by Coca-Cola bottling company. Success of intelligence services in Starbucks resulted in consistent revenue and strong customer satisfaction. Other benefits include precision marketing in banking, dynamic decision-making in social media, production planning in manufacturing, and real-time intuitions in sports.

An illustration of HCI design is provided for media analytics platform and web analytics. In the media industry, techniques such as filtering, summarizing, informatics, and decision-making contribute to the heuristic design [34]. Planners and advertisers aggregate behavioral data to improve user interface and experience. Selection of data range, comparison of demographic categories, program filter, and choosing dayparts are the options in interface design. Visualization includes composition of charts, highlighting, and color scheme. Web analytics comprises metrics such as duration, navigation, search, visits, information architecture, content design, and customer service [35]. Handling datasets, computing performance indicators and data-driven activities are the key points for interface design. New business solutions can be intended based on usability evaluation.

Innovative ways to attract customers consider user experience features and well-designed interface options. Augmented reality and natural language processing assist in adopting personalization and automation strategies. New models of collaborations include chatbots and language generation systems. Business can be improved by providing human-centric services and building personalized relationships using technical aspects.

9.6 Case studies

Interactive design aspects are specific to applications. An overview of practical case studies related to the HCI design for air traffic systems, automotive systems, virtual reality, and crisis management is provided in this section.

9.6.1 Air traffic systems

There has been a consistent and significant growth in airline systems to enhance various aspects of applications. The design is such that it is easily accessible to pilots on a modern aviation flight deck. A wide range of expertise is available at the fingertips and is mainly designed to assist pilots and designers in making intricate decisions, for effective communication, analyzing the situation, and providing assistance in flying the aircraft. These technologies are developed based on HCI. Airline applications have been prominent for long-term research to increase safety in aviation, since major reversals and hindrances in the form of fatal accidents and flight mishaps have been observed. Investigations related to flight accidents have considered user interaction as a major criteria, which demonstrates the influence of interface platforms on airline safety.

The air traffic system (ATS) is a service provided by ground-based air traffic controllers (ATCs) that provide guidance to aircraft on the ground and in airspace. The preliminary objective of ATCs is to avoid collisions between planes, to monitor and control the flow of traffic in airspace, and to provide necessary information and assistance to pilots. ATCs effectively coordinate the patterns of air traffic to make sure that aircraft have a safer distance between air and the ground. Recent years have seen a significant transformation in ATS that has resulted in the development of a next generation smart air traffic system (SATS) [36]. ATCs and pilots coordinate the tasks by synchronizing activities using scientific assistance. The development of modern and progressive HCI is required to perform these activities. The design of interface requires accurate synchronization, effective interpretation, and realization of hypothetical air traffic scenarios.

The effective implementation of SATS addresses a few research challenges. SATS must comply with the latest coordination strategies and policies for decision-making processes to increase the compatibility of aircraft trajectories with systematic air traffic [37,38]. The characteristics and functionalities along with certain task-oriented communication protocols must be followed for automating the process of traffic management systems. Modern interaction systems allow the users, namely pilots, crew of aircraft, and ATCs, to carry out designated tasks with proper guidance and assistance [39]. Additionally, the interactive tools employ elite and sophisticated languages to achieve error-free and ambiguous communication between pilots and ATC crew. It must be ensured that these languages must be easily interpretable and human readable [40]. User interface systems require innovative algorithms and mathematical models. The algorithms are used by air and ground systems to manage traffic flow. They also constitute the computational capacity of HCI and incorporate various functions that provide necessary information related to management of trajectory and collateral decision-making tasks such as trajectory estimation [41], detection and resolution of trajectory conflict [42], and appropriate trajectory guidance [43]. The information employed by HCI systems is mainly collected from multiple sensor-based inputs and intercommunication models [44]. The conceptual framework of SATS using HCI is illustrated in Fig. 9.5. Establishing good communication between

ATS Modules

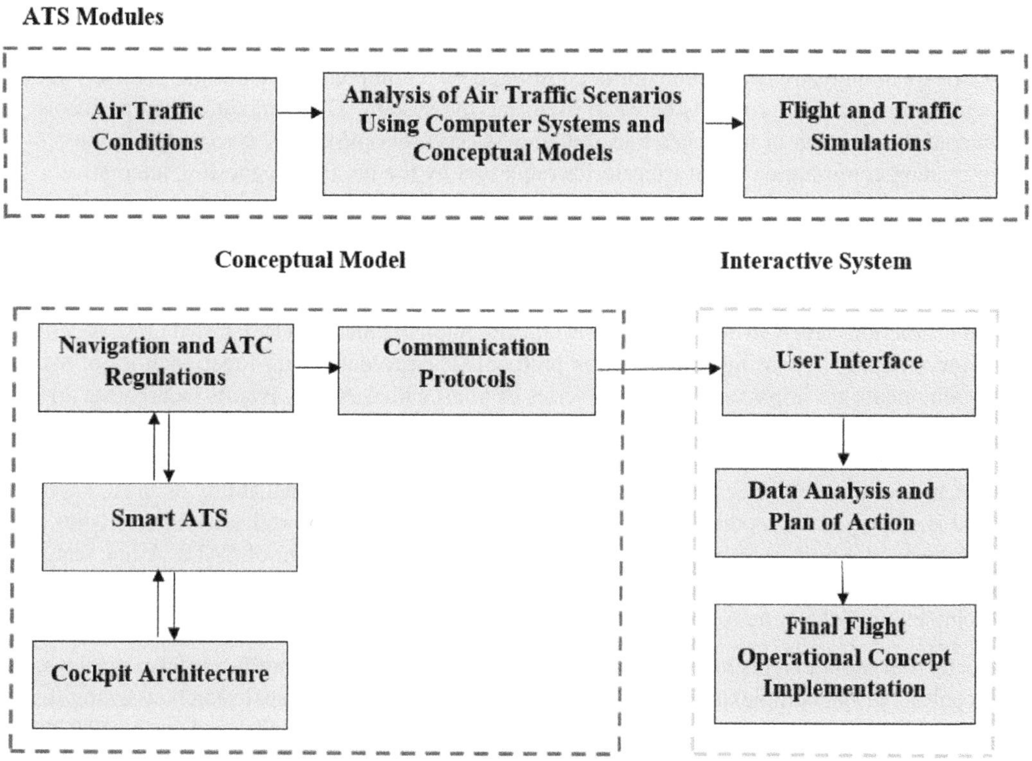

FIGURE 9.5

Framework of the SATS using HCI.

SATS and the user interface is significant. The plan of action and implementation aspects are based on protocols.

The framework of the SATS consists of three main stages, such as ATS modules, design of conceptual model, and interactive system.

(i) *ATS modules:* The system modules are designed to satisfy goals of SATS along with analysis of air traffic scenarios, which consist of different use cases. The requirements are usually categorized into different sub-scenarios for various levels and are specifically presented in HCI. To determine the most symbolic and paradigmatic scenarios, it is necessary to assign goals for each state. Further the goals and scenarios together assist in analyzing the main functionalities of the system such as potential for achieving desired goals, system—ground interface, system inputs, and actions for inputs. A few prominent subtasks of SATS are identified based on the operational point of view. The subtasks are aircraft, traffic control, airline operational control, meteorological service provider, and airspace resources provider [45]. HCI is employed for establishing an effective interaction between aircraft systems and ground environment. The most common air traffic scenarios are considered and evaluated based on controlling perspective.

(ii) *Conceptual model:* Design of a conceptual model comprises the static arrangement of elements such as navigation, ATC regulations, cockpit architecture, and dynamic communication protocols. The static structure of SATS links different users interacting with the system and data. Correspondingly, dynamic behavior is constituted by a comprehensive design, precisely HCI and communication protocols between users and the system. The communication protocols record the duration of messages transmitted between users [46]. ATC is responsible for providing confirmation about trajectories requested by the aircraft, suggesting alternative requested trajectories, accepting or rejecting the suggested alternatives by the aircraft system, and providing information about the final decision taken.

(iii) *Interactive framework:* In this stage, internal infrastructure and the process of smart ATC are displayed using an interfacing system. The interactive framework decides a plan of action based on instructions received and leads to final concept implementation. The internal process defines a fundamental view using an interaction protocol. The protocols with functionalities of user requirements are implemented using a series of plans called events. Events incorporate arrival of information or percept. The plans for implementing certain activities, decision-making agreement, and achieving correlation between users and system are categorized for defining the potential of an interacting system. The potential defines computational ability of an HCI system and is employed for modifying implementation process. Various correlated characteristics and attributes of a user interaction system are incorporated in the design of SATS. A few features might be segmented into multiple subtasks before being implemented, which reduces the complexity of the system in terms of plans, events, and data.

Special user requirements require novel interactions using graphical interfaces, large displays, and touch control. Visual complexity of cockpit displays, target detection, visual search, assisting loss of control, touch screen interaction, and automation are some of the issues addressed during HCI design on a modern flight deck [47].

9.6.2 Automotive systems

The evolution of information and communication knowledge in the automobile sector has resulted in remarkable growth of HCI systems. With the advancements in vehicular network technology, automotive applications are diversified. Applications allow vehicular data acquisition, information broadcasting, communication, and access to navigation systems [48]. Currently, the information automotive model has been developed from a single driving model to a convoluted model that includes data and communication technologies. Vehicle to vehicle (V2V) and vehicle to infrastructure (V2I) communication is tested along with the interoperability between manufacturers and service providers [49].

In a complex automobile communication system, it is necessary for drivers to carry out a greater number of secondary tasks that are not related to driving. Apart from primary tasks such as driving, controlling the car, observing the traffic scenarios, and maintaining the proper driving lane, various other secondary tasks such as navigation, AC controlling, and managing phone calls require a driver's attention. For accomplishing these tasks, the driver needs to have superior cognitive, visual, and action-based resources including a smart automotive interface [50]. Secondary tasks constituted by in-vehicle information interaction have a negative impact on the efficiency of a driver and majorly affect the safety of road traffic scenarios [51]. These factors have introduced sophisticated challenges to the drivers, especially while facing complex automobile interaction systems [52]. It is difficult for drivers to analyze the hierarchic relationship of vehicle-related data. Other tasks include obtaining relevant information from interactive systems and interpretation of information accurately and effectively, which have led to the research on automotive application-based HCI [53,54]. An approach of HCI design for automotive systems is shown in Fig. 9.6. Based on the input from interactive displays, information is processed, and relevant signals are communicated to an automotive controller as an important step. The controller is responsible for monitoring and navigation.

The traditional screen used for displaying the radio frequency of the car has been eliminated gradually and is being replaced by modern liquid crystal display screens and see-thru head-up displays [55]. The screen-based display technique has led to the visibility of clearer and larger images for drivers. There has been a significant development in projection-based displays [56]. Projection-based displays were initially used in aircraft applications to improve the interaction of an aircraft system. Based on the same motive, a projection-based display was deployed in vehicles to make sure that the driver can see current scenario clearly without any obstacles. It helps to overcome the complexities such as high illumination or inadequate lighting while looking at the windshield [57]. 3D displays using holographic projection are gaining prominence because of their ability to replay the light reflected from an object using a spatial light modulator [58]. Research on adaption of holographic projection in automotive applications is moving at a slower pace and provides a chance for further research and experimentation [59].

A fundamental interface system uses buttons, knobs, and brakes for controlling the vehicle. The controlling phenomenon is categorized under physical interaction. With the emergence of several progressive technologies, physical interaction is being replaced by HCI, and several activities can be performed using touch keys [60]. Physical interaction mode using buttons is highly challenging due to posing difficulties in reducing cognition, operational safety, and efficiency. Further, the aesthetic look of the vehicle dashboard is inferior and might result in nonoperation of keys after using for a long time

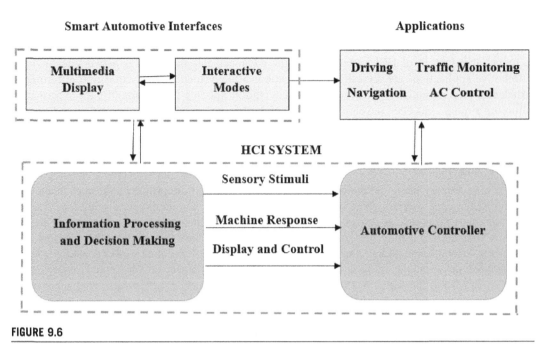

FIGURE 9.6

An approach of HCI design for automotive systems.

[61]. In touch screen—based interaction mode, the driver operates and controls the vehicle using gestures on the control screen. The screen enhances the interior look of the vehicle and has an intelligent way of operating [62].

Voice-based interaction refers to direct use of commands for controlling the vehicle equipment without requiring any physical controllers. This helps the driver to focus mainly on driving, thereby improving work efficiency and safety. One of the superior voice-based interaction approaches is the speech—user interface, which is successfully implemented for hand-free interaction [63]. Intelligence in the technology of automobiles has led to the design of vehicle-mounted products based on internet of things [64]. User HCI for functionalities such as telephone and navigation enhances the interactive experience. Other parameters for user experience include finger movement, facial expressions, and psychological scales.

9.6.3 Virtual reality systems

Development in virtual reality (VR) systems has gained significant attention in the field of potentially capable HCI-based research [65]. Considerable efforts have been made to elevate research to design higher productive techniques and reduce the technical barrier between humans and computer systems [66]. The main objective of VR systems in HCI is to design a beneficial platform that is feasible and reliable for establishing an effective interaction [67]. Techniques such as hand gesture-based recognition systems and action-based interactive systems play a vital role and are mainly employed in different engineering, empirical, and education-based applications. VR is expanding its base, and due to superior interfacing quality, it is a leading and widely used aspect of communication systems [68]. The capability of providing a comprehensive and clear picture of a concept is obtained by representing the object in a 3D spatial manner using computing devices. Users can interact, monitor, and control different objects in the virtual environment [69]. The systems mainly depend on 3 I's, such as interaction, immersion and imagination, which complement each other in terms of user attributes, interfacing capabilities, and interaction manners. The system has a head-mounted display, and information flows in these systems, which makes the user an integral part of the interfacing system. Fig. 9.7 illustrates different modules involved in the design of an HCI-based VR system.

An HCI-based VR system is a closed-loop system that artificially creates communication between the virtual environment and real-time scenarios. A VR system comprises a data acquisition and testing module that takes user instructions as input. Sensors act as an interacting system between user and interface. It collects and tracks different interaction modes such as gesture, voice, or touch. The control unit interacts with the virtual environment and provides feedback to users with virtual images being displayed. The user can interact with the virtual environment usually represented in the form of a 3D model. The innovation is that each user's interaction with the virtual environment is quantitatively and qualitatively analyzed using the simulation module for simple and complex tasks without the need of intermediate devices.

The research on HCI systems related to problem solving in VR is described as an application of computing [70]. Real-time experimental analysis is conducted to validate the efficacy of systems. Empirical research must be conducted such that hypothetical information is nearly identical to the real design. Implementation aspects must incorporate various technically verified hypotheses that include integrated conceptual models, facts, and techniques that act as connecting medium between the constructive solutions and theoretical aspects. Recent developments have created enormous interest in novel designs and cumulative works capable of facilitating robust communication [71]. Interaction through multiple platforms provides a broad scope and great impact on user experience in VR. Design of a multiuser VR system aids the manufacturing process in product structure and layout planning [72].

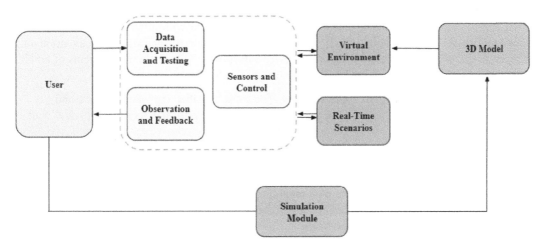

FIGURE 9.7

HCI-based virtual reality system.

The system supports globally distributed manufacturing companies in the design and review process through a collaborative platform.

9.6.4 Crisis management

The evolution of interactive computer-related technologies has made significant efforts in handling emergency conditions [73]. Since it is important to have an effective interaction for emergency situations, most of the applications implement intelligent algorithms that can accurately interpret user commands [74]. A reliable interfacing platform is required to communicate. Design of an automated system collaborating with users needs accurate responses in emergency situations. The latest techniques developed for HCI depend on accumulated large-scale data and quality of data. In case of emergencies or during uncertainties, there are chances that quality of data declines, which in turn affects the handling process. Thus, it is essential to identify issues from collective interaction to optimize the performance of interaction systems.

Crisis management requires accurate information in a short duration of time. It is essential to access effective response plans in a timely manner. In real-world scenarios, disaster situations are most common and suffer from resource allocation-related challenges [75]. To enhance the process and to reduce human error, computer systems play an eminent role in automating the procedure and plan event handling accordingly. Interactive systems must be trained appropriately for quick decision-making.

The aim of interface system is to replicate the information exchange process of human communication system with different modalities. Combination of voice- and gesture-based HCI shows substantial results, compared with individual usage. Collaborating speech and gesture has certain prominent advantages while dealing with complexities. The techniques are widely incorporated for achieving an effortless and expressive crisis management system. To manage the situation, a computer system must be able to understand multiple functionalities [76]. A multimodal HCI system enables the human user to interact with computing systems consisting of a large screen display [77]. The high-resolution display provides real-time visualization of current scenarios and events for plan of actions.

HCI used in emergency management systems is hypothesized with different characteristics and functionalities of critical situations. The operators have superior control, and significant attention must be given to the problem while ignoring all irrelevant information. The main requirements of an HCI system at each phase of emergency handling process are as follows:

(i) *Surveillance:* The HCI must focus on fusion and must visualize the value, impact, and reliability of surveillance data. The interface system has to prioritize its actions to deal with information overload.

(ii) *Crisis identification:* The identification of emergency situations is mainly related to risk perception where HCI systems enable the operators to assess the associated threats. It interacts with the emergency management team and gathers necessary information.

(iii) *Action planning:* A collaborative plan regarding the decision-making process and corresponding action based on the process is designed. This includes analysis of cognitive tasks and modeling of multicriteria decisions.

(iv) *Implementation plan:* HCI allows seamless interaction to outline a detailed execution plan that includes briefing and tasking on logistics, resource allocation, and situation awareness.

(v) *Cross-agency collaboration and sharing*: The task is mainly associated with deployment of HCI for performing various operations such as information fusion, data display, visualization, analyzing user perception of risk, handling the media, understanding the crowd behavior, and evaluation.

To design HCI for emergency management systems, it is essential to access the information at the precise time in the correct format. Computer interaction systems are employed for enhancing the capabilities of individuals and to design a potential interface to achieve effective interaction [78]. Universal design for crisis management uses tools based on information and communication technology that contribute to a larger sector of people including elders and disabled persons [79]. The requirements of diverse user groups are prioritized through iterations of prototyping and testing.

9.7 Conclusion

The chapter mainly deals with the role of HCI systems in the design of various applications. As inferred from existing literature, HCI has evolved as the most primitive technology that connects humans with computing devices. HCI is widely used in various applications based on artificial intelligence, computational intelligence, and design of an effective user interface. The design aspects are analyzed with respect to various applications. The study examines the design of HCI for healthcare systems, digital hearing, digital humanities, and business intelligence. Applied scenarios with reference to air traffic control, automotive systems, VR, and crisis management are outlined.

Application development for healthcare is a trending topic. Cognitive theories in HCI allow medical practitioners to exploit the information of patients using an effective interaction system. The study presents a comprehensive analysis of adaptive user interface and distributed computing based on HCI for consumer health. Application of computing devices in the healthcare sector and associated design aspects are presented. Artificial intelligence–driven decision-making tasks and physician-centered design provide an interactive solution to patients and support daily clinical routine [21].

Sign languages are based on native idioms and are different for every country. Hand gestures with face and head postures are analyzed. Many models exist involving modalities like text, speech, and sign language. An overview of HCI design for digital hearing is presented for speech to sign language conversion. Implementation of such interfaces in hospitals, airports, and major office areas would enhance the literacy for those who are hearing impaired. Interfaces could also include Kinect sensor and other assistive tools. Online captioning for streaming data in television and webcasts needs precise representation in sign language due to real-time parameters.

The distinctive contribution of digital humanities enhances scholarly interpretation, community practices, and traditional knowledge. Computational capabilities, differential approaches, ambiguity, and indexing need to be addressed at different levels. An interpretative framework is attained through aggregation of materials. New dimensions of knowledge and intellectual challenges promote innovation in this field. Business intelligence understands resource allocation, preferences, and trends to help data-driven enterprises. Online analytical processing supports multidimensional queries from data warehouses. State-of-the-art developments adapt cloud-based platforms, real-time processing, and big data analysis. With constant monitoring activity and communicating results, supply chain management can be improved. Cutting-edge systems incorporate machine learning techniques for prediction and automation. Implementing data-driven decision-making enhances business standards and performance in real-time scenarios.

Case studies are investigated to understand the developmental process of interactive systems. Smart ATS is realized based on the dynamic behavior and intelligent interference architecture, which provides an effective platform for users to interact with computing devices. Swift and seamless navigation is provided, thereby assisting the pilots to effectively coordinate with ATC to prevent possible collision between aircraft and ground systems. Current developments in airline applications such as cockpit voice recorders and flight data recorders have contributed to improving the aviation safety [80]. Automotive applications based on multimodalities are gaining huge attention among researchers. Interface and interaction models increase adaptability. Analysis of multimedia display modes such as screen, projection, and holographic projection are explored. The work discusses various facets of automotive HCI design such as physical, touch screen, and voice. Latest developments, such as in-cabin monitoring system in completely autonomous vehicles, have accounted for convictions in automotive applications [81]. VR-based concepts and research on HCI systems for problem solving are elaborated in this chapter. Skill-based visual exploratory technique, immersive approach for gaming, and physiologic sensing to measure human trust are the modern technologies that still need a deeper understanding of applying VR to different human-centric tasks. Effective design of HCI systems and essential criteria to accomplish an emergency management task are discussed. A multimodal HCI system for crisis management is explicated. Computer systems must be trained appropriately for a quick decision-making process. As a futuristic approach, technologic advancements can lead to superior interactive applications for societal and human needs.

References

[1] D. Fallman, Design-oriented human-computer interaction, in: SIGCHI Conference on Human Factors in Computing Systems, 2003, pp. 225–232.

[2] G.J. Kim, Human-Computer Interaction: Fundamentals and Practice, CRC press, 2015.

[3] F. Karray, M. Alemzadeh, J. Abou Saleh, M.N. Arab, Human-computer interaction: overview on state of the art, Int. J. Smart Sens. Intell. Syst. 1 (No.1) (2008) 137–159.

[4] H.M. Hassan, G.H. Galal-Edeen, From usability to user experience, in: IEEE International Conference on Intelligent Informatics and Biomedical Sciences, ICIIBMS), 2017, pp. 216–222.

[5] R.P. Sharma, G.K. Verma, Human computer interaction using hand gesture, in: Procedia Computer Science, Eleventh International Multi-Conference on Information Processing, vol 54, 2015, pp. 721–727.

[6] A. Ebert, N.D. Gershon, G.C. van der Veer, Human-computer interaction: introduction and overview, KI-Künstliche Intelligenz 26 (No.2) (2012) 121–126.

[7] Y. Yu, Z. Zhang, Contemporary social design principles in HCI design, in: IEEE *International Conference on Control, Automation and Systems Engineering*, CASE), 2011, pp. 1–4.

[8] G. Chao, Human-computer interaction: the usability test methods and design principles in the human-computer interface design, in: IEEE International Conference on Computer Science and Information Technology, 2009, pp. 283–285.

[9] V. Hinze-Hoare, The Review and Analysis of Human Computer Interaction (HCI) Principles, 2007 *arXiv preprint arXiv:0707.3638*.

[10] D.R. Kaufman, T.G. Kannampallil, V.L. Patel, Cognition and human computer interaction in health and biomedicine, in: Cognitive Informatics for Biomedicine, Springer, 2015, pp. 9–34.

[11] Y. Rogers, HCI Theory: Classical, Modern, and Contemporary. *Synthesis Lectures on Human-Centered Informatics*, Morgan & Claypool Publishers, 2012.

[12] J.M. Carroll, Introduction: toward a multidisciplinary science of human-computer interaction, in: HCI Models, Theories, and Frameworks: Toward a Multidisciplinary Science, Elsevier Science, 2003, pp. 1—9.

[13] M. Eslami, M. Firoozabadi, E. Homayounvala, User preferences for adaptive user interfaces in health information systems, Univers. Access Inf. Soc. 17 (No.4) (2018) 875—883.

[14] R. Alnanih, O. Ormandjieva, T. Radhakrishnan, A new methodology (CON-INFO) for context-based development of a mobile user interface in healthcare applications, in: Pervasive Health, Human—Computer Interaction Series, 2014, pp. 317—342.

[15] A.D. Fisk, S.J. Czaja, W.A. Rogers, N. Charness, J. Sharit, Designing for Older Adults: Principles and Creative Human Factors Approaches, second ed., CRC press, 2020.

[16] E. Machado, D. Singh, F. Cruciani, L. Chen, S. Hanke, F. Salvago, A. Holzinger, A conceptual framework for adaptive user interfaces for older adults, in: IEEE International Conference on Pervasive Computing and Communications Workshops, PerCom Workshops), 2018, pp. 782—787.

[17] H.B. Jimison, M. Pavel, A. Parker, K. Mainello, The Role of Human Computer Interaction in Consumer Health Applications: Current State, Challenges and the Future, Cognitive Informatics for Biomedicine, Springer, 2015, pp. 259—278.

[18] A. Mosenia, S. Sur-Kolay, A. Raghunathan, N.K. Jha, Wearable medical sensor-based system design: a survey, IEEE Trans. Multi-Scale Comput. Syst. 3 (No.2) (2017) 124—138.

[19] A.K. Triantafyllidis, V.G. Koutkias, I. Chouvarda, N. Maglaveras, Development and usability of a personalized sensor-based system for pervasive healthcare, in: 36th Annual International Conference of the IEEE Engineering in Medicine and Biology Society, 2014, pp. 6623—6626.

[20] V.L. Patel, T.G. Kannampallil, D.R. Kaufman, A multi-disciplinary science of human computer interaction in biomedical informatics, in: Cognitive Informatics for Biomedicine, Springer, 2015, pp. 1—7.

[21] L. Rundo, R. Pirrone, S. Vitabile, E. Sala, O. Gambino, Recent advances of HCI in decision-making tasks for optimized clinical workflows and precision medicine, J. Biomed. Inf. 108 (2020) 103479.

[22] H. Levitt, A historical perspective on digital hearing AIDS: how digital technology has changed modern hearing AIDS, Trends Amplif. 11 (Issue 1) (2007) 7—24.

[23] T. Harold, Understanding user centred design (UCD) for people with special needs, computers helping people with special needs, in: 11th International Conference ICCHP, LNCS 5105, 2008, pp. 1—17.

[24] B. Hans-Heinrich, Human computer interaction and communication aids for hearing-impaired, deaf and deaf-blind people: introduction to the special thematic session, computers helping people with special needs, in: 11th International Conference ICCHP, LNCS 5105, 2008, pp. 605—608.

[25] C. Anna, E.L. Richard, Hearing Impairments. *Web Accessibility*, 2008, pp. 25—35.

[26] E.G. Oussama, J. Mohamed, A Sign Language screen reader for deaf, HCI and usability for e-inclusion, in: 5th Symposium of the Workgroup Human-Computer Interaction and Usability Engineering of the Austrian Computer Society, USAB, LNCS 5889, 2009, pp. 476—483.

[27] A. Favre-Félix, C. Graversen, R.K. Hietkamp, T. Dau, T. Lunner, Improving speech intelligibility by hearing aid eye-gaze steering: conditions with head fixated in a multitalker environment, Trends Hear 22 (2018) 1—11.

[28] B. Ritika, Y. Sarthak, G. Sourav, B. Rajitha, Automated speech to Sign language conversion using google API and NLP, in: International Conference on Advances in Electronics, Electrical & Computational Intelligence, 2019.

[29] JSTORE, url: https://www.jstor.org/.

[30] A. JSTOR, Great leap forward in electronic journal access, Notices of the AMS 45 (No. 6) (1998) 713—716.

[31] Visual Geometry Group, University of Oxford, url: https://www.robots.ox.ac.uk/~vgg/.

[32] K. Thoden, J. Stiller, N. Bulatovic, H.-L. Meiners, N. Boukhelifa, User-centered design practices in digital humanities — experiences from DARIAH and CENDARI, ABI Tech. 37 (No. 1) (2017) 2—11.

[33] K. Baljit, S. Vikram, Business intelligence: need and usage in Indian corporate sector, J. Critical Rev. 7 (Issue 11) (2020) 2486–2498.

[34] H. Ajaz, D. Sara, S. Steve, A.G. Marcus, Y. Feng, D. Melissa, D. Lan-Xi, HCI design principles and visual analytics for media analytics platform, HCI international – posters, in: International Conference on Human-Computer Interaction, vol 1034, 2019, pp. 28–35.

[35] B. Claudia, R. David, M. Felix, What web analysts can do for human-computer interaction?, in: International Conference on HCI in Business, HCI in Business, vol 8527 LNCS, 2014, pp. 471–481.

[36] A. Bhat, M. Joseph, S. John, C. Dhas, Avionics interface unit-at the core of next generation avionics, in: 24th IEEE Digital Avionics Systems Conference, 2005.

[37] R. Lyons, Complexity analysis of the next gen air traffic management system: trajectory based operations, Work 41 (2012) 4514–4522.

[38] T. Todorov, P. Petrov, A study of sector configurations capacity for air traffic service, in: MATEC Web of Conferences, vol 133, EDP Sciences, 2017, p. 01003.

[39] T. Prevot, J.R. Homola, L.H. Martin, J.S. Mercer, C.D. Cabrall, Toward automated air traffic control—investigating a fundamental paradigm shift in human/systems interaction, Int. J. Hum. Comput. Interact. 28 (No.2) (2012) 77–98.

[40] G. Frontera, I. Campana, A.M. Bernardos, J.A. Besada, Formal intent-based trajectory description languages for quadrotor aircraft, IEEE Trans. Aero. Electron. Syst. 55 (No.6) (2019) 3330–3346.

[41] I. Lymperopoulos, J. Lygeros, Improved multi-aircraft ground trajectory prediction for air traffic control, J. Guid. Control Dynam. 33 (No. 2) (2010) 347–362.

[42] J.K. Kuchar, L.C. Yang, A review of conflict detection and resolution modeling methods, IEEE Trans. Intell. Transport. Syst. 1 (No.4) (2000) 179–189.

[43] E.D. Medagoda, P.W. Gibbens, Synthetic-waypoint guidance algorithm for following a desired flight trajectory, J. Guid. Control Dynam. 33 (No.2) (2010) 601–606.

[44] T. Cho, C. Lee, S. Choi, Multi-sensor fusion with interacting multiple model filter for improved aircraft position accuracy, Sensors 13 (No.4) (2013) 4122–4137.

[45] J.M. Canino-Rodríguez, J. García-Herrero, J. Besada-Portas, A.G. Ravelo-García, C. Travieso-González, J.B. Alonso-Hernández, Human computer interactions in next-generation of aircraft smart navigation management systems: task analysis and architecture under an agent-oriented methodological approach, Sensors 15 (No. 3) (2015) 5228–5250.

[46] S. Li, M.M. Kokar, Agent communication language, in: *Flexible Adaptation in Cognitive Radios*. Analog Circuits and Signal Processing, Springer, 2013, pp. 37–44.

[47] M. Carroll, N. Dahlstrom, Human– computer interaction on the modern flight deck, Int. J. Hum. Comput. Interact. 37 (No. 7) (2021) 585–587.

[48] A. Schmidt, A.K. Dey, A.L. Kun, W. Spiessl, Automotive user interfaces: human computer interaction in the car, in: CHI'10 Extended Abstracts on Human Factors in Computing Systems, 2010, pp. 3177–3180.

[49] W. Payre, C. Diels, Human-machine interface design development for connected and cooperative vehicle features, in: *International Conference on Applied Human Factors and Ergonomics,* Advances in Human Aspects of Transportation, Springer, 2017, pp. 415–422.

[50] D. Wilfinger, M. Murer, A. Baumgartner, C. Dottlinger, A. Meschtscherjakov, M. Tscheligi, The car data toolkit: smartphone supported automotive HCI research, in: 5th International Conference on Automotive User Interfaces and Interactive Vehicular Applications, 2013, pp. 168–175.

[51] R.J. Nowosielski, L.M. Trick, R. Toxopeus, Good distractions: testing the effects of listening to an audiobook on driving performance in simple and complex road environments, Accid. Anal. Prev. 111 (2018) 202–209.

[52] A.K. Kraft, F. Naujoks, J. Wörle, A. Neukum, The impact of an in-vehicle display on glance distribution in partially automated driving in an on-road experiment, Transport. Res. F Traffic Psychol. Behav. 52 (2018) 40–50.

[53] J. Zhang, S.L. Xu, F. Deng, Design and implementation of intelligent event-driven human-computer interface on vehicles, J. Adv. Comput. Intell. Intell. Inf. 19 (No.2) (2015) 247−254.

[54] M. Sun, H. Yu, Automobile intelligent dashboard design based on human computer interaction, Int. J. Perform. Eng. 15 (2) (2019) 571−578.

[55] K. Bark, C. Tran, K. Fujimura, V. Ng-Thow-Hing, Personal navi: benefits of an augmented reality navigational aid using a see-thru 3D volumetric HUD, in: 6th International Conference on Automotive User Interfaces and Interactive Vehicular Applications, 2014, pp. 1−8.

[56] L. Graichen, M. Graichen, J.F. Krems, Effects of Gesture-Based Interaction on Driving Behavior: A Driving Simulator Study Using the Projection-Based Vehicle-In-The-Loop. *Human Factors*, The Journal of the Human Factors and Ergonomics Society, 2020, pp. 1−19.

[57] T.T. Nguyen, K. Holländer, M. Hoggenmueller, C. Parker, M. Tomitsch, Designing for projection-based communication between autonomous vehicles and pedestrians, in: 11th International Conference on Automotive User Interfaces and Interactive Vehicular Applications, 2019, pp. 284−294.

[58] M. Yamaguchi, Full-parallax holographic light-field 3-D displays and interactive 3-D touch, Proc. IEEE 105 (No.5) (2017) 947−959.

[59] G. Wiegand, C. Mai, K. Hollander, H.I.C.A.R. Hussmann, A design space towards 3D augmented reality applications in vehicles, in: 11th International Conference on Automotive User Interfaces and Interactive Vehicular Applications, 2019, pp. 1−13.

[60] A. Shaikh, An interactive design using human computer interaction for autonomous vehicles, Int. J. Eng. Trends Technol. (2020) 160−172.

[61] L. Jianan, A. Abas, Development of human-computer interactive interface for intelligent automotive, Int. J. Artif. Intell. 7 (No.2) (2020) 13−21.

[62] J. DanNuo, H. Xin, X. JingHan, W. Ling, Design of intelligent vehicle multimedia human-computer interaction system, in: IOP Conference Series: Materials Science and Engineering, vol 563, IOP Publishing, 2019, p. 052029. No. 5.

[63] Y. Du, J. Qin, S. Zhang, S. Cao, J. Dou, Voice user interface interaction design research based on user mental model in autonomous vehicle, in: International Conference on Human-Computer Interaction, Springer LNCS, 2018, pp. 117−132.

[64] K. Wang, Human-computer interaction design of intelligent vehicle-mounted products based on the internet of Things, Hindawi Mobile Inf. Syst. (2021). Article ID 6795440, 2021.

[65] H.M. Sun, S.-P. Li, Y.-Q. Zhu, B. Hsiao, The effect of user's perceived presence and promotion focus on usability for interacting in virtual environments, Appl. Ergon. 50 (2015) 126−132.

[66] A.G. Sutcliffe, C. Poullis, A. Gregoriades, I. Katsouri, A. Tzanavari, K. Herakleous, Reflecting on the design process for virtual reality applications, Int. J. Hum. Comput. Interact. 35 (No. 2) (2019) 168−179.

[67] N. Ashtari, A. Bunt, J. McGrenere, M. Nebeling, P.K. Chilana, Creating augmented and virtual reality applications: current practices, challenges, and opportunities, in: CHI Conference on Human Factors in Computing Systems, 2020, pp. 1−13.

[68] J.L. Rubio-Tamayo, M.G. Barrio, F.G. García, Immersive environments and virtual reality: systematic review and advances in communication, interaction and simulation, Multimodal Technol. Interac. 1 (No. 4) (2017) 1−20.

[69] R. Galdieri, M. Carrozzino, Natural interaction in virtual reality for cultural heritage, in: International Conference on VR Technologies in Cultural Heritage, Springer, 2019, pp. 122−131.

[70] C. Boletsis, J.E. Cedergren, S. Kongsvik, HCI research in virtual reality: a discussion of problem-solving, in: International Conference on Interfaces and Human Computer Interaction, 2017.

[71] B.K. Szabo, Interaction in an immersive virtual reality application, in: IEEE International Conference on Cognitive Infocommunications, 2019, pp. 35−40.

[72] L. Gong, H. Soderlund, L. Bogojevic, X. Chen, A. Berce, Fast-Berglund, A and Johansson, B, Interaction design for multi-user virtual reality systems: an automative case study, in: Procedia 53rd CIRP Conference on Manufacturing Systems, 2020, pp. 1259−1264.

[73] Y. Kima, J. Park, Envisioning Human-Automation Interactions for Responding Emergency Situations of NPPs: A Viewpoint from Human-Computer Interaction, Transactions of the Korean Nuclear Society Autumn Meeting, 2018.

[74] S. Save, M. Gala, S. Patil, D.R. Kalbande, Applying human computer interaction to individual security using mobile application, in: IEEE International Conference on Communication, Information & Computing Technology, 2015, pp. 1−6.

[75] S. Fitriani, R.W. Poppe, A.G. Chitu, D. Datcu, R. Dor, D.H. Hofs, P. Wiggers, D.J.M. Willems, M. Poel, L.J.M. Rothkrantz, L.G. Vuurpijl, J. Zwiers, A multimodal human-computer interaction framework for research into crisis management, in: 4th International Information Systems for Crisis Response and Management Conference, 2007.

[76] J.F. Girres, Hazard-based images comparison methods for damage assessment in emergency mapping, Int. J. Cartogr. 5 (No. 2−3) (2019) 332−348.

[77] S. Kettebekov, R. Sharma, Toward natural gesture/speech control of a large display, in: IFIP International Conference on Engineering for Human-Computer Interaction, 2001, pp. 221−234.

[78] L. Carver, M. Turoff, Human-computer interaction: the human and computer as a team in emergency management information systems, Commun. ACM 50 (No.3) (2007) 33−38.

[79] T. Gjosaeter, J. Radianti, W. Chen, Universal design of ICT for emergency management from stakeholders' perspective, Inf. Syst. Front 23 (2021) 1213−1225.

[80] H.A. Inan, H. Topal, A comparison of crash investigation of two aircraft, one with flight data recorder and cockpit voice recorder and the other, without them, Int. J. Sust. Aviation 6 (No.1) (2020) 36−50.

[81] A. Mishra, J. Cha, S. Kim, HCI based in-cabin monitoring system for irregular situations with occupants facial anonymization, in: International Conference on Intelligent Human Computer Interaction, Springer, 2020, pp. 380−390.

Design and development of applications using human-computer interaction

10

Anunaya Pandey[1], Sanjeeb Prasad Panday[2] and Basanta Joshi[2]

[1]*Engineering Manager, Microsoft, Noida, India;* [2]*Pulchowk Campus, Institute of Engineering, Tribhuvan University, Kathmandu, Nepal*

10.1 HCI design principles

Human—computer interaction (HCI) design principles are used to design tasks and then to design the interfaces and the experiences that make those tasks possible. Identifying the tasks each application needs to solve is central to building something of value for end users. To discuss design principles that are broadly applicable, we need to investigate the process of identifying a user task. When we design a user interface or experience, we are trying to solve a task or job that a user has. There is a significant amount of research on how taking this approach is beneficial to both the design process and the business outcomes. A task is not just the actions that a user performs, but it is the combination of a user's motivations, goals, experience, and the context. Viewed from this lens, HCI practitioners are not just interface designers, but rather task designers. In this section, we will explore and build intuition around fundamental HCI themes, heuristics, and principles that will keep appearing throughout this chapter.

10.1.1 Feedback cycles

Feedback cycles are ubiquitous in all facets of life. They inform how we learn and adapt to our environments and the interfaces available to us. Don Norman [1] describes two important aspects of feedback cycles that we need to mitigate, as illustrated in Fig. 10.1.

Gulfs of execution cover how users go from personal goals to external actions. This is relevant when users are trying to figure out how something operates. It is especially important to get right when designing applications for emergency situations.

Gulfs of evaluation cover how users evaluate whether their actions resulted in their goals being met. This is relevant when users are trying to figure out the result of their action and whether something expected or unexpected happened.

We can basically describe most of HCI as designing ways to bridge these two gulfs: helping users accomplish their goals more easily, and helping users understand that their goals have been accomplished more quickly. A recent example involves rapid advances in artificial intelligence (AI) text to image generation capabilities in the form of Dall-E 2, Imagen, and Stable Diffusion [2] [3]. As the AI

Innovations in Artificial Intelligence and Human-Computer Interaction in the Digital Era. https://doi.org/10.1016/B978-0-323-99891-8.00011-5

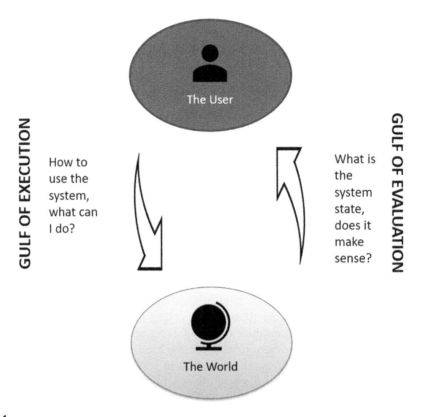

FIGURE 10.1

Gulfs of execution and evaluation, as described by Don Norman.

models keep getting better, companies like Microsoft, Canva, and Google are actively experimenting with user experiences that incorporate image, audio, and video generation into their existing line of products while trying to reduce the gulfs of execution and evaluation for users.

10.1.2 Direct manipulation and invisible interfaces

Direct manipulation gives us one way to create interfaces with small gulfs of execution and evaluation. This notion of creating interfaces where users feel like they are directly interacting with the object of the task is most relevant when building virtual reality (VR) applications. Instead of typing commands or selecting operators, users would physically interact with the interface. The goal of any good interface design is to create interfaces that become invisible. Invisible interfaces allow the user to focus completely on the task instead of the interface. Any interface can become invisible when the user has enough practice and expertise, but our goal is to create interfaces that vanish sooner because of good design.

HCI has a long and rich history, drawing from several fields like cognitive sciences and human factors engineering before becoming a field of its own. During that history, it developed lots of principles and heuristics for how to design good interfaces. Lots of great principles came from Don Norman, Jakob Nielsen, Larry Constantine, Lucy Lockwood, and the Center for Universal Design. We will talk about three of those principles used to support the creation of an invisible interface: simplicity, mapping, and affordances.

10.1.2.1 Simplicity

Simple user interfaces help reduce both gulfs of execution and evaluation. Keeping a user interface simple is arguably the biggest challenge in HCI these days. As AI-powered experiences keep pushing the boundaries of what is possible, keeping things simple is as important as it is challenging. In a simple user interface, common tasks are easy to perform, and possible actions are communicated clearly in the users' own language. This helps a user plan their actions, reason about what actions they can take, and how they can manipulate the interface to accomplish their objectives. Every piece of information in a user interface needs to compete for inclusion because irrelevant or noncontextual information can reduce the relative visibility of more relevant pieces of information. Focusing on displaying contextual information makes simple interfaces intuitive and easy to understand, which also helps reduce the time and cognitive effort needed for users to perceive, interpret, and compare the results of their actions.

10.1.2.2 Mapping

Mappings help establish the relationship between the elements of the user interface and the tasks a user wants to accomplish. A good mapping can make an interface intuitive and invisible because the user does not need to reason about how they operate the interface to perform their task. Interfaces that use good mappings also focus on the language used to emphasize the users' needs and tasks before the interface itself. Instead of using system- or interface-focused language, well-mapped interfaces use the same words, phrases, and concepts that users are already familiar with. When information is presented to users in a natural and logical order, it lowers the cognitive load on users and helps lower the gulf of execution. We will explore the concept of mapping further in Section 10.3 on designing for automotive applications.

10.1.2.3 Affordances

Good affordances help address both gulfs of execution and evaluation. According to Don Norman [1], affordance describes the relationship between an object's properties and the capabilities of a user. That relationship eventually establishes how the object can be used. When used properly, affordances let the user know what they can do and what they need to do just by looking; there is no need for instructions, documentation, labeling, or diagrams. This helps users easily plan their actions, specify which actions they can take, and perform the action they are interested in taking, thereby easing each step involved in the gulf of execution to keep the interface invisible. Similarly, affordances help users interpret what happened after they took an action, which helps lower the gulf of evaluation.

10.1.3 Mental models and representations

Every user has some mental understanding of their task, as well as where our interfaces fit into that task. We call this their mental model. They use the mental model to simulate and predict the effects of their actions. Our goal is for the user's mental model to match the reality of the task and the interface.

To accomplish that goal, we try to design representations with clear mappings to the underlying task. That is how we can ensure the user's mental model of the system is accurate and useful. There are a couple of challenges that can arise in trying to help users build accurate mental models. One of these is an expert blind spot that occurs when we lose sight of our own expertise and forget what it is like to be a novice. The other is learned helplessness, which is when users learn that they have no real ability, or control over the interface, to accomplish their goals. In designing representations that lead to accurate mental models, we need to make sure we avoid both. These principles are especially important when designing healthcare applications.

10.1.4 Distributed cognition

Cognitive load is the idea that humans have finite cognitive resources, and if they are overloaded, their performance suffers, and they get frustrated. By reducing cognitive load, we can make a user's task easier. We could also add to their cognitive resources. That is the principle of distributed cognition: the interactions of humans and interfaces together have more cognitive resources than individuals. We will talk more about this concept in Section 10.5 on designing for airline applications. Devices and interfaces can exhibit cognitive properties like memory and reasoning, offloading those demands from the user. There are also three related theories: social cognition, situated action, and activity theory [4]. All three of these put a strong emphasis on the context of a task, whether it be the physical context, social context, or societal context.

These principles are important, but we cannot just create intelligent interfaces by applying these principles to new problems. These principles can help us make progress much faster, but to design good experiences, we must involve the user. This is the most important principle of HCI: user-centered design. User-centered design advocates keeping the user at the heart of all our design activities. For HCI practitioners, that is not just the person using the tool, but it is also the people affected by the tool's very existence. To keep the user in mind, we use an iterative design life cycle that focuses on getting feedback from the user early and often. Since good design causes interfaces to become invisible, to appreciate the importance of good design, sometimes it is worth looking at examples of poorly designed user interfaces.

Take the example of an online shopping portal http://arngren.net/. It is comically bad and yet, millions of people use it every year. The website violates all the criteria of a good representation. There are no physical electronics stores where the items are randomly laid out on the floor or the shelves. And yet, that is seemingly what Arngren does. The user is not able to form a good model for understanding the layout of the items on the site because it violates the criteria of familiarity. The menus on the left of the website use different fonts, colors, and typography, so the criteria of consistency are violated. The violation of good representation is not just limited to the menu system. It is pervasive throughout the site. Since the site does not use a grid system or a consistent navigational structure, the criterion of predictability is also violated. Not all pages are the same size and for most product details pages, the user needs to scroll both horizontally and vertically to see all the content on a given page. Since most other e-commerce websites use responsive grid layouts that do not require horizontal scrolling, Arngren's website also violates the criteria of generalizability. The colors for the different menu items and products are seemingly chosen at random. The website is like a case study in what not to do when designing a user interface, which is how we are planning to use it.

10.2 Designing VR applications

> Reality leaves a lot to the imagination.
>
> **—John Lennon**

HCI is of interest in VR applications because of the rapid growth of games and other applications that leverage VR technology. VR experiences provide sensory input to a user and mimic the feeling of presence. The sensory input is most commonly visual, auditory, and in some cases, haptic. With the help of innovative devices and state-of-the-art AI modeling, VR technology offers a highly immersive experience, which lends itself well to gaming and entertainment experiences. For this chapter, included under the umbrella of VR applications are augmented reality (AR) applications, mixed reality (MR) applications, VR video game experiences, and VR experiences deployed in healthcare. Also important are VR applications in education (improved learning experiences), architecture (experiencing a virtual building before it is built, iterating on the design), and business (for meetings, virtual events, and remote engagements).

10.2.1 Current VR landscape

The global VR market size was valued at USD 15.81 billion in 2020 and is expected to grow at a compound annual growth rate of 18.0% from 2021 to 2028. Although gaming helped pave the way for most VR experiences before 2020, the healthcare sector is expected to witness the fastest growth rate from 2021 to 2028, which is attributed to the wide spectrum of opportunities for VR in the healthcare sector, such as in medical learning and training, medical marketing, and disease awareness [5].

Within the realm of games, instead of focusing on making experiences faster, safer, and more efficient, HCI places greater emphasis on making them enjoyable to use. For over 2 decades at Microsoft, researchers, designers and engineers in Xbox and other games teams have been constantly applying, refining, and experimenting with different HCI techniques to improve not only the usability of their games, but more importantly, the enjoyability.

10.2.2 VR application design considerations

Technology development in the context of VR has consistently borrowed and integrated concepts from HCI research. Here are some HCI principles to apply in VR settings [6].

10.2.2.1 Invisibility

This notion of creating interfaces where users feel like they are directly interacting with the object of the task is most relevant when building VR applications. When users are engaging with a VR experience, whether for play, work, or learning, they want the controls to disappear, and they want the interface to become invisible and for the user to be fully and completely immersed in the task at hand. For an interface to become invisible, the physical form, and properties, of the interface should be able to efficiently convey its intended function. Viewed from this lens, VR interfaces are inherently more expressive because they can add new layers of information and meaning on top of the physical world. By the same token, VR interface designers can build on top of interaction patterns already established with other digital and physical interfaces to arrive at novel designs that lead to faster learning times and improved user satisfaction.

10.2.2.2 Reducing cognitive load

The more working memory resources users need to spend when interacting with an application, the more cognitive overheard there is. Reducing cognitive load allows users to focus on the actual task at hand and helps to make the user interface invisible. For VR systems that introduce or require new kinds of interaction techniques (e.g., giving the user "magic" or superhuman-like capabilities), Rizzo et al. [7] posits that new interaction metaphors that require additional cognitive effort to understand and master might be a liability. Especially for nonexpert users, who must go through a learning curve to figure out how to reason about and navigate an application, new and untested interaction metaphors only serve to increase cognitive load. This will eventually lead to decreased user satisfaction and engagement.

10.2.2.3 Low physical effort

This principle is especially relevant in the context of VR applications that typically ditch the typical keyboard, mouse, phone screen interactions with gestures, or body movements in the 3D space. While amusing at first, user interactions that are inefficient increase the likelihood of fatigue and cause a drop in engagement over time. Having users interact with a VR application using comfortable, lightweight, and intuitive controls is more likely to increase user satisfaction and prevent exhaustion [8]). Simulator sickness is also a real challenge in VR environments. For example, several video games of the first-person shooter variety score low in the physical effort scale because they tend to induce simulator sickness in virtual environments, which can drastically diminish usability of a system.

10.2.2.4 Learnability

As we explored in the previous section, research by Ref. [9] suggests that learnability in virtual environments is often compromised because of cognitive overhead. Especially for VR applications where learning and training are the end goals, it is imperative that designers spend the time to reduce perceptual and cognitive load. Kaufmann and Schmalstieg [8] argues that for AR and VR applications targeted toward students, learnability should be a primary design goal because students cannot be expected to focus on mastering the interface.

Even for VR applications that are not primarily aimed at students, learnability should be a core priority. Being an expert user of 3D user interfaces should not be a requirement for using VR applications. Even nonexpert users who do not have prior training or experience with 3D user interfaces should be able to navigate their way through VR-based technology [7]. Designers can always borrow ideas from interaction methods in existing real-world applications to limit the amount of learning needed to pilot a new application for a new user. For example, the basic interaction technique for Virtual Tennis allows users to hit the ball by swinging the controller. Anyone new to Virtual Tennis will intuitively be able to start playing the game by mimicking the interactions from a real game of tennis.

Consistency is an important component of learnability. Especially for VR applications, where new methods of interaction are likely involved, consistency in the visuals, controls, and behavior makes users feel more at home. For example, an e-book application in a VR environment can either choose between using gestural feedback to navigate back and forth between pages or a click-based interaction, akin to using a mouse. Mixing the two interaction patterns in different parts of the application will lead to confusion and increased cognitive load for the users.

10.2.2.5 Error tolerance

VR systems and applications are gradually transitioning from the category of demo/trial/beta applications to production applications that solve unique user needs and pain points. As a result, user expectations from VR applications are also up. Gone are the days when VR applications could be glitchy, instable, or error prone. At the very least, VR applications need to be error tolerant and provide the user a clear path forward when unexpected behaviors happen. Tracking stability is an especially challenging issue for VR applications in the context of gaming. Even though accurate algorithms exist to track spatial registration of real and virtual environments in high fidelity, inaccuracies such as virtual information "jumping," jittering, or sudden disappearance when in the middle of a VR experience are still possible. As a result, these inaccuracies need to be accounted for, and baked into, the design process so users can have as smooth an experience as possible. Technologies like hybrid tracking and parallel tracking using multiple trackers can help alleviate user gripes related to buggy and unexpected application behavior.

10.2.3 VR application evaluation

Since the field of VR interface/applications is rapidly evolving, researchers, game designers, and game studios are constantly experimenting with novel methods for evaluating the usability and enjoyability of VR applications. Sutcliffe and Gault [10] describes a heuristic method for evaluating VR user interfaces that is widely used in the video game industry. The method proposes 12 heuristics, as shown in Fig. 10.2, to address usability/presence issues and is primarily based on [11] usability heuristics.

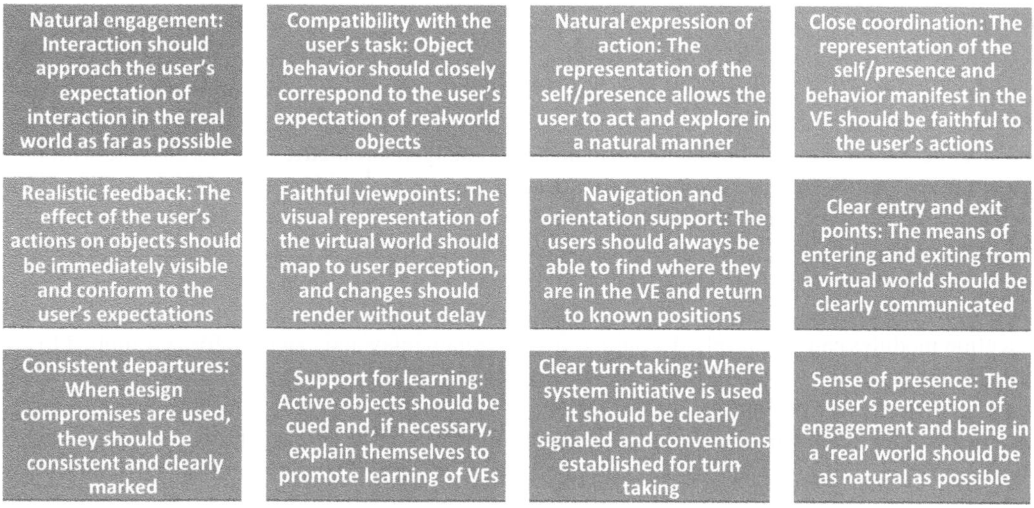

Natural engagement: Interaction should approach the user's expectation of interaction in the real world as far as possible	Compatibility with the user's task: Object behavior should closely correspond to the user's expectation of real-world objects	Natural expression of action: The representation of the self/presence allows the user to act and explore in a natural manner	Close coordination: The representation of the self/presence and behavior manifest in the VE should be faithful to the user's actions
Realistic feedback: The effect of the user's actions on objects should be immediately visible and conform to the user's expectations	Faithful viewpoints: The visual representation of the virtual world should map to user perception, and changes should render without delay	Navigation and orientation support: The users should always be able to find where they are in the VE and return to known positions	Clear entry and exit points: The means of entering and exiting from a virtual world should be clearly communicated
Consistent departures: When design compromises are used, they should be consistent and clearly marked	Support for learning: Active objects should be cued and, if necessary, explain themselves to promote learning of VEs	Clear turn-taking: Where system initiative is used it should be clearly signaled and conventions established for turn taking	Sense of presence: The user's perception of engagement and being in a 'real' world should be as natural as possible

FIGURE 10.2

Heuristics to address usability and presence issues in VR applications.

The model describes an evaluation method where multiple evaluators score a given heuristic on its applicability and validity. Multiple such evaluations are then correlated to arrive at a final rating.

10.2.4 Case study on VR Game difficulty adjustment

Despite all the hype associated with VR applications and games, VR technology has inherent usability concerns that need to be solved before widespread and multisector adoption of VR can happen. VR game applications are at the forefront of this effort to understand and address these usability concerns. Games have always driven innovation in technology and research. Recent examples include innovations in high-end GPUs, haptic feedback, head tracking, hand gesture interface, and innovations in the AR/VR space. Games are also a tremendous source of interface innovation. While the mouse and keyboard interface for desktops has mostly remained unchanged for the last 30-plus years, video game controllers have been evolving over the years as dramatically as the consoles themselves. The net effect of all these innovations is that the gaming tent is getting bigger. Games are not just for the "gamers" anymore, and VR is only going to accelerate that trend. More diverse users, in terms of skill, experience, and demographics, will enter the fold. This presents an additional challenge for VR application designers: being able to adjust game difficulty based on user performance and engagement.

Because AR/VR systems provide instant feedback about user perception and engagement, application designers can use those signals to create a performance- and engagement-sensitive system that optimizes for high enjoyability. Bian et al. [12] describes a similar approach for autism intervention. It is worth noting that similar approaches have already been integrated into several VR games like "Until You Fall" in PlayStation VR, "Chess Club" in Oculus Quest, and "Minecraft VR" in Windows Mixed Reality.

Fig. 10.3 sheds light on how we design a task switching mechanism that considers both user performance and engagement level. In this engagement-sensitive system, performance and engagement metrics are combined with state information on the current difficulty level to reason about how to adjust game difficulty level. In the context of a VR game, a user can only move up to a higher level with increased difficulty if they demonstrate good performance (GP) and high engagement (HE). Conversely, a user will be moved to a low difficult level if they demonstrate either poor performance (PP) or low engagement (LE).

In some other cases, where the performance and engagement metrics are out of sync with each other, the switching strategy becomes more nuanced. For example, when a user displays GP and LE, the system recommends maintaining the same difficulty level at least until the next adjustment. At the next adjustment point, if the user still displays GP and LE, the system decreases the difficult level. The figure above also describes other edge cases where the system is already at the highest or lowest difficulty level. A big advantage of this approach is that the engagement and performance detection modules can be entirely decoupled from VR gameplay and can therefore be applied to any learning scenario. Whatever the game-specific means of capturing engagement signals, engagement level predictions can be sent as JSON strings over the network, which can be read and applied generically. Once the difficulty levels are defined for a given task, the state transition logic to move between different difficulty levels can be applied based on the performance and engagement level of the user [12].

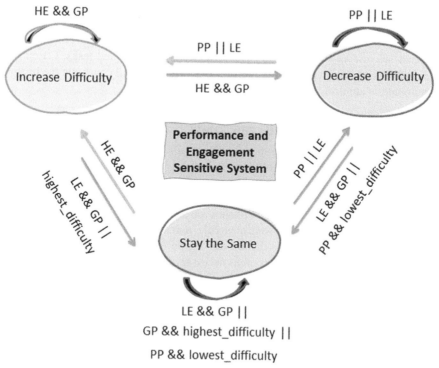

FIGURE 10.3

Performance- and engagement-sensitive system. *GP*, good performance; *HE*, high engagement; *LE*, low engagement; *PP*, poor performance.

Adapted from Bian, D., Wade, J., Warren, Z., & Sarkar, N. (2016). Online engagement detection and task adaptation in a virtual reality based driving simulator for autism intervention. In M. Antona & C. Stephanidis (Eds.) Universal Access in Human-Computer Interaction: Users and Context Diversity. UAHCI 2016. Lecture Notes in Computer Science, 9739: pp. 538–547. Switzerland: Springer. https://doi.org/10.1007/978-3-319-40238-3_51.

10.3 Designing automotive applications

> Your mind is an automobile and words are your wheels.
>
> —**Sara Evans**

HCI has been a critical component of automotive research for decades. Automotive applications are especially interesting from an HCI perspective right now because of what is ahead of the fold: the impending changes in automotive interface and applications caused by the self-driving car revolution. Automobile applications and interfaces currently encompass an entire operating system comprised of a navigation system, a music system, a temperature control system, communication modules, phone interface, and onboard diagnostics, among others. Naturally, today's automotive applications are orders of magnitude more feature-rich and complicated than automotive interfaces from a couple of decades ago. The proliferation of automated driving will only accelerate this trend. As interface designers, we need to understand how to organize all this information on driver interfaces. In their classic paper on usability, Ref. [13] identified three key principles to be followed when designing products for ease of use that are just as relevant today: (1) early focus on users and tasks, (2) empirical measurement, and (3) iterative design. At a high level, these principles still constitute the bedrock of HCI design for automotive applications.

10.3.1 Automotive interfaces and road safety

According to Ref. [14], over 1.3 million people die because of road traffic crashes every year, and traffic accidents cost most countries 3% of their gross domestic product. Road traffic injuries are also the leading cause of death for people aged 5−29 years. The proliferation of mobile phones in recent years has also increased the specter of distracted driving. Because phone use can slow down reaction times, data shows that drivers using mobile phones are approximately four times more likely to be involved in a crash than drivers not using a mobile phone. A rapidly changing technologic and automotive experience landscape means that drivers are performing more tasks in their automobiles than ever before. As a result, cognitive resources necessary for performing the most important task of driving are getting scarcer. In this landscape, it is important for HCI to focus on the most pressing research questions. After reviewing research from the last 50 years on human-automation interaction, Ref. [15] proposes that future human-automation interaction research needs to primarily focus on the following: (1) issues of function and task allocation between humans and machines, (2) issues of trust, incorrect use, and confusion, (3) the balance between focus, divided attention, and attention management. With these research questions in mind, the next few sections will discuss who the users of automotive applications are, what kinds of tasks they perform, and how we evaluate automotive applications and interfaces.

10.3.2 Users of automotive applications

Barring country-specific laws, most licensed adults can operate automotive vehicles. When designing automotive applications and interfaces, almost all adults need to be included in the design process. As a result, users of automotive applications are some of the most diverse in terms of age, skill, ability, and other demographics. To account for this diversity, design needs to be inclusive to account for significant differences in individual performance and cognitive load. Two factors are especially important to consider: driver's age and the driving context. As part of the University of Michigan Transportation Research Institute telematics studies, Nowakowski et al. [16] reported that older drivers typically require one and a half to two times longer to complete similar tasks when driving. Since human lives are at stake, we need to broaden our definition of acceptable reaction times and task completion times in the context of automotive application design.

On driving context, good progress has been made in terms of developing and deploying adaptive systems to detect driver cognitive load, distraction levels, and myriad driver tasks, as shown in Fig. 10.4. When designing such adaptive systems that require interplay and cooperation between humans and automation, a design needs to ensure that appropriate feedback cycles exist to ensure automotive safety. This is particularly important when automation reliability is suspect because of driving conditions, weather, or other contextual factors. Several vehicles today already offer autopilot

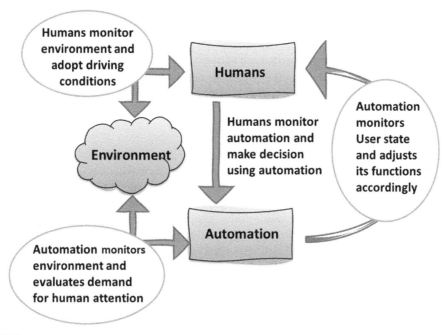

FIGURE 10.4

Adaptive in-vehicle systems to monitor driver state and adjust function accordingly.

functionality like hands-free lane-centering capabilities and traffic-sensitive adaptive cruise control. But reliability of the automated driving assistance can degrade depending on weather conditions like snow, heavy rain, and hail. When such conditions are detected, driving assistants typically respond by slowing down and providing the driver feedback to assume driving control. But there is still more room for automation to contribute to adaptive in-vehicle systems. Modeling cognitive load of user interaction based on ocular parameters has become a dominant method for exploring usability evaluation of interfaces for systems and applications. With the growing importance of AI in HCI, research has proposed many approaches to enhance the human-centric method for automotive interface design and identified key parameters like age, fixation count, saccade count, saccade rate, and average pupil dilation for modeling estimated cognitive load levels.

10.3.3 Automotive application tasks and problems

Obviously, the most important and safety-critical automotive user task is driving. Since most of the driving controls are already standardized, we need not reason about HCI design principles for these controls. We will instead focus on the following automotive tasks.

10.3.3.1 Menu interface tasks

All the major automakers either build or license their own in-car menus and infotainment systems. So, there is little consistency in the controls or displays used for automotive applications. Unlike the days of yore, the physical buttons for controlling temperature, music, system settings, and other options have been replaced with a menu-based system that borrows heavily from desktop and mobile interfaces. Most of these menus deploy existing mappings from desktop and mobile applications. When information is presented to users in a natural and logical order, it lowers the cognitive load on users and helps lower the gulf of execution. But the context in which these menu systems are accessed in an automobile is entirely different, which makes it even more important to simplify menu access and interface tasks.

10.3.3.2 Navigation system tasks

Operating a navigation system in an automobile is as critical as it is fraught with dangers. According to a survey of more than 1000 drivers done by Esurance, operating navigation devices is the most distracting thing users can do while driving [17]. Almost 77% of drivers who identify as being "rarely distracted" say they view GPS navigation apps. That number jumps to 96% for drivers who identify as being distracted. In recent years, car manufacturers have started to disable the ability to enter a new address or change the destination in navigation apps while a car is in motion. The proliferation of voice commands has also helped instances of distracted glances at navigation systems. This is a major focus area for HCI research.

10.3.3.3 Cell phone tasks

According to a 2013 National Safety Council study, cellphone use is estimated to be involved in 26% of all motor vehicle crashes. Drivers using features such as voice-based and touchscreen technology took their hands, eyes, and mind off the road for more than 24 s to complete tasks [17]. Voice commands have the potential to curb driver distraction and the potential for accidents. The current implementation of voice commands is neither accurate enough nor deeply integrated enough into the automotive experience to have a significant impact on driver and passenger safety. Therefore, this is another major focus area for HCI research to address how automotive interfaces and applications can be better designed to account for the severe physical, cognitive, and perceptual constraints placed on users by the task of driving.

10.3.3.4 Web access

This is mostly an extension of the last section because most users continue to access the web through their cellphones. But as more vehicles with semiautonomous driving capabilities start to roll off the factory floors, we are seeing users use the web from their automobile applications. Checking in and engaging in social media accounts while driving is a growing hazardous trend. Specific design and regulatory guidance to curb web access by drivers, especially when engaged in high-workload scenarios like changing lanes, merging onto the freeway, turning at an intersection, parking, or braking in response to another vehicle, might be in order.

10.3.3.5 Autonomous driving

Using AI to automate the process of driving naturally is fraught with challenges. To help reason about the different tasks that need to be automated, Parasuraman et al. [18] describes four corresponding functions that are also relevant to autonomous driving: information acquisition (sensory data gathering), information analysis (processing of acquired information), decision selection (choosing an option), and action implementation (execution of selected decision). To reason about the different levels of autonomy powered by AI systems, Flemisch et al. [19] proposes an automation spectrum with five levels: manual > assisted > semiautomated > highly automated > fully automated. As we march toward building and adopting fully automated driving systems, it is important to consider that AI-powered automation in general comes with a batch of well-known human factor challenges. We will continue to address this theme in Section 10.6 on designing for airline applications.

10.3.4 Empirical measurement of safety and usability

Empirical measurement of safety and usability is critical to being able to iteratively improve automotive interfaces and applications. Most automakers have developed their own in-vehicle telemetry systems that keep track of automotive application usage. Vehicles can track how much time users are spending navigating to different parts of the menu system, what slips/mistakes users make when trying to operate the navigation system, and how much time is spent operating the infotainment module versus the temperature control module. In addition, all this application usage data includes metadata about the driving context as well. As most car manufacturers have already realized, drivers are most likely to be cognitively and perceptually overburdened when changing lanes, merging onto the freeway, turning at an intersection, parking, braking in response to another vehicle, or accelerating from a traffic light. This juxtaposition of safety and usability signals provides automakers with critical insights on pushing the boundaries of HCI research and application. Tesla Autopilot, for instance, has been in the news a few times following vehicle crashes where they were able to gather data logs recovered from crashed vehicles and understand what led to a given accident.

In addition, automakers also make use of usability labs to iterate on their designs before automotive applications are released. Since automotive applications have started to follow more frequent release cycles in recent years, usability lab studies for automotive interfaces and applications are more common in the automotive industry. A typical usability lab would include a simulated environment where users can engage with automotive applications, a couple of rooms (one for the subject and one for an experimenter), cameras, and audio-visual equipment for recording the sessions.

10.3.5 Evaluating automotive applications and interfaces

The assessment of automotive applications used to occur in contexts other than simulators and real roads. Nowadays with in-built telemetry in most vehicle operating systems, vehicle manufacturers can tap into a multitude of primary and secondary signals for driving and interface effectiveness. In addition, there are multiple devices that plug into the onboard diagnostic connector of the engine computer to enable easy recording of empirical driving metrics like speed, gear selection, throttle, brake, and engine RPM. Taken together, empirical metrics provide a wealth of data that allows designers and engineers to iterate on making automotive applications and interfaces safe and effective.

Although feedback from empirical metrics described above is important, it is important to understand that automotive design is strongly influenced by both international and domestic standards and regulations. To ensure compliance with design guidelines when designing enterprise applications, operating systems include application program interfaces (APIs) to guide consistent interaction with available user interface elements like windows, widgets, menu systems, and systems settings. Even though automobile manufacturers do not release similar public interfaces for driver interfaces, documents for evaluating automotive interfaces can take the form of standards documents, information reports, guideline documents, recommended practices, or automotive design principles [16]. In addition, automobile manufacturers need to constantly evaluate whether their applications meet regulatory requirements. Even though technically voluntary, guidelines written by the International Organization for Standardization (ISO) are used by most automobile manufacturers as evaluation metrics. Compliance with ISO standards also makes economic sense for major automobile manufacturers with global sales because building and evaluating noncompliant country-specific systems is often much more expensive.

10.3.6 Procedures for iterating on automotive application design

This section describes two specific procedures used to iterate on, and improve, the efficiency of automotive interfaces.

10.3.6.1 SAE J2365 task time calculations

SAE J2365 defines a method for calculation of the time to complete in-vehicle navigation and route guidance tasks [20]. Developed by Green in 1999, the method allows engineers and designers to calculate task completion times early in the design life cycle when most elements in the user interface are still malleable. SAE J2365 applies to both OEM (Original Equipment Manufacturer) and after-market equipment. The calculation method is based on the goals, operators, methods, and selection rules (GOMS) model described by Ref. [21] with task time data from several sources. Section 10.5.4 goes into more detail on the specifics of the GOMS model. Similar time task calculations can be used to assess the efficiency of two or more competing design options when integrating automotive application interfaces.

10.3.6.2 SAE J2364 Pettitt's occlusion time calculation

SAE J2364 defines an extended keystroke level model (KLM) for use in predicting the visual demand of in-vehicle information systems, such as GPS navigation systems, and estimating occlusion task times [22]. In the occlusion procedure, the subject's vision is occluded using goggles with LCD shutters that open and close for 1.5 s each, intending to mimic the way a driver glances back and forth between the road scene and an in-vehicle system. After running straight occlusion tests of two different navigation systems and comparing those results with their new method, Pettitt et al. concluded that their extended KLM model can be successfully used for evaluating GPS navigation systems. By developing additional actions used in vehicle information systems, methods like this could be extended to predict task performance and effectively iterate on automotive application design.

10.3.7 Case study on GPS and distributed cognition

To understand the concept of distributed cognition, imagine a time before GPS navigation and think of a navigation system comprised of a married couple in a car and a map. To highlight the role of HCI in designing safe and useable automotive applications, let us start by analyzing this system from the perspective of distributed cognition and reason about what cognitive activities, including perception, memory, reasoning, and acting, each part of the system performs.

The driver is continuously monitoring the speed and the direction of the car, perceiving which other vehicles are in the road and maintaining situational awareness of passengers, road conditions, weather, and traffic. All the perception activities described also require the driver to reason about whether the car is traveling safely. The driver also needs to perceive and understand the navigational directions given by the passenger and act to make changes to the steering, braking, or throttle response. In addition, the driver needs to perceive changes in car conditions like warning lights about low fuel, tire pressure, or hazardous road conditions. If such changes are perceived, the driver then needs to decide whether it is safe to continue traveling. And at any point during the journey, the driver may act to slow the car, take the next exit, or ask for directions to the nearest gas station from the passenger.

The map serves as a memory aid for the navigator. Using landmarks, exit locations, points of interest, and other signs on the map, the navigator can continually perceive and maintain awareness of the car's location. Similarly, road signs function as another integral part of this distributed cognitive system for navigation. Both maps and road signs, in and of themselves, do not perceive, act, or reason but help create the structure in this distributed cognitive environment that provides much more than external memory. In this system, both maps and road signs are examples of long-term memory that is constant and cannot be changed by the actions of the driver or the navigator. The navigator's memory is more likely to be affected by other tasks like playing music or finding the closest gas station. The breakdown of such a memory may lead to more cognitive load because of the need to re-plan a route.

When considering the same navigation task with a lone driver using a GPS, the creation and the maintenance of the representational state that is used to organize route planning has now shifted from the navigator and the map to the GPS. GPS provides a memory for the car's current location and a memory for all the navigation activities performed by the driver during the trip. In this context, the GPS memory is malleable because it changes based on the car's current location and the driver's actions. In the prior example, the driver had to perceive visual and auditory cues from the navigator to drive the car. With a GPS, the driver is perceiving and reasoning about symbols in the GPS interface instead of recalling those symbols from her memory. Because the GPS memory is malleable and not vulnerable to being affected by other tasks like having a conversation or playing music, memory in the GPS as a cognitive system is more reliable.

There is also communication overhead between the driver and the navigator in the first example without a GPS. This overhead can lead to a breakdown in communication between the two components of system. The simple act of being lost in conversation can result in the navigator forgetting to check the map or road signs, which can lead to missed exits or turns. Since GPS memory is more reliable, there is less chance of a breakdown in the distributed cognitive system when a GPS is involved. The previous system relied more heavily on the perception, memory, reasoning, and actions of both users being directed toward the task of navigation. The benefit of the GPS system is that it allows a reconfiguration of the distributed system that reduces the requirements of scarce cognitive resources from human actors. Deploying HCI principles like distributed cognition when designing applications ensures the same outcome when designing all other automotive applications.

10.4 Designing healthcare applications

> Healthy citizens are the greatest asset any country can have.
>
> —**Winston Churchill**

Healthcare applications run the whole gamut from (1) provider-centric applications for recording electronic health, medical, and patient data, (2) medical personnel-centric applications for medical database, research, and diagnosis, (3) hospital-centric applications for medical imaging, billing, and equipment management, (4) communication-centric applications for appointment booking and virtual consultation services to (5) consumer-centric applications for keeping track of health, personal fitness, and personal health records. Depending on the type of application being developed, almost all adults need to be included in the design process when designing healthcare applications. There is also a separate category of applications and interfaces for operating medical devices at home, which is equally critical from an HCI perspective.

Challenges like an expert blind spot can arise when expert healthcare practitioners design, or provide feedback to design, healthcare applications. Similarly, challenges like learned helplessness can arise when patients or caregivers are unable to navigate, understand, or construct proper mental models to effectively use healthcare applications, which leads to application users being disengaged. In designing representations that lead to accurate mental models, we need to make sure to avoid both. These principles are especially important when designing healthcare applications because people's health and lives are at stake.

10.4.1 Healthcare applications and public health

To maximize public health outcomes, HCI should inform a two-pronged approach to increase both the effectiveness of healthcare professionals to deliver safer care and the quality of service experienced by patients. At a high level, HCI for healthcare applications should prioritize the following core principles.

10.4.1.1 Equity

Application design should be able to accommodate varied user abilities, needs, and preferences. According to the principles of universal design [23], equitable design is about creating applications, products, and experiences that are identical to the extent possible and equivalent when not. Design should make it a priority to avoid segregating or stigmatizing any users based on their abilities. As we will discuss in the next section, consumers of healthcare applications are truly diverse, and design should respect this diversity. Optimizing for universal accessibility can increase the diversity of people for whom a healthcare application is viable.

10.4.1.2 Constraints

Don Norman [1] describes constraints as powerful clues for limiting the set of possible actions. Even when users encounter a novel situation when using an application, the thoughtful use of constraints helps users easily determine the correct action to take. In that sense, constraints help lower the barrier of execution for users. Especially when thinking about provider-centric healthcare applications where slips and mistakes on the part of the user can adversely affect health outcomes, design needs to include necessary safeguards to reasonably prevent such outcomes. This could be as simple as introducing a semantic constraint by flashing a red light in a machine to signal that the results are not yet available. Another example is automated external defibrillator (AED) machines that allow users to administer a shock only after it has detected the casualty's heart rate and determined it is safe to do so (Fig. 10.5). The designer can also introduce additional skill-level constraints to healthcare applications when applications are being used by new employees or healthcare employees undergoing training.

10.4.1.3 Multimodal

This refers to the ability to display and accept information in a combination of visual, aural, and haptic modes. Research shows that multimodal interfaces exhibit several advantages: (1) they reduce instances of slips and errors, thereby making applications and interfaces more robust, (2) they help users

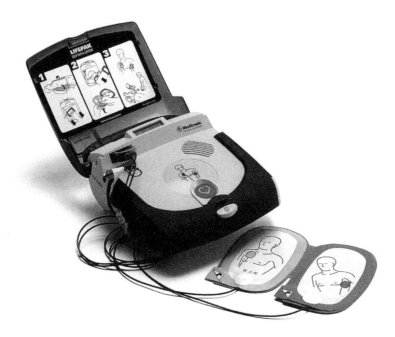

FIGURE 10.5

Automated external defibrillator (AED) machine with in-built safety constraints for safe operation.

more easily recover from errors, (3) they increase the bandwidth of the communication, and (4) they add additional methods of communication to different situations and environments. When users are dealing with error-prone or low-sensitivity modalities, it is especially useful to have multiple modalities complement each other to make the system more robust. The case study on healthcare applications with AR technology (Section 10.4.5) will also cover this aspect in more detail.

10.4.1.4 Mental models and natural mappings

HCI principles can be used to build intuitive user interfaces that allow users to leverage existing mental models to understand and master the use of new applications. In the context of healthcare interfaces, a good mapping allows users to borrow from symbolic or natural analogies from other physical or digital interactions. This has the effect of lowering the cognitive load required to make sense of, and operate, an interface. A natural mapping also requires a proper and natural arrangement for the relations between controls and their manipulation to the outcome of this manipulation. Medical training simulation is one of those areas where natural mappings are especially useful. When students train to use virtual scalpels or surgeons use virtual interfaces to perform remote surgeries, having a natural mapping of the physical and virtual surgery space is critical.

10.4.1.5 Personalized

Personalized applications and interfaces can be tailored to respond in a manner best suited to the current user and his or her needs. This principle also includes tolerance or design for error. For users who are more likely to perform inadvertent actions because of age, medical preconditions, or the environment, having the application request confirmation of critical or irreversible actions is extremely beneficial. This can also help prevent negative health outcomes because of improper use of applications or interfaces. With the help of AI-powered algorithmic analyzers, personalized medicine can now be used to treat patients based on their individual parameters, including their biometric data, gender, diet, known preconditions, family history, or the results of DNA testing.

10.4.2 Users of healthcare applications

Users of healthcare applications are a truly diverse group. Designing for healthcare is unique in that there are two distinct stakeholders: providers and consumers. The design considerations for these two sets of users are also unique. Therefore, we must analyze them separately. A third layer is the facilitation of effective communication between the providers and consumers, where HCI also comes into play. Users' ability to reason about, and operate, an application or a device depends on several factors [24].

- physical attributes like size, strength, dexterity, flexibility, and coordination
- vision, hearing, tactile sensitivity, and other sensory capabilities
- memory, attention, reasoning, and other cognitive capabilities
- comorbidities (i.e., multiple conditions or disease)
- literacy, language, education, and training as it pertains to a given medical condition
- state of physical, mental, and emotional health
- knowledge of, and experience with, a particular device or application
- ability to learn and adapt to a new interface or application

HCI also needs to account for a user's emotional state, especially when a healthcare application or device is meant for use by a patient or by a loved one. Stress, emotions, and cognitive load may make processing information and operating devices more difficult. Slips or mistakes can also happen more frequently when users are overwhelmed, stressed, or emotionally fatigued. This can result in potential harm to the patient, the caregiver, or a device. Good design that is rooted in the needs of the user can be useful in such situations to gather, process and communicate information, to increase the user's confidence and to improve their decision-making. To effectively prioritize the needs of users during the design process, Hancock et al. [25] proposed a "hierarchy of ergonomics and hedonomic needs." They define hedonomics as a being devoted to the promotion of not just functional, but pleasurable, HCI. They also proposed a model to prioritize user need for safety and functionality before addressing the need for pleasure, which is especially relevant in the context of healthcare applications and illustrated in Fig. 10.6.

The core philosophy is still to keep the user in the center of the design process, but this framework offers additional guidance on the hierarchy among user safety, accessibility, and usability. Safety is the primary requirement for healthcare applications and interfaces, whether intended for use by trained medical professionals, caregivers, patients, or the public. The secondary requirement is that they be functional and accessible for their intended users. This is especially important for users with any sort of physical, locomotor, cognitive, emotional, intellectual, or sensory disability because if a user cannot access an application for whatever reason, it is, by definition, not functional for them. For example, diagnostic facilities are not functionally accessible to a suspected COVID-19 patient who does not have access to at-home test kits and is not capable of visiting a testing facility. Abouyoussef et al. [26]

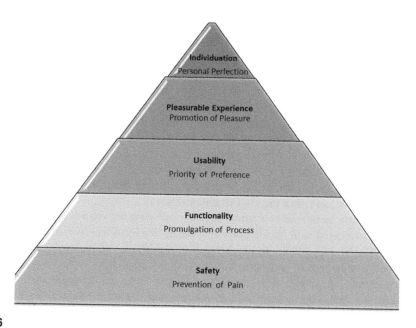

FIGURE 10.6

A hierarchy of ergonomics and hedonomic needs derived from Maslow's conception.

describes an online automated platform that can remotely collect the symptoms needed for a rapid diagnosis in such situations. Ideally, healthcare applications would not only be safe and functional, but also useable, pleasurable, and customizable. That way, an application can satisfy all levels of the pyramid. But for practical reasons, the last two levels are more important in the context of consumer healthcare applications like fitness trackers, health logging applications, scheduling applications, and applications for getting information on health conditions. The ability to deliver a pleasurable and customizable experience can help differentiate a consumer healthcare application from a sea of competitors. Plus, building a pleasurable application that enables users to better manage or to take better care of their health is a good design goal in and of itself.

10.4.3 Medical applications and interfaces in home healthcare

The US Food and Drug Administration (FDA) defines a home medical device as a device to be used in a home or nonclinical environment and as such may require the user to be trained by a healthcare professional on the safe and effective use of the device [27]. Patients who are still in need of medical attention are increasingly being released from hospitals and healthcare facilities because of greater proliferation of medical devices for use at home. As a result, both professional caregivers and household members are making use of a wide variety of technologies in nonclinical settings to manage their own health or to assist a loved one with theirs [28]. This presents both challenges in terms of safe operation of medical interfaces at home and opportunities in terms of being able to improve the usability of existing healthcare applications and interfaces to make them safer for the home.

According to a study commissioned by the National Institute of Aging (NIA), the world's older population, aged 65 and over, is expected to grow from 617 million in 2015 to 1.6 billion by 2050 [5]. Given this context, the need to invest in medical applications for use in home healthcare to solve aging-related concerns cannot be understated. The NIA report also stresses the need to conduct research and usability studies on medical applications that are targeted toward older adults. More recently, designers and researchers have built home healthcare applications targeted toward older adults by using voice-assistant systems. For example, Rath and Chandna [29] describes building a high-fidelity prototype mobile health application to track varied health metrics like blood pressure, glucose level, and body temperature using voice commands. More importantly, the psychological and physical characteristics of the elderly were considered during application design. When designing applications for the elderly, extra attention needs to be paid to details like screen sizes, touchscreen interactions, typeface, volume of information, labels, etc., to honor the HCI design ethos.

The FDA collects data on the use of medical devices, including data on adverse usage events. 1059 of the adverse events reported with device usage had the device location reported as "home." Devices like mechanical walkers, implantable pacemakers, insulin infusion pumps, cardioverter defibrillator, ventricular bypass devices, piston syringes, and continuous ventilators were involved in the most reported adverse events [28]. Some of the devices in the list above, for example infusion pumps and continuous ventilators, are quite complicated to operate and require a thorough assessment of the patient's home environment before accepting a patient for in-home device use. Both devices are generally used on patients who are sicker that the typical home healthcare recipient, which further means that the margin for error when operating the device is small.

Several existing standards, like "Human Factors Design Process for Medical Devices" (ANSI/AAMI HE74:2001), "Medical Devices—Application of Usability Engineering to Medical Devices" (ISO/IEC 62366:2007), and "Human Factors Engineering—Design of Medical Devices" (ANSI/AAMI HE75:2009) already provide ample guidance to designers and engineers to help design a good medical interface and validate it. In addition to guidance specific to medical devices, there are other attempts to provide specific guidance for designing Human—AI interactions. For instance, the People + AI Guidebook by Ref. [30] makes it a point to only focus on deploying AI solutions when they can be used to support user needs. Instead of adding AI functionality for marketing, technical feasibility, or branding, it is imperative that designers balance the need to augment and automate user tasks. These design guidelines also factor in the needs and requirements of a wide variety of potential users when considering medical applications and interfaces for use in home healthcare [28].

10.4.4 Evaluating healthcare applications

The last section introduced some existing standards that device manufacturers and interface designers already consult when building healthcare applications. The design lifecycle process introduced here will provide additional guidance on evaluating healthcare applications and introduce tools that applications designers can leverage to get feedback from users while iterating their designs. Once again, the core idea of the design lifecycle is to integrate the user into every phase of the life cycle. Even though we are talking about the design lifecycle in the context of healthcare applications here, these concepts are broadly applicable and can be used to build all kinds of applications. There are four design phases to consider: need finding, design alternatives, prototyping and evaluation.

10.4.4.1 Need finding

This is where we build a comprehensive understanding of the task a user is trying to perform. It is crucial not to jump into the design process before we have a deep understanding of user needs, tasks, and task context. It is generally a good idea to start with a data inventory to gather the data necessary to kick-start the design process. Some examples include user demographics, user environment, task context, user goals, user needs, collaboration needs, and breakdown of user tasks and subtasks (physical, cognitive, social). Some tools for need finding include interviews, surveys, focus groups, think-alouds, participant observation, and naturalistic observation. For example, in naturalistic observation, we observe users in their natural context. If we are trying to design a better health tracker, naturalistic observation might involve observing people interacting with their health trackers at the park.

10.4.4.2 Design alternatives

This is where we explore, generate, and synthesize early ideas on how to approach the task. The core idea here is to explore lots of ideas to broaden the design space as much as possible and avoid settling on a single design idea or a design idea of an existing solution. By starting with lots of ideas and a broad design space, we are more likely to land on a design that borrows strong elements from multiple alternatives. Some tools for exploring design alternatives include brainstorming (individual or group), scenarios and storyboards, persona exploration, user profile exploration, and user modeling. For example, in using user modeling to explore design alternatives for a medical diagnosis software, we reason about how doctors achieve each of their goals in the interface and the likelihood of success for each goal. This will give us ways to compare the effectiveness of different design alternatives under consideration.

10.4.4.3 Prototyping

The goal of prototyping is to get user feedback as quickly and rapidly as possible. We usually start with low-fidelity prototypes that are easy to change, help us evaluate risks early, and make it reasonably clear that the user is interacting with a prototype. With low-fidelity prototypes, the expectation should be that we are prototyping for feedback. This allows us to weed out bad ideas, interactions, and designs earlier in the design life cycle. Some examples of low-fidelity prototyping methods include verbal prototypes where the interface is verbally described to the user, paper prototypes that include a representation of the interface on paper, and Wizard of Oz where a user interacts with a system while a human does the work behind the scenes to supply functionality that has not been implemented. Wireframing tools like Balsamiq and Figma and physical prototypes feature greater fidelity and are used to evaluate the intuitiveness of software and hardware interfaces respectively. At the other end of the fidelity spectrum are functional prototypes that tend to be high fidelity and approach the live interface in terms of functionality and usability (Fig. 10.7).

10.4.4.4 Evaluation

This is where we evaluate a prototype in terms of its efficiency, accuracy, learnability, memorability, and satisfaction. There are primarily three types of evaluation methods: qualitative, empirical, and predictive. Qualitative evaluation emphasizes the totality of a phenomenon, whereas empirical is based on numeric summaries or observations of a phenomenon. Predictive evaluation is based on systematic application of preestablished principles and heuristics. The prototype evaluation process typically involves defining the task and performance measures, developing the experiment, recruiting participants, and performing the experiment to gather salient data. Design and engineering can then analyze

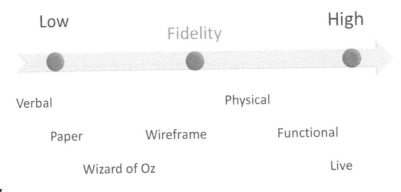

FIGURE 10.7

Different methods for prototyping plotted along a prototype fidelity axis.

the data, which feeds into the next stage of need finding. The iterative design life cycle of need finding, design exploration, prototyping, and evaluation continues until the application is finalized.

10.4.5 Case study on the role of HCI in experiential learning through augmented reality

This section intends to explore the potential of emerging technologies like AR and AI for building healthcare applications to enhance personal and clinical change. We explore the entire spectrum of VR, AR, and MR in more detail in Section 10.2.1. This discussion will be focused on AR, which allows the use of technology to augment our real-world experience with digital data, stimuli, and experiences. One could think of AR as a technology with which we could see more than others see, hear more than others hear, and perhaps even touch, smell, and taste things that others cannot. The novel opportunities lie in building technology to perceive abstract computational elements and objects within our real-world experience that can help us in our daily activities. In Section 10.2, we discussed how the ability to experience more through VR leads to a heightened sense of presence and emotional engagement when users are playing AR/VR video games. But the same effect is also achieved when AR technologies are leveraged to enable experiential learning. Some examples include effecting personal change through clinical psychology, poststroke recovery, physical rehabilitation, social and emotional training for children with autism, and pain reduction.

Riva et al. [31] describes the potential to create, using technology, experiences that lead to learning and knowledge that can only be unlocked through experience and that can potentially change a person's worldview. In each of the healthcare situations mentioned above, recovery and rehabilitation involve the patients going through a process of personal change, which helps patients manage the symptoms of distress produced by life transitions and adapt to a new reality. High levels of personal change are associated with psychosocial well-being. Kolb [32] has proposed a model on experiential learning that consists of four stages: concrete experience, reflective observation, abstract reconceptualization, and active experimentation. Botella et al. [33] describes an experiment where AR was used to support experiential learning to treat cockroach phobia. For the "experience" stage, the patient is exposed to cockroaches in an AR environment. This experience forms the basis of the rest of the stages of experiential learning. The patient can now process the experience and think about the actions they took, the emotions they experienced, and compare the current AR experience with more traumatic prior experiences with cockroaches. This is where the therapist comes into play to help the patient conceptualize or generalize the experience and create recommendations for the next exposure. These recommendations form the basis for new actions and strategies, which can be duly tested to achieve the desired healthcare outcome of treating cockroach phobia.

AR offers support to all stages of the experiential learning cycle through a cyclical interaction of concrete experience, reflective observation, thought, and active experimentation, as shown in Fig. 10.8. This is quite similar to how feedback cycles are used in HCI in an iterative fashion to improve application design (Section 10.4.4). Going back to the cockroach phobia example, AR enables real-time interactivity because the therapist can actively monitor the patient's physical and emotional state and suggest behavior changes like slow breathing in real time. At the same time, AR provides targeted and patient-centered suggestions that help users develop knowledge and learn more effectively. Finally, since AR experiences can be deployed in the same context where the patient has experienced phobias or difficulties previously, AR can help with effective real-world skill transfer.

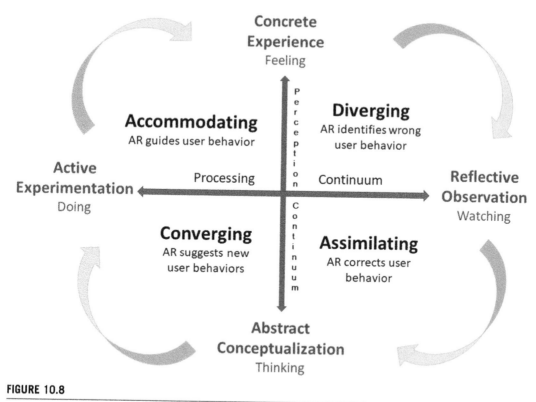

FIGURE 10.8

The role of AR in the experiential learning cycle.

Adapted from Kolb, D. A. (1984). Experiential Learning as the Science of Learning and Development. Englewood Cliffs, NJ: Prentice Hall.

Viewed from this lens, AR is a powerful tool for experiential learning, especially in the context of developing healthcare applications. Since the use of AR calls for new interaction patterns as they relate to healthcare applications, this is an area that is ripe for future HCI research.

10.5 Designing airline applications

> Flying starts from the ground. The more grounded you are, the higher you fly.
>
> —**J.R. Rim**

Research in HCI has often proposed that there are many similarities between the modern automated office and the high technology flight deck because both sets of workers are managers of complex suites of automation [34]. But designing airline applications and interfaces is quite different from designing applications for the office environment for two primary reasons: (1) the airline industry is highly regulated and proceduralized, so designers must contend with more industry-specific constraints, and (2) the risk involved in flying necessitates additional design considerations. Nonetheless, airline interfaces should follow the same golden [13] principles used to design everyday desktop or phone apps: (1) early focus on users and tasks, (2) empirical measurement and (3) iterative design. Since HCI in the context of cockpit and air traffic control (ATC) concerns all the interactions between human and computer-based actors to communicate information, give instructions, and accomplish goals, poorly designed HCI results in increased cognitive load for airline pilots and ATC. Only by placing the users' needs, interests, and knowledge in the center of the design process will HCI designers be able to support optimal task performance and situational awareness. One key challenge for HCI is to maximize situational awareness while minimizing cognitive load for both ATC and airline pilots. As we will discuss in the following sections, optimizing for both is a hard problem. Section 10.5.5 will expound on the idea of distributed cognition to solve this problem.

10.5.1 Airline interfaces and flight safety

Pilots on modern aircraft today have access to a range of high-tech systems at their fingertips, like flight management systems for overall flight management, electronic flight bag for improved information management, and automated collision avoidance maneuvering for improved aircraft control [35]. All these technologies are designed to maximize the pilot's situational awareness and minimize their cognitive load. But as with all complex systems, there is a learning curve associated with the operations and management of these systems. The longer-term trend toward increased safety in aviation continues, and the consistent innovation in high-tech flight systems has certainly helped. But advances in airline interface and application HCI have led to temporary setbacks in the form of accidents and incidents [36]. Flight AF447 from Rio to Paris crashed into the Atlantic Ocean on June 1st, 2009. The safety investigation report written by the French Office of Investigations for Civil Aviation Safety concluded that human factors played an important role in the accident [37]. More recently, airline HCI came into sharper focus again after the accidents of Lion Air Flight 610 and Ethiopian Airlines Flight 302. Independent investigations in both accidents pointed to prevalent HCI concerns as part of the investigations [35]. These are just a few prominent examples where HCI concerns were central to airline accidents. Taken together, these accidents demonstrate the importance of HCI issues on the flight deck and on ATC for flight safety.

10.5.2 Mental models and situational awareness

Situational awareness (SA) in aviation refers to the pilot's accurate perception of the current state of the flight environment. There is a significant body of research related to SA because safety in aviation is contingent on the pilot being actively aware and developing an accurate internalized mental model of the environment inside and outside the aircraft. Loss of SA has been a major contributing factor to several accidents in the history of aviation. Endsley has proposed a breakdown of SA into three discrete levels [38].

1. *Level 1* concerns the perception of what is happening. This is necessary to build an accurate mental model of the environment. Factors like high cognitive load, distractions and interruptions, attention deficit, visual illusions, and confirmation bias can lead to a loss of SA. This can lead to the activation of wrong or inappropriate mental models despite contradictory real-world evidence. To help pilots maintain a high level of SA, designers and researchers have experimented with several variables like the number of displays in cockpits, single-instrument versus integrated displays, the arrangement of displays, the volume of information displayed to pilots and ATC, the spatial relationships between the information in different displays, and autopilot functionality.
2. *Level 2* concerns the understanding of what has been perceived. This is tied to the HCI principle of bridging the gulf of evaluation so that pilots and ATC can easily reason about the result of their actions or the result of a change in the environment. The same factors mentioned in level 1 are also applicable here and can lead to the formation of incorrect mental models. Lack of experience, knowledge, and know-how can also be a contributing factor. To prevent pilots from losing SA, it is important to design applications and interfaces that are consistent, so pilots can rely on established patterns and associations to aid perception. This is another reason for the frequent use of checklists, procedures, and best practices in aviation.
3. *Level 3* concerns the use of what is understood to think ahead and act. This is tied to the HCI principle of bridging the gulf of execution. Since the feeling of directness is directly proportional to the amount of cognitive effort it takes to manipulate and evaluate a system, the arrangement of displays and controls within the cockpit plays a crucial role in ensuring that pilots can act quickly when time is of the essence. Wickens and Carswell [39] further expanded this idea of distance in their "proximity compatibility principle," which states that when attempting to integrate information from multiple locations, greater workload is induced by greater separation, as the physical proximity of the sources should mimic the cognitive proximity of the information.

10.5.3 Airline automation and usability heuristics

Air traffic has continued to grow unabated for the last few decades, and the next couple of decades will see air traffic more than double. This introduces challenges for both pilots and ATCs. To meet the demands for ever greater levels of traffic and capacity, we will continue to rely more on automated systems. To successfully scale aviation traffic and capacity, automation must be based on sound usability heuristics and principles. Nielsen and Molich [40] developed a set of usability principles and heuristics to aid the design of effective user interfaces. These principles ensure that applications and interfaces are designed so that they are "easy to learn, effective to use, and enjoyable from the user's perspective." Out of the 10 most cited HCI principles for interface design, four principles are especially applicable in the context of airline automation, as summarized in Table 10.1.

Table 10.1 Summary of principles applicable to airline automation.

#	Principle	Description
1	System status visibility	Keep the user situationally aware and adequately informed by means of appropriate and timely feedback.
2	Favor recognition over recall	Minimize user cognitive load by ensuring that the user does not need to memorize information from one screen to the next.
3	Help users diagnose/ recover from errors	Use simple language to communicate errors without resorting to error codes and assist the user in understanding the available courses of actions to arrive at the best decision.
4	Empower users with a sense of control and freedom	Support options like undo and redo so users can easily recover from slips and mistakes without having to go through extensive menu options to leave the undesired state.

Even though automation has generally been a boon for aviation, automation surprise is often presented as an issue that has adversely affected the aviation industry for decades. Several fatal aircraft accidents like Air Inter 148, Flash Airlines Flight 604, and Asiana 214 have been attributed to the rise of airline automation and autopilots. As a result, research and design efforts have focused on breaking down the problem of airline automation into different levels and prescribing the appropriate level of automation for different classes of functions within the cockpit. A model proposed by Ref. [18] groups automation functions into four classes, which also map neatly with the HCI heuristics presented above. The four classes are as follows:

1. Information acquisition, which concerns acquiring and presenting flight-related signals to the pilot or ATC. This class is closely tied to the "system status visibility" heuristic because automation needs to continually provide users with timely and appropriate feedback.
2. Information analysis, which relates to integrating or transforming information to aid decision-making. This class is closely tied to the "recognition rather than recall" heuristic because automation needs to help lower the cognitive load of the user.
3. Decision and action selection, where automation assists in outlining possible courses of actions and in decision-making. This class is the counterpart of the "help users diagnose/recover from errors" heuristic because automation can help users focus on the right set of problems and priorities to arrive at a reasonable solution in time.
4. Action implementation, where automation performs actions on behalf of the user. While this is powerful and convenient, automation needs to leave room for "user control and freedom." In situations where the reliability of automation is a concern or where automation chooses a course of action by mistake, the user should be able to take control, undo a mistake, and rectify the situation.

10.5.4 GOMS model for evaluating airline applications

The GOMS (goals, operations, methods, and selection rules) model was developed by Ref. [21] and published in the book *The Psychology of Human Computer Interaction*. It is a seminal model that has been used in real-world design and evaluation situations across a variety of applications. Originally conceived to provide an engineering model of human performance, the model has been extended several times, and there is a subset of GOMS models that have reached enough maturity to be effective tools in HCI application design [41]. Going back to the notion of design life cycle introduced in Section 10.4.4, the GOMS model can produce quantitative predictions of performance at an earlier stage in the design life cycle of an application using a low-fidelity prototype. This is crucial when developing airline applications, which are generally complex and expensive to produce. By predicting execution time, learning time, errors, task sequence, and identifying parts of an application or interface that enable these predictions, designers can front-load the task of identifying and iterating crucial parts of the application. These models are straight-forward enough for computer designers to use without extensive training in psychology, and they are integrated enough to cover total tasks [41].

In the context of airline applications, goals represent a user's intentions defined in layman's language, like wanting to pilot an aircraft. Subgoals for this task would include intentions like wanting to take off, wanting to reach 10,000 feet, or wanting to land. Operators are the actions that a user can perform when using an airline application. Operators can be detailed like mouse clicks, screen taps, and menu-level interactions or more high level like clearing the current route. But GOMS models typically use more detailed operators. Methods are the steps to achieve a goal. Finally, selection rules are required to choose between alternate methods. If there are multiple methods to accomplish the same goal or subgoal, we turn to selection rules.

10.5.4.1 GOMS model analysis of intelligent airline tutoring system

Simulation technology has completely revolutionized training in the airline industry, whether it is training Air Force pilots, maintenance staff, air traffic management staff, or airport design personnel. Different variants of GOMS models have been used over the years to iterate designs of airline applications using quantitative signals from modeling exercises. Steinberg and Gitomer [42] describes a specific GOMS model analysis to improve the interface for an intelligent tutoring system for training Air Force maintenance personnel. As part of their jobs, the maintenance personnel move around the aircraft, examine aircraft components, manipulate different controls in the aircraft, observe the effect of these operations, and troubleshoot aircraft hydraulic systems such as the flight control systems. The tutoring system provided an application in which a trainee could "travel" to different parts of the aircraft using a menu system to carry out the set of operations described to troubleshoot potential issues.

An earlier version of the interface evaluated using the GOMS model had an in-built assumption that maintenance personnel would troubleshoot one component or location at a time. The assumed modus operandi was that a user would "travel" to one location of the aircraft, interact with a component or control, observe the effect of the interaction, and perform troubleshooting activities all within the same location of the aircraft. But a GOMS model analysis showed that support personnel often needed to move to different locations of the aircraft to accomplish the task of troubleshooting a single aircraft component. A typical activity was an input–output test, in which inputs would be supplied to one set of components, and then several other components, often in an entirely different location, would be observed. For example, the troubleshooter would enter the cockpit, set several switches, and then start moving the control stick, and then observe the rudders to see if they moved [41].

Because of a faulty assumption about how maintenance personnel performed their jobs, the version of the interface being evaluated required users to traverse a complicated and hierarchic menu system to perform multiple-component input—output operations. This allowed applications designers to build an improved tutoring system that more closely aligned with the jobs performed by Air Force maintenance personnel. The improved application interface allowed users to more easily view and act on different locations of the aircraft. This, in turn, made the tutoring system more accurate and efficient in terms of training maintenance personnel.

10.5.4.2 GOMS model analysis of the advanced automated cockpit

Ref. [34] posits that there are many similarities between the modern automated office and the high-technology flight deck because both sets of workers are managers of complex suites of automation. Their paper analyzes the skills needed to perform tasks using the flight management computer (FMC) on an advanced commercial aircraft. The authors point out that advanced aircraft entail high complexity and cognitive load for using FMC, and they require extensive training, followed by months of line experience, for efficient and skilled use of FMC. Therefore, the authors built a training program and did a detailed analysis of FMC tasks using the GOMS model to test the efficiency of this training program. They trained subjects to perform tasks in a full motion simulator and compared them to other pilots.

The top-level method in the GOMS model is a task acquisition loop that models a set of user steps. As part of these steps, we scan the environment to select a task, understand/categorize the task, select an appropriate method to accomplish the task, execute the task, and then return to the task acquisition loop [34]. Two primary tasks are identified at the top-level: "Preflight FMC" and "Modify Route." The first task involves initializing the FMC with data about the flight route. Fig. 10.9 summarizes the GOMS model for one of the subtasks in "Preflight FMC" called "INSTALL ROUTE," which involves entering the route the aircraft needs to take. By comparing the percentage of subjects who could complete each task without experimenter intervention and by further diving into the kinds of errors and issues different groups of users experience for each subtask, the authors were able to gain insights into user cognitive loads, learning curves, skill transfer, and common errors, all of which can be leveraged to iterate on the application design. Similar methods and principles can be deployed to obtain quantitative data on the effectiveness and efficiency of airline applications to perform rapid design iterations.

10.5.5 Case study on how a cockpit remembers its speeds

"Remembering" is generally thought of as a uniquely human or biologic trait. But given the dynamic nature of flight, it is interesting to reason about how a cockpit remembers its speeds. The title of the paper by Ref. [43] hints that in an airplane, it is not just the pilot remembering, but rather the entire cockpit remembering. The cockpit here is a distributed system composed of a collection of controls, sensors, and interfaces, and the pilots themselves. The contention is that this system, in its entirety, is remembering the speeds, not just the human pilot or pilots inside the cockpit. That is also the essence of distributed cognition. The cognition involved in landing a plane is distributed across the components of the system. This is a deeper notion than just using interfaces to help us do tasks. The important thing here is that these different interfaces in the cockpit serve cognitive roles in the system and add additional cognitive resources needed for flight. The cockpit system remembers the aircraft speed, and the memory process emerges from the activity of the pilots. But the memory of the cockpit is not primarily made of pilot memory.

Method to Accomplish Goal of INSTALL ROUTE

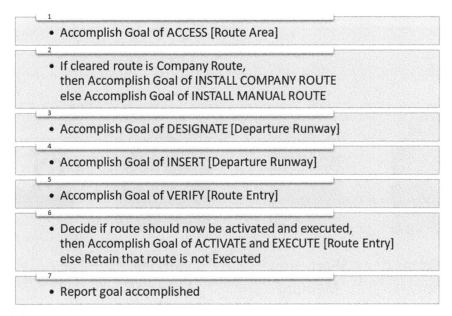

1
- Accomplish Goal of ACCESS [Route Area]

2
- If cleared route is Company Route,
  then Accomplish Goal of INSTALL COMPANY ROUTE
  else Accomplish Goal of INSTALL MANUAL ROUTE

3
- Accomplish Goal of DESIGNATE [Departure Runway]

4
- Accomplish Goal of INSERT [Departure Runway]

5
- Accomplish Goal of VERIFY [Route Entry]

6
- Decide if route should now be activated and executed,
  then Accomplish Goal of ACTIVATE and EXECUTE [Route Entry]
  else Retain that route is not Executed

7
- Report goal accomplished

FIGURE 10.9

GOMS model breakdown for method of install route.

It is also worth noting that Hutchins describes the airplanes' speeds in the paper title in plural: "How a Cockpit Remembers Its Speeds." This is because for every flight, there are a unique set of speeds that must be remembered. When a plane is descending for landing, there exists several different changes the pilots need to make to the wing configurations. These changes are made at different speeds during the descent. When the plane slows down to a certain speed, it demands a certain change to the wind configuration. The speeds at which these configuration changes must happen differ based on several different variables. So, the cockpit is not just remembering how fast it is going now, but rather a sequence of speeds at which multiple changes need to happen. The configuration changes to the wings must be made during the descent at narrowly defined times, which means pilots must act quickly. Unfortunately, this creates a high cognitive load and mistakes under these circumstances can be fatal.

In the cockpit, cognition is distributed in at least three ways: (1) between the two pilots, (2) between the pilots and the dashboard instruments, and (3) over time. Ref. [43] describes the task of controlling the configuration of the airplane to match the changes in speed required for maneuvering in the approach and landing. The cockpit features several different cognitive components to remember speeds:

1. long-term memory: a booklet of different speeds for different parameters that is used by pilots to find speeds that correspond to their parameters;
2. short-term memory: one sheet from the booklet that contains a specific configuration that represents the current speeds and is accessible to both the pilots;

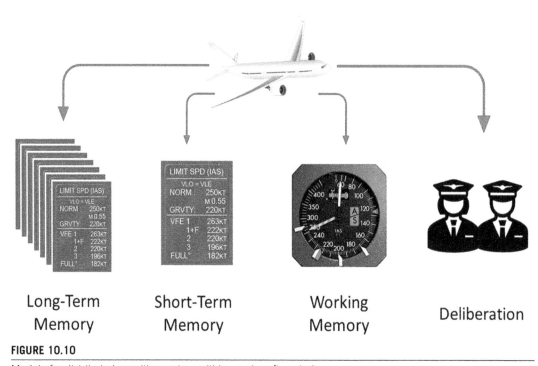

FIGURE 10.10

Model of a distributed cognitive system within an aircraft cockpit.

3. working memory: as pilots begin descent, they mark the different speeds on the speedometers with the help of speed bugs; when the speedometer passes a speed bug, the pilots know it is time to make a certain change;
4. deliberation: the two pilots in the cockpit.

Each one of these components helps in remembering the speed of a plane by serving as an individual cognitive component in the cognitive system, as illustrated in Fig. 10.10.

10.6 HCI for emergencies

Laughter, along with madness, seemed to be the only way out, the emergency exit for humans.

—Matt Haig

10.6.1 Users of emergency applications

Emergency applications are a powerful tool to help in case of emergency. With the advent of mobile devices and digital emergency applications, people giving emergency assistance, whether professional or not, have more avenues to help. In this context, HCI design for specific emergencies contexts needs to put users, the people in danger, and the emergency environment in the center of the design process.

HCI can also help to plan for emergency response. Ref. [44] describes a methodology for a precise and reliable COVID-19 forecast that can be used by public health officials and government officials to effectively plan and budget resources for COVID-19 relief in the future. Having an accurate predictive model is the first piece of the puzzle. HCI comes into play when we need to build visualizations, data pipelines, and applications to support decision-making. Depending on these different contexts and factors, we face different challenges and need to prioritize different design considerations.

10.6.1.1 EMTs and trained personnel

Emergency medical technicians (EMTs) are trained health professionals that provide emergency medical services. Most commonly, EMTs and other trained emergency personnel work as part of an ambulance crew and deal with different kinds of personal emergency situations. Since their job involves lifting patients and handling transportation via ground or air vehicles, they need hands-free interaction capabilities to coordinate emergency response efforts with other members of the crew. Equally important, their interactions with communication systems should not distract from the primary task of providing prehospital treatment, stabilization, or transport to medical care. Therefore, it is necessary to understand these primary tasks, and the context in which these tasks are performed, in sufficient detail and design interfaces and applications for the use of EMTs around those tasks.

10.6.1.2 Collaborative emergency management

When disaster strikes, emergency management (EM) aims to manage risks to communities and the environment by focusing on four fundamental elements: prevention, preparedness, response, and recovery. It is not uncommon for different groups of professionals, who would not otherwise collaborate daily, to coordinate EM efforts. This can include volunteers, medicos, firefighters, and policymakers, among others. This heterogeneity in terms of expertise and exposure to different technologic systems presents a big challenge for HCI. As a result, interface and applications used for EM also need to be context aware and adapt to the user, the environment, and the devices at hand. For instance, applications used by field response teams need to focus more heavily on being able to capture the current state of emergency and transmit that data to a command center, whereas command center-based applications need to be able to quickly process incoming signals and help with resource prioritization. At the same time, EM applications should also be able to distinguish between experienced and novel users to address the complexity challenge by reducing the cognitive load according to the experience level and the user's task.

10.6.1.3 Health at home

To care for a loved one at home, families have been increasingly relying on operating health care devices, interfaces, and services at home. Some of these include medical administration equipment, test kits, first aid equipment, meters/monitors, respiratory equipment, feeding equipment, voiding equipment, telehealth equipment, and healthcare apps. While some users must deal with health emergencies frequently, others are highly unfamiliar with how these devices operate. From an HCI lens, that means the user interfaces must support the whole spectrum from novices up to very experienced, well-trained users. Another significant area of concern relates to the stress, emotions, and cognitive load associated with responding to a medical emergency at home. Consider an example of a young couple needing to perform infant CPR at home and relying on an app for instructions. In this emergency, the parents are seldom trained, so they are lacking in skill and expertise, and they are experiencing tremendous emotional strain, which can cloud their judgment. So, design for healthcare emergencies at home needs to pay special attention to stress, emotions, lack of skill, and cognitive load.

10.6.1.4 Driving and flying

SA is a concept that is relevant to both driving and flying. It refers to the driver's or the pilot's accurate perception of the current state of the environment. In case of driving, this environment has to do with the state of the roads, the traffic conditions, the weather, and other conditions that would affect the safety of the moving vehicle. In the case of flying, the environment encapsulates the airplane's physical location in space and extends out to include conditions like weather, air traffic, communications, and resource management that relate to the safety of the flight. Loss of SA has been a major contributing factor to several emergencies, and subsequent accidents, in the history of both aviation and automobiles. Therefore, a key challenge for emergency HCI in the context of driving and flying is to maximize SA while minimizing cognitive load for both drivers and pilots.

10.6.2 Challenges for emergency HCI

Emergencies, by definition, require immediate action. As a result, time is a critical factor in most of the challenges with the application of HCI principles in emergency situations. Whether we are talking about mobile devices that support individual emergency response scenarios, applications that alert users about impending emergencies, or distributed information systems that support emergency response or disaster recovery scenarios among a group of people, the following are major challenges that HCI needs to address.

10.6.2.1 Bridging the gulf of execution

Section 10.1.1 covered the concept of gulf of execution in more detail. The core idea here is that in an emergency, the interface or application in question needs to clearly communicate the action that a user needs to take to handle or mitigate an emergency. For example, fire extinguishers include concise and specific 4-step instructions on the use of PASS technique: pull the pin, aim at the base of fire, squeeze the lever, and sweep side to side. Design that facilitates lowering the gulf of execution is critical in an emergency context. Similarly, emergency applications that require complex instructions or the use of a manual to operate can instead opt to integrate a language-agnostic conversational AI or chatbots to guide users through the process of using or troubleshooting the application.

10.6.2.2 Dealing with the ironies of automation

The expression "ironies of automation" was coined by Ref. [45]. Even though automation has benefited several industries in the last few decades, paradoxically integration of technically sophisticated automated systems has resulted in increased cognitive load for operators, especially in emergency situations. The introduction of computerized airplanes slowly led to a formalization of all segments of the flight in the language of the machine. Over the course of decades, substitutive automation of the human operator in different aspects of flight management resulted in a rupture in the professional culture of the pilots, to the detriment of the pilots' own thinking. As a result, when pilots find themselves in an emergency, they find it hard to reason about what has gone wrong and what corrective action needs to be taken. Staying with the airline example, the challenge here is to strike the right balance between automating enough functions but also helping pilots maintain SA so they are always ready to respond in the face of emergencies.

10.6.2.3 Adverse physical environments

Design must consider the physical conditions under which an emergency response needs to happen. For example, first responders need to be able to find and operate fire extinguishers in smoky environments, emergency personnel need to be able to easily remove the helmet on a motorcyclist after an accident, and an elderly person needs to be able to use a mechanical walker to find a phone to report an emergency. Therefore, we need to focus on the specific emergency and the surrounding physical context when designing for emergencies. Designing for tasks that are situated in a larger context, as opposed to designing for items on a list that do not have context, can lead to drastically different design outcomes.

10.6.2.4 Stress, emotions, and cognitive load

All three of these factors lead to a wider gulf of execution and evaluation in an emergency context. A user operating an interface, device, or application will find it harder to both process information around them and reason about what action they need to take. This is another reason why the concept of situated action is so important when designing for emergencies because design needs to consider not just the task the user is performing but the larger context and the conditions under which a user is performing the said tasks as well as what effects, if any, this context can have on the ability of the user to perform the emergency task [4].

10.6.2.5 Unintended side effects of technology

This is the unending debate about privacy versus safety and about adding constraints versus affordances to applications. On the one hand, technology empowers design to come up with creative solutions that leverage real-time location tracking, facial recognition, data mining, and other innovative AI techniques. Use of these technologies for contact tracing during the COVID-19 outbreak or for emergency messaging for severe weather alerts were lifesaving. But the unintended side effect of technology and data science is that custodians of data can extract a lot of useful information from other people's data and, in many cases, have broad leeway on what they can do with users' personal data. Similarly, technology makes it easy to add new features to everything, but when building applications to be used in a specific emergency context, adding more constraints as clues can be more powerful than adding more functionalities. So emergency design needs to inform and guide practices on defining the line vis-à-vis public safety and privacy and between adding versus removing features.

10.6.3 Case study: cognitive task analysis for an emergency management game

The Bethesda Hospital decided to design a training system for hospital EM situations [46]. In particular, the hospital wanted to train staff for multiple roles in procedures for handling highly infectious diseases. Since immersive simulations are quite effective at creating engaging and transformative learning experiences, a game-based approach was selected for the simulation. Furthermore, well-designed game-based simulations that retain training efficacy are much more economical when compared with real disaster exercises. Since serious game design is a complex process that requires marrying effective gameplay and storytelling with effective learning outcomes, this effort required assembling a multidisciplinary team with expertise in gameplay, programming, pedagogy, interaction design, and human cognition.

Often, expert users of applications and interfaces are unaware of how much unconscious knowledge they deploy when doing their jobs. For some, their actions and decisions rely on as much as 70% automatic, unconscious knowledge to complete a task, which is why methods like cognitive task analysis (CTA) are to capture this rich unconscious knowledge necessary for proficient task performance. From an instructional design perspective, the CTA output needs to describe the implicit and explicit knowledge to support the actions and decisions made by the expert as well as the context in which the task is performed [47]. CTAs are especially useful in the context of developing a serious EM game because CTAs emphasize mental processes, and they are formal enough for interface design. Moreover, CTAs are generally better suited for experts, and this case study targeted professional and experts in the hospital setting.

Depending on the problem and the task context, different CTA methods can be chosen. Ref. [48] identified three broad families of methods for knowledge elicitation to support a CTA: (1) observations and interviews rely on watching and talking to experts, (2) process tracing is suited for tracking specific tasks via data sources like eye movements and nonverbal user actions from which cognitive inferences can be made, and (3) conceptual techniques are focused on developing domain concepts, structures, and interrelationships. The case study CTA exercise used observations and interviews to get continual feedback from hospital staff while they relied on an agile methodology that leaned heavily on rapid prototyping and iteration. To effectively transfer knowledge from the CTA exercise to the game developers and to complete the design feedback cycle, the team relied on the following process.

1. collect existing documentation and preliminary knowledge
2. develop interview protocol questions
3. conduct CTA interviews
4. analyze and verify data acquired
5. format results and identify training requirements
6. create storyboards

Based on their experience developing a simulation-based roleplay game to respond to hospital emergencies, the authors recommend using a CTA approach for iteratively building similar training systems for EM scenarios. Since effective coordination between a multidisciplinary team was a top priority, they also recommend using an agile approach for rapid prototype development to keep everyone informed of the latest design, development, and timeline requirements [46]. The hospital staff were able to use the simulated game environment to effectively learn the process for donning and doffing personal protective equipment in response to a hospital emergency. And because a CTA is domain independent, similar simulated environments can be built for other emergency applications as well.

10.7 Conclusion

"Good design is like a refrigerator—when it works, no one notices, but when it doesn't, it sure stinks."

—Irene Au

HCI principles enable good design. HCI is used to design user interfaces that are intuitive and easy to use, so that users can easily interact with a system and understand its output. HCI principles can also be used to develop AI systems that are able to adapt to the needs and preferences of individual users, so that they can provide personalized experiences. Additionally, HCI principles can be used to design AI systems that are able to communicate with users in a natural and intuitive way, so that they can provide information and assistance in a way that is easy for users to understand and act on.

We started the chapter with a discussion of the fundamental, domain agnostic HCI principles used in the design and development of intelligent applications. Concepts like feedback cycles, direct manipulation, invisible interfaces, mental models and representations, and distributed cognition are fundamental to HCI. These concepts feature extensively throughout the chapter when discussing application design in different domains. But no matter which HCI principle we deploy for a given application domain, there is one constant in HCI: putting the user in the center of the design process. This is the essence of user-centered design. To design applications and interfaces that are better than existing designs, it is important to take into consideration the user's needs at every stage of the design process. There are also multiple dimensions to consider when designing applications and interfaces. But the most important one is to ensure that design is principally informed by a thorough understanding of users, user needs, and user environments. Therefore, we must gather information about the users, the tasks they perform, and where they perform those tasks, and we need to leverage that knowledge throughout the design process.

Sometimes application designers will go through the entire design process believing they already understand the needs of the user without actually getting user feedback. This is a dangerous trap. In HCI, user-centered design is about prioritizing the user's needs while also recognizing that we do not know the user's needs. Before we start, we need to examine user needs in depth, both by observing them and by asking direct questions. After we start designing, we need to present our design alternatives and prototypes to the user to get substantive feedback. And when we have a design that we like, we need to evaluate the quality of the design with actual users. Having a good working knowledge of HCI principles helps us go through several iterations of the design lifecycle involving need finding, design alternatives, prototyping and evaluation more quickly and effectively. Techniques like GOMS model, time task calculations, telemetry data analysis for empirical evaluation, and surveys for qualitative evaluation are typically used to rate how good a design or a prototype is. Because of the introduction of newer interaction patterns and interactive technologies in recent years, HCI research is constantly evolving to find new ways to design, prototype, and evaluate applications and interfaces.

Looking ahead, rapid evolution toward more intelligent interactive technologies means that HCI will be increasingly called upon not just to aid interface design but also to solve broader societal and technology-related challenges. Several researchers have written about the future of HCI to guide further research and exploration. In his book *The Design of Future Things*, Ref. [49] explored the ongoing tug-of-war vis-à-vis automation and control. There is a similar dilemma unfolding between machine and human intelligence. As these dilemmas unfold, they gradually reshape the landscape of product design. A few years later, Ref. [50] published "Artificial Intelligence: Think Again" as artificial intelligence was starting to look increasingly impactful, following a number of cycles bemoaning the death of AI. In recent years, there has been a great deal of conversation, concern, and consequently myths around machine learning in popular media. Through his publication, Kaplan seeks to address common misunderstandings and refocus the conversation on pragmatic design choices that address relevant cultural, social, economic, and ethical concerns. As current VR experiences mature, they will pave the way for newer interaction patterns in the form of brain–computer interfaces that raise further questions about how we humans understand our expanding capabilities and think about the trajectory of human evolution. Similarly, the impending changes in automotive interface and applications caused by the self-driving car revolution will require HCI research to reason deeply about safety and security in Human–AI interaction. Since robotic technology is slowly proliferating across the healthcare sector, safety, security, and reliability are also critical to address in the context of healthcare. Since we are progressively marching to an age where machine intelligence and AI increasingly shape application experiences, future HCI research should also study and inform regulation activities about how safe, secure, and private these emerging technologies are.

Considerations related to human safety are especially important in the context of smart environments, which are becoming increasingly autonomous in nature. This is applicable to smart environments in the realm of applications for airlines, automobile, healthcare, and emergencies. Human safety is therefore a prime candidate for future HCI research. Human safety should be accounted for during the design and implementation of applications, but the design process should also be forward-looking. In particular, the development and deployment of artificially intelligent systems that can learn and evolve over time is inherently risky because designers and developers might not be able to fully control this process of evolution [2]. Moreover, technology misuse or poor design only compound these concerns. To this end, a recommendation is that advanced intelligent systems should be "safe by design." The core being that safety is baked into the design lifecycle as early as possible by using known safe and more safe technical paradigms [2].

The nature of HCI design is that different design principles and considerations might have significant connections, not just to the design of the application, but to the very core of the task that we are trying to support. For each application domain covered in this chapter, we discussed case studies to explore the right principles and considerations that best support user tasks, goals, and environments for a given domain. HCI principles can be used to make applications more safe, functional, useable, pleasurable, and customizable, all of which add to the richness of the user experience in varied ways. To accomplish this, it is important to think of application design as a conversation instead of a monologue, aided by an iterative life cycle. The more we engage with our users, the better we understand their needs, and how to design solutions that best meet their needs. Through this iterative approach informed by HCI, we can design applications that improve public health outcomes, enhance automotive and airline safety, streamline emergency response, and refine VR experiences.

References

[1] D.A. Norman, Cognitive engineering, in: D.A. Norman, S.W. Draper (Eds.), User Centred System Design, Lawrence Erlbaum Associates, New Jersey, 1986.

[2] A. Ramesh, P. Dhariwal, A. Nichol, C. Chu, M. Chen, Hierarchical Text-Conditional Image Generation with Clip Latents, 2022 *arXiv preprint arXiv:2204.06125.*

[3] C. Saharia, W. Chan, S. Saxena, L. Li, J. Whang, E. Denton, M. Norouzi, Photorealistic Text-To-Image Diffusion Models with Deep Language Understanding, 2022 *arXiv preprint arXiv:2205.11487.*

[4] B.A. Nardi, Studying context: a comparison of activity theory, situated action models, and distributed cognition, in: B.A. Nardi (Ed.), Context and Consciousness: Activity Theory and Human−Computer Interaction, MIT Press, Cambridge, MA, 1996, pp. 69−102.

[5] Virtual Reality Market Size, Share and Trends Analysis Report by Technology (Semi and Fully Immersive, Non-immersive), by Device (HMD, GTD), by Component (Hardware, Software), by Application, and Segment Forecasts (2021 − 2028), 2021.

[6] A. Dünser, R. Grasset, H. Seichter, M. Billinghurst, Applying HCI Principles to AR Systems Design, 2007.

[7] A.A. Rizzo, G.J. Kim, S. Yeh, M. Thiebaux, J. Hwang, J.G. Buckwalter, Development of a benchmarking scenario for testing 3D user interface devices and interaction methods, in: The Proceedings of the 11th International Conference on Human Computer Interaction, 2005.

[8] H. Kaufmann, D. Schmalstieg, Designing immersive virtual reality for geometry education, in: IEEE Virtual Reality Conference (VR 2006), 2006, pp. 51−58, https://doi.org/10.1109/VR.2006.48.

[9] C. Dede, M.C. Salzman, R.B. Loftin, ScienceSpace: virtual realities for learning complex and abstract scientific concepts, in: Proceedings of the IEEE 1996 Virtual Reality Annual International Symposium, 1996, pp. 246−252, https://doi.org/10.1109/VRAIS.1996.490534.

[10] A. Sutcliffe, B. Gault, Heuristic evaluation of virtual reality applications, Interact. Comput. 16 (4) (2004) 831−849, https://doi.org/10.1016/j.intcom.2004.05.001.

[11] J. Nielsen, R.L. Mack, Usability Inspection Methods, Wiley, New York, 1994.

[12] D. Bian, J. Wade, Z. Warren, N. Sarkar, Online engagement detection and task adaptation in a virtual reality based driving simulator for autism intervention, in: M. Antona, C. Stephanidis (Eds.), Universal Access in Human-Computer Interaction: Users and Context Diversity. UAHCI 2016. Lecture Notes in Computer Science, 9739, Springer, Switzerland, 2016, pp. 538−547, https://doi.org/10.1007/978-3-319-40238-3_51.

[13] J.D. Gould, C. Lewis, Designing for usability: key principles and what designers think, Commun. ACM 28 (3) (1985) 300−311, https://doi.org/10.1145/3166.3170.

[14] World Health Organization, Road Traffic Injuries, June 21, 2021. Retrieved from, https://www.who.int/news-room/fact-sheets/detail/road-traffic-injuries.

[15] C.P. Janssen, S.F. Donker, D.P. Brumby, A.L. Kun, History and future of human-automation interaction, Int. J. Hum. Comput. Stud. 131 (2019) 99−107, https://doi.org/10.1016/j.ijhcs.2019.05.006.

[16] C. Nowakowski, D. Friedman, P. Green, An experimental evaluation of using automotive HUDs to reduce driver distraction while answering cell phones, in: Proceedings of the Human Factors and Ergonomics Society 46th Annual Meeting, vol 46, 2002, pp. 1819−1823, https://doi.org/10.1177/154193120204602209.

[17] Q. Fottrell, GPS, Smartphones and Speed Keep Road Deaths at 10-year High, February 16, 2018. Retrieved from, https://www.marketwatch.com/story/forget-texting-the-most-dangerous-distractions-for-drivers-come-with-the-car-2017-10-05.

[18] R. Parasuraman, T.B. Sheridan, C.D. Wickens, A model for types and levels of human interaction with automation, in: IEEE Transactions on Systems, Man, and Cybernetics—Part A: Systems and Humans, vol 30, 2000, pp. 286−297, https://doi.org/10.1109/3468.844354.

[19] F. Flemisch, J. Kelsch, C. Löper, A. Schieben, J. Schindler, Automation spectrum, inner/outer compatibility and other potentially useful human factors concepts for assistance and automation, Hum. Factors Assist. Autom. (2008) 1−16, 2008.

[20] P. Green, Estimating compliance with the 15-second rule for driver-interface usability and safety, Proc. Hum. Factors Ergon. Soc. Annu. Meet. 43 (18) (1999) 987−991, https://doi.org/10.1177/154193129904301809.

[21] S. Card, T.P. Moran, A. Newell, The Psychology of Human Computer Interaction, Lawrence Erlbaum Associates, New Jersey, 1983.

[22] M. Pettitt, G. Burnett, A. Stevens, An extended keystroke level model (KLM) for predicting the visual demand of in-vehicle information systems, in: CHI '07: Proceedings of the SIGCHI Conference on Human Factors in Computing Systems, 2007, pp. 1515−1524, https://doi.org/10.1145/1240624.1240852.

[23] M.F. Story, J.L. Mueller, R. Mace, The Universal Design File: Designing for People of All Ages and Abilities, Raleigh: The Center for Universal Design, NCSU, 1998.

[24] FDA, Human Factors Considerations, 2017. Retrieved from, https://www.fda.gov/medical-devices/human-factors-and-medical-devices/human-factors-considerations.

[25] P.A. Hancock, A. Pepe, L.L. Murphy, Hedonomics: the power of positive and pleasurable ergonomics, Ergon. Des 13 (1) (2005) 8−14.

[26] M. Abouyoussef, S. Bhatia, P. Chaudhary, S. Sharma, M. Ismail, Blockchain-enabled online diagnostic platform of suspected patients of COVID-19 like pandemics, IEEE Intern. Things Magaz. 4 (4) (2021) 94−99.

[27] U.S. Food and Drug Administration, Medical Device Home Use Initiative, 2010. Retrieved from, https://www.fda.gov/media/78647/download.

[28] M.F. Story, 8 medical devices in home health care, in: National Research Council (US) Committee on the Role of Human Factors in Home Health Care. The Role of Human Factors in Home Health Care: Workshop Summary, National Academies Press (US), Washington (DC), 2010.

[29] Rath, S., & Chandna, S. Leveraging Voice Assistive Technology to Enhance Health Monitoring of Older Adults.

[30] Google: People + AI Guidebook: User Needs + Defining Success, 2020.

[31] G. Riva, R.M. Baños, C. Botella, F. Mantovani, A. Gaggioli, Transforming experience: the potential of augmented reality and virtual reality for enhancing personal and clinical change, Front. Psychiatr. 7 (2016) 164, https://doi.org/10.3389/fpsyt.2016.00164.

[32] D.A. Kolb, Experiential Learning as the Science of Learning and Development, Prentice Hall, Englewood Cliffs, NJ, 1984.

[33] C. Botella, J. Breton-Lopez, S. Quero, R. Banos, A. Garcia-Palacios, Treating cockroach phobia with augmented reality, Behav. Ther. 41 (3) (2010) 401−413, https://doi.org/10.1016/j.beth.2009.07.002.

[34] S. Irving, P. Polson, J.E. Irving, A GOMS analysis of the advanced automated cockpit, in: CHI '94: Proceedings of the SIGCHI Conference on Human Factors in Computing Systems, 1994, pp. 344−350, https://doi.org/10.1145/191666.191780.

[35] M. Carroll, N. Dahlstrom, Human computer interaction on the modern flight deck, Int. J. Hum. Comput. Interact. 37 (7) (2021) 585−587, https://doi.org/10.1080/10447318.2021.1890495.

[36] Boeing, Statistical Summary of Commercial Jet Airplane Accidents: Worldwide Operations | 1959−2019, 2019. Technical report. Retrieved from, http://www.boeing.com/resources/boeingdotcom/company/about_bca/pdf/statsum.pdf. (Accessed 15 July 2021).

[37] S. Conversy, S. Chatty, H. Gaspard-Boulinc, J.L. Vinot, The accident of flight 447 Rio-Paris: a case study for HCI research, in: HCI-aero '16: Proceedings of the International Conference on Human-Computer Interaction in Aerospace, 2016, pp. 1−8, https://doi.org/10.1145/2950112.2964586.

[38] M.R. Endsley, Toward a theory of situation awareness in dynamic systems, Hum. Factors J. Hum. Factors Ergonom. Soc. 37 (1) (1995) 32−64, https://doi.org/10.1518/001872095779049543.

[39] C.D. Wickens, C.M. Carswell, The proximity compatibility principle: its psychological foundation and relevance to display design, Hum. Factors 37 (3) (1995) 473—494, https://doi.org/10.1518/001872 095779049408.

[40] J. Nielsen, R. Molich, Heuristic evaluation of user interfaces, in: CHI '90: Proceedings of the SIGCHI Conference on Human Factors in Computing Systems, 1990, pp. 249—256, https://doi.org/10.1145/97243.97281.

[41] B.E. John, D.E. Kieras, Using GOMS for user interface design and evaluation: which technique? ACM Trans. Comput. Hum. Interact. 3 (4) (1996) 287—319, https://doi.org/10.1145/235833.236050.

[42] L.S. Steinberg, D.H. Gitomer, Cognitive task analysis, interface design, and technical troubleshooting, in: W.D. Gray, W.E. Hefley, D. Murray (Eds.), Proceedings of the 1993 International Workshop on Intelligent User Interfaces, ACM, New York, 1993, pp. 185—191.

[43] E. Hutchins, How a cockpit remembers its speeds, Cognit. Sci. 19 (3) (1995) 265—288, https://doi.org/10.1207/s15516709cog1903_1.

[44] S. Namasudra, S. Dhamodharavadhani, R. Rathipriya, Nonlinear neural network-based forecasting model for predicting COVID-19 cases, Neural Process. Lett. (2021), https://doi.org/10.1007/s11063-021-10495-w.

[45] L. Bainbridge, Ironies of automation, IFAC Proc. Vol. 15 (6) (1982) 129—135, https://doi.org/10.1016/S1474-6670(17)62897-0.

[46] S. Dass, J. Barnieu, P. Cummings, V. Cid, A cognitive task analysis for an emergency management serious game, in: The Interservice/industry Training, Simulation, and Education Conference: I/ITSEC, 2016. PMID: 29629430.

[47] D.H. Jonassen, H. Tessmer, W.H. Hannum, Part IV cognitive task analysis—introduction, in: D.H. Jonassen, H. Tessmer, W.H. Hannum (Eds.), Task Analysis Methods for Instructional Design, Routledge, New York, 1999, pp. 107—109.

[48] N.J. Cooke, Varieties of knowledge elicitation techniques, Int. J. Hum. Comput. Stud. 41 (1994) 801—849.

[49] D. Norman, The Design of Future Things, Basic Books, New York, 2007.

[50] J. Kaplan, Artificial intelligence: think again, Commun. ACM 60 (2016) 36—38, https://doi.org/10.1145/2950039.

Further reading

[1] R. Chatila, J.C. Havens, The IEEE global initiative on Ethics of autonomous and intelligent systems, Intell. Syst. Contr. Autom. Sci. Eng. (2019) 11—16, https://doi.org/10.1007/978-3-030-12524-0_2.

[2] M. Crutchfield, Phases of Disaster Recovery: Emergency Response for the Long Term, 2013. Retrieved from, https://reliefweb.int/report/world/phases-disaster-recovery-emergency-response-long-term.

[3] W. He, D. Goodkind, P. Kowal, An Aging World: 2015, 2016, https://doi.org/10.13140/RG.2.1.1088.9362.

Challenges and future work directions in artificial intelligence with human-computer interaction

Mahesh H. Panchal and Shaileshkumar D. Panchal

Graduate School of Engineering and Technology, Gujarat Technological University, Ahmedabad, Gujarat, India

11.1 Introduction

Human—computer interaction (HCI) is a multidisciplinary field that deals with study of the interaction between humans (the users or any other stakeholders) and computers. Initially HCI was thought to be with only computers, but now it has been expanded to cover almost all forms of advanced information technology design. The term HCI was coined in early 1980s when the Apple Macintosh and IBM PC 5150 were started to enter offices for personal computing. The size of computers in those early years was large and not easily movable from one place to another. But people were comfortable with them for their regular work in word processing and accounting software. As the time elapsed, with the advancement in hardware technology (such as VLSI) and other peripheral devices, the computer systems came in smaller sizes. Whether there were large-size computers or compact ones, the HCI has played a very important role for easy and efficient access of computer systems. As shown in Fig. 11.1, HCI covers mainly the following major disciplines: (i) computer science, (ii) human-factors engineering, (iii) design, (iv) sociology and psychology, (v) cognitive science, (vi) natural language processing, and (vii) ethnography.

There is always trade-off between user interface and development difficulty. The early command line interfaces were very easy to develop but as far as users' interaction with them is concerned, it was very difficult. Nowadays, it is expected to provide a very easy interface to the users, but at the same time, it is very difficult to build such interfaces. The modern interfaces with digital gadgets are easy to use for naïve users too, but they are very hard to design, develop, and test. The main reason is that such programs are complex in nature and have many execution paths, many exit points, etc. To tackle this complexity of programs, the concepts from computer science are very useful. The role of computer science in HCI is to understand, apply, and develop the tools and techniques that can reduce the complexity of programs. The design of user interface modules for the interactive system of any gadget has to pass through four distinct levels: (1) conceptual, (2) semantic, (3) syntactic, and (4) lexical. All these levels have their own design and user interface modules that have to pass through these designs.

Voice is one of the interfaces by which humans can interact with the computers. The virtual assistants (e.g., Google Assistant, Apple's Siri, etc.) are commonly used for searching on the web, finding nearby places, searching for details of favorite players, etc., just by voice interface. It is

FIGURE 11.1

HCI as multidisciplinary field.

assumed that in coming years the applications based on voice interface will be heavily used by users across the web. Compared with touch interface, voice interface keeps the user's body parts free, and that is why it is the first choice. Considering the demand of voice-based interfaces, the supporting applications and software will also be required to be developed.

The field of artificial intelligence (AI) is gaining popularity due to rich set of machine learning (ML) algorithms. Basically, ML is a data-driven approach where the algorithms learn from given data. The things that are learned are characteristics of data, correlation among data, and causality between data. The outcome of learning is an ML model in which learned things are represented in different forms like trees, rules, cluster of neurons, and weights. Online financial fraud detection, prediction of loan approval, chat bots, virtual personal assistant, speech recognition, image recognition, traffic prediction, and self-driving cars are some of the application areas of ML.

Although ML algorithms are applied successfully in different applications and models are developed with high predictive accuracy, there is a demand for transparent AI systems to make the HCI more trustworthy. The purpose of transparent AI is to explain the user internal functioning of the ML model, the way predictions are made by model. By this way, the trust toward the AI system of every stakeholder will be increased and finally will create a bonding of HCI. The transparent AI system in literature is termed explainable artificial intelligence (XAI). XAI is to enable the artificially intelligent systems to provide meaning, purpose, and reasons behind the outcomes predicted by it. These explanations form a basis for various stakeholders to understand and then trust the outcomes/decisions derived by artificially intelligent systems. By means of XAI, it is also expected to produce more explainable learning models, while maintaining a high level of learning performance (prediction accuracy), as mentioned in Refs. [1–3]. It is also to be ensured that algorithmic decisions as well as any data driving those decisions can be explained to end users and other stakeholders in nontechnical terms. The "interpretability" is normally used with ML models, while "explainability" is more general than it and used with artificially intelligent systems. XAI expects that the ML models are interpretable as well as that their internal operations are also provided to the user for understanding purpose. XAI also serves as a base for responsible AI that takes into account societal values and moral and ethical considerations. Accountability, responsibility, and transparency are considered to be three main pillars of responsible AI, as shown in Fig. 11.2.

Nowadays, the availability and usage of AI-based smart devices, smart appliances, and smart environments has increased the intentional and unintentional interactions of humans with them. These interactions mainly include location tracing, pictures uploading on clouds, chatting on social media platforms, making profiles on social media websites, etc. Due to such interactions, big data is generated, and it is a cream for companies providing the AI services in the sense of mining these data and reaching to further depth with humans to increase the interactions. To make the AI system explainable, there are many challenges that open the windows of research. Looking at the ease of use and ability of bringing the humans on a common platform, these AI-based systems are facing the challenges on which the researchers are working. As shown in Fig. 11.2 and also mentioned above, the AI systems are providing accurate outcomes. But still in life critical applications (law, defense, medicine, etc.) and explanations about the decisions made by an AI system and its working are required to be known by the stakeholders. Explanations with the output of ML model are crucial, e.g., in precision medicine, where experts require far more information from the model than a simple binary prediction for supporting their diagnosis, as mentioned in Refs. [2,4].

In general, there is need of XAI for following reasons: (i) justification, (ii) control, (iii) improvement, and (iv) discovery.

Justification: The end user of an AI system asks about the justification of a specific outcome. For example, after getting details of nearby restaurants from Google Assistant, a user may ask why details of particular restaurant are not shown? Here, the user is not interested to know about inner working details of the decision-making process but wants the justification/reason about the outcome. If when using XAI, the said justification is provided, then it will create trust in users on AI system and its decisions. Furthermore, the "right to explanation" also demands the justification about explanations. The "right to explanation" is a regulation included in the General Data Protection Regulation that came into effect across the European Union on May 25, 2018, as mentioned in Refs. [1,5].

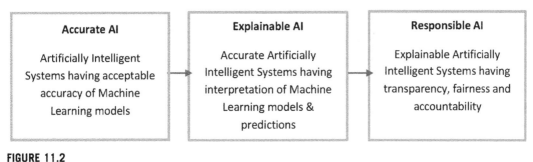

FIGURE 11.2

From accurate AI to responsible AI.

Control: When the algorithm(s) followed by an AI system goes wrong because of any reason, then for controlling its behavior, explanations about present working steps and complete flow are required. This also presents unknown vulnerabilities and flaws to the users and thus can be controlled by user.

Improvement: If explanations about outcomes are provided to the stakeholders particularly to ML engineers (one of the stakeholders of AI systems), then the performance of the ML models can be improved or can be made smarter after understanding the explanations. This will lead to more robust AI systems.

Discovery: Explanations are useful to learn new facts and thus gain knowledge. This will lead to the discovery of new facts that can be incorporated in the development of new ML models. Therefore, XAI systems are creating a foundation for discovering new AI systems in the same domains.

During development of the ML model, consideration of interpretability is advantageous for the following three reasons.

- It helps to ensure impartiality in decision-making.
- It increases robustness by highlighting to stakeholders the potential adversarial perturbations that could change the prediction.
- It ensures that only meaningful variables/features infer the output; i.e., there exists actual causality.

11.2 Research challenges in AI with HCI

As far as interpretability is concerned, the ML models are categorized based on the following factors, as mentioned in Ref. [6].

1. time (intrinsic versus post-hoc)
2. scope (local versus global)

Based on time when the interpretation or explanation is provided, ML models are categorized into two types: (i) intrinsic and (ii) post-hoc. In intrinsic, the interpretation of the model is prepared simultaneously with the process of model construction, as in the case of decision tree or rule-based ML algorithms. In contrast to it, the interpretation is prepared after the model is constructed, and it is known as a post-hoc model. The examples are artificial neural network (ANN), deep learning (DL), and support vector machine. As far as intrinsic and post-hoc categorization is concerned, there is straightforward trade-off between accuracy of the model and level of explanation provided by the model. Intrinsic models provide an accurate explanation but suffer from lower predictive accuracy. On the other hand, post-hoc models provide high predictive accuracy but lack the model explanation.

Considering the scope of explanation, ML models are categorized into two types: (i) local and (ii) global. In local interpretability, the explanation is provided for a particular decision problem regarding why only this outcome. In global interpretability, the explanation of a complete learned model (i.e., its structure and parameters) is provided to the user irrespective of a particular decision. In the case of a deep neural network (DNN), understanding the representation of neurons at the intermediate layer serves the purpose of global interpretation, while explanation of the contribution of each feature in predicting the output of particular input serves the purpose of local interpretation. Global interpretation indicates the transparency of the model as it explains the inner working of the model. Local interpretation indicates the causal relationship between specific input and its prediction. It can be said that global interpretability increases the trust in model, while local interpretability increases the trust in prediction.

As discussed earlier, the intrinsic ML models save the explanation about learning during the model construction itself. Therefore, once the model is constructed, they provide complete explanation about what the model learned so far. Now, based on scope of learning, they can be further divided into two categories: (i) intrinsic global interpretable models and (ii) intrinsic local interpretable models. The global models are again constructed into two ways: (i) adding interpretability constraints and (ii) extracting the explanation from a model.

The interpretability constraints are added to increase the comprehensibility of the model for the user. The example is pruning the decision tree by replacing the subtree with a leaf node where fewer samples are involved. Therefore it will create deep tree instead of a wide tree by providing more explanation to the user. As more constraints are added to provide more satisfactory explanation to user, it will degrade the performance of the model (i.e., predictive accuracy will reduce) because of a trade-off between explanation and accuracy.

Extracting the explanation from the model is carried out by approximating the learned model into another model that is interpretable without compromising the predictive accuracy. As an example, a tree-based ensemble ML model is approximated into a single decision tree. As another example, the learning in ANN or DNN can be transformed into a decision tree, so the predictive accuracy is not compromised, and explanation is achieved.

Local interpretable models, as discussed earlier, provide explanations about why such decisions are made by a model for particular input. As an example, recurrent neural network employs an attention mechanism that explains to the user which parts of the input were attended by the model to make the prediction. The attention mechanism visualizes the explanation in the form of a matrix called an attention weight matrix for every prediction made by a model.

As mentioned earlier, the post-hoc interpretable models provide higher accuracy because the major concern of such models is on correct prediction not explanation. But without explanation, the ML models are just like a black box. When a model fails to predict the correct output, then it becomes necessary for the ML experts to know that how such output was derived by the model. Therefore, for researchers as well as for users (to increase the trust on prediction), explanation of the model and prediction is required. For post-hoc interpretable models, there are two levels. In first level, considering only the predictive accuracy, the ML model is constructed. It means that the learning algorithms that are providing higher accuracy like DNN are used. In second level, the models that provide more explanation like decision tree or regression tree are constructed based on the model prepared in level one.

The post-hoc global interpretable models explain the inside of model, what it learned from training dataset, and effect of parameters on learning and prediction. Based on the generalized explanation and model-specific explanation, there is further division: (i) model-agnostic explanation and (ii) model-specific explanation. Model-agnostic explanation is a generalized explanation irrespective of the model and its internal working. Such an explanation mainly concentrates on how the individual features of the training dataset are co-related with each other, which are redundant features and are most promising features. Based on the relevance of feature with outcome, rank is assigned to each feature of a training dataset, and redundant features will not be considered while constructing the ML model. On the other hand, a model-specific explanation provides information about internal structure and working of a learned model. It also provides the explanation of model-specific parameters.

Given below are some of the research challenges when AI is integrated with HCI.

11.2.1 Lack of unified concept for XAI systems

In recent years, the black box ML models (like developed DNNs, random forest, ANNs, SVMs) have been applied for real applications in different domains (e.g., image classification, speech recognition, language translation, automatic vehicles) with acceptable performance. The risk is involved when the outcomes from such black box models are applied without justification. There are interpretable ML models (like developed from decision trees, k-nearest neighbors, rule-based learning, Bayesian network), but their performance is not as good as black box ML models. Therefore, it can be said that there is trade-off between performance of the model and its transparency.

As mentioned in Ref. [2], there are different stakeholders of artificially intelligent systems, shown in Fig. 11.3, who expect the explainability from the ML models:

End users are those who are expecting to fulfill their requirements and get comfort after use of AI systems. Explainability of AI system's outcome to them will add their trust. End users can also verify the fairness of outcomes given by AI systems.

FIGURE 11.3

Stakeholders of an artificially intelligent and explainable system.

Managers are collecting end users' requirements and work with domain experts and ML engineers. If the system is explainable, then it will help them to rethink certain requirements of users, and appropriate messages can be provided further to data scientists and ML engineers.

Domain experts are experienced people in their own work domain. Examples are automobile engineers, investment planners, farmers, etc. They are helping to provide necessary knowledge about the system based on their experience. The explanation provided by the ML model will help them to check the completeness of the system. It will also help them to gain new knowledge.

Data scientists and ML engineers are involved in analyzing of data and development and evaluation of ML models. Model explanations will help them to improve the performance of an existing model, to add new functionalities in it, and to further research in the direction of designing new methods.

AI system developers are those who are developing the modules by coding under the supervision of ML Engineers. If the AI systems are explainable, then it will help the developers to easily debug the code and correct the errors. It will also help them to optimize the code wherever required.

Regulatory bodies are government-approved or competent agencies that are certifying the AI-based products. If explanations are available from AI systems, then it will help these authorities to check the compliance of the models with existing legislation.

As far as XAI is concerned, there is difference between similar looking words: interpretability, explainability, understandability, and transparency. The difference lies in how much interaction between stakeholder and model is involved. For black box models, post-hoc explainability is required. It explains the functioning of the model after it is built. In general, post-hoc explainability can be either model-agnostic or model-specific. Even for interpretable models (e.g., decision tree), post-hoc explainability is required when a model is developed from an ensemble of decision trees. For DNNs, feature relevance method of providing the post-hoc explanation is becoming more popular.

One of the objectives of XAI systems is to provide the understanding of how the different stakeholders of XAI systems characterize the problem of explainability. To meet this objective, the author of Ref. [7] has conducted interviews with the 40 stakeholders of XAI systems. These stakeholders are technologists, academicians, people in oversight or policy roles in organizations currently using ML or AI technologies, and individuals who are or will be the end users of ML and AI systems. During interviews, the stakeholders have used following terms for "explainability": accountable, auditable, certifiable, fair, inspectable, interpretable, justifiable, operational, ready-to-use, reliable, repeatable, reproducible, responsible, self-service, tested, transparent, trusted, unbiased, understandable, and verifiable. Therefore, it seems that there is no consensus on the capabilities of the term XAI, as well as there are different interpretations of the same term. One stakeholder used two terms from above like synonyms, while another was able to distinguish between the same. From some stakeholders' perspective, XAI is only related to ANN and DNN, but actually that is not the case. The data scientists expect that the XAI system should be fair enough in terms of model performance, but the naïve user may understand the fairness as how the model is used in some social application. The training data may contain the bias toward a specific class/group of samples. The traditional AI system learns from such biased training data and provides a biased prediction. The goal of XAI is to detect the bias present in training data and provide it to the stakeholder to avoid the blind acceptance of a biased prediction.

The main categories of explanation methods are (i) model-agnostic and (ii) model-specific. But the AI community does not rely only on this categorization. For example, model-agnostic method SHAP is widely used to explain deep learning models. Locally interpretable model explanation (LIME) that is not exclusive to use with images can be used for convolution neural networks. Therefore the research challenge is to develop an XAI system that is not specific to the algorithm's inherent characteristic but can be as general as possible. Another research challenge is to satisfy the requirement of a unified concept of explainability and its terminology. There should be a common platform where the researchers can contribute by providing new techniques of XAI. For that common concept, first the needs are to be expressed, and accordingly a common structure can be proposed for every XAI system.

11.2.2 Biased decisions and explanation from AI systems

The model explanation methods like feature-oriented, local, global, model-agnostic, and model-specific are not representing the functions of a model in human understandable form. The explanations from a model expected by humans should be decision oriented, have associations, and have it be possible to evaluate similarities among them, as well as having the ability to be produced in court or to another expert. Such explanations are called human-centric instead of relying completely on statistics. Per right to explanation of the European Union's General Data Protection Right, the automated systems must avoid inequality and bias in their decision. Further, they must fulfill the safety and security in safety-critical tasks. It has been reported in Ref. [8] that the researchers have proposed an explainable DL approach to detect the COIVD-19 based on CT scans. This approach has proven to be better in terms of accuracy, F1 score, and other performance measures. It also represents a CT scan that a radiologist can clearly understand. Further, classes like low, mild, and severe can be added to add more explanations. In countries like the United States, there is an automated system based on XAI for predicting the places where crime is most likely to occur, the person who is most likely to commit a violent crime, the person who fails to appear for a hearing in court, etc. Of course, the data on which the system is working does not include race of individual, but other attributes of people may correlate to race, and a bias prediction based on race may come out. It is expected that such biases can be detected before prediction so that the system maintains its fair identity. Neuroscience and psychology can help to build simplified and efficient XAI models that are more easily understood by humans. XAI models derived from DNNs can also help in understanding the mechanisms of intelligence in the human brain. Therefore, XAI can help to bridge the gap between DL and neuroscience and also to fully understand a way of how human intelligence originates from neurons.

From the perspective of cognitive effort and cognitive learning theory, the explanations can be classified in four types, as shown in Ref. [9]: (i) type 1, trace or line of reasoning that explains why only particular decisions were made and not others, (ii) type 2, justification or support that justifies the reasoning process by linking the explanation with knowledge from which it was derived, (iii) type 3, control or strategic that explains the system's problem solving strategy, and (iv) type 4, terminological, which provides definitions and terminological information. Explainability is important to evaluate in the AI system for detecting its working behavior and unknown vulnerabilities and flaws to avoid some spurious correlations. Explainability is also important for designers to improve the system. If they know the inner working of the system, they can try for its enhancement. One of the goals of XAI is to learn from the algorithm's working that results in gaining deep knowledge. The explanations from an AI system can be used to discover unknown correlations with causal relationships in data. The quality criteria to be used for personalized explanations from XAI system are fidelity, generalizability, explanatory power, interpretability, comprehensibility, plausibility, effort, privacy, and fairness.

When an AI-based system is used for criminal justice systems, then there is a possibility of biased decisions based on certain characteristics of citizens like race. Of course, the data on which the system is working does not include race of individuals, but other attributes may correlate to race, and a biased prediction may come out. The research challenge is to detect such biases before prediction so that the system maintains its fair identity. There is potential of XAI to be explored in the applications of natural language processing and self-driving vehicles. It has been reported in Ref. [7] that for road conditions that are not part of training data, DL-based methods make incorrect predictions with high confidence that may have harmful consequences for self-driving vehicles, passengers, legal outcomes, and trust. Therefore a research challenge is to detect the biasing of confidence and provide transparent explanation systems for DL-based methods.

11.2.3 Lack of stakeholder-specific explanations

A framework is proposed in Ref. [10] to characterize and systematically assess the explainable systems by five key dimensions: functional, operational, usability, safety, and validation, as shown in Fig. 11.4. Such a framework is named explainability fact sheets, which provides a platform for researchers to assess their XAI system to find the capabilities and limitations.

The operational requirements include how the XAI system presents its output to the stakeholders. It contains an association between antecedent and consequent, contrasts, differences,

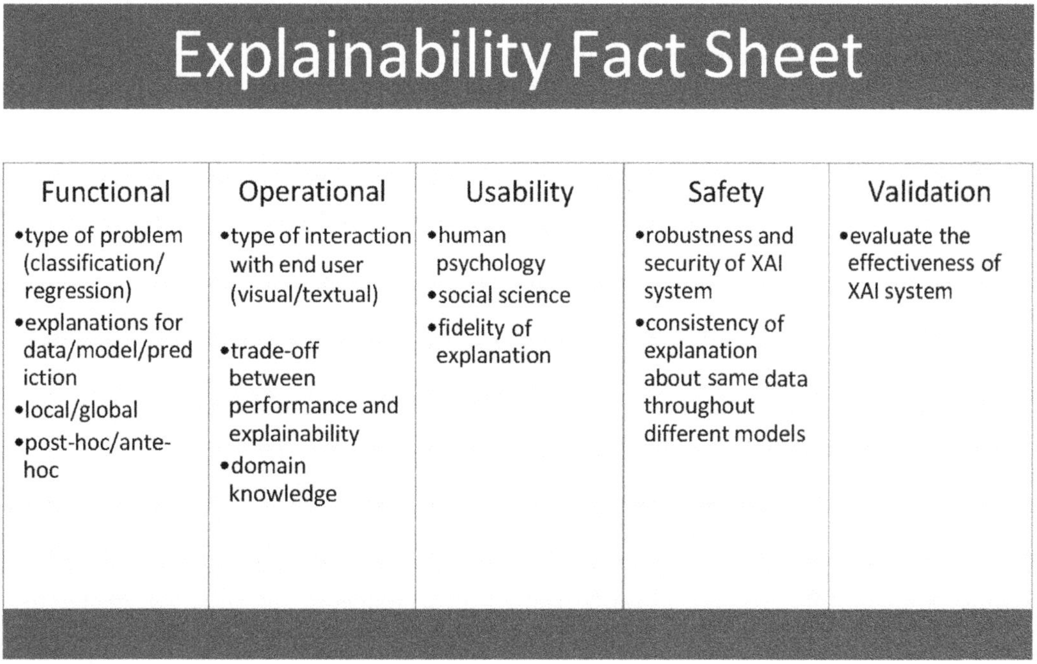

Explainability Fact Sheet

Functional	Operational	Usability	Safety	Validation
•type of problem (classification/ regression) •explanations for data/model/pred iction •local/global •post-hoc/ante- hoc	•type of interaction with end user (visual/textual) •trade-off between performance and explainability •domain knowledge	•human psychology •social science •fidelity of explanation	•robustness and security of XAI system •consistency of explanation about same data throughout different models	•evaluate the effectiveness of XAI system

FIGURE 11.4

Five key dimensions of explainability fact sheets.

causal mechanism, summarization, visualization, textualization, static explanations, interactive explanations, dialog form, explanation in original domain or transformed domain, etc. As far as the user is concerned, the XAI system is to be designed in a way that it should provide appropriate explanation to the stakeholders based on their language skill and cognitive capacity. The measurement of soundness between explanations and predictions is required only in post-hoc explanation, not in ante-hoc explanation. The value of performance metric between predictive model and explanatory model is calculated. Its high value ensures the consistency of explanation with the predictions of underlying model. If the explanations are not looking to be generalized, then its context within the specific application should be mentioned so that trust of the user in the XAI system is maintained. By means of explanation, partial information about the training data and functions of a predictive model are reveled. Therefore, it is essential to check the effect of explanations on security, privacy, and robustness on predictive systems. When explanations are provided to the user from multiple systems, then the explanations should be clearly distinguishable, possibly by highlighting the changes. A model-agnostic approach of explanation forces it to be post-hoc. Such an approach creates an extra layer on the top of the predictive model that is harmful to the fidelity of the explanations. When there is a trade-off between completeness and soundness in a model-agnostic approach, one should prefer completeness over soundness. A comprehensive list of requirements for XAI systems from computational and social points of view is needed. Such a single list can benefit designers of system and users too through the fact sheets. Such fact sheets assist in development, implementation, evaluation, and comparison of XAI systems in a systematic and consistent manner. The fact sheets also identify the gap between theoretical capabilities and corresponding implementation limitations. The authors in Ref. [10] have just proposed the framework and therefore called it "fact sheet" instead of standards, guidelines, or recommendations. The authorized professional body like IEEE can take this fact sheet as a base, and standards can emerge from it in future. The fact sheet concept proposed in the paper is made open and available on GitHub. Further research can revise the fact sheet based on new requirements of explainability, and therefore natural evolution is possible.

As far as the philosophy, psychology, and cognitive science is concerned, the explanation should be (i) counterfactual so that humans can understand why certain events happened and not other events, (ii) focus on a few causes instead of many causes, and (iii) in the form of social conversation and interaction, according to Ref. [11]. Expert systems are considered to be a first realization of applied AI that helps the human in decision-making processes in a specific domain. The knowledge acquisition in expert system is not an easy task, and the successful working of a system depends on the knowledge base. The explanations from an expert system are in the form of descriptions coupled with reasoning from the system or may be decoupled from the reasoning process, but in any way, it is a story behind the decision-making process. ML systems solve the problem of data acquisition that was observed in expert systems. The algorithms are learning from the large amount of data presented to it. Some ML algorithms create the black box models that are highly accurate in prediction but not able to explain the function of algorithms or prediction itself. The role of explanation is to make the stakeholders aware about the working of the system and final predictions. The stakeholders should be able to know that why only a particular prediction is given by the system instead of another. The present explainable systems are not accurate in terms of providing the truthfulness and closeness to the underlying model. The present metrics to evaluate the truthfulness and closeness are not reliable. Fidelity is one of the measures of closeness, but it is limited in its capacity and capability to find the meaningful representations for transparent reasoning. The importance of explanations from an XAI system to the end users (external stakeholders) was ignored for years even though they are the actual users. The explanations were limited to only the ML engineers (internal stakeholders) who are using it for debugging the systems. Therefore, there is a gap between explainability provided by XAI systems and the goal of transparency. The transparent systems should consider each stakeholder equally and provide the relevant and selected explanations to each one of them. If it happens, then only the purpose of responsible AI will serve.

The research challenge is that based on the language skill and cognitive capacity of a stakeholder, the XAI system should deliver the explanations to all the stakeholders, and that is not found in existing systems. The present metrics to evaluate the truthfulness and closeness of XAI systems with their underlying mode are not reliable. One of the measures to evaluate the closeness of an XAI system with its underlying mode is fidelity, but it is limited in its capacity and capability to find the meaningful representations for transparent reasoning. The research challenge is to develop uniform metrics that evaluate the performance of XAI methods. Human psychology mainly prefers to understand the situations in form of counterfactual or contrastive explanations. The research challenge is to provide the explanations in such way, and it will vary from application to application. The present explanation methods are designed mainly for data scientists or ML engineers for debugging the systems. Therefore, it is not completely fulfilling the goal of a transparent AI system. The research challenge is to develop the transparent systems that consider each stakeholder equally and provide the relevant and selected explanations to each one of them.

11.2.4 Exploring research areas in XAI

The research directions for XAI are shown in Fig. 11.5. The research can be explored and narrowed down in the following four overlapping directions.

- methods of explanations
- validating/measuring quality of XAI models
- applications of XAI systems
- stakeholder-centric explanations

In all above five possible areas, the further narrow directions are also shown in Fig. 11.5.

11.3 HCI for speech-impaired people: a case study

The HCI plays a vital role for providing smooth communication between a speech-impaired person and a normal person as well as among speech-impaired people. The heart of such a system is to convert the signs of a speech-impaired person into speech. The hand gloves or other such wearable can sense the signs and convert them into speech of a desired natural language. The text input from signs of a speech-impaired person can be achieved with dictation systems. The HCI research in the domain of technology for speech-impaired people is limited. In some cases a communication aid creates synthesized speech messages from the person's dysarthric speech. Speech synthesis is useful to get smooth interaction with a computer. It is also successful in certain constrained applications.

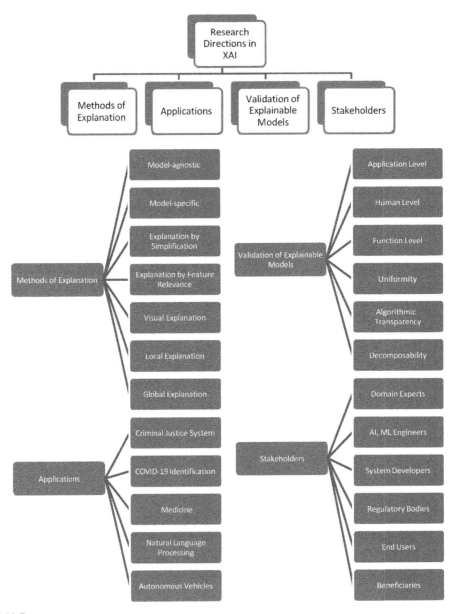

FIGURE 11.5

Possible research areas in XAI.

11.3.1 Issues and challenges

- The challenge is that enough training from given data is required to develop a robust ML model. The robust model is in the sense that irrespective of the size of the wearable device, it should give accurate speech output based on input signs.
- Another challenge is, as hand sizes vary from person to person, the size of wearable also varies. The gestures of different people are somewhat different even if they want to say same words. Despite these challenges, there are such wearables in the market that can be used by speech-impaired people to communicate.
- The set of concepts or theories for understanding user sign languages in speech interface interactions is lacking in the literature.
- The evaluation of speech interfaces in the real world context is one of the complex tasks.
- Another challenge is the handling of the distorted pronunciation of words and variation in pronunciation itself. This distortion and variation in pronunciation can be long-term because of progressive impairments or short-term because of fatigue.
- One issue in designing a system for dysarthric speech is stuttering and elaborate pauses during commands. A time-out is required once the start of the command is given, and there may be elaborate pauses during commands. These time-outs for dysarthric speakers are required to be much longer than those for normal speakers. In an ideal case, these time-outs are adjusted for each user.

11.4 Beyond HCI

There are many expectations by users to feel that computer systems have the form of smooth interfaces. There is also much scope whereby minimum efforts and maximum interactions with the computers can be made.

- There is an increase of interest to have personalized interfaces. When working on social networking or online shopping websites, it seems that the webpage(s) displayed to the user are specially developed for individuals. The designers and developers behind the scenes are developing such smart software modules, so every single click of the users are recorded, and once the user logs in next time, they feel continuity. Of course, there may be the issues of user privacy in such cases, but it is to be taken care of by the developers.
- There is huge demand and usage of video games. The video games are developed in such a way that users feel comfortable and have a smooth interface while playing them. The future of such video games will be on eye-tracking. Eyes of humans show the intention of the work and also action. Therefore, instead of using a mouse, the user can play the games with eyes. Wherever from the screen user wants a response, just rest the eyes at that position, and the highly intelligent interfaces detect it, and the user will quickly get the response. This is the future of HCI.
- There may be the case that two ML models having same predictive accuracy are providing different explanations for the same input. Therefore, a challenge is to decide which explanation is the best. The performance measures may include user's satisfaction level, faith in a model, and a model's ability to recover from explanation after failure.

- For post-hoc explanation, at present the methods of model explanation are approximating the model. But it should be precise and truly reflect the model behavior so that user's trust on a model increases. There should be a balance between the actual working of a model and the explanation provided to a user.
- For local interpretable models, the explanation is in terms of input features of a training dataset. This explanation is useful to ML researchers not to end users. For end users, the explanation is expected in the format and/or language that is understandable by them.
- For different types of users, a different explanation is required for the same prediction. It depends on a user's background and working domain. As an example, while predicting the risk score of approval of a loan for a customer, the explanation required by a finance manager and ML engineer is different for the same risk score.
- Users can ask the explanation in terms of comparison. As an example, a user can ask to explain why the return value on his portfolio is predicted to be down while other person's shows up even though both have invested the same amount. Present interpretable models are not able to explain in such a comparative way. For the previous example, the features cause the up/down result for both persons' portfolios to be found and provided to them in explanation form.
- Present interpretable models explain everything about the outcome to the user in the case of local interpretation. But users are interested to know only the most important causes. Therefore, from a complete set of causes, the most promising cause that affects the outcome is to be extracted and explained to the user.
- The explanation can be demanded in conversation form. Depending on the question and explanation asked by a user, an appropriate answer in proper format depending on type of user is to be provided.
- Scalability of interpretable ML models is one of the challenging tasks. LIME constructs a local explanation model for a prediction of every instance. If there are thousands of such instances for which a prediction is required, then it becomes computationally expensive. Shapley values check the contribution of a particular input feature for prediction by considering all possible combinations of input features in a training dataset. When the training dataset has thousands of input features, then again it becomes computationally expensive to create an explainable model.

11.5 Future work directions in AI with HCI

There are lots of opportunities for exploration of research work when the state-of-the-art techniques of AI, knowledge representation, reasoning, ML, and natural language processing are applied for HCI. Given below are some of the future work directions.

- Conversational user interfaces deal with transforming the theoretical concepts and paradigms into actual practices as well as in research. When multiple users are working on the same AI-based system and conversation is in the form of voice, then there are obvious differences in tones, frequency of signals, etc. All the users are expecting a productive solution, and the interactions should be simple to understand. Therefore, there is a great demand for creating a delightful experience for the users. Even the user interfaces should be accessible to every human (apart from actual users) regardless of their mental or physical capability. To make uniformity and valid, correct responses from the AI-based system to all the users, the user interface is to be designed with proper care.

- Most of the HCI methods available at present are mostly non-AI. There is need of joint teamwork of HCI professionals with AI, ML, and NLP experts. The HCI professionals include information architects, user interface developers, researchers, and accessibility designers. The teamwork will integrate the existing methods in the disciplines of AI, ML, and NLP with the opportunities in HCI for multidisciplinary research work. There may be some misconception in individual disciplines, but after such integration, it can be resolved.
- AI-based systems have complex decision-making algorithms. Though these algorithms are complicated, they are the most powerful in terms of their inference capability and decision-making ability. They are solving the problems of human bias, which can negatively impact the lives of millions of people. The AI-based decision-making algorithms are capable of being fairer and more efficient than decisions by humans. There is also a need to ensure that the AI system has an unbiased perspective of a biased world. The other merits of AI-based decision-making methods are reliability, affordability, and being time efficient. But at the same time, it is a challenging task to apply such complicated decision-making algorithms for designing and development of HCI.
- Due to the complexity of AI-based algorithms, there is great demand for transparent and explainable interface design. As we know, there are black box ML models (e.g., DNN) that have high accuracy but are poor in providing explanations to the users. Of course, to provide high accuracy, the mechanisms followed by such algorithms are complex. Therefore, add-in modules in such black box models are required to be developed that can explain the causes of inferences to the users. The efforts are always made to balance between the performance of such a black box model and its explainability and transparence. Once it is done, then only powerful AI-based algorithms can give appropriate and proper outcomes to the user in an understandable form. And if understandable outcomes are available to users, then their trust in the AI-based system and interaction with such systems can increase.
- In HCI, there is always the importance of bidirectional conversation between human and computers. While taking the feedback from the users, the modules responsible for receiving the feedbacks are to be designed in such a way that there must be synchronization with previous modules in hierarchies. Therefore, the responses from the users are to be tackled with proper care with any loss of data.
- The stakeholders of HCI can be AI engineer, doctor, businessman, data scientist, farmer, or government official. To meet each individual's requirements and expectations about interaction with the AI-based system, it is required to develop relevant solutions and understanding who will be using the AI-based system, what is their scope, role, use, etc. Every stakeholder is making significant and life-altering decisions every day, and therefore it is very important to understand who is getting what type of explanations about the outcomes from AI-based systems.

11.6 Conclusions

This chapter explored the tremendous opportunities in the area of applying AI for providing intelligent interfaces in HCI. Different disciplines intersect to contribute to the growth of HCI, and how HCI touches the different disciplines to make it a multidisciplinary field of research work is detailed in this chapter. The important part is, if complex AI algorithms are applied to provide intelligent interfaces, then the human must know how the interface is working and what its consequences are. The XAI provides various mechanisms and methods to give explanations of every event occurring during the human interactions with a machine. Once the AI-based system is explainable, then it receives the trustworthiness of stakeholders, and thus it becomes more responsible. To make the interpretable ML models, the scope of possible research work direction is also shown in this chapter. Instead of providing common explanations of inferences, the reasons behind stakeholder-wise explanations are detailed in this chapter. The possible research areas under XAI are also shown, and they are open research areas for further exploration. The future possibilities of integration of AI and HCI are also mentioned, and they can be considered open research challenges.

References

[1] A. Adadi, M. Berrada, Peeking inside the black-box: a survey on explainable artificial intelligence (XAI), IEEE Access 6 (2018) 52138−52160, https://doi.org/10.1109/ACCESS.2018.2870052.

[2] A. Barredo Arrieta, N. Díaz-Rodríguez, J. Del Ser, A. Bennetot, S. Tabik, A. Barbado, S. Garcia, S. Gil-Lopez, D. Molina, R. Benjamins, R. Chatila, F. Herrera, Explainable Artificial Intelligence (XAI): concepts, taxonomies, opportunities and challenges toward responsible AI, Inf. Fusion 58 (2020) 82−115, https://doi.org/10.1016/J.INFFUS.2019.12.012.

[3] P. Linardatos, V. Papastefanopoulos, S. Kotsiantis, Explainable AI: a review of machine learning interpretability methods, Entropy 23 (1) (2021) 1−45, https://doi.org/10.3390/e23010018.

[4] R. Roscher, B. Bohn, M.F. Duarte, J. Garcke, Explainable machine learning for scientific insights and discoveries, IEEE Access 8 (2020) 42200−42216, https://doi.org/10.1109/ACCESS.2020.2976199.

[5] P. Hacker, R. Krestel, S. Grundmann, F. Naumann, Explainable AI under contract and tort law: legal incentives and technical challenges, Artif. Intell. Law 28 (4) (2020) 415−439, https://doi.org/10.1007/s10506-020-09260-6.

[6] M. Du, N. Liu, X. Hu, Techniques for interpretable machine learning, Commun. ACM 63 (1) (2019) 68−77, https://doi.org/10.1145/3359786.

[7] A. Brennen, What Do People Really Want when They Say They Want "Explainable AI?" We Asked 60 Stakeholders, Conference on Human Factors in Computing Systems—Proceedings, 2020, https://doi.org/10.1145/3334480.3383047.

[8] P.P. Angelov, N.I. Asrnold, E.A. Soares, P.M. Atkinson, R. Jiang, Explainable artificial intelligence: an analytical review, Wiley Interdiscip. Rev. Data Min. Knowl. Discov. (2021) 1−13, https://doi.org/10.1002/widm.1424. January.

[9] C. Meske, E. Bunde, J. Schneider, M. Gersch, Explainable Artificial Intelligence: Objectives, Stakeholders, and Future Research Opportunities, Information Systems Management, 2020, https://doi.org/10.1080/10580530.2020.1849465.

[10] K. Sokol, P. Flach, Explainability fact sheets: a framework for systematic assessment of explainable approaches. FAT* 2020—Proceedings of the 2020 Conference on Fairness, Accountability, and Transparency, 2020, pp. 56−67, https://doi.org/10.1145/3351095.3372870.

[11] R. Confalonieri, L. Coba, B. Wagner, T.R. Besold, A historical perspective of explainable artificial intelligence, Wiley Interdiscip. Rev. Data Min. Knowl. Discov. 11 (1) (2021) e1391, https://doi.org/10.1002/WIDM.1391.

Index

Note: Page numbers followed by "*f*" indicate figures and "*b*" indicate boxes.

A

A/B testing, 191
Accuracy percentage, 81
Action planning, 248
Activity theory, 258
Adolescence, 180
Advanced automated cockpit, GOMS model analysis of, 282
Aesthetic appeal, 233
Affordances, 257
Air traffic control (ATC), 242, 278
Air traffic systems (ATS), 242–244
   modules, 244
Airline
   automation and usability heuristics, 279–280
   interfaces and flight safety, 278
Algorithms, 40
   decisions, 296–297
   lack of algorithmic transparency, 183
   testing, 118
Amalgamation process, 116
Amazon (company), 39
Analytical AI, 36–37
Annotated labels, 106
Annotation process, 104
   predicting amount of annotation required, 107–108
Annotators
   from crowdsourcing, 105
   hired on contract, 105–106
ANOVA analysis, 21
Application program interfaces (APIs), 267–268
Architectural design process, 10
Arngren's website, 258
Artificial intelligence (AI), 1, 31, 69, 95, 133, 173, 221, 255–256, 295–298. *See also* Computational intelligence (CI); Human-centered artificial intelligence (HCAI)
   for achieving required accuracy of faster, 99
   advantages and disadvantages of, 41–42
      availability, 41
      data maintenance, 42
      decrement in human error, 41
      expensive, 42
      faster decision, 41
      impartial decisions, 41
      lethargic humans, 42
      losing creativity, 42
      no risk, 41
      unemployment, 41
   AI research prospects and future directions, 61–63
   AI-based decision-making methods, 309
   AI-based frameworks, 42
   AI-based human-centered app, 118
   AI-based smart devices, 297
   AI-based system, 303, 309
   algorithm, 100
   applicability of AI in recommendation systems, 39–40
      common obstacles encountered by recommender system, 40
      machine learning in recommendation systems, 40
      recommender systems with AI, 40
      system recommendations function, 39–40
   applications, 57–61
      expert systems, 57–59
      gaming, 57
      natural language processing, 57
      speech recognition, 59–61
   background studies, 208–217
      effect of COVID-19 outbreak, 209–217
   characteristics of AI waves, 2–3
   evolutionary computing, 43–48
      application in real world, 47–48
      benefits and limitations of genetic algorithm, 46
      EA, 44–46
   evolving HCI interaction in era of, 3–5
   examples of hybrid designs involving humans and, 111–116
   explainable AI, 37–39
   future works, 228–229
      directions in AI with HCI, 308–309
   growth of, 31–35
      AI becomes thriving industry, 34
      early excitement, incredible assumptions, 32–33
      information-based frameworks, 33–34
      portion of real world, 33
      recent events, 35
      return of neural networks, 34–35
   beyond HCI, 307–308
   HCI as multidisciplinary field, 296f
   HCI for speech-impaired people, 305–307
   history of, 31–35
   and human rights, 183–186
      cybersecurity vulnerabilities, 184
      intellectual property issues, 184

Artificial intelligence (AI) (*Continued*)
  lack of algorithmic transparency, 183
  lack of contestability, 184
  liability for damage, 185—186
  privacy and data protection issues, 184—185
  unfairness, bias, and discrimination, 184
  user-centered system development, 186—187
importance of, 134—137
for increasing accuracy of, 99
industry 4.0 and AI revolution, 35—37
intelligent robots, 61
logic-based reasoning, 48—50
managing effects of
  blended learning, 222—224
  e-learning, 224—227
  work from home, 217—222
models of knowledge representation based on structural
    analysis, 50—52
  frames, 50—51
  scripts, 52
  semantic networks, 50
NN, 55—57
obtaining annotated data from existing AI design model,
    108—109
pattern recognition and cluster analysis, 54
programming, 58
recommender systems with, 40
research challenges in AI with HCI, 298—305
  biased decisions and explanation from AI systems,
      302—303
  exploring research areas in XAI, 305
  lack of stakeholder-specific explanations, 303—305, 303f
  lack of unified concept for XAI systems, 300—302
revolution, 35—37
role in psychology, 174—186
rule-binding systems, 52—53
solution with, 79—84
symbolic AI and computational AI, 42—43
system, 296—297, 302
  biased decisions and explanation from, 302—303
  coupled with society, 109—110
  developers, 301
winter, 35
Artificial linguistic internet computer entity (ALICE), 175
Artificial neural network (ANN), 298
Assistive intelligence. *See* Intelligence amplification (IA)
Associated Chambers of Commerce & Industry of India
    (ASSOCHAM), 78
Attention weight matrix, 299
Audio-based interfaces, 234
Augmented reality (AR), 10—11, 19, 21, 23—24, 259. *See also*
    Virtual reality (VR)

case study on role of HCI in experiential learning through,
    276—278
comparison spatial skill gains between university groups
    training by AR and between training types, 23—24
pilot study with, 12—14
technologies, 12
Automated external defibrillator (AED), 270, 271f
Automatic facial recognition, 63
Automatic speech recognition, 59
Automotive application tasks and problems, 265—267
  autonomous driving, 266—267
  cell phone tasks, 266
  menu interface tasks, 265—266
  navigation system tasks, 266
  web access, 266
Automotive interfaces, 264
Automotive systems, 245—246
  approach of HCI design for, 246f
Autonomous driving, 266—267
Autonomous vehicle, 102—103
  HAI in, 116

B
Back-end recognition, 61
Big data, 198
Biometric technology, 63
Black box ML models, 300
Blended learning
  managing effects of, 222—224
    advantages of blended learning, 223—224
Bloom's taxonomy, 14
Business intelligence, 113, 241—242

C
Canva, 255—256
CAPTCHA, 107
CART, 83
Cattell-Horn-Carroll Model of Intelligence, 7
Cell phone tasks, 266
Character recognition, 139
Chatbots, 175—177
  advantages and limitations, 176—177
  history of, 175
  Pacifica, 176
  Woebot, 175
  Wysa, 176
CIBIL score, 120—121
Citizen science app, 118
Classification techniques, 83
Classroom evaluation process, 222—223
Clause form, 49
Clear analytics (tools), 241

Cluster analysis, 54
Clustering approaches, 79–80
CMutation, 46
Cockpit remembering, 282–284
Cognitive augmentation. *See* Intelligence amplification (IA)
Cognitive behavioral strategies, 176
Cognitive behavioral therapy (CBT), 175
Cognitive load, 258, 287
Cognitive science, 211
Cognitive task analysis (CTA), 288
    for emergency management game, 287–288
Collaborative AI design, 110
Collaborative emergency management, 285
Collection rate, 120–121
Communication process, 178
Competitive analysis, 189
Complex data labeling, 104
Computational AI, 42–43
Computational intelligence (CI), 43, 69–79. *See also*
        Artificial intelligence (AI)
    case study in higher education system, 68–69
    framework, 79–84
        application of model on all datasets, 84
        approach, 80–81
        data sets, 79–80
        experimental setup and measures, 81–83
        machine learning algorithms implemented in model, 83
    potential aspects to resolve issues with, 68–69
    problems faced by higher education system for
            employability, 70–79
    results, 84–88
        future possibilities, 88
    review of literature, 70
Computer
    processing technologies, 175
    technologies, 17
Conjunctive normal form (CNF), 49
Connectionist AI, 42
Consequence network formalism, 35
Consistency, 235
Constraints, 270
Content-based filtering, 40
Contestability, lack of, 184
Context analysis, 187
Conventional concepts, 195
Conventional HCI, 2–3
Convolution neural networks (CNNs), 56, 95, 139–141
COVID-19, 208–210, 214
    epidemic, 225
    outbreak, 224
    effect of, 209–217
        fake news and misrepresentation, 215

human services impacts, 213–214
        imbalance of interpersonal, 215–216
        monetary effect, 210–211
        psychological impacts, 217
        social impacts, 214–215
        sociological relevance, 216–217
        stay-at-home orders, 211–213
    physiologic impacts of, 182–183
    problem, 208
Crisis
    identification, 248
    management, 248–249
Cross-agency collaboration and sharing, 249
Crossover probability, 46
Crowdsourcing technique, 105, 117–118
Cutting-edge technologies, 37
Cyber security vulnerabilities, 184
Cyberpsychology, 178–181, 199
    addiction to internet and technologies, 178–179
    FOMO, 180–181
    negative relationships and online vulnerability, 179–180
    online behavior, identity, and comparison, 179
    phubbing, 180
Cyberspace, 178

D

Dall-E 2, 255–256
DAT5-SR, 13
    tests, 18
Data
    analysis, 102–109
        data labeling, 103–104
        obtaining annotated data from existing AI design model,
            108–109
        predicting amount of annotation required, 107–108
        quality control in data labeling, 104–107
    annotation, 104–107
        using end users, 106–107
    data-driven AI technology, 183
    data-driven approach, 296
    labeling, 103–104
        complex data labeling, 104
        finding appropriate people for, 105–106
        quality control in, 104–107
        simple data labeling, 104
    mining, 67, 69, 175
    scientists, 301
Debt
    collection process, 120–121
    proposed case study of HAI in loan approval and debt
            recovery, 120–123
    recovery process, 120–121

Decision-making algorithms, 297, 309
Deep learning (DL), 63, 134, 207, 298. *See also* Machine learning (ML)
  DL-based methods, 303
Deep neural networks (DNNs), 95, 298–299
Demand-based AI design, 111
Democratization of information technology, 195–199
  distribution of information, 195–199
    enhance user experience, 198
    social media, 197
    social media and big data, 198
    study human condition, 199
    target advertising, 198
    Web 1.0, 195
    Web 2.0, 196–197
DENDRAL rules, 33–34
Design, 3–4
  alternatives, 275
  approaches of HAI, 109–111
    AI system coupled with society, 109–110
    collaborative AI design, 110
  cycle process, 47
    i nteraction-based AI design, 110–111
    demand-based AI design, 111
  thinking approach, 117–118
Designing, 109–116
Differential Aptitude Test (DAT5-SR), 13
Digital Equipment Corporation (DEC), 34
Digital gadgets, 295
Digital hearing, 238–240
  interface for digital hearing considering speech to sign language conversion, 240f
Digital humanities, 240–241
Digital psychology. *See* Cyberpsychology
Direct manipulation, 256–257, 268–269
Distributed cognition, 258
Diversified parallel design, 189
Documentation repository, 59
Domain experts, 301
Domo (tool), 241
Driving, 286

E

Education, 68
Effect of COVID-19 outbreak, 209–217
e-Learning
  managing effects of, 224–227
    benefits, 226
    drawbacks, 226
    inequalities in ethnicity, 226–227
Electrooculography (EOG), 239
ELIZA, 175

Emergencies, HCI for, 284–288
Emergency management (EM), 285
Emergency medical technicians (EMTs), 285
  and trained personnel, 285
Emotions, 41, 287
Empirical measurement of safety and usability, 267
Employability, problems faced by higher education system for, 70–79
Employees, 219
Employers, 212
End users, 300
Engineering design, 47
Enhanced intelligence. *See* Intelligence amplification (IA)
Enthralling user experience, 233
Equity, 270
Errors, 104–105
Ethical technologies, 109–110
Ethnicity, inequalities in, 226–227
EU Agency for Fundamental Rights, 184
European countries, 24
Evaluation, 275–276
  and strategies, 116–119, 151–152
Evolutionary algorithms (EAs), 44–46
  pseudopodia of evolutionary algorithms, 44b
Evolutionary computation, 43
Evolutionary computing, 42–43
Experiential learning, case study on role of HCI in experiential learning through augmented reality, 276–278
Experimental design, 12–13, 16
Expert annotators, 106
Expert systems, 57–59
Explainable artificial intelligence (XAI), 1, 37, 296–297
  exploring research areas in, 305
  models, 302
  systems, 298, 301
    lack of unified concept for, 300–302, 300f
Explanatory module, 59
Extended COVID, 208

F

Facebook, 215
Fact sheet, 303–304
Fake news and misrepresentation, 215
Farming, 211
Fear of missing out (FOMO), 180–181
  FOMO-prone humans, 180
Feature extraction, 152–153
Feed-forward NNs, 56
Feedback, 235
  cycles, 255–256
Females, 215–216

Fifth-Generation project, 34
Finance companies, 121
First-order logic description of world, 48–49
First-order logic language (FOL language), 48
    specific forms of FOL calculative formulas, in reasoning
        systems, 49
Flight management computer (FMC), 282
Flying, 286
Fourth industrial revolution, 35–36
Frames, 50–51
Frequency baseline, 106
Front-end speech recognition, 61
Functional AI, 37
Functionality, 233
Fuzzy ensemble modeling, 67

G

Gaming, 57
General Data Protection Regulation (GDPR), 185, 297
Generalized prediction model, 80
Genetic algorithm, 47
    benefits and limitations of, 46
Gesture-based interfaces, 234
Global epidemic, 210
Global interpretable models, 299
Global interpretation, 298–299
Goals, operators, methods, and selection rules model (GOMS
        model), 268
    for evaluating airline applications, 280–282
        advanced automated cockpit, 282
        intelligent airline tutoring system, 281–282
Good data, 241
Good performance (GP), 262
Google, 255–256
Google. com, 193
GPS, case study on, 268–269
Gross domestic product (GDP), 210
Ground truth, 106
GTZAN dataset, 152–153
Gulfs of evaluation, 255, 256f
Gulfs of execution, 255, 256f
    bridging, 286

H

Head mounted display (hmd), 181
Health at home, 285–286
Healthcare
    applications and public health, 270–272
        constraints, 270
        equity, 270
        mental models and natural mappings, 271
        multimodal interfaces, 270–271
        personalized applications and interfaces, 271–272
    HAI in, 113–115
    impacts, 213–214
    systems, 236–238
        adaptive user interface–based HCI for healthcare, 237f
        smart wearable sensing device, 236f
Healthcare workers (HCWs), 213
Herbert Gelernter's Geometry Theorem Prover, 32
Heuristic method for evaluating VR user interfaces, 261, 261f
Hidden Markov models (HMMs), 35
Hierarchic methods, 54
High engagement (HE), 262
High usability, 233
Higher education system
    case study in, 68–69
        contributions of chapter, 69
        issues of higher education system in India, 68
        potential aspects to resolve issues with computational
            intelligence, 68–69
    problems faced by higher education system for
        employability, 70–79
Home medical device, 273
Homepage interface, 152
Homo sapiens, 31
Human-centered AI experiences (HAX), 125–127
    playbook, 127
    toolkit, 125–127
    project, 125–127
Human-centered artificial intelligence (HCAI), 2–3, 95–98
    in autonomous vehicles, 116
    case studies, 120–127
        HAX toolkit, 125–127
        human-centered AI at Netflix, 125
        proposed case study of HAI in loan approval and debt
            recovery, 120–123
        transformation from simple AI to human-centered AI at
            LinkedIn, 123–125
    data analysis, 102–109
    design flow, 117–118
    designing and prototyping, 109–116
        different design approaches of HAI, 109–111
        examples of hybrid designs involving humans and AI,
            111–116
    different design approaches of, 109–111
    evaluation and strategies, 116–119
    human-in-the-loop machine learning, reasoning, and
        planning, 98–102
        for achieving required accuracy of AI model faster, 99
        for increasing accuracy of AI model, 99
        models, 100–102
    in industry, 113
    limitations of HAI, 127

Human-centered artificial intelligence (HCAI) (*Continued*)
  in medicines and healthcare, 113—115
  proposed case study of HAI in loan approval and debt
    recovery, 120—123
  in public safety, 115
Human—computer interaction (HCI), 1, 67, 173, 233, 255,
    295
  beyond, 307—308
  business intelligence, 241—242
  case studies, 242—249
    on role of HCI in experiential learning through
      augmented reality, 276—278
  concepts of HCI system with interaction and interface, 234f
  designing airline applications, 278—284
    airline interfaces and flight safety, 278
  designing automotive applications, 263—269
    adaptive in-vehicle systems, 265f
    automotive application tasks andproblems, 265—267
    automotive interfaces and road safety, 264
    case study on GPS and distributed cognition, 268—269
    empirical measurement of safety and usability, 267
    evaluating automotive applications and interfaces,
      267—268
    procedures for iterating on automotive application
      design, 268
    users of automotive applications, 264—265
  designing healthcare applications, 269—278
    evaluating healthcare applications, 274—276
    healthcare applications and public health, 270—272
    medical applications and interfaces in home healthcare,
      273—274
    users of healthcare applications, 272—273
  designing VR applications, 259—262
  digital hearing, 238—240
  digital humanities, 240—241
  direct manipulation and invisible interfaces, 256—257
    affordances, 257
    mapping, 257
    simplicity, 257
  distributed cognition, 258
  for emergencies, 284—288
    challenges for emergency HCI, 286—287
    cognitive task analysis for emergency management
      game, 287—288
    users of emergency applications, 284—286
  feedback cycles, 255—256
  future work directions in AI with, 308—309
  healthcare systems, 236—238
  and importance, 1—5
    characteristics of HCI and AI waves, 2—3
    evolving HCI interaction in era of AI, 3—5
    possible research areas, 5

  mental models and representations, 257—258
  principles, 234—235
  research challenges in AI with, 298—305
  role in psychology, 174—186
  solution with, 79—84
  for speech-impaired people, 305—307
    issues and challenges, 307
  techniques, 67
Humans, 41, 100, 190, 208
  AI and human rights, 183—186
  blunder, 41
  decrement in human error, 41
  examples of hybrid designs involving humans and AI,
    111—116
  factors, 217
  human-centered design, 117—118, 128
  human-centered systems, 118
  human-centric AI, 2
  human-centric approach, 117—118
  human-centric explanations, 302
  human-in-the-loop machine learning, reasoning, and
    planning, 98—102
  intelligence, 7
  resources, 109
  services impacts, 213—214
Hybrid designs involving humans and AI
  examples of, 111—116
  HAI in
    autonomous vehicles, 116
    industry, 113
    medicines and healthcare, 113—115
    public safety, 115
Hybrid HAI public security system, 115

I

IBM (Company), 241
icCube (tool), 241
Image annotation, 61
Imagen, 255—256
Immersive virtual reality, 11
  pilot study with, 16—18
  training sessions, 19
Impact on medical employees, 212
Implementation plan, 248
Inclusive design, 110
Incorporated operational strategies, 212—213
India, issues of higher education system in, 68
Industry
  HAI in, 113
  industry 4.0, 35—37
Inference engine, 59
Informatic technologies, 10

Information technology, democratization of, 195–199
Information-based frameworks, 33–34
Infusion of computational intelligence, 69
Integrated circuit (IC), 195
Intellectual property issues, 184
Intellectual property rights, 184
Intelligence, 7, 211
Intelligence amplification (IA), 174, 181–182
Intelligent agents, 4
Intelligent airline tutoring system, GOMS model analysis of, 281–282
Intelligent decision-making process, 38
Intelligent robots, 61
Intelligent software, 39
Intelligent teaching technologies, 224
Intelligent user interfaces, 133
    importance of artificial intelligence and machine learning, 134–137
    recent innovations in, 139–153
        objective answer evaluation, 142
        for online examination system using NLP techniques, 141–152
        for online music genre classification system using ML techniques, 152–153
        subjective answer evaluation, 151–152
        for tamil letter recognition using ML techniques, 139–141
    strategies required for efficient, 133–137
Intensive care units (ICUs), 213
Interaction process, 1, 178
    interaction-based AI design, 110–111
Interactive AI, 37
International Organization for Standardization (ISO), 267–268
Internet, 178
    addiction to internet and technologies, 178–179
    inventions, 176
Internet psychology. *See* Cyberpsychology
Intrinsic local interpretable models, 299
Intrinsic ML models, 298
Invisible interfaces, 256–257
Ironies of automation, 286–287
Iterative design, 187

J

Journal storage (JSTOR), 240–241

K

k-fold cross-validation, 81
K-means clustering, 54
K-nearest neighbors, 300
K-star, 83

Kappa statistics, 83
Keystroke level model (KLM), 268
Knowledge, 135
    acquisition, 59
    models of knowledge representation based on structural analysis, 50–52
Kolmogorov–Smirnov test, 19
Kruskal–Wallis analysis, 21

L

Label, 100, 135–137
Lambda abstraction, 50
Lambda calculus (λ-calculus), 49–50
Large multinational companies process, 183
Learning process, 4, 178
    module, 59
Lethargic humans, 42
Lexical analysis, 57
LinkedIn, transformation from simple AI to human-centered AI at, 123–125
Local interpretable models, 299
Locally interpretable model explanation (LIME), 301–302
Logic-based programming languages, 34
Logic-based reasoning, 48–50
    reasoning as computation of symbols, 49–50
    theorem proof by reasoning, 48–49
        first-order logic description of world, 48–49
        reasoning by method of resolution, 49
        in reasoning systems, specific forms of FOL calculative formulas, 49
        techniques for converting formulas to normal forms, 49
Logic-based systems, 52
Low engagement (LE), 262

M

Machine learning (ML), 4, 69, 134, 173, 296. *See also* Deep learning (DL)
    algorithms, 221, 296–297
        implemented in model, 83
    engineers, 298, 301
    importance of, 134–137
    intelligent interface for online music genre classification system using machine learning techniques, 152–153
    intelligent interface for tamil letter recognition using machine learning techniques, 139–141
    methods, 40
    model, 296, 298
    paradigm, 135
    in recommendation systems, 40
Machine-augmented intelligence. *See* Intelligence amplification (IA)
Magnetic resonance imaging (MRI), 99

MagVi concept, 63
Man-computer symbiosis, 181–182
Mandel's golden rules, 131–132
Mapping, 257
Medical applications and interfaces in home healthcare, 273–274
Medicines, HAI in, 113–115
Memory-based principle, 235
Mental models, 271
  and representations, 257–258
  and situationalawareness, 279
Mental rotation (MR), 8
Mental Rotation Test (MRT), 13, 18
Menu interface tasks, 265–266
Microsoft, 241, 255–256
Minsky and Papert's *Perceptron*, 33–35
Misinformation, 215
Mixed reality (MR), 10–11, 259
Mobile computing, 1
Mode baseline, 106
Model
  model-agnostic approach, 303–304
  model-agnostic explanation, 299
  model-specific explanation, 299
Monitoring technologies, 214–215
Moore's law, 195
Multicriteria shortest path problems (MSPPs), 47–48
Multilayer perceptron, 56
Multilinkages concept, 207–208
Multimodal interfaces, 270–271
Mutation process, 46
MYCIN rules, 33–34

N

National Digital Infrastructure for Teachers Diksha, 222
National Institute of Aging (NIA), 274
Natural language processing (NLP), 37, 57, 141, 175
  intelligent interface for online examination system using NLP techniques, 141–152
Natural mappings, 271
Navigation system tasks, 266
Negative relationships, 179–180
Netflix, human-centered AI at, 125
Neural networks (NNs), 31, 55–57, 95
  return of, 34–35
Neurons, 55
Non-playable characters (NPCs), 57
Non-probabilistic sampling, 13
Normal forms, techniques for converting formulas to, 49

O

Online

examination system, 141
  intelligent interface using natural language processing techniques, 141–152
instructional methods, 227
intelligent interface for online music genre classification system using machine learning techniques, 152–153
vulnerability, 179–180
Ontology, 50
Oracle, 241
Original Equipment Manufacturer (OEM), 268
Outsourcing, 105
Oxford University, 209

P

Pacifica, 176
  mediation tool, 176
Pandemic, 209, 213
Parallel design, 189
Parametric statistical tests, 19–21
Participatory design (PD), 187, 190
Pathfinding technique, 57
Patients, 208, 215
Pattern recognition, 54
Performance Assessment, Review, and Analysis of Knowledge in Holistic Development Program (PARAKH Development Program), 222
Performance metrics, 81
Personal computer (PC), 2–3
Personalized applications and interfaces, 271–272
Personalized organizations, 220
Personalized protective equipment (PPE), 212
Perspective taking/SOT, 16–17
Persuasive technology concept, 110–111
Phubbing, 180
Physical environments, 287
Physical interaction, 245–246
Physiologic systems, 216
Pilot study
  with augmented reality, 12–14
  with immersive virtual reality, 16–18
PLANNER (logic-based programming languages), 34
Poor performance (PP), 262
Post-hoc categorization, 298
Post-hoc explainability, 301
Post-hoc explanation, 308
Post-hoc interpretable models, 299
Post-hoc ML models, 298
Post-hoc models, 298
Postpandemic financial system, 207–208
Predictive generalized model, 80
Presidential commission, 193
Process approach within UCDD, 187

Product recommendation algorithm models, 40
Progressive methods, 4
Projection-based displays, 245
Prolog (logic-based programming languages), 34
Prototyping, 109—116, 189—190, 275
Psychology
    challenges, 199—200
    contribution, 173—174
    democratization of information technology, 195—199
    motivation, 173
    preliminaries, 174
    role of HCI and AI in psychology, 174—186
        AI and human rights, 183—186
        chatbots, 175—177
        cyberpsychology, 178—181
        intelligence amplification, 181—182
        physiologic impacts of COVID-19, 182—183
    usability engineering and verification, 188—195
Public safety, HAI in, 115

Q

QlikView, 241
Quality control in data labeling, 104—107
    applying checks to approve labels before entering system, 106
    crowdsourcing, 105
    data annotation using end users, 106—107
    finding appropriate people for data labeling, 105—106
Quality data, 102—103
Question generation process, 151—152

R

Random baseline, 106
Random forest, 83
Random tree, 83
Reasoning process, 52
Reasoning systems, specific forms of FOL calculative formulas in, 49
Recall value, 81
Recommendation
    engine, 39
    systems
        applicability of AI in, 39—40
        machine learning in, 40
Recommender system
    with AI, 40
    common obstacles encountered by, 40
Recurrent neural networks (RNNs), 56
    RNN-based models, 63
Regions of interest (ROIs), 63
Regulatory bodies, 301
Rehabilitation modalities, 47—48

Reinforcement learning, 137
Reminders, 235
Remote tutoring, 222
Resolution, reasoning by method of, 49
Right to explanation, 297
Risk indicators, 213
Road safety, 264
Robotics, 47
Root-mean-squared error (RMSE), 81, 83
Root-relative-squared error (RRSE), 81, 83
Rule-based learning, 300
Rule-based ML algorithms, 298
Rule-based systems, 52—53
    model of, 52—53
Rule-binding systems, 52—53
    model of rule-based systems, 52—53

S

SAE J2364 Pettitt's occlusion timecalculation, 268
SAE J2365 task time calculations, 268
Sales-oriented businesses, 47
SAP, 241
Science, technology, engineering, and mathematics (STEAM), 10
    importance of spatial skills in, 9—10
Science, technology, engineering, and mathematics field (STEM field), 9—10
Scripts, 52
Semantic networks, 50
Semi-supervised learning, 137
Shapiro—Wilk test, 19
Shifra (AI-based human-centered app), 118—119
Sign separation approach, 54
Simple data labeling, 104
Simplicity, 257
Sisense, 241
Situated action theory, 258
Situational awareness (SA), 279
Smart air traffic system (SATS), 242
    framework of SATS using HCI, 243f
Social cognition theory, 258
Social loan quotient (SLQ), 121—122
Social media, 173, 197—198
Social networking sites, 215
Society, AI system coupled with, 109—110
Software models, 117—118
Solver, 241
Spatial intelligence, 7
Spatial orientation (SO), 8, 19—21
Spatial Orientation Test (SOT), 16—17
Spatial perceptions (SP), 8
Spatial relation (SR), 8, 13

Spatial skills, 7
 definition of spatial skills and components, 7—8
 employing virtual and augmented reality, 11
 importance of spatial skills in STEAM, 9—10
 measurement data, 16
 measurement tests, 16
 methodology, 12—18
  pilot study with augmented reality, 12—14
  pilot study with immersive virtual reality, 16—18
 motivation and contribution, 12
 results, 19—24
  comparison spatial skill gains between university groups training by AR and between training types, 23—24
 training, 10—11
Spatial visualization (SV), 8, 19—21
 component, 25
Speaker dependent (speech recognition software), 60
Speaker independent (speech recognition software), 61
Speaker recognition framework, 60
Speech
 HCI for speech-impaired people, 305—307
 recognition, 35, 59—61
  software, 60
 speech to message, 59
 speech-impaired person, 305
Stable diffusion, 255—256
Stakeholder-specific explanations, lack of, 303—305
Statistical analysis, 19, 69
Statistical ML techniques, 5
Stay-at-home orders, 211—213
Stress, 287
Structural analysis, models of knowledge representation based on, 50—52
Supervised learning techniques, 137
Surrendered speech recognition, 61
Surveillance, 248
SWAYAM (National online education platform), 222
Symbolic AI, 42—43
 awareness, 42
System recommendations function, 39—40

T

Tamil character recognition system, 169
Tamil letter recognition using machine learning techniques, intelligent interface for, 139—141
Task, 235
Technology
 technology-centric design approach, 2—3
 technology-centric strategy, 2—3
 unintended side effects of, 287
Test budget, 191

Testing, 191
Textual AI, 37
Theory of mental modeling, 67
Three Mile Island accident, 192
Three Mile Island Nuclear Generating Station-2 (TMI-2), 192
Three-dimensional visual (3-D visual), 11
Touch-based interfaces, 234
Training process, 104—105
 comparison spatial skill gains between university groups training by augmented reality and between training types, 23—24
Transfer learning technique, 103
Transmission, 209
Tree-based ensemble ML model, 299
Turing's theory of computation, 31—32
Twitter, 215

U

United Health Group, 199
United Nations policy documents, 183
Universal Declaration of Human Rights (UDHR), 184
Universidad Católica San Pablo (UCSP), 12
Universidad de La Laguna (ULL), 12
Unsupervised learning, 137
US Environmental Protection Agency, 219
US Food and Drug Administration (FDA), 273
Usability, 4
 engineering and verification, 188—195
  A/B testing, 191
  competitive analysis, 189
  google homepage over 20 years, 193—195
  importance of user-centered design, 192—193
  know user, 189
  parallel design, 189
  participatory design, 190
  prototyping, 190
  setting usability goals, 189
  test budget, 191
  test goals and test plans, 191
  usability, 188
  usability engineering lifecycle, 188—190
  usability heuristics, 190—191
  usability testing, 191
 interface design, 182
 process, 189
Used-centered design development (UCDD), 174
 process approach within, 187
User experience (UX), 1—2
 research methodology, 191
User familiarity, 132—133
User information-based principle, 235

User interface (UI), 59, 131, 309
User interface design (UID), 131
   principles, 132—133
   process, 132—133
User-centered design, 258
   importance of, 192—193
User-participating experimental assessment, 4
User—centered system development, 186—187
   context analysis, 187
   iterative design, 187
   key elements of, 186—187
      levels of user participation, 187
   process approach within UCDD, 187
Users of automotive applications, 264—265
Users of healthcare applications, 272—273
   hierarchy of ergonomics and hedonomic needs, 273f

V

Vehicle to infrastructure communication (V2I
      communication), 245
Vehicle to vehicle communication (V2V communication), 245
Video magnification program, 63
Virtual assistants, 175
Virtual employment, 219
Virtual reality (VR), 10—11, 23—24, 256. *See also*
      Augmented reality (AR)
   application design considerations, 259—261
      error tolerance, 261
      invisibility, 259—260
      learnability, 260—261
      low physical effort, 260
      reducing cognitive load, 260
   application evaluation, 261—262
   case study on VR game difficultyadjustment, 262
      performance-and engagement-sensitive system, 263f
   designing VR applications, 259—262
      current VR landscape, 259
   systems, 246—248

HCI-based virtual reality system, 247f
   technologies, 12
Visual AI, 37
Voice-based interaction, 246

W

Watson's system, 113—114
Wealth, investments in, 219
Web
   access, 266
   analytics, 242
   Web 1.0, 195
   Web 2.0, 196—197
   web-based UI, 142
Web psychology. *See* Cyberpsychology
Weight matrix, 139
Weighted mean precision, 81
Weighted mean recall, 81
Woebot, 175
Work from home (WFH), 208
   benefits, 218—220
      autonomy of location, 219
      balance of work and life, 218
      environment effects, 219
      improve efficiency and throughput, 220
      investments in wealth, 219
      more tolerance and diversity, 219
      personalized organizations, 220
      reduced amount of travel trauma, 219
      secure work life, 220
      significant influence of nature, 219
   drawbacks of, 220—222
   managing effects of, 217—222
World Health Organization (WHO), 209
Wysa, 176

Z

Zoom Solutions, 120—121

Printed and bound by CPI Group (UK) Ltd, Croydon, CR0 4YY

03/10/2024

01040331-0001

Implementing 802.11 with Microcontrollers:

Wireless Networking for Embedded Systems Designers